A Complete Guide to the
Freshwater
Fishes
of Southern Africa

A Complete Guide to the
Freshwater Fishes
of Southern Africa

Paul H. Skelton

Illustrated by Dave Voorvelt and Elizabeth Tarr

SOUTHERN
BOOK PUBLISHERS

Copyright © 1993 by the author

All rights reserved. No part of this publication may be reproduced or transmitted in any form or by any means without prior written permission from the publisher.

ISBN 1 86812 350 2 (Soft cover)
ISBN 1 86812 493 2 (Hard cover)
ISBN 1 86812 494 0 (Collectors' edition)

First edition, first impression 1993

Published by
Southern Book Publishers (Pty) Ltd
PO Box 3103, Halfway House, 1685

Published in Zimbabwe by
Tutorial Press (Pvt)
16 George Silundika Avenue, Harare 1993
ISBN 0 7974 1241 9

Cover design by Insight Graphics
Cover illustration by Dave Voorvelt
Illustrations by Dave Voorvelt and Elizabeth Tarr
Set in Souvenir medium
by Unifoto
Printed and bound by Singapore National Printers Ltd

CONTENTS

Foreword vii
The J.L.B. Smith Institute of Ichthyology ix
Acknowledgements x
How to use this book xi
An introduction to freshwater fishes of Southern Africa 1
Introduction 3
  A brief history of southern African freshwater ichthyology 3
  Geographical background 6
  Aquatic systems and habitats 10
  Factors affecting fish distribution 16
  What is a fish? 19
  Aspects of biology and ecology 34
  Fishes and man in southern Africa 45
  Threatened fishes and conservation 51
  Classification, taxonomy and nomenclature 59
  Collection, preservation and measurement 63
Southern African freshwater fishes: introduction and classification 69
Key to families 81
Species accounts 87
  Protopteridae – African lungfishes 89
  Mormyridae – snoutfishes 92
  Megalopidae – tarpons 102
  Anguillidae – freshwater eels 104
  Clupeidae – herrings 109
  Kneriidae – knerias 112
  Cyprinidae – barbs, yellowfishes, labeos 117
  Distichodontidae – citharines 193
  Characidae – characins 199
  Hepsetidae – African pike 208
  Suborder Siluroidei – catfishes 210
  Claroteidae – claroteid catfishes 211
  Austroglanididae – rock catfishes 215
  Amphiliidae – mountain catfishes 218
  Schilbeidae – butter catfishes 224
  Clariidae – air-breathing catfishes 227
  Malapteruridae – electric catfishes 238
  Mochokidae – squeakers, suckermouth catlets 240
  Galaxiidae – galaxiids 258
  Salmonidae – trouts 260

Order Cyprinodontiformes – killifishes, topminnows 266
Aplocheilidae – annual killifishes 267
Cyprinodontidae – topminnows 273
Poeciliidae – live-bearers 278
Spiny-rayed fishes 283
Centrarchidae – sunfishes 283
Percidae – perches 289
Cichlidae – cichlids 291
Anabantidae – labyrinth fishes 333
Mastacembelidae – spiny eels 339
Coastal and estuarine species that may occur in freshwaters 343
Carcharhinidae – requiem sharks 343
Pristidae – sawfishes 345
Ambassidae – glassies 347
Atherinidae – silversides 350
Mugilidae – mullets 351
Syngnathidae – pipefishes 354
Sparidae – seabreams 356
Monodactylidae – moonies 358
Eleotridae – sleepers 360
Gobiidae – gobies 363
Glossary 369
Selected references and reading list 377
Useful addresses 379
Index to scientific and common names 381

FOREWORD

Living fish species outnumber all other vertebrates combined, yet fishes are among the least known of the backboned animals. The mammals and birds of southern Africa, and to a lesser extent the reptiles and amphibians, are well studied, but research on our marine and freshwater fishes is still in an exploratory phase.

William Burchell's *Travels in the Interior of Southern Africa* (1822) was the first publication in which southern African freshwater fishes are described. Other noteworthy early descriptions were made by Dr Andrew Smith (1849), the first Director of the South African Museum, the French Consul Count F. Castelnau (1861), the visiting German Professor Dr Wilhelm Peters (1868), and others. In 1896 Dr G.D.F. Gilchrist was appointed as Government Biologist in the Cape. Although he was primarily a marine biologist, he stimulated freshwater ichthyology by encouraging fieldwork and collections, and by inviting the British ichthyologist, Dr G.A. Boulenger, to South Africa in 1905. Gilchrist and his assistant W. Wardlaw Thompson produced the first book specifically on southern African freshwater fishes in 1913–17.

Dr Keppel Barnard, also a Director of the South African Museum, was a superb all-round naturalist who studied marine and freshwater invertebrates and fishes as well as terrestrial invertebrates. His *Pictorial Guide to the Fishes of South Africa* (1947) was the first field guide to our marine and freshwater fishes. Dr Rex Jubb, a meteorologist originally based in Zimbabwe, spent some of his most productive years (1958–late 1970s) at the Department of Ichthyology, Rhodes University, and the Albany Museum in Grahamstown. He published extensively on the taxonomy and biology of southern African freshwater fishes, culminating in his authoritative book *Freshwater Fishes of Southern Africa* in 1967. He also selflessly encouraged many other freshwater ichthyologists, including Graham Bell-Cross, Alan Bowmaker, Bob Crass, Peter Jackson and more recently Mike Coke, Ian Gaigher, Paul Skelton, Ben van der Waal and myself.

Paul Skelton has emerged as Jubb's natural successor and is now recognised as the leading expert on the freshwater fishes of southern Africa. The high regard in which he is held by his scientific colleagues is shown by the frequent invitations that he receives to write chapters in books, attend scientific conferences and collaborate in international research programmes. Besides being a noted fish taxonomist, he has played a leading role in fish conservation and is the author of the *South African Red Data Book – Fishes*. The *Complete Guide to the Freshwater Fishes of Southern Africa* is his most significant publication to date, and continues the fine tradition of great natural history books that have been produced in South Africa.

The scientific illustration of southern African freshwater fishes also has a long tradition, starting with the unpublished paintings of the sharptooth catfish and banded tilapia by William Burchell and the colour illustrations of Sir Andrew Smith. The drawings of J. Green and A.H. Searle in Boulenger's *Catalogue of the Freshwater Fishes of Africa* and Gilchrist & Thompson's books were excellent examples of accurate scientific drawings. Rex Jubb took high quality photographs of many southern African freshwater fishes and his wife, Hilda, used these as a basis for her brilliant paintings in his books. Notable recent freshwater fish illustrators have included Esme Hennessy and Rosemary Ahren for Bob Crass's book on Natal, Janet Duff for Bell-Cross & Minshull's book on Zimbabwe, and Penny Meakin for Paul Skelton's Red Data book. Margaret Smith began the fine tradition of fish paintings in the J.L.B. Smith Institute of Ichthyology, which has been continued by Dave Voorvelt and Elizabeth Tarr, who have both developed distinctive styles. Their meticulous attention to detail has produced outstanding works of scientific illustration.

The text and paintings clearly illustrate the diversity of form and function of our freshwater fishes, as well as their economic importance, and a strong plea is made for their conservation and rational utilisation. We have greatly complicated the ecology of our freshwater fishes by impounding and channelising waterways, linking and polluting rivers and by the introduction of alien fishes and parasites and the over-utilisation of water resources. As a result, determined efforts now have to be made to conserve our freshwater fishes and their habitats. The area covered by this book is bounded in the north by the Cunene and Zambezi systems and includes 14 countries; clearly the resolution of freshwater fish conservation issues will have to be an international affair.

Modern freshwater anglers need to be knowledgeable about their potential catch in order to be successful. This book contains a wealth of information about the feeding and breeding behaviours of fishes as well as their habitat preferences and daily and seasonal cycles which will inform the inquisitive angler. An increased knowledge of our freshwater fishes may also lead to a greater variety of species being caught using bait-casting, spinning and flyfishing techniques.

The mission of the J.L.B. Smith Institute of Ichthyology is to "contribute to the knowledge and understanding of fishes and to promote the conservation and wise use of the aquatic environment". Paul Skelton, Dave Voorvelt and Elizabeth Tarr have contributed significantly to that mission by producing an informative and accurate book of outstanding appeal; all the people of southern Africa will benefit from their achievement.

M.N. Bruton
J.L.B. Smith Institute of Ichthyology, Grahamstown
March 1993.

THE J.L.B. SMITH INSTITUTE OF ICHTHYOLOGY

The Institute is a national museum specialising in the study of fishes. It houses the largest collection of preserved marine and freshwater fishes in Africa. The Institute traces its origins to the work of Professor J.L.B. Smith, after whom it is named, beginning in the late 1920s. In 1939 Professor Smith described the first coelacanth and in 1946 established the Department of Ichthyology at Rhodes University in Grahamstown. In 1969 the Institute was established by Rhodes University and the Council for Scientific and Industrial Research in memory of J.L.B. Smith. Professor Margaret Smith, his widow, served as the first director from 1969 to 1982.

Today the Institute conducts research ranging from marine and freshwater fish taxonomy to the ecology and conservation of marine, estuarine and freshwater fishes, management of threatened fishes, problems of invasive aquatic animals, fisheries in African wetlands, and aspects of aquaculture and the aquarium industry. Several major publications, such as *Smiths' Sea Fishes* and *Fishes of the Southern Ocean*, have been produced. The Institute is active in the education of students and the public in all aspects relating to fish and the aquatic environment. The Society of Friends of the Institute, ICHTHOS, produces a quarterly newsletter and a variety of books, posters and other items relating to fishes and the Institute.

The J.L.B. Smith Institute of Ichthyology

Acknowledgements

This book is built on a 20 year foundation of experience during which numerous people have actively and unselfishly assisted me to explore the freshwater fishes of southern Africa. To all these friends and colleagues I express my sincere appreciation and gratitude.

Professor Mike Bruton supported and encouraged the project from the outset. Dave Voorvelt has produced wondrous illustrations from what is often the flimsiest of sources. I have enjoyed and appreciate greatly the opportunity of working closely with Dave throughout the active compilation of the book. Paintings by Elizabeth Tarr were done during an earlier attempt to launch this project, and her work also is of the highest standard.

As the project crystallised I received direct assistance, photographs and answers to my requests for specimens, information and photographs from a wide variety of friends and colleagues including Graham Bell-Cross, Mike Bruton, Jim Cambray, Mike Coke, Johan Engelbrecht, Humphry Greenwood, Kas Hamman, Clinton Hay, Tom Hecht, Nick James, Neels Kleynhans, Glenn Merron, John Minshull, Peter Jackson, Tom Pike, Sharon Pollard, Shirley Roberts, Tony Ribbink, Tony Smith, Stewart Thorne, Denis Tweddle, Ben van der Waal, Des Weeks, and Alan Whitfield. In particular Denis Tweddle and Ben van der Waal provided numerous specimens and colour transparencies of fishes, for which I would not otherwise have obtained the information needed to prepare the text and illustrations. In the laboratory I have been helped by Daksha Naran, Robin Stobbs and Billy Ranchod. Mike Bruton kindly read and critically reviewed the entire text; various chapters were read, commented on and improved by Eric Anderson, Humphry Greenwood and Alan Whitfield. Humphry Greenwood has helped to clarify for me many technicalities regarding the anatomy, biology and systematics of fishes. Sharon Tweddle kindly edited a draft of the text.

I undertook several specific trips to gather information for the book. In Zimbabwe I was warmly hosted and assisted by John and the late Jacqui Minshull, in Malawi by Denis and Sharon Tweddle, and, at various times, in Namibia by Justice and Mrs Ken Bethune and Shirley Roberts. I have spent many trips exploring the fishes of the Okavango with Glenn Merron. My research on southern African freshwater fishes is supported by the Foundation for Research Development.

I am very grateful to Basil van Rooyen of Southern Book Publishers for enthusiastically accepting the project, and for his patience in seeing it through. I am grateful to Rita van Dyk and Louise Grantham who both managed the project with understanding and patience. Frances Perryer has ably edited the text and tolerated the changing whims of the author. Anna Jonker, translator of the Afrikaans text, has made many useful suggestions and helped clarify many ambiguous phrases and meanings.

How to Use This Book

This book is a guide to all the currently recognised freshwater fish species from southern Africa. All the freshwater species and a selection of prominent or more commonly encountered estuarine and marine species in freshwaters are described and illustrated. Our aim is to provide a source of basic biological information and the means to recognise and identify southern African freshwater fishes. The following notes explain the scope and foundations of the book.

Classification and groupings The family classification used is based primarily on J.S. Nelson's *Fishes of the World* (1984), with certain adjustments. Genera follow W.N. Eschmeyer's *Catalogue of the Genera of Recent Fishes* (1990), published by the California Academy of Sciences.

Keys Keys for the identification of species are provided at the beginning of each family, genus or group of species. These keys are constructed within a southern African context and may not apply to fishes beyond this region. Most of these keys are new and based on the author's personal experience, a few are adapted from keys published in the literature. In cases where the fishes are difficult to identify it is possible that the couplets do not lead to unambiguous identification of a species. Users experiencing problems with the keys are invited to contact the author with suggestions to improve the keys.

As far as possible clearly evident external or accessible internal (e.g. the number of gill rakers) morphological characters are used in the keys. Line sketches are sometimes used to clarify various characters. Usually dichotomous couplets are used but in a few instances tri- or polychotomies have been used.

Common names are used to introduce each species. The common name is based on Peter Jackson's 1975 list, with additions and adjustments for recent name changes.

Scientific names are given for each species in italics according to accepted practice. A scientific name includes a genus name that always begins with a capital letter (e.g. *Hydrocynus*) and a species name that always begins in the lower case (e.g. *vittatus*). The original author with the year of publication of the name follows the species name (e.g. *Hydrocynus vittatus* Castelnau, 1861). The author and date are placed within brackets if the original genus name has been changed since it was published, e.g. *Oreochromis mossambicus* (Peters, 1852), which was originally described as *Chromis mossambicus*.

Abbreviations are used for standard length (SL), total length (TL) and fork length (FL), dorsal fin (D), anal fin (A), degrees Centigrade (° C) and the usual metric length and mass units: millimetres (mm), centimetres (cm), metres (m), kilometres (km), grams (g), kilograms (kg).

Symbols indicating the recorded size of the species, its conservation status, alien species and man's use of the species are given with each account.

following symbols are used:

Size: one of seven scales

- ✊ 1. to 40 mm SL
- ✌ 2. 40–100 mm SL
- ☝ 3. 101–150 mm SL
- 👤 4. 151–300 mm SL
- 👤 5. 301–600 mm SL
- 👤 6. 601–1000 mm SL
- 👤 7. above 1 m SL

Conservation: one of three symbols of status as defined on p.51

- ⚠E 1. Endangered
- ⚠V 2. Vulnerable
- ⚠R 3. Rare

Alien species (as defined on p.69) are indicated by the following symbol:
⬆

Human use: one or more of three categories:

- 🐟 1. aquarium species
- 🎣 2. angling species
- ✋ 3. aquaculture species

Illustration Each species is illustrated in colour. These illustrations were prepared from actual specimens with the colour taken usually from published or unpublished colour photographs or colour transparencies in the collections of the J.L.B. Smith Institute of Ichthyology or the Albany Museum. Where colour photographs were not available (only a few cases) the species illustrations are based on published colour descriptions or collector's notes.

Readers are cautioned that the colour of fishes is extremely variable depending on a variety of factors such as the nature and condition of the environment, the condition, age and social status of the specimen and even the conditions under which the fish is photographed or held prior to being photographed. The colour of the illustration may differ from a specimen of the same species encountered in the field or in captivity and the identification of a species should thus not be made on colour alone.

Description Descriptions are prepared from field notes and preserved specimens and include the dorsal (D) and anal (A) fin formulae (as explained on p.66); the maximum size reached as recorded in the literature in terms of length and/or mass, and the open angling records for South Africa, Zimbabwe and Malawi. Addresses of the respective records officers for each of these countries are given in the section **Useful addresses** on page 379.

Distribution maps are given for each species. These maps have been compiled from museum records and the literature and are as accurate as the scale allows. We welcome possible new distribution records from the public.

Uses This section records the specific known use of a species by man in a broad context. Excluded are non-specific uses such as in the catches of traditional fisheries where practically every species caught is used.

Notes This section caters for special points that are made, especially as regards the species' taxonomy or nomenclature.

Measurements of fishes Attention is drawn to p.65, where details on various measurements that may be taken of a fish are given.

Glossary The meaning of various words as used in this book, especially technical words, is given in the Glossary.

Selected references and reading list Readers who are interested in finding out more about any particular aspect may refer to this section, which is not a comprehensive list of all the literature used to compile the book. In addition, readers are invited to contact the author at the given address with new or interesting information about freshwater fishes or in connection with any particular query that may arise and is not answered in the book.

Introduction

INTRODUCTION

A BRIEF HISTORY OF SOUTHERN AFRICAN FRESHWATER ICHTHYOLOGY

The recognised scientific descriptions of animals began with the publication of the tenth edition of Linnaeus's *Systema Naturae* in 1758. No indigenous southern African species were described by Linnaeus but two introduced species, the brown trout *(Salmo trutta)* and the European perch *(Perca fluviatilis)*, were described in this seminal edition. The smallmouth yellowfish *Barbus aeneus* and the barbel or sharptooth catfish *Clarias gariepinus* were the first freshwater fishes described from southern Africa, in William Burchell's (1822) account of his travels.

Archaeological excavations and cave paintings show that, well before the first Europeans arrived, the inhabitants of southern Africa were familiar with river fishes. Soon after the settlement of Europeans in the Cape prominent species such as the whitefish *(Barbus andrewi)* were noted in the records of early expeditions to the interior. The names given to the fishes in these early accounts were often based on those of well-known European species or on outstanding features of the fishes themselves. The whitefish and Clanwilliam yellowfish *(Barbus capensis)*, for example, were both referred to as "a type of carp", and the redfin minnows as "gudgeons" or "rooivlerkies".

Scientific interest in freshwater fishes began in the early 1800s when several naturalist-explorers including Henry Lichtenstein, William Burchell and Ludwig Krebbs made expeditions into the interior to collect animal and plant specimens. Burchell's classic account of his travels in 1811–12 included the description of the first two species of southern African freshwater fishes. In 1825 steps were taken to establish a museum in Cape Town, and a young medical doctor, Andrew Smith, was appointed as superintendent. Smith conducted an expedition into the interior in 1834–36 and later published illustrations and descriptions of many of the animals collected, including several freshwater fish species, between 1840 and 1845.

Between 1842 and 1848 the famous German scientist Professor Dr Wilhelm Peters led an expedition to the lower Zambezi area in what is now Mozambique. Peters described many new species during and after the expedition and provided new insight into the anatomy and biology of several more interesting fishes of that area such as the many-spined climbing perch *(Ctenopoma multispine)*, the lungfish *(Protopterus annectens)* and the electric catfish *(Malapterurus electricus)*. Peters also described two species from the Cape (the eastern Cape redfin *Pseudobarbus afer* and the sawfin *Barbus serra)* collected in the 1820s by Ludwig Krebbs.

4 HISTORY OF ICHTHYOLOGY

In 1861 the French Consul at the Cape, Count F. Castelnau, described 21 freshwater species from the Cape and as far afield as the Okavango Delta area. Castelnau's species included such well-known fishes as the tigerfish *(Hydrocynus vittatus)* and the eastern Cape rocky *(Sandelia bainsii)*, and one of his new species *(Cyprinus longicaudis)*, supposedly from a river in Namaqualand, was subsequently shown to be a goldfish!

Several other European scientists, among them Dr Franz Steindachner (Vienna), Dr Max Weber (Amsterdam), Dr Albert Günther and Dr George Boulenger (both of the British Museum), made important contributions during the latter half of the 19th and early 20th century.

Dr G.D.F. Gilchrist and his assistant Mr W.W. Thompson at the South African Museum were the first resident scientists to work on southern African freshwater fishes. They wrote the first comprehensive catalogue in 1913–17. Their successor, Dr Keppel Barnard, revised the fishes from the south-west Cape region and described several new species in 1938 and 1943. Between 1930 and 1960 a number of local and overseas scientists made taxonomic contributions. Dr Rex Jubb was the next major authority, writing numerous papers that described new species and clarified the identity of others between 1953 and the late 1970s. Jubb's chief contribution was the book *Freshwater Fishes of Southern Africa* published in 1967. During the same era several other important regional accounts were published by southern African scientists, including Peter Jackson *(The Fishes of Northern Rhodesia,* 1961), Bob Crass *(The Fishes of Natal,* 1964) and Graham Bell-Cross *(The Fishes of Rhodesia,* 1976, now reprinted with co-author John Minshull as *The Fishes of Zimbabwe,* 1988). A Belgian scientist, Dr Max Poll, published an authoritative account of the fishes of Angola in 1967.

Over the past hundred years or so fish hatcheries and Inland Fisheries Departments (later assimilated into Nature Conservation authorities) have played an important role, conducting surveys, studying the biology of species and sending the specimens to the museums. Until 1950 the South African Museum in Cape Town led the taxonomic study of freshwater fishes in southern Africa, but since 1950 this research has been conducted by the J.L.B. Smith Institute of Ichthyology and the Albany Museum in Grahamstown. The South African Museum collection as well as smaller collections from other South African museums have now been sent to the Grahamstown museums. Another important collection is housed in the Zimbabwe Museum of Natural History in Bulawayo, and there is a small collection in the State Museum of Namibia in Windhoek.

Systematic ichthyology in southern Africa is now focused on revisions and studies of phylogenetic relationships. In addition new approaches and techniques are being applied and studies of early life history, behaviour, chromosomes and biochemical characters are advancing our knowledge of these interesting organisms. The practical aspects of aquaculture and fisheries science are rapidly expanding studies and are being actively pursued by a new generation of scientists.

HISTORY OF ICHTHYOLOGY 5

Fig.1 (Clockwise from top): William J. Burchell (1781–1863), Dr Andrew Smith (1797–1872), Dr Wilhelm K. H. Peters (1815–1883), Dr John D. F. Gilchrist (1866–1926), Dr Keppel H. Barnard (1886–1963), Dr Rex A. Jubb (1905–1987).

6 HISTORY OF ICHTHYOLOGY

Much of our knowledge on the biology and ecology of southern African freshwater fishes has its roots in the writings of naturalists and anglers. Over the past few decades scientific research on freshwater fish biology, ecology and physiology has been conducted by the nature conservation departments, universities and institutions such as the J.L.B. Smith Institute of Ichthyology. Major studies have included the fishes from the Vaal–Orange system, Lake Sibaya in Maputaland, the Phongolo floodplain, rivers of the Kruger National Park and the Zambesi and Okavango systems. Information from all these studies has been used in presenting the species accounts in this field guide.

GEOGRAPHICAL BACKGROUND

Physical features (Fig.2)
In this book southern Africa is defined as that part of the African continent south of the northern watershed of the Cunene, Okavango and Zambezi rivers, excluding Lake Malawi and the Shire River above the Kapachira Falls.

Southern Africa extends south as a broad but narrowing landmass, from a latitude of about 10° S to 34° S and longitude 12° E to 36° E. It is surrounded by sea on three sides: to the east and south lies the Indian Ocean, to the west the Atlantic. The east coast is brushed by the southerly flowing warm Mozambique-Agulhas current, the west coast by the northerly flowing cold Benguella current.

Structurally the land consists of a low-lying coastal plain and an elevated interior plateau separated by a short steep escarpment. The coastal plain is narrow in the far south and broadest in the north-east (Mozambique). In places the coastal plain has been deeply dissected by river valleys. The valleys of the larger rivers such as the Zambezi, Limpopo and Orange penetrate deep into the interior. The Great Escarpment forms a mountain belt surrounding the plateau, reaching its greatest elevation in the Drakensberg of Natal and Lesotho. In the far south the Cape Fold Mountains are interposed between the coast and the Great Escarpment. They consist of a double east–west orientated arc from Algoa Bay to the south-west Cape and a north–south arc parallel to the west coast. These ancient mountains are the most prominent fold mountains in Africa apart from the Atlas Mountains in Morocco and Tunisia. Other highlands of note in southern Africa are the Eastern Highlands of Zimbabwe, the Angolan Highlands and the Khomas Highlands in Namibia.

Drainage
The drainage pattern consists of a few large systems that drain the interior, each separated by a series of shorter river systems that drain the coastal plain. From the north the major systems are, draining eastwards, the Zambezi, Save and Limpopo and draining westwards, the Cunene (or Kunene) and the Orange.

Rising in the Angolan Highlands, the Okavango flows south and east to the

GEOGRAPHICAL BACKGROUND 7

Fig.2 Countries, major centres and geographical features of southern Africa.

Delta in Botswana. At times of high water the Delta overflows through the Selinda spillway into the Linyanti–Chobe, and is therefore usually considered to be a part of the Zambezi system. Waters passing through the Delta enter the Botletle River which drains to Lake Dow and the Magadikgadi. The Zambezi system is divided into the upper, middle and lower Zambezi on the basis of natural geographic barriers to the freshwater fishes. The Victoria Falls forms the natural barrier between the upper and middle Zambezi and the Cahora Bassa rapids (now the Cahora Bassa dam) the division between middle and lower Zambezi.

The coastal systems separating these larger drainages are a north-east belt including the Busi, Pungwe and Save rivers, a south-east coastal belt including the Incomati, Phongolo, Tugela and smaller rivers up to and including the Umtamvuna system, a southern coastal belt including all rivers between the Umtamvuna and the Eerste in False Bay, a west coastal drainage from False Bay to the Orange including the Clanwilliam Olifants River, and a Namibian coastal drainage from the Orange to the Cunene.

8 GEOGRAPHICAL BACKGROUND

Southern Africa has only a few natural freshwater lakes, of which Lake Sibaya in Maputaland is the largest (65 km^2) and best known. On the other hand several large man-made lakes have been created by dams on large river systems. Lake Kariba and Lake Cahora Bassa on the Zambezi and Lake Verwoerd and Lake Le Roux on the Orange are the best known. In addition, there are over 550 large river impoundments in South Africa alone that create lentic – standing water – habitats for fishes. Major floodplains and wetlands include the Okavango Delta, the coastal reaches of the Zambezi, Pungwe, Buzi, Save, Limpopo, Incomati and Phongolo river systems in Mozambique and the Mkuze swamps in north-east Zululand. The coastal lakes of southern Mozambique, northern Zululand and the southern Cape also provide important habitats for freshwater fishes in their upstream reaches.

Temporary water bodies that may sometimes have fishes in them include rain-filled pans in the dry Kalahari, the Karoo and the coastal plain of northern Natal and Mozambique as well as the large Etosha and Makarikari pans of northern Namibia and Botswana. Isolated sinkhole lakes, cave lakes and natural springs or river "eyes" are also found in certain regions, and these sometimes hold interesting fish communities. The most notable examples are Lakes Guinas and Otjikoto in Namibia, Aigamas Cave lake in Namibia and the Molopo and Kuruman Eyes in the northern Cape.

Climate

The climate of southern Africa varies from warm tropical in the north-east to a temperate Mediterranean-type in the south-west Cape. Tropical climates predominate across the northern sector and down the lowveld reaches of the east coast to central Natal. Under the influence of the warm Mozambique-Agulhas ocean current a narrow band of subtropical climate extends along the east coast south to the eastern Cape. Moving inland the effects of altitude moderate the climate, especially over the highveld region where warm temperate conditions prevail. In winter low nocturnal temperatures are typical of this region; coupled with generally dry conditions and low river flows, this has an important effect on fish distribution. In winter the southern and south-west Cape are subject to the low-pressure cyclonic cells of the westerlies which bring rain and snow to the higher lying areas.

Summer rainfall is normal for most of the subcontinent except the southern and south-west Cape, where all-year and winter rainfall respectively occurs. Rainfall is generally greatest in the east and across the northern sector, especially in Angola, and least in the west. Desert and semi-desert conditions are found along the west coast and adjacent interior. Local rainfall is highest along the escarpment and in the mountains. The regularity and degree of rainfall is highly variable from region to region so that drought and flood conditions are both common and generally unpredictable. The larger rivers across the northern sector of the subcontinent have a fairly reliable seasonal flood cycle resulting from the summer rainfall in their catchments.

GEOGRAPHICAL BACKGROUND 9

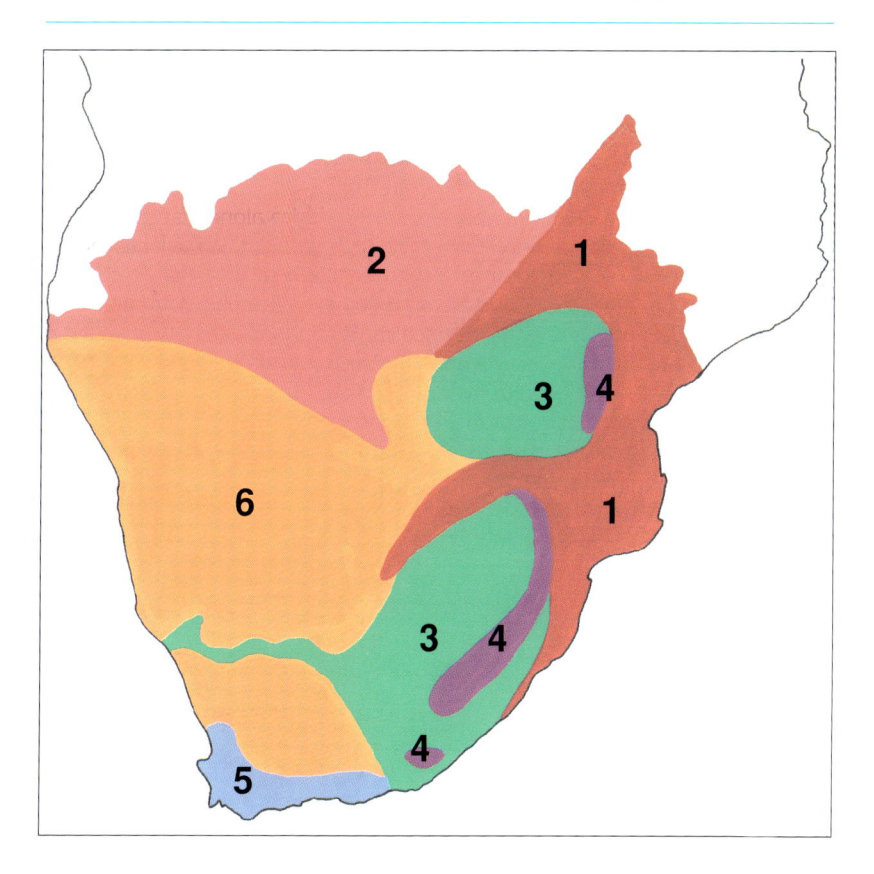

Fig.3 Aquatic ecoregions of southern Africa (see numbered list below).

Aquatic ecoregions (Fig.3)
When several environmental factors combine to create similar conditions over broad areas the animals and plants often form characteristic communities or biomes. Factors that may contribute to defining such regions for the aquatic systems of southern Africa include climate, vegetation, geology, altitude and the nature of the biological communities. The aquatic ecoregions of southern Africa include the following:
1 Tropical east coast region, including extensions along the Zambezi and Limpopo valleys. The rivers are generally low-gradient mature systems with floodplain reaches. Other water bodies include coastal lakes, swamps and temporary rain-filled pans.
2 Tropical interior region. These are relatively large, well-watered catchments with a distinct annual flood regime in response to seasonal rainfall cycles. The rivers include young as well as mature stretches with extensive flood-

plain and swamp reaches.
3 Highveld (temperate) region. Includes two subregions based on fauna: (a) the interior plateau regions of Zimbabwe with comparatively higher numbers of tropical species as a result of the connections to the Zambezi system, and (b) the Transvaal–Orange Free State region extending to the coast in southern Natal and Transkei.
4 Montane-escarpment region. Generally high-gradient streams with cool temperatures and low or moderate concentrations of dissolved solids. The region is fragmented into "islands" arranged like an archipelago along the escarpment. The fish fauna is of low diversity and includes several characteristic species like mountain catlets and chiselmouths.
5 Cape Fold Mountain region. Generally clear cool-temperate acid water streams, but influenced by marine-based geological deposits in lowland valleys and coastal reaches. The fish fauna is highly endemic and distinct.
6 Kalahari–Karoo–Namib region. Generally arid with intermittent rivers and temporary pans. Isolated permanent springs and sinkholes also occur. Waters are usually alkaline and turbid when flowing. The fishes are mostly hardy species or relicts.

AQUATIC SYSTEMS AND HABITATS

Water covers more than 70% of the earth's surface, and is an essential medium for life on earth. On the land freshwater bodies such as rivers and lakes cover only a small percentage of the total surface. Much of Africa is generally arid with abundant surface water only present in the huge lakes of the Great Rift Valley and in the lowland tropical forest regions of Zaire and West Africa. Southern Africa is also comparatively dry; perennial rivers occur along the northern, eastern and southern sectors but the rivers of the interior and western areas are generally either periodic (flowing during certain periods of the year only) or episodic (flowing at varied and unpredictable intervals).

Water as a living medium
By comparison with air, water is a dense, heavy medium. This means that it provides greater physical support to an organism but also creates greater resistance to forward movement. Consequently, fishes are generally smooth and streamlined; they have light bones and their fins serve as hydrofoils, keels or brakes.

Water is also an excellent solvent and contains dissolved minerals and ions from the soil. Minerals are essential for life, but high concentrations may be harmful or toxic. In freshwaters the level of ions in the body fluids of fishes must be maintained at a higher concentration than in the medium, both by retention of ions and by control of water flux. Different combinations of dissolved minerals determine the pH (degree of acidity or alkalinity) of water. Most southern African waters are neutral or alkaline (pH 7 to about 8) but those draining the sandstone formations of the Cape Fold Mountains are naturally acidic (pH 5 to 6,9).

Water contains only about 1–20 mg/*l* of dissolved oxygen, much less than the 200 mg/*l* of oxygen in air. The amount of dissolved oxygen decreases with increasing water temperature so that cool, moving waters contain more oxygen than warm, standing waters. Fishes that live in poorly oxygenated waters such as tropical swamps often have accessory air-breathing organs, or may use behavioural mechanisms, such as breathing from the thin surface layer of water, to increase the available oxygen.

Because water is a denser medium than air, light penetrates less and is more rapidly diffused. Some fishes, e.g. catfishes and mormyrids, depend less on eyesight than other senses for survival and the detection of prey or predators. Fishes in midwater are visible from both below and above, so that in order to blend in with the habitat they are countershaded, lighter below and darker above. In turbid waters, where light is scattered, fishes are often very pale and silvery in colour.

Sound is much more readily conducted through water than air. Fishes are extremely sensitive to sound or pressure waves and the lateral line system is a specialised sensory organ to detect such waves. The swimbladder of some species acts as a sound amplifier.

Water, especially with dissolved ions, is a good conductor of electricity. The mormyrids and certain catfishes are able to generate and receive electric signals that are used for different functions such as communication, or to locate prey or potential enemies and, by the electric catfish *(Malapterurus electricus)*, for self-defence or to stun prey.

Temperature plays a very important role in water as a living medium by affecting the rate of chemical reactions and the metabolic rate of organisms. Water absorbs and releases heat much more slowly than air so that temperature changes in water are relatively more gradual. Consequently fishes are often very sensitive to rapid changes in temperature, and a sudden cold snap or hail storm may cause widespread mortalities. Being "cold-blooded" organisms, the body temperature of fishes, and hence their metabolism, is largely determined by the ambient temperature of the water. Because metabolic rates and other vital functions are temperature dependent, the distribution of many fishes is determined by the temperature regime.

Problems of feeding and breeding are different in water. Eggs can be fertilised after being laid in water but they are in danger of being carried away by currents and need to be protected or secured in some way. Special adaptations are also required by the embryos and larvae to ensure they are not swept away into undesirable habitats, or damaged by currents.

Fishes in rivers, especially predators like the tigerfish, often congregate at the head of a pool or the tail of a rapid where the current naturally carries food items. Other species like trout take advantage of the protection of rocks and boulders to avoid the current while feeding. Quiet places such as backwaters and bays are important feeding grounds for bottom feeders.

12 AQUATIC SYSTEMS

Fig.4
A spectrum of southern African freshwater systems:

(a) A Cape Fold mountain stream, the Twee River, Cedarberg Mountains.

(b) The Kouga River, Baviaanskloof Mountains, eastern Cape.

(c) The Levhuvu River, Kruger National Park.

AQUATIC SYSTEMS 13

(d) A riverine floodplain, the Okavango River at Rundu, Namibia.

(e) A swamp channel, Okavango Delta, Botswana.

(f) A natural lake, Lake Bangazi in Maputaland.

Rivers

Rivers are extremely dynamic entities, constantly changing in form through diverse landscapes and over time with the seasons and rainfall. Typically a river system begins in mountains or elevated areas as many small headwater streams which combine to form larger rivers, eventually with one mainstream entering an estuary, lake or the sea. Distinct zones along a river are defined by the gradient and the nature of the river bed.

Headwater streams are often, but not always, found within deep valleys on steep mountain slopes; they have narrow channels with rocky beds often forming cascades, waterfalls and rapids. The current is usually fast flowing, the water cool, clear and well oxygenated. Some headwater streams arise on low-gradient plateaux such as the highveld. These streams also have narrow channels but the bed consists of gravel, pebbles or cobbles; bushes and grass line the banks.

As the river descends to the foothills of the mountains the gradient declines, boulders and large rocks form the bed structure, waterfalls and cascades are less frequent and pools are generally larger. Trees are more frequent along the banks. As the gradient declines further the bed nature changes to smaller cobbles and pebbles with sandy patches in pools. Deep runs interspersed with short rapids are more common and waterfalls are uncommon.

In the middle stretches of the river the bed widens, flow decreases and submerged and emergent vegetation such as palmiet and reeds becomes part of the environment. In southern Africa it is here that the rivers are exposed to man: many weirs have been built and the water is extracted for irrigation. The river meanders increasingly and finer deposits appear, with mud and silt being typical of the more mature sections. During rains the combined input of the tributaries may cause the mainstreams to flood their banks, and in the larger systems such as the Zambezi and Okavango, extensive floodplains are formed.

Lakes

Lakes may be natural or man-made. In southern Africa there are few natural lakes and most are formed by the damming of rivers. Man-made lakes are important habitats for fishes, providing deep, open waters with relatively narrow bands of inshore environments that offer food and cover. The shorelines of man-made lakes are often unstable because of fluctuating water levels due to the many uses to which their water is put. Riverine lakes also act as nutrient traps and their waters can become very enriched as a result of the sediment and chemicals accumulated from the catchment. Algal blooms may develop and cause oxygen depletion and toxification. Temperature regimes in large lakes are quite different to those in rivers. The deeper waters of lakes are often much colder than the upper layers and may also be de-oxygenated as a result of the decomposition of organic sediments.

Temporary waters

Some lakes, pans and rivers do not have a reliable water supply and are only filled on a temporary basis, either after sufficient rain or following a river flood.

Temporary waters may be inhabited by fishes provided that there is some access for them in the first place. Some fishes are specially adapted to live in temporary waters, either by being able to air-breathe and aestivate in the mud during the dry period, like lungfish *(Protopterus* species), or, as with killifish *(Nothobranchius* species), by laying drought-resistant eggs which hatch once the habitat is filled with water again. Temporary pans may form rich habitats for the short time that they exist, with abundant food derived from decaying plant and animal matter and newly hatched insects.

Estuaries

Estuaries occur at the mouth of the river where it enters the sea. In the upper reaches of an estuary the water may be quite fresh, grading to sea water at the mouth. Even higher concentrations than sea water can occur in estuaries under conditions of reduced freshwater inflow. Estuarine fishes are typically tolerant of a wide range of salinities and usually include freshwater species as well as specialised estuarine and marine species. Cichlid species such as the Mozambique tilapia *(Oreochromis mossambicus)* are tolerant of salinity and frequently occur in estuaries. Gobies and sleepers (eleotrids) such as the tank goby *(Glossogobius giuris)*, the river goby *(G. callidus)*, the golden sleeper *(Hypseleotris dayi)* and the dusky sleeper *(Eleotris fusca)* are found in many estuaries and rivers. Other common estuarine fishes like the mullets, including the freshwater mullet *(Myxus capensis)* and the flathead mullet *(Mugil cephalus)*, often spend part of their life cycle in freshwaters. For eels the estuaries are important areas where they adjust to the changing salinities of the environment during their migrations to and from the sea.

Special environments

Lakes in caves and underground waters are sometimes inhabited by fishes. They form special environments because many of the usual factors, such as light, plants and food organisms are not present and water temperature may be constant throughout the year so that regular cycles and cues for breeding are absent.

Fishes in such environments often become stunted and lose pigment; their eyes degenerate and, after many generations, their sight may be lost entirely, the senses of smell and touch increasing considerably. They feed on whatever falls or washes into the water, such as insects and the droppings of bats or baboons. Because of the restricted food supplies they do not generally form large populations and may cannibalise their own young.

16 DISTRIBUTION FACTORS

Fig.5
Some factors affecting fish distribution:

(a) Waterfalls such as the Tsitsa Falls, north-east Cape, form barriers.

(b) Turbidity is harmful to many species.

FACTORS AFFECTING FISH DISTRIBUTION

Freshwater systems are usually restricted and well defined in extent. Consequently the distribution of freshwater fishes is often more distinct and restricted than that of amphibious and terrestrial animals. Besides the physical limits of water bodies, there are other factors that govern the distribution of fishes within the systems themselves. Chief amongst these are physical barriers, physico-chemical tolerance, ecological barriers, and biological and behavioural factors.

The physical boundary of a particular water body is the most obvious limit to fish distribution. Rivers and lakes do, however, change over time in accordance with geological processes such as mountain building, rifting and erosion. An actively eroding river may capture adjacent drainages, transferring the fauna of

(c) Swamps such as in the Okavango Delta form barriers to some riverine species.

(d) Weirs, dams and other man-made structures form barriers to fish movement.

one system to the next. River basins may be connected by the retreat of sea-level during cooler periods of the earth's history. Conversely, connected systems may be separated by rising or advancing sea-levels. Lakes may be formed by rockfalls, as was the case with Lake Fundudzi in Venda. Faulting of the earth's surface can block or redirect a river's course, as when a fault disrupted the Okavango River to form the Okavango Delta, and faulting redirected the upper Zambezi towards the Batoka Gorge and the Victoria Falls.

Waterfalls develop over time and may divide a fish fauna and prevent upstream or downstream movement. A vertical fall of about two metres will be an effective barrier to most free-swimming fishes. Some species such as eels and suckermouths *(Chiloglanis* species) may overcome barriers which are too high to jump, by climbing wet surfaces using their mouths or fins. Some of the better known waterfall barriers to fishes in southern Africa include the Victoria Falls on the Zambezi, the Kapachira Falls on the Shire, the twin Chibirira and

Selawandoba Falls on the Save and Runde rivers respectively, and the Augrabies Falls on the Orange.

The gradient of a river can form a barrier to different fish species depending on their swimming abilities and habitat preferences. A strong-swimming form with high oxygen requirements will be discouraged from moving into a downstream zone where slow-flowing waters and low oxygen conditions prevail. Brown and rainbow trout, for example, are usually restricted to the cooler upland reaches of rivers. Conversely, lowland species such as carp *(Cyprinus carpio)* are restricted from moving too far upstream into the fast-flowing tributaries.

The thermal tolerance of fishes is often a factor limiting their distribution. Southern African freshwater fishes are broadly categorised into temperate and tropical fauna. The temperate fauna is restricted to areas where maximum temperatures are generally below about 25–28° C during the summer months. The tropical fauna is restricted to areas where temperatures do not decline below about 15–18° C during the cooler winter months.

In recent times man has modified the natural distribution ranges of many species, increasing them through introduction and translocations, or decreasing them by destroying their habitat and introducing alien fishes that displace or eliminate the indigenous ones. Pollution may directly eliminate fishes from long stretches of rivers. Severely increased turbidity of many rivers is detrimental to fishes by reducing light, clogging their gills and smothering the river bottom, which affects their feeding and breeding requirements. Water extraction, especially during dry periods, may cause rivers to dry out, while the building of dams changes habitats from riverine (flowing waters) to lacustrine (standing waters).

Water transfer schemes linking different river basins also allow fishes to move from one basin to another. Some well-known cases of indigenous fishes extending their distribution range by these and other means are, for example, the smallmouth yellowfish *(Barbus aeneus)* from the Orange system to rivers such as the Gourits, Great Fish and Kei; the common or sharptooth catfish *(Clarias gariepinus)* is now well established in the Sundays, the Great Fish and the Keiskamma rivers of the eastern Cape as well as in the Eerste River and the Cape Flats area. The nembwe *(Serranochromis robustus)* has been introduced throughout Zimbabwe as well as to Swaziland and Natal.

The range of several indigenous species has declined following the introduction of alien species. In the southern and south-west Cape several redfin minnows *(Pseudobarbus* species) have been eliminated from large parts of their natural range following the introduction of largemouth, smallmouth and spotted bass *(Micropterus* species). Two indigenous fishes, the Berg river redfin *(Pseudobarbus burgi)* and the Cape kurper *(Sandelia capensis)* have been eliminated from the Eerste, which is polluted and degraded after passing through Stellenbosch, since the introduction of trout and bass.

WHAT IS A FISH?

In broad terms a fish is a cold-blooded vertebrate animal, living in water, breathing by means of gills, and having fins for stability and movement. Fishes are by far the most numerous and diverse group of vertebrates and differ from this basic plan in a variety of ways. It is only possible to consider briefly a few basic points about them here.

Body sections (Fig.6)
The body of a fish consists of a head, trunk and tail. Unlike many other vertebrates, it is not always easy to tell where one region ends and the next begins. The head, which bears the eyes, nostrils, mouth and gills, is usually measured from the tip of the snout to the end of the gill covers. The trunk comprises the body from behind the head to the end of the body cavity, as usually indicated by the anus or the start of the base of the anal fin. The tail region comprises the caudal peduncle and the caudal or tail fin. The caudal peduncle is measured from the hind end of the anal fin to the base of the caudal fin, which is taken along the line of flexure of the fin rays and the body.

Shape (Fig.7)
A fish's shape gives an indication of its biology and habitat requirements. For example, an anguilliform or eel-like shape is suited to living in holes or crevices or to moving through dense or tangled root stocks or vegetation; an eel swims by moving the body in a series of waves, the fins playing relatively little part.

Active swimmers like minnows, trout or the tigerfish usually have a fusiform body, broadest in the middle and tapered towards either end. These fishes move by wave-like thrusts passing along the body to the tail fin. The fins play an important stabilising role by preventing the fish from yawing, rolling or pitching; the pectoral fins also act as rudders and brakes. Fishes living in fast currents or those that are very swift swimmers have slender bodies, curved, pointed fins and a deeply forked or crescent-shaped caudal fin.

A deep-bodied fish, like most cichlids, swims by beating its tail and is also capable of slow, gentle manoeuvering or hovering by paddling with the fins, especially the pectorals. The long dorsal and anal fins serve as keels or as organs of display. Selective feeding by picking or grazing from rock surfaces and complex behavioural displays are important in the biology of such fishes.

African pike (*Hepsetus odoe*) have a slender, pointed body with the dorsal and anal fins placed far back. This shape is particularly suited for short, quick bursts as when attacking their prey.

Butter catfish (*Schilbe intermedius*) shoal in midwater and have depressed heads like other catfishes but their body is narrow and deep, with a very long anal fin. Progressive waves along the fin provide a gentle upward and forward thrust.

Benthic fishes, like gobies and many catfish, have broad, flattened heads,

20 WHAT IS A FISH?

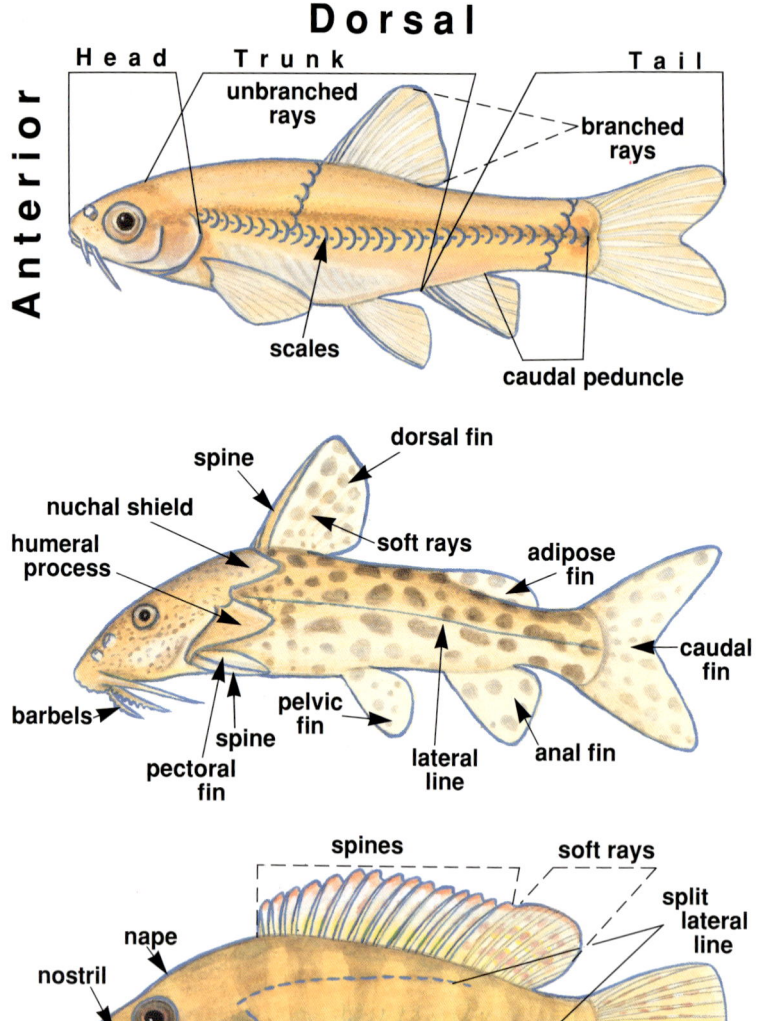

Fig.6 Parts of a fish illustrated from three different fishes, a cyprinid, a catfish and a cichlid.

WHAT IS A FISH? 21

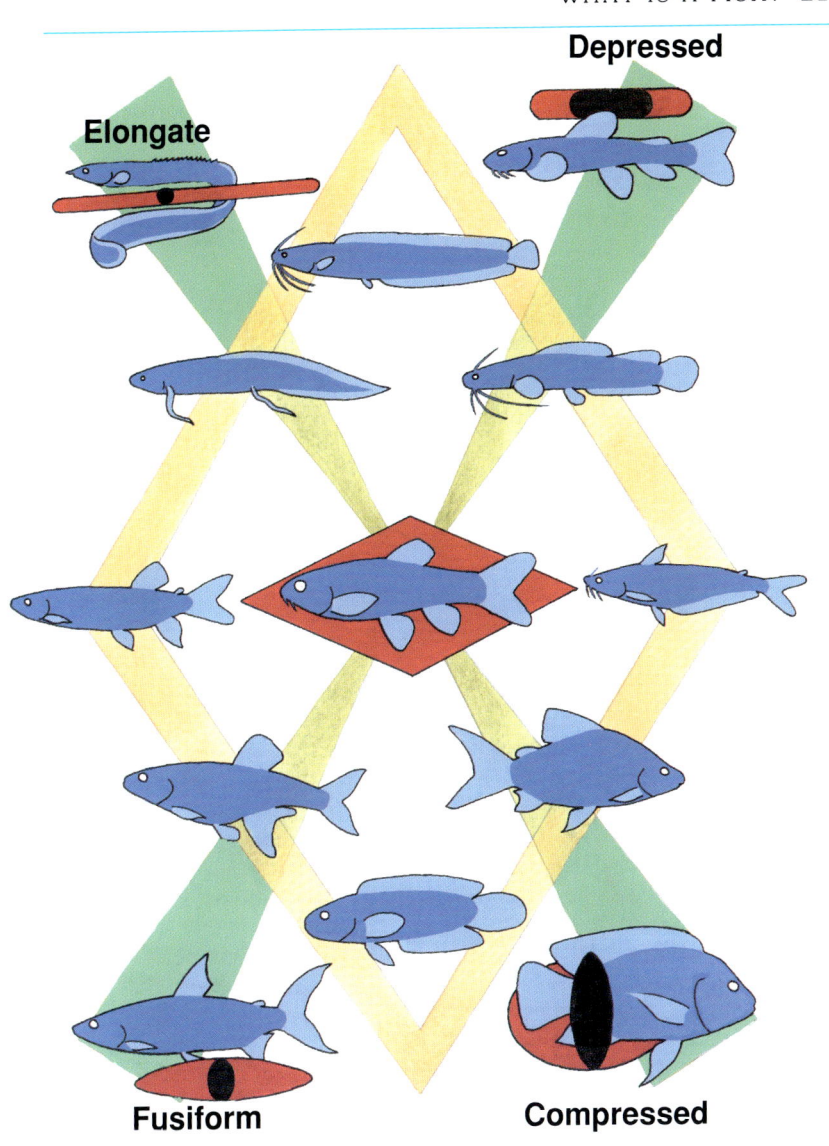

Fig. 7 Shapes of fishes. Body shapes of fishes trend along different axes from a generalised form: active swimmers have streamlined fusiform shapes with pointed fins and oval profiles; agile forms tend to be deep and compressed with broad fins; sedentary forms are broad and flattened; elongated eel-like bodies are suited to entering crevices, burrows or entwined root- or vegetation mats. Intermediate trends are also present: the midwater-living butter catfish have flattened heads and compressed bodies; the snake catfish is flattened and elongated; the African pike has a pointed streamlined body; the blackspot climbing perch is compressed and oval-shaped.

and the pectoral and pelvic fins are often modified to form supports. In the mountain catfishes (*Amphilius* species) the broad pectoral and pelvic fins help keep the fish on the bottom in currents.

Size
The smallest fishes in southern Africa, like the upjaw barb *(Coptostomabarbus wittei)*, the sicklefin barb *(Barbus haasianus)*, and the sand catlets *(Leptoglanis* species*)*, reach maturity at about 20 mm SL (standard length). The largest species, such as the vundu *(Heterobranchus longifilis)* and the sharptooth catfish *(Clarias gariepinus)*, vary in the size at which they mature but can attain a length of about 1,5 m and a mass of 50–60 kg or more. The actual size reached by individuals of a species depends on several factors including genes, age (a fish continues to grow throughout almost all of its life), living space (a large fish requires a spacious habitat like a major river or a lake to reach full size), food resources (both quantity and quality are important), and general ecological and biological factors (for example, fishes living in degraded habitats, or where their energy is channelled into reproduction rather than growth, will not reach their potential full size).

Skin and scales (Figs 8,9)
The skin of fishes provides physical protection and serves as an impermeable barrier between the body fluids and the external medium. Mucus is secreted in order to provide a smooth, friction-reducing layer, for protection against diseases and parasites, for initial healing of wounds and, in many cases, providing toxic secretions for defence against predators. The mucous layer of mormyrids forms a distinctive outer film when they are preserved.

Scales, which consist of a bony plate covered by a thin layer of skin (epidermis), are present in the skin of most fishes. They protect the body and sometimes have an ornamental function. There are several different kinds of scales including the dermal denticles of sharks and sawfishes, placoid scales of the bichir and reedfish (found in tropical Africa), and the cycloid or ctenoid scales of most bony fishes. Cycloid scales are simple and round or ovoid in shape, ctenoid scales have fine teeth on the free edge.

Bony scales increase in size by adding concentric outer layers. Scientists study the pattern of these growth rings to determine the age of a fish in the same way that foresters determine the age and history of a tree from the rings on its trunk. Other important features of scales are thin lines or striae which may radiate from a focus, run in parallel or semi-parallel lines or form a network over the scale. The pattern of these striae is useful in taxonomy and for identifying fossils and fish remains at archaeological sites.

Tubercles occur on the head, body and fins of some fishes. They may appear singly, in groups or in bands, as tiny pimples or as prominent conical or asteroid (star-shaped) wart-like projections. These tubercles have a hard outer layer of keratin, the same substance that forms the nails, feathers and hair of mammals and birds. Various tubercles have different functions depending on their

WHAT IS A FISH? 23

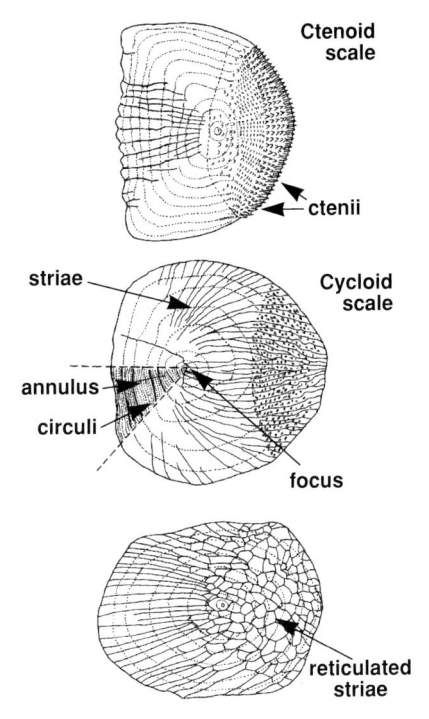

Fig. 8 (left) Scales of fishes: a ctenoid scale from the many-spined climbing perch; a cycloid scale from the cyprinid *Labeo altivelis*; a cycloid scale with reticulate striae from the bulldog *(Marcusenius macrolepidotus)*.

Fig. 9 (above) Tubercles on the head of *Barbus amatolicus*.

size, form and position. They often serve to improve contact between breeding fishes, in butting and sparring between territorial males, and as hydrodynamic aids to reduce turbulence and drag in currents. Unculi are microscopic horny projections from single cells found around or on the mouth and fins of certain cyprinids and catfishes. They assist in protection of the skin, in rasping and providing firm bottom contact in swift currents. Unculi are best seen on the mouthparts of suckermouth catlets (*Chiloglanis* species) and the pectoral fin pads of amphiliid mountain catlets.

Fins (Fig.10)

Fins perform a variety of different functions, mainly in producing and controlling movement, but also in defence, display and communication, spawning activities, and for holding and touch. Their shape, size and position are important identifying characters. Fins are either paired (pectoral and pelvic fins) or lie in the midline (dorsal, caudal and anal fin). Fins are supported by spines and soft rays; spines are either true spines (as found in percoid and other spiny-rayed fishes), or are modified soft rays, as found in the cyprinids and catfishes. Spines may be simple or serrated, i.e. provided with barbs along one or both edges. The spines of many catfishes can be held firmly erect by means of a special locking mechanism, and form a very effective defence. Soft rays are divided into two halves and are segmented; they may be simple or branched.

24 WHAT IS A FISH?

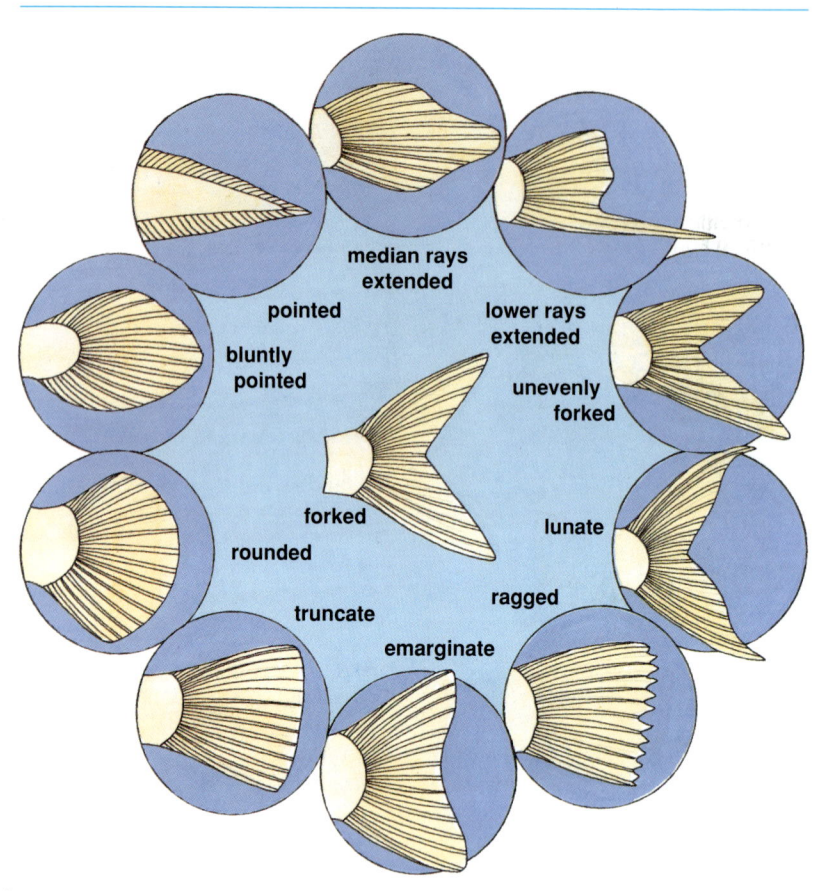

Fig.10 Shapes of caudal fins.

Many fishes have a second dorsal fin which is soft and fleshy, called an adipose fin. The adipose fin may be small and lobate like that of a trout or tigerfish (*Hydrocynus vittatus*), or it may be large and firm like that of the vundu *(Heterobranchus longifilis)* and the squeakers (*Synodontis* species).

Mouth and teeth (Fig.11)
In fishes the mouth may be above (dorsal or superior), at the end of (terminal) or below (inferior or ventral) the tip of the snout. In many fishes the upper and lower jaws can both be moved and the mouth actively extended (protruded) during feeding. In others, like the catfishes, the upper jaw is fixed. The lips indicate the feeding style of the species. Fishes that scrape their food from firm surfaces have firm sharp lips, grubbers have large soft lips, predators have thin lips that may cushion the teeth but allow them to be exposed when feeding. Some fishes, like the yellowfishes (*Barbus* species), which have a wide range of

WHAT IS A FISH? 25

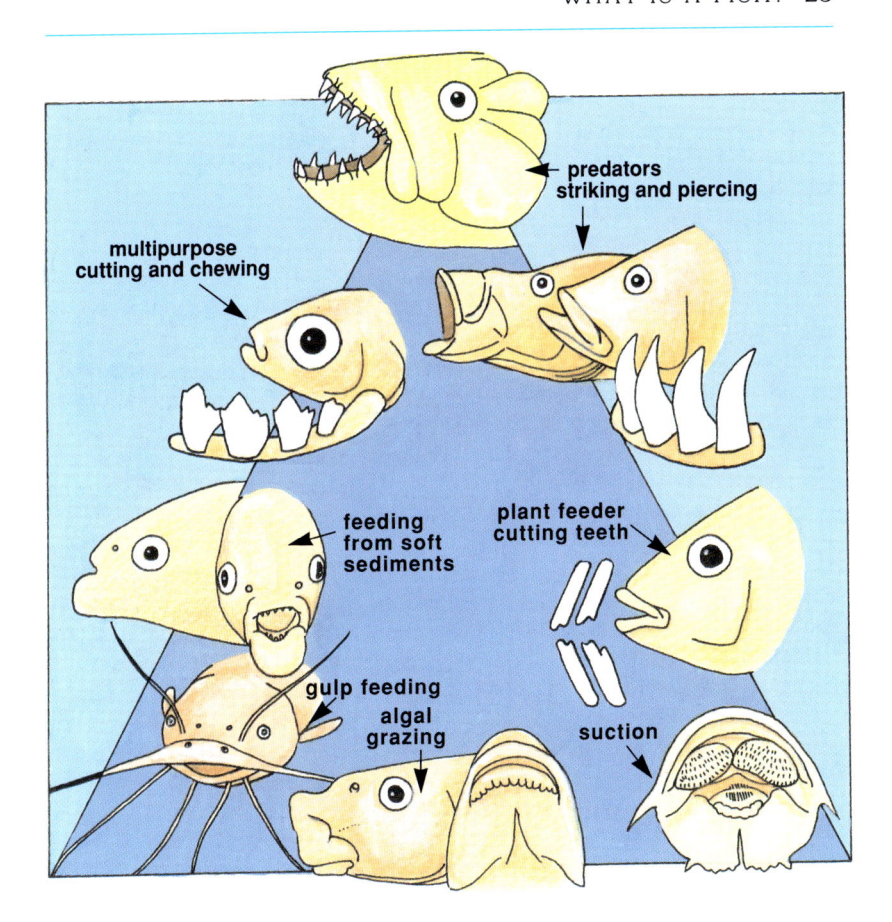

Fig.11 The mouths, jaws and teeth of fishes are shaped according to the functions they perform. Predators have large, often protrusible mouths with sharp, pointed teeth. Omnivores may have multicuspid teeth. Herbivores like *Tilapia rendalli* have teeth suited for biting or nipping plants. Mormyrids have small mouths with small teeth suitable for extracting insects from soft sediments. Catfishes have large mouths with sensory barbels suited for feeding on a range of live or inactive food. Bottom feeders may scrape algae from rocks or use their mouth for attachment in flowing water.

feeding habits, are able to develop different forms of lip, depending on the circumstances.

Teeth occur along the jaws and in the mouth and throat (pharynx) of some fishes. They provide useful identifying characters and indicate the feeding habits of many species. The cyprinids do not have teeth on their jaws, but do have well-developed throat or pharyngeal teeth. Predators like the brown trout *(Salmo trutta)*, tigerfish *(Hydrocynus vittatus)* and African pike *(Hepsetus odoe)* have large pointed teeth in one or a few rows. Catfishes have pads or strong bands, generally of fine pointed teeth. Teeth are replaced several times during the life cycle, either gradually or in a rapid, synchronised fashion. Replacement teeth can be readily seen in species like the squeakers (*Synodontis* species), and occasionally in a tigerfish when it is caught without teeth or with newly erupting teeth.

The teeth in the mouth and throat of fishes serve the important function of crushing and masticating the food prior to its digestion in the gut. In cyprinids the fifth gill arches are modified to form strong, arched, teeth-bearing bones that masticate food against a padded plate at the base of the skull. In the cichlids the fifth gill arches are also modified and joined to form a single triangular unit (pharyngeal bone) with teeth. In these fishes the pharyngeal bones operate in conjunction with two teeth-bearing plates in the palate, each supported by separate bones at the base of the skull.

Some fishes have a tongue but it is not a muscular structure like that of mammals and is never protrusible. It consists of a fleshy pad overlying a medial bone in front of the gill arches.

Sight and eyes

Sight is an important sense for fishes: colours and patterns of body pigments are clearly correlated with finely tuned vision. Besides its obvious role in the detection of predators and food, sight also helps maintain close cohesion between schooling fishes and plays an important part in behaviour and communication between individuals.

In free-swimming forms the eyes are placed on the sides of the head but in bottom-living or shallow stream species the eyes are on top of the head. The mormyrids and the catfishes are mainly active at night and have small eyes. These fishes have other well-developed senses and probably are not capable of fine visual focusing on objects, but can detect varied light conditions and moving objects.

Fishes do not have movable eyelids but some species, like the tigerfish (*Hydrocynus vittatus*) and the flathead mullet (*Mugil cephalus*), have clear protective adipose sheaths covering part of the eye.

Pigment and colour

Some fishes are brightly coloured or have distinct pigment patterns whereas others are dull or camouflaged in tune with the environment. Larvae and small fishes are often transparent or translucent. Generally fishes are countershaded, with the upper parts dark and the lower parts light. This has the effect of cancelling out the brighter light coming from above and makes the fish more difficult to see from all angles. Many fishes control and change their colours rapidly and in some groups, like the cichlids, body colour is an important means of communication.

Colours of fishes are mainly due to the presence of specialised pigment cells in the skin containing red, orange, yellow or black pigment. These cells can expand or contract to form a fine but highly variable mosaic of colours and intensities. The cells respond to both nerve and hormonal controls so that short-term and long-term colour changes are possible. In addition reflective cells containing crystals of guanin provide for the silvery sheen of many fishes.

Smell
Because fishes live in water the sense of smell is highly refined. The nostrils (or nares) open into a chamber containing the main olfactory organs which consist of a series of lamellae or "leaves" over which a water current passes. There is usually a separate inlet and outlet for each organ, but the cichlids only have a single opening on each side.

Fishes use smell not only to detect food items in the water but also to locate familiar places in their environment and to communicate with each other by means of pheromones. Certain migratory fishes like the salmon (*Oncorhynchus* species) are known to home accurately to the stream of their birth using smell. Cyprinids release an alarm substance or pheromone that rapidly alerts other individuals to danger. Pheromones are also used for communicating during breeding activities.

Taste
In addition to the olfactory organs, there are specialised cells for the detection of chemical elements in the water that are concentrated around the mouth and lips as well as on the barbels of catfishes and cyprinids. Barbine and labeine cyprinids may have one or two pairs of simple barbels from the upper jaw. Catfish barbels include a maxillary pair from the upper corners of the mouth and two pairs of mandibular barbels on the lower jaws. An additional pair extends from the base of the nostrils in some catfish species. In the squeakers (*Synodontis* species) the mandibular barbels are branched. Barbels are often mobile and used for touch and taste and sometimes for collecting food. Clariid catfishes extend their barbels to form a basket or net around the mouth.

Gills and air-breathing organs
Fishes breathe by means of gills, which are feather-like filaments arranged in rows along four or five pairs of gill arches at the back of the mouth. The gills of a healthy fish are bright red in colour due to the rich supply of fine blood vessels. On the inside of the gill arches are a number of gill rakers which form an intermeshing sieve to strain the water that passes between the arches and over the gills. The shape, size and number of gill rakers, particularly those on the first gill arches, are useful taxonomic characters.

Fishes frequenting poorly oxygenated waters may have accessory air-breathing organs of one form or another. In the lungfish the swimbladder forms a lung. Clariid catfishes have branching air-breathing organs in a pair of chambers above the gill arches. Anabantid fishes have rosette-shaped air-breathing organs also in a pair of chambers above the gill arches. In some species of air-breathing families the need for air-breathing is redundant and the organ is reduced or lost. This has happened in the case of the Cape kurper and eastern Cape rocky (*Sandelia* species) and the smoothhead catfish *(Clarias liocephalus)*.

Lateral line system

The lateral line system is a specialised feature of fishes and some amphibians that serves to detect water currents or moving bodies at close range. The lateral line consists of interconnected sensory cells lying within a series of mucus- or gel-filled tubules on the head and along the body. The tubules lie near the surface and at intervals have pores opening to the surface. The lines of pores are usually visible along the body and over the head. The lateral line system is often well developed in active-swimming schooling fishes and fishes from running waters and is reduced or absent in certain species. In the cichlids and anabantids it is divided into two separate sections on the body, one along the back and the other along the middle of the caudal peduncle.

Genital appendages (Fig.12)

Some fishes have prominent external genital appendages. The males of many catfish species have an elongated conical papilla, and in the greenhead tilapia (*Oreochromis macrochir*), breeding males develop a tasselled papilla. A separate genital opening is characteristic of catfishes, but a single opening for the anus and genital system is more usual in southern African freshwater fishes. Fins may be modified to serve as sexual appendages. The pelvic fins of male sharks form claspers. In the live-bearers like the guppy and swordtail the male anal fin is highly modified to form a gonopodium or intromittent organ.

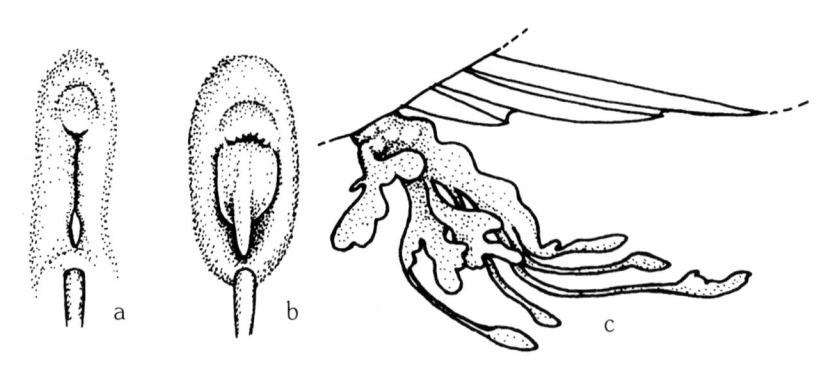

Fig.12 (a) Female and (b) male genital appendages of *Chiloglanis anoterus*; (c) genital tassel of a male *Oreochromis macrochir*.

Skeleton (Fig.13)

Fishes are vertebrates with an internal bony or cartilaginous skeleton made up of head components, vertebral column and fin-supporting elements.

In cartilaginous fishes the head skeleton consists of a box-like braincase with upper and lower jaws, a hyoid arch which suspends the lower jaws and five branchial or gill arches. The fins of sharks are quite different to those of bony fishes and consist of a series of basal cartilages supporting more numerous outer cartilaginous radial elements. These fins are covered by thick skin; they

WHAT IS A FISH? 29

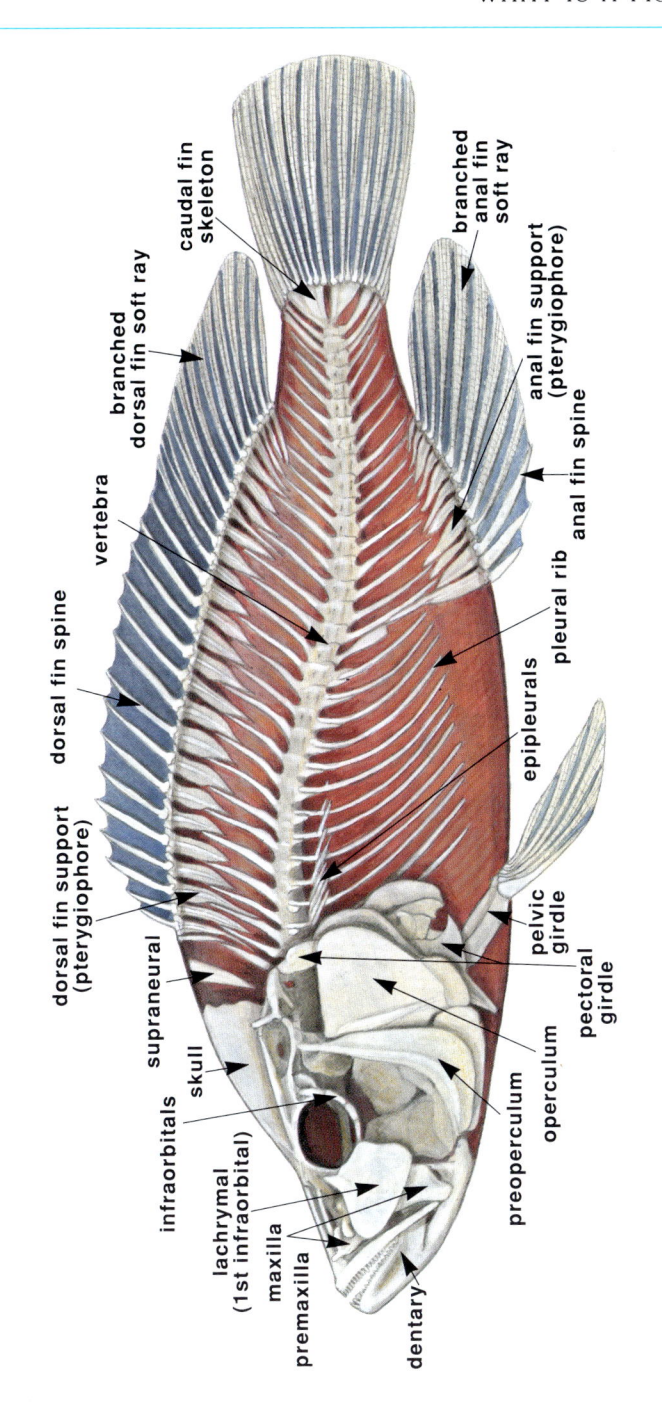

Fig.13 The skeleton of a bony fish (*Serranochromis meridianus*).

30 WHAT IS A FISH?

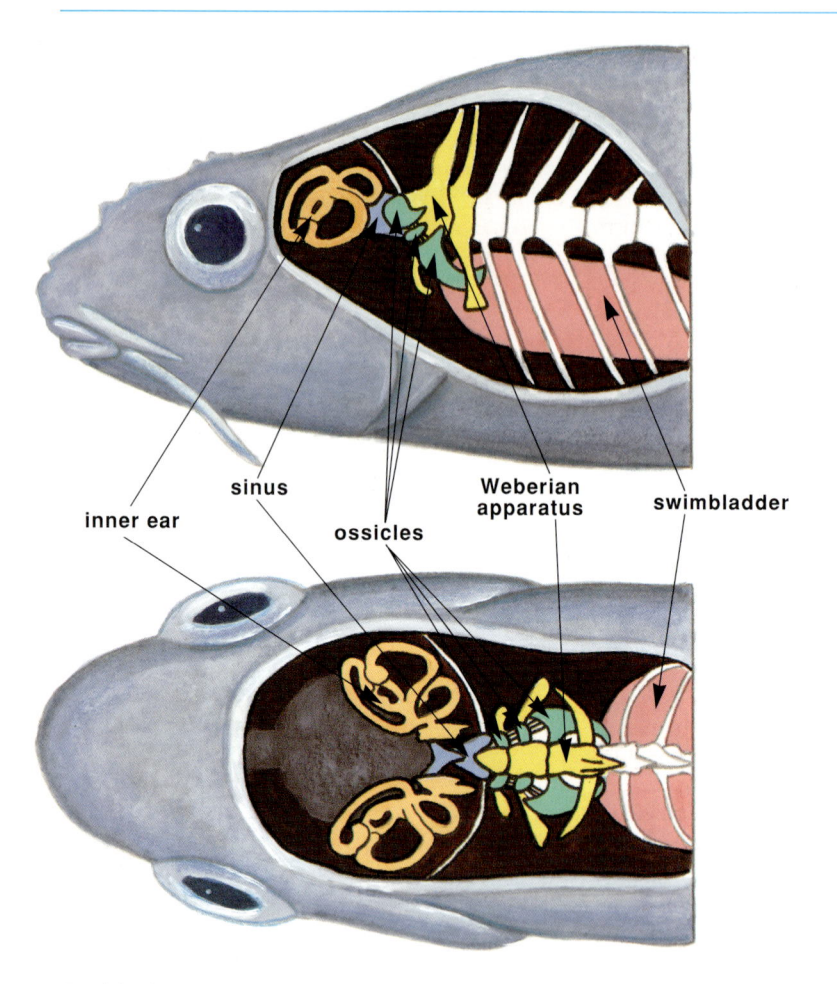

Fig.14 The Weberian apparatus forms a link beween the swimbladder and the inner ear of otophysan fishes.

cannot be folded or expanded and act chiefly as hydrofoils.

In bony fishes the skeleton is more complex. The skull consists of a series of bones forming a neurocranium or braincase housing the inner ears and brain and supporting the eyes and olfactory organs. The upper jaws, the bones of the palate and lower jaws, the gill arches, gill covers and pectoral girdles are attached to or suspended from the neurocranium. The vertebral column consists of a series of abdominal (rib-bearing and without haemal arches) and caudal (with haemal arches) vertebrae and the caudal skeleton. There are often a series of separate bones (inter- or supraneurals) in the midline between the skull and the dorsal fin. The fins are supported by pterygiophores, which are pointed blade-like bones, and small cartilaginous elements. In addition to the main ribs some bony fishes like the cyprinids and characins have fine rod or Y-shaped bones between the muscles that are responsible for the "bony" reputation of such species.

The Weberian apparatus (Fig. 14) is an important modification of the vertebral column found in all the otophysan fishes (cyprinids, characins and catfishes). This complex structure is derived from the first four to six vertebrae, and connects the swimbladder to the inner ear by means of a chain of small bones and ligaments to act as a sound amplifier.

Body cavity (Fig.15)

On opening up the body cavity of a fish the main organs to be seen are the alimentary canal, the liver and the gonads (either the ovaries or the testes). Above these in the roof of the cavity are the swimbladder, which may be reduced or absent in some species, and the kidneys.

The alimentary canal consists of a short oesophagus followed by the expanded stomach (except in cyprinids, which lack a true stomach), intestine and rectum. The length and size of each of these sections varies greatly between species. Generally, predatory fishes have a short intestine, whereas herbivorous or plant- and detritus-eating species, like labeos and tilapias, have a long coiled intestine. The liver lobes usually wrap around the front (head) section of the alimentary canal, and the canal itself is often surrounded by fatty tissue. A small gall bladder is often clearly visible. Some predators, like the trout and basses, have a number of finger-like extensions, called pyloric caeca, which increase the area of the intestine for absorption of food, at the point where the stomach and intestine join.

Unlike the relatively discrete organ of mammals and birds the kidney of fishes is a long irregular band of deep red tissue closely applied to the roof of the body cavity. The gonads are usually paired structures, often only clearly evident in mature or semi-mature individuals. The ovaries appear as creamy or yellowish granular tubes or bags, and in ripe females the mature ova (eggs) are readily visible. The testes are usually whitish in colour, in immature fishes they form a thin tube that is difficult to locate but increase in size with maturity and ripeness. In catfishes the testes often have a series of finger-like projections.

The swimbladder, also called the airbladder or gasbladder, when present, is usually a long gas-filled bladder along the roof of the body cavity. In the cyprinids, characins and catfishes it is divided into two chambers. It normally functions to maintain buoyancy, but may also serve as a sound resonator and amplifier and it forms the "lung" of lungfishes.

Heart and circulation

The circulatory system of fishes is essentially a single circuit with a one-way pump (the heart). The heart is situated in a small chamber behind and below the gill arches and consists of two chambers in series, the atrium and the ventricle. In the lungfish the two chambers are partially divided in accordance with the use of the lungs as the main respiratory organ.

32 WHAT IS A FISH?

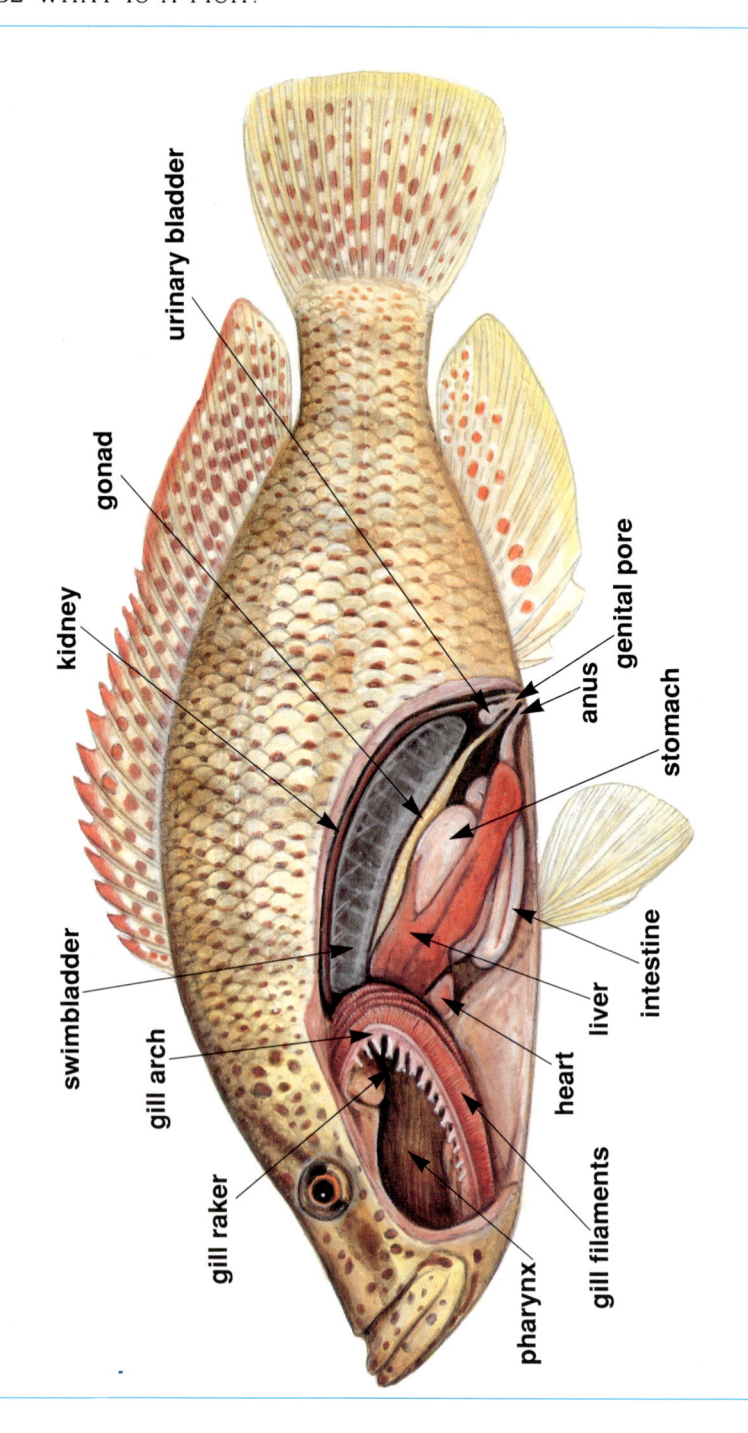

Fig. 15 Body organs of a bony fish, the cichlid *Serranochromis thumbergi*.

Brain and nervous system
The brain of fishes consists of three major sections, the forebrain or cerebral hemispheres, the midbrain or optic lobes, and the hind brain or cerebellum and medulla. The brain passes directly to the spinal cord, which runs within the neural arches of the vertebral column. There are 10 pairs of major cranial nerves stemming from the brain, and paired spinal nerves pass out from the spinal cord at each vertebra.

Inner ear
Unlike other vertebrates, fishes do not have an outer or middle ear, but they do possess a pair of inner ears that serve as organs of balance and hearing. Each inner ear rests within the braincase and consists of three semicircular canals linked to basal chambers in which are found the earstones or otoliths, the lapillus, the sagitta and the asteriscus. The otoliths are useful in the study of age and growth because they increase in size with age, adding distinct layers that form characteristic rings or bands.

Endocrine organs
The endocrine system consists of hormone-producing glands that control the various metabolic functions of the body. Most endocrine glands are small or diffuse tissues that are not easily examined. The chief endocrine glands are the pituitary, located at the base of the brain, which secretes various hormones that control growth, colour changes, maturity and water balance; the thyroid, along the ventral aorta (metabolism, maturity and water balance); ultimobranchial bodies, between the oesophagus and the heart (calcium balance); suprarenals, along the kidneys (blood pressure); adrenals, at the head of the kidney (fat metabolism, and water and ion balance); sex glands, in the body cavity (maturity and sexual characters and behaviour).

Electrical organs (Fig.16)
The mormyrids and certain catfish species are capable of producing and receiving electrical pulses. In the mormyrids these pulses are generally of very low amplitude, although they may be felt from some species like the bottlenoses (*Mormyrus* species) and the Cornish Jack *(Mormyrops anguilloides)* when being handled alive out of the water. The electric catfish *(Malapterurus electricus),* on the other hand, can generate a dangerous shock of 300–400 volts. Divers have reported being stunned by them.

The electrogenic organs consist of modified muscle cells called electrocytes that are connected to the central nervous system. In mormyrids the electrocytes are arranged in two columns along the caudal peduncle. The cerebellum of mormyrids is greatly enlarged to control this specialised system. In the electric catfish the electric organ is derived from anterior muscles which wrap around the body of the fish. In this species the organ is controlled by a single giant nerve cell on each side of the spinal cord which ensures a rapid synchronised discharge.

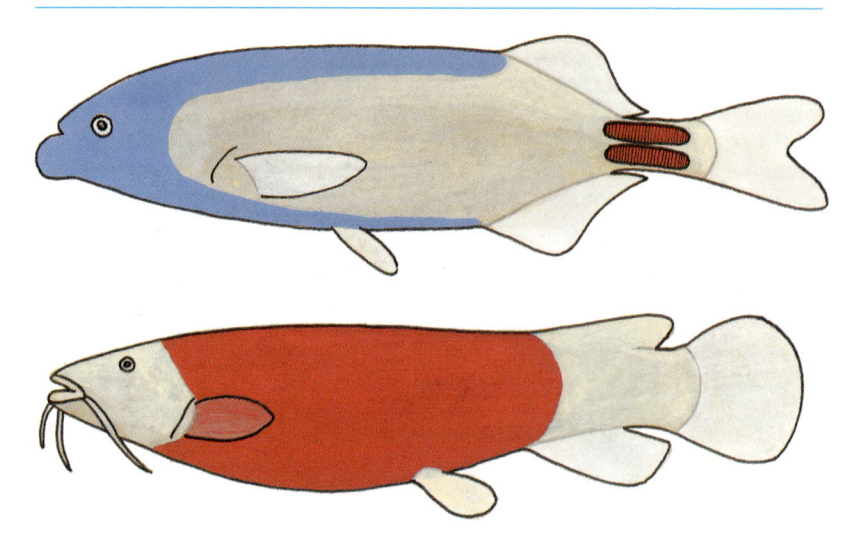

Fig.16 Electric organs of a mormyrid (the bulldog, *Marcusenius macrolepidotus*) and the electric catfish. Electroreceptor organs of the mormyrid are distributed in the skin within the blue area.

Mormyrids have three types of electroreceptor organs consisting of specialised cells and organelles in the skin connected to the central nervous system. These receptors are distributed in species-specific patterns over the body, most often on or around the head region. The function of the different receptors is to detect electric pulses coming from the fish's own or another individual's electric organ or other electric currents in the environment. In mormyrids electricity is used for communication, and for electrolocation of possible prey or of threatening predators. Certain catfishes, including the sharptooth catfish *(Clarias gariepinus)*, can also detect electric currents.

ASPECTS OF BIOLOGY AND ECOLOGY

Life-history cycles (Figs 17,18,19)
Fishes have a wide range of life cycles, some far more complex than others. A simple life cycle is that of an average small minnow species. The cycle begins with the fertilised egg, one of many scattered amongst the submerged vegetation in a stream pool. The embryo takes about 48 hours to hatch into a small larva that continues to absorb egg yolk for another 36 hours or so. Once the larva is able to swim freely it begins to feed on tiny creatures like rotifers and microplankton. After a few weeks all signs of larval characters such as fin folds have disappeared and the fish is a fully formed juvenile. Further growth takes place over several months and by the next summer or two, depending on the species, it will be mature and able to breed.

BIOLOGY AND ECOLOGY 35

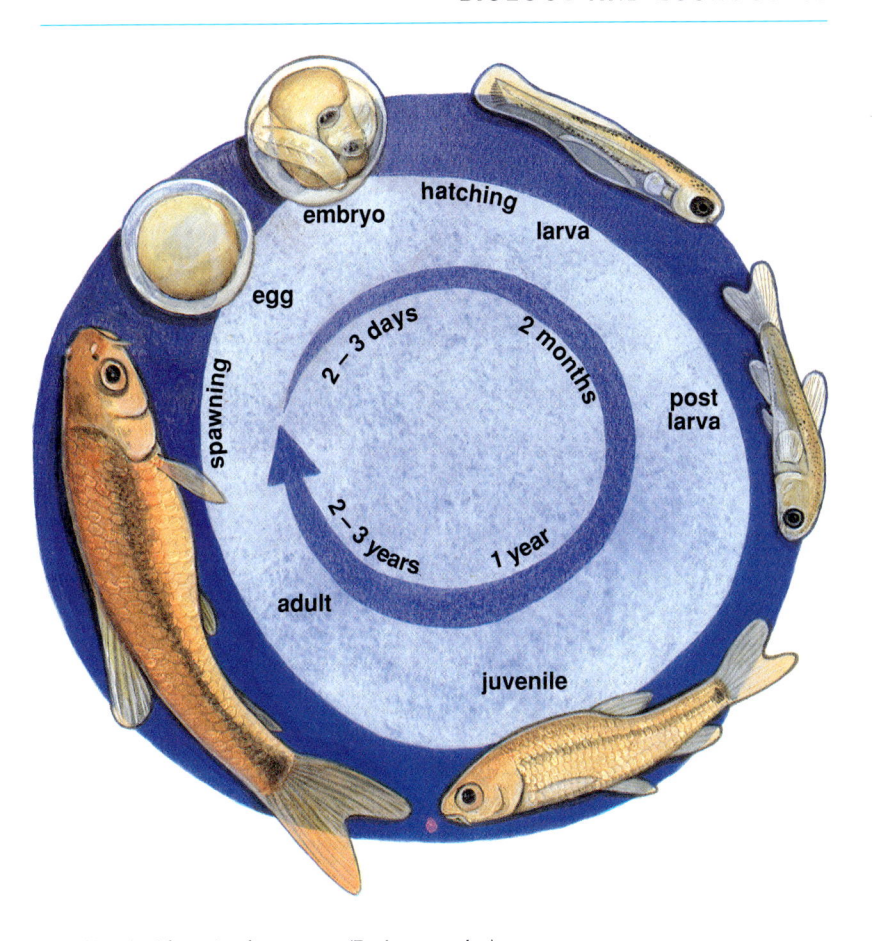

Fig. 17 The life cycle of a minnow *(Barbus anoplus)*.

Other life cycles are variations on this theme, becoming ever more complex in one aspect or another, especially as regards breeding biology. Long larval stages involving lengthy migrations are characteristic of the eels (*Anguilla* species). Eels breed at sea and the eggs and the leaf-like larvae (called leptocephali) are borne by the currents towards the shore where they change into transparent "glass eels" and move into estuaries. They may remain in the estuary for a while before migrating into the rivers and changing into elvers. Upstream migration continues until a suitable pool is found where the growing eel may remain for 10 to 20 years before returning to the sea to breed.

The life cycle of annual killifishes (*Nothobranchius* species) involves a short active phase of only several weeks from hatching to adulthood and a long inactive phase of several months when the eggs lie dormant but viable in the dry bed of a temporary pan. When the eggs are laid and fertilised development

36 BIOLOGY AND ECOLOGY

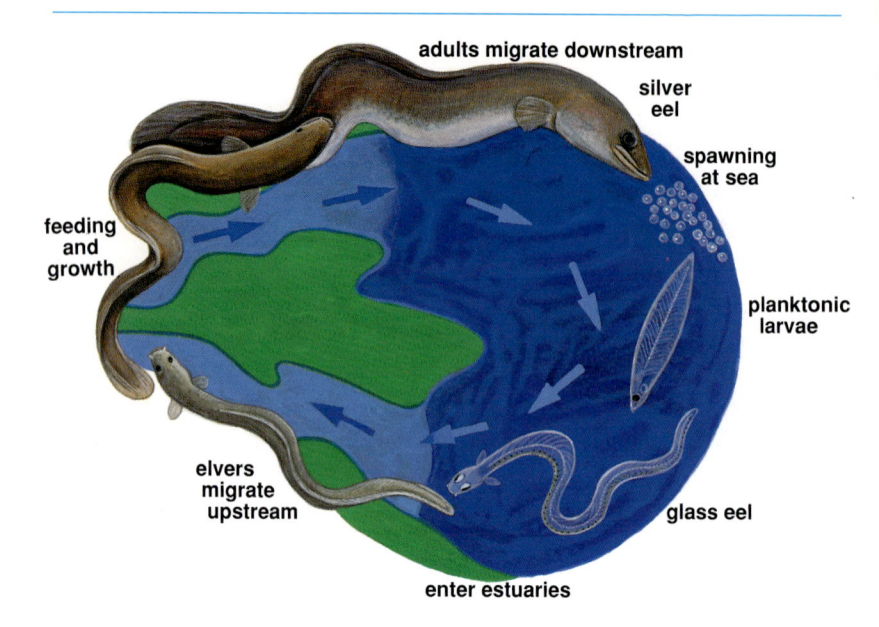

Fig.18 The life cycle of an eel (*Anguilla* species).

proceeds to a pre-hatching stage before being arrested. The eggs enter diapause and remain dormant in the dry mud of the pan until the following rainy season six months to even a year or two later. When the rains reflood the habitat development proceeds, the eggs hatch and, in a rich environment, the small fishes grow quickly to adulthood. Breeding occurs before the pan dries out again.

For many species spawning involves a special gathering of ripe adults in suitable places. The males may each establish and defend a breeding territory to which the females are attracted. In certain species the males gather in a nuptial school in order to attract the ripe females. Mass migration to a spawning site is a feature of many riverine fishes. Both instream and temporarily flooded areas may be used as spawning sites. Some species scatter the eggs without any particular preparation of the spawning site, others prepare the spawning site or select special sites such as crevices in which to lay their eggs. A more advanced habit is nest construction and active guarding and tending of the eggs and larvae.

Nests may be simple or fairly elaborate structures. Male bass (*Micropterus* species) simply clear a suitable area for the egg-laying site and guard the brood alone, leaving the female to mate with other partners. The banded tilapia *(Tilapia sparrmanii)* and many other cichlids form breeding pairs, excavate a depression in the bottom sediments, and both parents tend the brood. The redbreast tilapia *(T. rendalli)* excavates a large nest and may dig separate brood chambers or tunnels for the eggs and larvae. The African pike (*Hepsetus*

BIOLOGY AND ECOLOGY 37

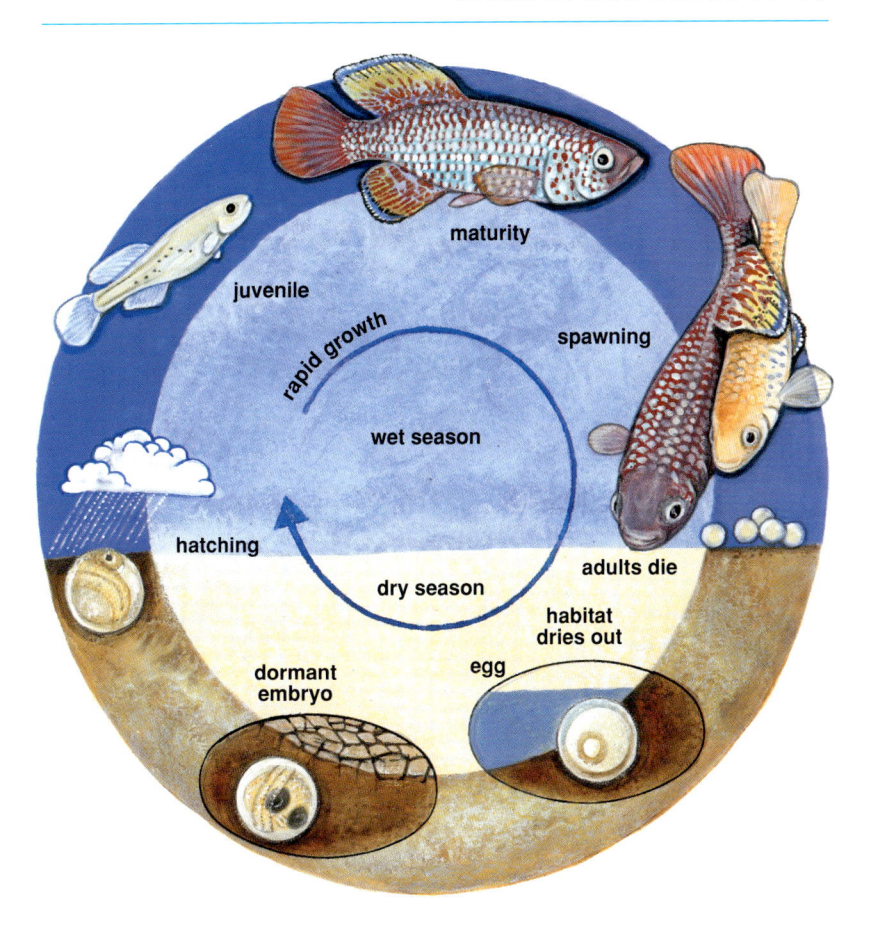

Fig.19 The life cycle of an annual killifish (*Nothobranchius* species).

odoe) and the blackspot climbing perch *(Ctenopoma intermedium)* construct a floating nest of foam or froth and guard the brood from below.

Mouthbrooding of eggs and larvae is an advanced breeding style practised by certain genera of cichlids. It is usually the male that establishes a territory and builds a nest, with the female mouthbrooding the eggs. Another form of egg-brooding occurs in pipefish, where the male has a pouch along its abdomen in which the eggs and larvae are incubated. In all these cases the eggs are fertilised once they have left the female's body.

Apart from bull shark *(Carcharhinus leucas)*, internal fertilisation does not occur in any indigenous freshwater fish from southern Africa. However, internal fertilisation is a feature of several livebearers, such as the guppy *(Poecilia reticulata)* and the swordtail *(Xiphophorus helleri)*, introduced from Central and South America. These fishes are termed viviparous or live-bearing because

Fig.20 Behaviour in fishes: aggression. A territorial male southern mouthbrooder advances from his nest in bright colours and with fins erect to chase off an intruder.

the eggs are fertilised and develop within the female, the young being born as fully developed juveniles.

Behaviour (Figs 20,21)
Like other animals, many fishes communicate by means of behavioural displays. Colours and pigment patterns, the erection of fins and branchiostegal membranes, movement and stance are all used in the process of conveying messages. Ritual displays of aggression and submission are used to establish a dominance hierarchy within a community. Breeding fishes especially have interesting courtship and territorial rituals, and of all the fishes in southern Africa the cichlids are best studied in this respect.

In the southern mouthbrooder *(Pseudocrenilabrus philander)* a mature male will chase all other individuals from a chosen area. On being approached by an intruder the resident male raises his fins and extends his branchiostegal membrane to display himself fully to the intruder. He then actively pursues the intruder and chases him beyond the boundaries of the territory. Once his dominance

BIOLOGY AND ECOLOGY   39

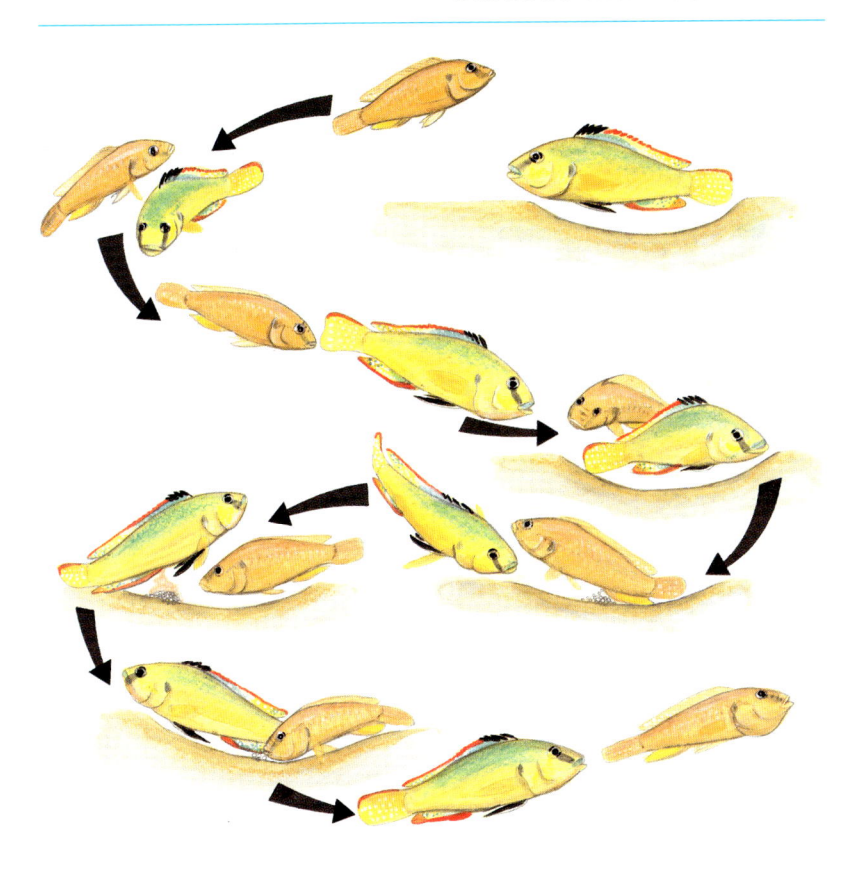

Fig. 21 Behaviour in fishes: breeding. A territorial male southern mouthbrooder attracts a ripe female to his nest, induces her to lay eggs which he fertilises as she picks them up in her mouth. Finally he drives her from the nest area and prepares to repeat the sequence with another suitable female.

in the territory is assured he digs a depression nest by taking bites of sand and spitting them out around the edges. In full breeding dress he follows a complex ritual of displays involving body shakes, fin-quivering and positioning of the body to attract a gravid female to the territory and entice her to lay eggs in the nest. Within the nest the pair circle, butt and prod each other until the eggs are laid and fertilised. The female then gathers the eggs in her mouth and is driven from the territory by the male. He proceeds to court other females while she seeks a suitable nursery to brood the eggs and larvae.

Mormyrid fishes do not require bright colours as they are active at night and communicate by means of electrical impulses. The behaviour of the southern African species is not well known, but interesting and complex patterns of behaviour and communication using electric signals can be expected.

40 BIOLOGY AND ECOLOGY

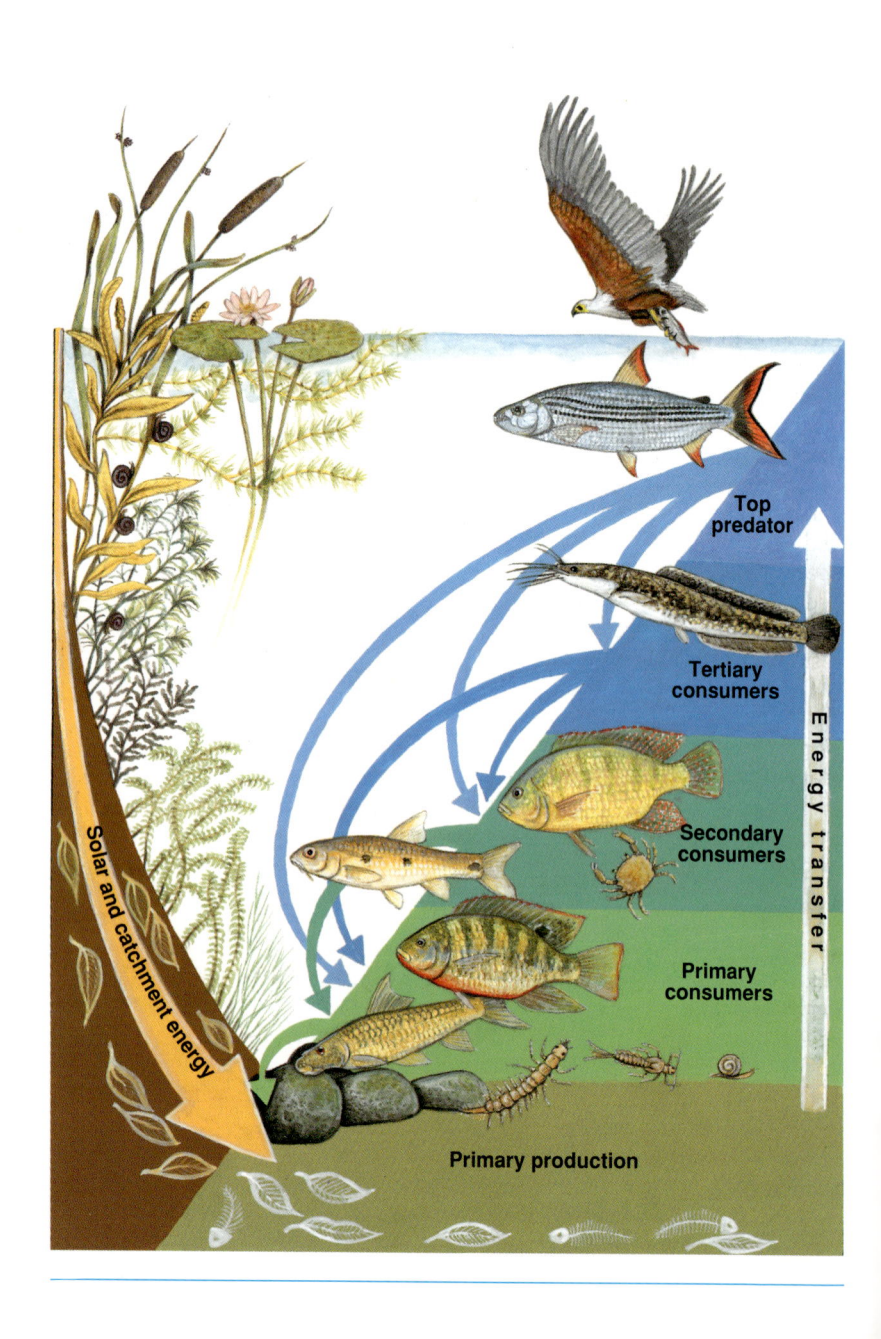

Feeding

Freshwaters are productive environments that provide a wide range of foods from microscopic detritus and algae, plants, insects, snails, shrimps and crabs to vertebrates like frogs and fishes. Items such as leaves, seeds and adult insects that enter from the surrounding land add to the available foods. Fishes are often opportunist feeders but within a community will comprise a spectrum of feeding types ranging from detritivores and herbivores to predators.

A typical freshwater food pyramid or chain (Fig.22) starts with the energy derived from sunlight and minerals on which plants, bacteria and unicellular organisms feed. These primary producers are in turn consumed by secondary producers like insects, crustaceans and other small invertebrates and fishes. The links continue through larger members of the community until one or more top predators exist at the apex of the pyramid. Aquatic food chains often extend to the terrestrial environments through predators like crocodiles, birds, otters and man.

Specialist feeding types occur in the complex fish communities of the larger tropical rivers of our area. In the Zambezi and Okavango rivers there may be as many as 20 or 30 different fish species present in local communities. Specialist feeders include detritivores, algal grazers, herbivores, insectivores, molluscivores (snail and mussel feeders), scavengers, small piscivores (fish predators) and large specialised piscivores like the largemouth breams (*Serranochromis* species) the pike *(Hepsetus odoe)* and the tigerfish *(Hydrocynus vittatus)*. In addition, the different species feed from different substrata and levels of the water column, at different times and in different ways. Other aquatic and terrestrial animals like terrapins, crocodiles, otters, hippos, birds and man add to the complexity of interactions regulating the community.

Migrations and movements

Many fishes have a home range in which they freely move about in the course of their daily activities. The size of the home range depends on the species and the nature of the environment; in the case of small minnows it may only be a single pool in a stream, but for larger fishes it can be an entire lake or a long stretch of river. The localised movements of some species have been studied by

Fig.22 (opposite) A simple aquatic food pyramid. Energy enters the system in the form of sunlight and organic matter from plants and animals in the catchment and forms the nutrients for bacteria, algae and higher plants (primary production). These organisms provide food for primary consumers such as insects, snails and herbivorous and detritivorous fish such as labeos and the redbreast tilapia. Secondary consumers are carnivores or scavengers such as crabs, predatory insects and various fishes that feed on primary consumers and producers. Larger or more specialised predators in turn feed on the secondary consumers and so on up the pyramid, depending on the composition of the community concerned. Top predators such as tigerfish, African pike and bass feed on suitable prey from any supporting level of the pyramid. Ultimately even top fish predators are preyed on by terrestrial creatures such as birds, crocodiles, otters and man.

42 BIOLOGY AND ECOLOGY

monitoring the population through regular netting programmes and by tagging individuals and then recapturing them later. More recently the use of implanted radio tags has allowed fishery biologists to record the daily movement of individual fishes within a water body.

Migrations are distinct movements of whole populations or sections of populations for a specific purpose such as breeding, feeding or dispersal. Many fishes make seasonal migrations in accordance with the seasonal flood cycles of larger rivers like the Okavango and the Zambezi. These movements are made so that the fishes may avoid less favourable conditions in one area and take advantage of more favourable conditions in a different part of the system as a result of the seasonal changes.

Many riverine fishes make breeding migrations soon after the first major rains of spring or summer when the rivers are in spate and conditions are most favourable for the survival, growth and feeding of the offspring. These migrations often take place at night and thus may not be seen except when their passage is blocked by a waterfall, weir or dam and the massing fishes jump to clear

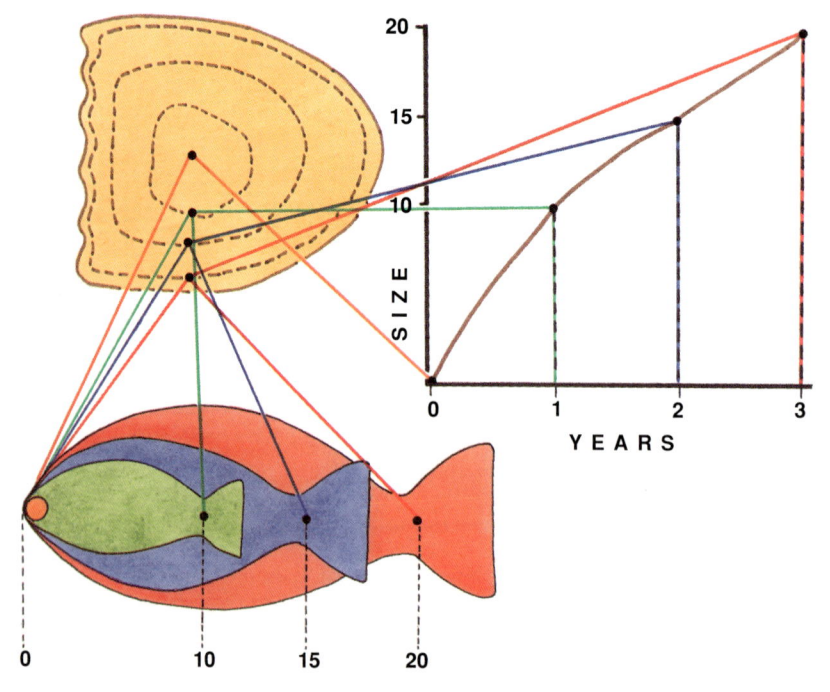

Fig.23 Aging a fish from growth rings on scales: the number of growth rings on a scale (or bone, spine or otolith) is counted and correlated with the length or mass of the fish. By plotting the age of different specimens against length or mass a growth curve can be devised for a particular population of a species.

the barrier. During migrations species like the redeye labeo *(Labeo cylindricus)* and the suckermouth catlets *(Chiloglanis* species) have been seen climbing dam walls by clinging with their mouths and fins. Fish ladders have been built at a few weirs in southern Africa to assist migrating fishes to overcome man-made barriers.

The life cycle of eels involves long-distance migrations in two directions, firstly from the breeding area at sea to the rivers where they live and grow to adulthood, and then a return migration of adults to the breeding grounds at sea. Similar but shorter migrations from the sea to rivers and back to the sea (catadromy) are made by the mullet species. Some cyprinid species in the African Great Lakes migrate from the lake to the rivers for breeding.

Age, growth and longevity (Fig.23)

"How long do fishes live?", "How old are fishes when they mature and breed?" Answers to these questions are important to fishery biologists wanting to manage stocks efficiently.

How do you tell the age of a fish? One way is to keep track of the age of captive fishes. The age of discrete size-groups of free stocks can be estimated by plotting the lengths of large numbers of individuals in a population. The age of individual fishes can be established by a study of the growth rings laid down on scales, otoliths, spines or bones, and correlating the number of rings with a known sequence of ecological events. Once a sufficient number of individuals has been aged, a graph can be drawn of age against length, from which the age of further specimens of known length can be established.

Relatively few age and growth studies have been done on southern African freshwater fish species. Some, especially small species like killifishes *(Nothobranchius* species) and topminnows *(Aplocheilichthys* species), are short-lived, surviving for a year or two at most. Minnows *(Barbus* species) usually live for three to six years. Five to 10 years is probably the normal life span of most larger southern African freshwater fishes. A few, including the large yellowfish species, carp, tench and eels, are recorded as living for more than 10 years, even for as many as 20 years in a few instances.

The longevity of individual fishes depends largely on ecological circumstances. Captive fishes free from the dangers and stresses of the natural world may live for many more years than those in the wild. In one case a Cape galaxias *(Galaxias zebratus)* survived in an aquarium for more than 10 years.

Parasites and diseases (Fig.24)

Fishes are subject to a wide range of diseases and parasites, some of which are fairly well known in southern Africa and have had a great impact on the aquaculture industry or have caused losses to fish keepers and aquarium traders. In the wild, deteriorating river conditions throughout southern Africa are causing stress to populations with a consequent rise in parasite infestations and disease. Some of the more commonly encountered diseases and parasites are briefly described.

44 BIOLOGY AND ECOLOGY

Fig.24 Some common parasites of freshwater fishes: from the top, nematode worms in the body cavity of a mountain catfish *(Amphilius)*; "black spot" trematode cysts on a smallmouth yellowfish *(Barbus aeneus)*; "anchorworm" (*Lernaea* sp.) on the flanks of a Manyame labeo *(Labeo altivelis)*; a free-living crustacean parasite *Chonopeltis minutus* on a Clanwilliam redfin *(Barbus calidus)*; fish leeches.

Fungus disease *(Saprolegnia)* affects stressed and injured fishes during winter and appears as outbreaks of a furlike growth on the body and gills. The mucus secreted by the skin of a fish is an important protection against fungal infections.

Bacterial infections may appear as lesions, haemorrhages, "popeye" and a bloated appearance as a result of affecting water balance.

Protozoan parasites such as *Ichthyophthirius*, otherwise known as "Ich" or "white-spot" disease, are common in aquarium and pond fishes. These persistent unicellular parasites burrow under the skin and generally debilitate the individual. Typically they spread rapidly throughout an infected water body.

Nematode worms (roundworms or threadworms) sometimes infect the ali-

BIOLOGY AND ECOLOGY 45

mentary canal and body cavity of fishes in dense concentrations. Although they may not kill the host these worms are very debilitating to the fish and make it unsuitable for humans to eat.

Trematodes (flukes) occur either as adults within the internal organs or as larvae in the form of white- or black-spot cysts in the skin. Heavy infections can affect the swimming ability of the fish itself, so that it may be an easier prey to birds, which are the parasite's final host.

Tapeworms such as the Asian species *(Bothriocephalus acheilognathi)*, which was introduced with imported grass carp *(Ctenopharyngodon idella)* in 1975, infect many species in southern Africa. The intermediate hosts of this parasite are small copepods, which in turn may be eaten by zooplankton-feeding fishes. Birds eating infected fish, as well as the translocation of infected stock by man, assist in the rapid spread of such parasites.

Leeches parasitise fishes in much the same way that they do other vertebrates, by attaching themselves to the body, usually in the gill chamber or at the base of the fins, and then sucking blood from the host.

Copepods are small crustacean parasites that often infest the gills of fishes. The adult parasite partly embeds itself in the gill filaments, leaving only the egg sacs protruding. The anchor worm *(Lernaea)* protrudes from the body of its host, destroying the mucus layer and causing lesions in the skin and flesh.

Free-living crustacean ectoparasites such as the "fish lice" *Argulus, Dolops* and *Chonopeltis,* are also found on many southern African fish species in tropical and temperate waters. The parasites infect protected places like the bases of the fins and in particular the mouth and gill chambers but also occur on the exposed body. Adults of these parasites grasp the host by means of paired suckers and the immature stages have strong claws for this purpose. Individual parasites appear to cause relatively little damage to the host but heavy infestations may be debilitating in the long term.

FISHES AND MAN IN SOUTHERN AFRICA

Traditional fishing activities (Fig. 25)
Fishes have been caught from the rivers of southern Africa for as long as man has been in the area. Archaeologists working riverside middens of early San (Bushman) and Khoi (Hottentot) cultures frequently find evidence of fish remains. However, only in the tropical regions of southern Africa, where the rivers and the fish communities are sufficiently large, have traditional fishing activities endured. The best examples of traditional fisheries are found on the coastal lowlands of Mozambique and Maputaland and the floodplains of the upper Zambezi and Okavango rivers in Angola, Zambia, Namibia and Botswana.

Traditional fishing involves both active and passive methods using traps, fences and funnels woven from reeds and grasses. Individuals use rod and line,

46 FISHES AND MAN

bow and arrows, fishing spears, and woven grass or reed scoops or plunge baskets. Groups of men or women combine to drive fish into bays and backwaters where they are more easily caught with baskets. Traditional fish drives involving several hundred people are an important social activity along the east coast. On the Save River a long line of men push before them a reed fence that drives the fish into a confined space where they are caught. Similar fish drives take place along the Phongolo floodplain in Maputaland but here the men and women each carry a "fonya" or plunge basket. As the line of people advances the basket is plunged into the water and any trapped fish are removed through an opening at the top. In the upper Zambezi and Okavango floodplains small groups of 10 to 20 women using thrust baskets made of reeds or grass form lines to drive and catch fish. All these fish drives take place when the water level is receding or low and the fish are concentrated in pools and pans. A wide variety of fish is usually caught by traditional fisheries, including both large and small species, all of which are generally relished.

Subsistence and commercial fisheries
Gill nets and other more modern equipment are also used by subsistence and commercial fishermen along the larger floodplains and in man-made impoundments. In Lake Kariba up to 16 000 tonnes of fish are caught each year by the commercial fishery. Several hundred tonnes are also gathered from smaller impoundments in Zimbabwe such as Lake McIlwaine near Harare. In 1980 over 450 commercial fishermen were operating along the Zambezi-Chobe floodplains in the Caprivi area. River fisheries are extremely valuable to the local inhabitants and yields of 840 tonnes per annum have been reported for the Okavango River in Kavango, Namibia. On the Phongolo floodplain in Maputaland an estimated 400 tonnes per annum may be harvested by the traditional subsistence fishery.

One of the most important impoundment fisheries is the "kapenta" or Lake Tanganyika sardine fishery in Lake Kariba. The kapenta *Limnothrissa miodon* was introduced into Lake Kariba from Lake Tanganyika in 1967/8 and by 1972 was sufficiently established for experimental fishing to begin. Commercial fishing between 1973 and 1982 landed over 38 000 tonnes of this species.

Fishing safaris for sportsmen operate from several fishing camps in the Okavango Delta in Botswana, the Caprivi and at Lake Kariba in Zimbabwe. Private and commercial facilities for bass and trout fishing are well established in South Africa and Zimbabwe.

Angling
Angling is probably the largest participator sport in southern Africa. In the Transvaal alone over 68 000 licences were issued in 1964, and by 1977/8

Fig.25 (opposite) Traditional fishing methods in southern Africa. Top left: Hlengwe palisade fish drive, Save River; top right: Sintunga corral trap, Okavango River; centre left: Sikuku fish baskets, Okavango River; lower right: isifonya thrust basket, Phongolo flood plain; lower left: umono valve traps set into barrier, Phongolo floodplain.

this number had increased to over 117 000.

A few important early milestones in the development of freshwater fish angling in southern Africa are:
1859 - first reported introduction of carp
1890 - first successful introduction of brown trout
1894 - establishment of the Jonkershoek and Pirie trout hatcheries
1897 - first successful introduction of rainbow trout
1928 - first introduction of largemouth black bass
1937 - first introduction of smallmouth black bass.

About 20% of the indigenous freshwater fishes are suitable angling species. This is a relatively low proportion for the size of the subcontinent. The most important indigenous angling species are tigerfish *(Hydrocynus vittatus)*, Cornish Jack *(Mormyrops anguilloides)*, eels *(Anguilla* species), *Barbus* species such as the yellowfish (largemouth, smallmouth, Clanwilliam) and the scaly, chessa *(Distichodus shenga)*, nkupe *(D. mossambicus)*, African pike *(Hepsetus odoe)*, sharptooth catfish *(Clarias gariepinus)*, vundu *(Heterobranchus longifilis)*, threespot tilapia *(Oreochromis andersonii)*, Mozambique tilapia *(O. mossambicus)*, the largemouth breams (*Serranochromis* species) especially the thinface bream *(S. angusticeps)* and the nembwe *(S. robustus)*. Sporadic marine species such as the ox-eye tarpon *(Megalops cyprinoides)* and the Zambezi or bull shark *(Carcharhinus leucas)* are also important angling targets.

Rainbow trout *(Oncorhynchus mykiss)* and brown trout *(Salmo trutta)* are the chief targets of the very popular flyfishing enterprise in both rivers and dams. Trout fishing is restricted to the cooler upland mountain or escarpment regions and is absent from Botswana, Namibia and Mozambique. Fly-fishing is not restricted to trout and there is a strong trend towards this sport in places like the Okavango and in estuaries.

The American basses *(Micropterus* species), the largemouth *(M. salmoides)*, the smallmouth *(M. dolomieu)* and the spotted *(M. punctulatus)*, are also highly valued as angling species. Several big bass fishing tournaments are held each year by enthusiasts. Largemouth bass, including the subspecies known as Florida bass, are caught mainly in dams and impoundments, whereas smallmouth and spotted bass are mainly riverine species. Spotted bass are probably the least well-known of the basses and it seems that they are generally confused with either the smallmouth or the largemouth. Bluegill sunfish *(Lepomis macrochirus)* occur in many bass waters and are also often caught by anglers. Their relatively small size counts against their popularity.

Carp *(Cyprinus carpio)* is regarded by many as the premier angling species in the inland waters of the Cape, Orange Free State and Transvaal.

Angling clubs and societies form the backbone of the sport and are well established in many places. Tournaments are very popular and attract large followings, especially with the advent of big-time sponsorships in recent years. The annual Lake Kariba Tigerfish Tournament in Zimbabwe has been running for several decades and is now the premier international gamefish tournament in Africa. Several hundred anglers converge on Lake Kariba each September or October for the event and it is an important source of revenue for the country.

National angling records are maintained by the national angling body or a fish records association in several countries. In South Africa the records are published in a list available from the South African Angling Union (SAAU) and updated every few years. The Zimbabwe Fish Records Association also provides an updated fish record list. Information regarding freshwater angling in southern Africa can be obtained from the addresses given on page 379.

Fish farming (aquaculture)

Fish farming is a rapidly growing sector of agriculture and a South African Aquaculture Association was formed in 1989. Rainbow trout *(Oncorhynchus mykiss)* and sharptooth catfish *(Clarias gariepinus)* are the two main species that are cultured at present. Others include various "tilapias" such as the Mozambique tilapia *(Oreochromis mossambicus)*, the greenhead tilapia *(O. macrochir)*, threespot bream *(O. andersonii)* and the redbreasted tilapia *(Tilapia rendalli)*, as well as common carp *(Cyprinus carpio)*, grass carp *(Ctenopharyngodon idella)*, largemouth bass *(Micropterus salmoides)*, goldfish *(Carassius auratus)* and a wide variety of ornamental species. Research on new aquaculture candidates is constantly being done and further species are likely to be added to this list in future.

At present there are about 30 major producers of trout, located chiefly in the eastern Transvaal and the Cape, producing about 750 tonnes with a value of about R11 million per year. The initial importation of trout and other gamefish was done by private individuals and associations. The first hatcheries, such as Pirie and Jonkershoek in the Cape, were built in the 1890s and used for the production of game and fodderfish for angling purposes. Most state hatcheries no longer produce gamefish, a function that is increasingly being carried out by private fish farmers.

Catfish farming is a rapidly growing industry and the sharptooth catfish *(Clarias gariepinus)* is likely soon to become the major local production species. The sharptooth catfish has many favourable attributes for an aquaculture species: it is extraordinarily hardy, can be bred artificially, eats practically all foods, is fast growing and provides a large, white fillet. Current catfish production in southern Africa is about 120 tonnes per annum, worth over R1 million. Experimentally produced hybrids of the vundu *(Heterobranchus longifilis)* and the sharptooth catfish have even faster growth rates than either parent species and may become important aquaculture products.

Although tilapias are important aquaculture species in certain countries local use has not been very successful, and production in 1988 amounted to about 11 tonnes with a market value of R33 000. Attempts to use indigenous tilapias were made before production principles for such species were developed and lack of control over breeding and stocking resulted in overbreeding, hybridisation and stunting of stock. The potential of indigenous tilapias for aquaculture remains high, however, and they are likely to be used more extensively in future.

The aquarium trade is a huge international industry and several local producers are now culturing "ornamental" fishes for the local and export markets. Ornamental fish farms range from small private breeders using backyard or garage facilities to large commercial companies. The largest ornamental fish farm in South Africa produces over 1,5 million fishes each year, and the total production of ornamental fish in South Africa is currently about 3–4 million. At present about 80 species are produced commercially in South Africa, covering a wide range from goldfish to gouramis. The total value of ornamental fishes produced is in excess of R6 million per annum, and is now about equal to the value of imported aquarium fishes.

Aquariums and ponds
Keeping fish has been practised in South Africa since the early days of the Cape when "Japanese goldfish" were kept in the Governor's garden ponds. Outdoor ponds with goldfish *(Carassius auratus)* and koi *(Cyprinus carpio)* are still popular features throughout the region. The development of frameless glass aquariums with electric pumps and lights has boosted the popularity of the hobby.

People keep fishes for different reasons, usually because they are attractive and enhance the garden or home. Many aquarists try to learn something about their pets, either from books or magazines or by joining a club and meeting with other enthusiasts. It is also true that many people remain ignorant about fish and do not maintain a healthy aquarium. As a result their tanks are neglected and the fish suffer and die prematurely. Survivors are sometimes released into local streams or other natural water bodies in the mistaken belief that this is the best thing for them. Many aquarium fishes will not survive in local habitats but survivors do threaten indigenous species by introducing diseases or by competition. Even small species like the guppy *(Poecilia reticulata)* can be very harmful by preying on the eggs and larvae of indigenous species.

Unwanted fishes should be returned to the place where they were bought or given to another hobbyist. Alternatively they could be handed in at the nearest nature conservation office or aquarist club, or destroyed.

Very few indigenous fishes are available on the local market, partly because of restrictions on collecting fishes from the wild and also because few are bred commercially. Collecting and trading of indigenous species is not generally encouraged, mainly because of the dangers of overexploitation of natural stocks and of translocation of species into river systems other than those from which they were originally collected.

Some indigenous species are attractive and could be suitable aquarium or outdoor pond subjects. Some species are more suitable for community tanks whereas others are predators or aggressive and should be kept alone or only in large aquariums or ponds. A distinction between tropical or warm-water species and cool-water species is necessary because in the case of tropical species the water temperature should not drop below about 20° C, and for cool-water species the water temperature should not exceed about 25° C.

Small-sized species such as minnows, topminnows, annual killifishes, robbers, certain catfishes and dwarf cichlids make the most suitable aquarium subjects. Larger fishes such as lungfish and various catfish including the electric catfish are also kept by experienced hobbyists as curiosity pets but these fishes are usually very expensive and are seldom available through local dealers.

> **It illegal and a threat to conservation interests to collect fishes from private or public waters anywhere in southern Africa without a permit from the relevant nature conservation authority.**

THREATENED FISHES AND CONSERVATION

Threatened   The status of a species or population which has deteriorated through natural or unnatural causes to the point where it may be considered as Rare, Vulnerable or Endangered.

Endangered   Species in danger of extinction and whose survival is unlikely if the causal factors continue operating.

Vulnerable   Species believed likely to move into the Endangered category in the near future if the causal factors continue operating.

Rare   Species with small or restricted populations which are not at present endangered or vulnerable but which are at risk.

Safe   Species formerly included in a threatened category but that are now considered to be relatively secure.

Indeterminate   Species that are suspected of being threatened but for which insufficient information is currently available.

52 CONSERVATION

Over the past few centuries man has changed the landscape of southern Africa in many ways, and as a result many plant and animal species have declined and been eliminated from much of their natural range. In a mostly dry subcontinent, springs, rivers and other freshwater bodies have always been the focus of human activities, but too often not in a respectful way. Thus the habitats of fishes and other aquatic organisms have been drastically changed and often destroyed. Fishes provide us with an indication of the health of their environment – if they are dying then so is the system. The survival of several southern African fish species is now threatened. In this book the conservation status of threatened species has been indicated by means of a letter, either E for endangered, V for vulnerable, or R for rare (see above for definitions of these categories).

Threatened freshwater fishes

There are 24 freshwater fish species from southern Africa listed in the 1988 IUCN Red List. These include seven Endangered, seven Vulnerable and 10 Rare species. No known species has become extinct in historical or recent times in southern Africa although some local populations of threatened species have been completely eliminated. Many threatened species are small and naturally restricted in their distribution. The majority are endemic species from mountain streams in the Cape, especially the south-west. In Namibia the cave catfish *(Clarias cavernicola),* Guinas tilapia *(Tilapia guinasana)* and Caprivi killifish (*Nothobranchius* species) each occur in a single or very few water bodies. These water bodies are all important sources of water for man, and so the species are threatened with extinction.

Besides the listed threatened species, many other freshwater fish in southern Africa have declined or had their ranges reduced in recent years. Even well-known species like the tigerfish *(Hydrocynus vittatus)* no longer occur in places where they were once common, the Cape kurper *(Sandelia capensis)* has been eliminated from the Eerste River and other rivers of the south-west Cape, and the eastern Cape redfin *(Pseudobarbus afer)* is now restricted to small tributaries of the Gamtoos and other coastal rivers.

IUCN Red List freshwater fishes from southern Africa

SPECIES	COMMON NAME	STATUS
Austroglanis barnardi	Barnard's rock catfish	Endangered
Clarias cavernicola	cave catfish	Endangered
Nothobranchius sp.	Caprivi killifish	Endangered
Pseudobarbus burgi	Berg River redfin	Endangered
Pseudobarbus phlegethon	fiery redfin	Endangered
Pseudobarbus quathlambae	Drakensberg minnow	Endangered
Tilapia guinasana	Otjikoto tilapia	Endangered
Barbus andrewi	whitefish	Vulnerable
Barbus erubescens	Twee River redfin	Vulnerable

Barbus serra	sawfin	Vulnerable
Barbus treurensis	Treur River barb	Vulnerable
Barbus trevelyani	Border barb	Vulnerable
Chiloglanis bifurcus	Incomati rock catlet	Vulnerable
Sandelia bainsii	eastern Cape rocky	Vulnerable
Chetia brevis	orange-fringed largemouth	Rare
Austroglanis gilli	Clanwilliam rock catfish	Rare
Austroglanis sclateri	rock catfish	Rare
Barbus capensis	Clanwilliam yellowfish	Rare
Barbus calidus	Clanwilliam redfin	Rare
Barbus hospes	Namaqua barb	Rare
Labeo seeberi	Clanwilliam sandfish	Rare
Pseudobarbus burchelli	Burchell's redfin	Rare
Pseudobarbus tenuis	slender redfin	Rare
Serranochromis meridianus	lowveld largemouth	Rare

Threats to freshwater fishes (Fig.26)
Only a few of the many threats to freshwater fishes caused directly or indirectly by human actions can be mentioned here. Within southern Africa the widespread destruction of habitat is a serious problem. Draining wetlands or vleis, which often form the source of streams, is a common agricultural practice. The water in many rivers is pumped out for agricultural, domestic and industrial purposes. Stream beds are channelised using bulldozers.

Dams and weirs or other obstructions such as concrete causeways have been built on all our rivers. These obstructions restrict the passage of migrating fishes and fragment populations into small units that are more susceptible to other threats. These structures change a river from a flowing system to one of standing waters. Fishes that prefer flowing waters tend to be replaced by species preferring still-water habitats.

During the dry season water is drawn directly from dams and rivers for agriculture. In times of drought, or in areas such as the south-west Cape where the summers are dry, many rivers are pumped completely dry for long periods of time. Once again fish populations are fragmented or eliminated, and cannot recover since summer is the breeding period.

Overpopulation, overgrazing, deforestation and the inefficient cultivation of crops cause soil erosion and the introduction of heavy sediment loads into the rivers. This results in turbid water conditions and smothering of the river bed, eliminating food organisms, breeding sites, eggs and larvae.

Fertilisers and insecticides enter the system from the lands, polluting the water and destroying the living organisms. Pollution from mines, industry and urban centres destroys or degrades long stretches of rivers and is an ever-increasing threat to freshwater environments. Air pollution results in acid rain which can, in time, develop into a major conservation problem. Air pollution in the eastern Transvaal highveld is particularly serious.

Invasive alien plant and animal species are a serious problem in freshwater

54 CONSERVATION

Fig. 26
Threats to freshwater fishes.

(a) Pollution and eutrophication kill fishes.

(c) Erosion, especially river bank erosion, destroys river habitats.

CONSERVATION 55

(b) Sand exploitation and channelisation degrades or destroys the habitats of fishes.

(d) Invasion by alien organisms, such as water hyacinth in the Crocodile River, eastern Transvaal, eliminates fishes and other aquatic life.

56 CONSERVATION

Fig.27 Conservation activities in freshwater systems.

(a) State Nature Conservation hatcheries are being used to breed threatened fishes (a pond for breeding whitefish *Barbus andrewi*, Jonkershoek Hatchery, South West Cape).

(b) A fish ladder on the Engelhard dam, Letaba River, in the Kruger National Park (photo A. Bok).

(c) Sanctuaries to conserve threatened species have been established, such as above this waterfall on the Treur river, a proclaimed National Heritage Site.

CONSERVATION 57

(d) A simple fish ladder for small fishes on a weir in the Gamtoos river system, Eastern Cape (photo A. Bok).

(e) Collecting fishes by means of an electrofisher for research on the impact of alien fishes on indigenous species.

habitats. Plants like water hyacinth *(Eichhornia crassipes)*, Kariba weed *(Salvinia)* and the fern *Azolla* can completely cover a water body and smother habitats, reducing light and oxygen and ultimately eliminating the fishes. Invasive trees like wattles *(Acacia* species) along the banks of rivers also destroy the habitat by reducing light and eliminating natural vegetation.

Invasive predatory fishes such as bass *(Micropterus* species) and trout *(Salmo trutta* and *Oncorhynchus mykiss)* have had a severe impact on indigenous species in places such as the south-west Cape. Trout and bass were introduced widely in streams that had a small natural fish community of a few species such as minnows or Cape kurper *(Sandelia capensis)*. Not only did the indigenous species lack natural defenses against large specialised predators, but the predators themselves had no natural controls. Consequently populations of indigenous species were quickly eliminated from many water bodies and some threatened species now survive only in refuge streams beyond the reach of introduced predators. Similar problems are being caused by the translocation of indigenous fishes like the sharptooth catfish *(Clarias gariepinus)* into systems beyond their natural range.

Carp *(Cyprinus carpio)* are popular angling species, but they are not favoured by the conservation authorities because of the harm they cause by stirring up bottom sediments and creating turbid conditions in impoundments. Parasites and diseases have been introduced with alien fishes, e.g. the Asian tapeworm *(Bothriocephalus acheilognathi)* which was probably introduced together with grass carp *(Ctenopharyngodon idella),* in 1975.

Conservation of freshwater fishes (Fig.27)

In order to conserve a species it is necessary to conserve its environment. Conservation may be defined as "the wise management of human use of the biosphere so that it may yield the greatest sustainable benefit to present generations while maintaining its potential to meet the needs and aspirations of future generations".

Although in the long term it is essential to redress root causes of the decline of many species, in the short term this is usually impractical or economically impossible. Scientists have only recently started to understand the processes that sustain river ecosystems, from which they will be able to recommend catchment and water-management practices, in order to improve degraded systems and conserve those that are still functioning adequately. Water managers in southern Africa now recognise that some allocation of water resources must be made to rivers for natural ecological functions.

Sometimes, in order to ensure the survival of a species, short-term measures such as captive propagation or the creation of sanctuaries are required. River surveys have revealed where species occur and what threats they are facing. Some threatened species have been translocated to safe sites elsewhere, or are being bred at state hatcheries and re-stocked into the rivers. Sanctuaries, in the form of National Heritage Sites, have been declared by the landowners of several important localities for fish conservation.

With rapidly increasing human populations and concomitant industrial, agricultural and domestic demands on water resources in southern Africa, the prospects for improvements in freshwater ecosystems are slender. Fish populations will continue to decline, further species will be added to the Red List and some of the endangered species may become extinct. It is important that people adopt the right attitude towards the conservation of freshwater systems. Freshwater is a precious resource on which all life depends, and to pollute or destroy it should be nothing less than a criminal offense. Individuals must play an active part in this process. For example, anglers should ensure that they do not litter dams and streams, and aquarists must not dispose of unwanted pets by releasing them into natural waterbodies.

CLASSIFICATION, TAXONOMY AND NOMENCLATURE

Systematics and Taxonomy
Systematics is the study of the diversity of living organisms and the relationships between those organisms. Any information about organisms may be used to determine diversity and understand their interrelationships.

Taxonomy is the theory and practice of describing, naming and classifying living organisms. The naming of a species or subspecies is strictly regulated by the International Code of Zoological Nomenclature (a similar code exists for botany and microbiology). The basic principle on which the code operates is one of priority, namely that the earliest name given to a species is the valid one. Only names published after 1758 are valid, as this is the year in which the famous Swedish naturalist Carolus Linnaeus published the 10th edition of his work *Systema Naturae,* in which he used for the first time a dual, or binomial, name for each species.

Classification (Fig.28)
Many classifications operate by grouping subjects together, on the basis of shared similar features, into progressively larger groups, or hierarchies. The closer the similarity, the more likely the subjects will be placed in the same group. Traditionally the same principle applied to the classification of living organisms, and this worked reasonably well up to a point. However, living organisms differ from inanimate objects in that individuals are members of a species which has evolved over time, and which is related to other species according to their shared genealogical (or phylogenetic) history. Species which share the same ancestor form a related lineage known as a monophyletic lineage.

A problem arises in the case of classifying living organisms in that obvious similarities between organisms may obscure finer but more significant similarities with other organisms. In addition relatively large changes can occur between species during evolution, and even closely related species may therefore not appear to be similar. In other words general similarity does not neces-

60 CLASSIFICATION

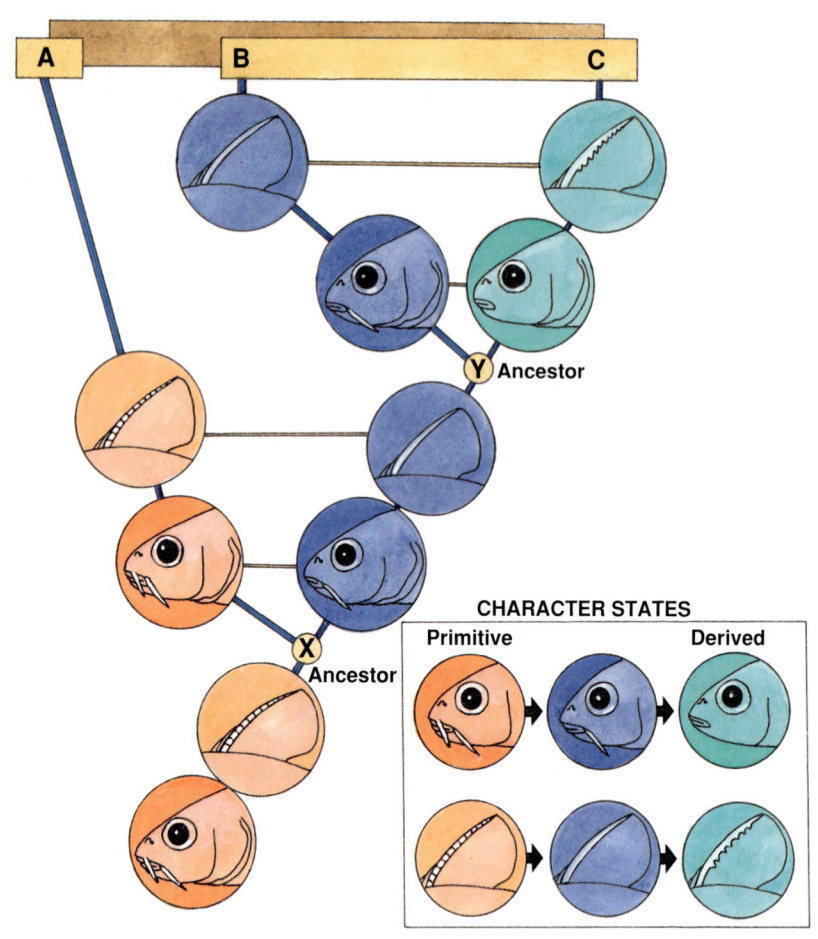

Fig.28 Establishing phylogenetic relationships using the cladistic method. Species A, B and C form a monophyletic lineage because they share the common ancestor "X". But because species B and C share relatively derived character states and the common ancestor "Y" they are more closely related to each other than either is to species A.

sarily indicate closest relationship. Studies have shown that close or sister relationships between species, or monophyletic lineages, can only be established on the basis of shared characters derived from the same ancestor. More and more, shared derived characters, and not general similarity, are the prime criteria on which modern classifications are built.

Categories and scientific names
The species is the basic category or taxon of biology. Although there is disagreement among biologists as to what a species actually is, it may be defined

as a group of a distinct kind of organisms that share a common evolutionary history not shared by any other such group. A general characteristic of a vertebrate species is that individual members of the opposite sex are able to interbreed freely with each other. Members of a species usually share a set of biological characteristics that differs from that of other species, including the means to recognise and interact with other members of the same species.

How do taxonomists select names and describe species? One or more specimens, called the type specimens, are chosen to represent the species being described. One of the types is chosen to be the holotype or name-bearing type. Type specimens must be deposited in a museum collection and serve as the reference for the described species and its name.

Each species must be placed in a genus, which is a taxonomic category containing at least one species or a monophyletic group of species. The name given to a species therefore consists of at least two words (binomen); the first word refers to the genus and the second to the species itself. In cases where taxonomic differences are evident between populations within a species a third name is added to designate a subspecies. A subgenus may also be designated and its name inserted into the name of a species, but this name is always placed within brackets and is not formally part of the species name e.g. *Serranochromis (Serranochromis) robustus*. Higher categories like families and orders are not formally included in the name of the species.

The name of the person or persons who describe the species (called the author or authors) and the year when the description was published is customarily given after the name of the species the first time it is referred to in a scientific publication. This is done so that there is no doubt as to which species is being referred to and so that another scientist or reader may look up the description of the species with certainty. The layman is often confused by the fact that the author's name is placed in brackets for some species and not for others. The presence or not of brackets is important: they indicate that the genus allocation has changed since the species was first described – for example, the Mozambique tilapia (originally described by Peters in 1852) was known as *Chromis (Tilapia) mossambicus* Peters, 1852; now it is known as *Oreochromis mossambicus* (Peters, 1852). If there are no brackets it indicates that the name is unchanged, for example *Tilapia sparrmanii* A. Smith, 1841.

Why do scientific names of a species change? There are two common reasons. First, a species may be "discovered" more than once. When it is correctly identified, only the earliest name is valid. Second, a change in understanding of the relationships of the species to other species may necessitate a change of genus for one or other of the species.

Taxonomic categories above the genus exist only in classifications. Some higher categories may be recognised by a distinct suffix or termination to their name but not every available category is necessarily used in a particular classification. The main classificatory categories used in this book, together with their Latinised endings, are:

Subspecies (varied endings)

Species (varied endings, in agreement with the gender of the genus)
Genus (varied endings, determined by gender)
Tribe (- ini)
Subfamily (-inae)
Family (-idae)
Order (- iformes)
Class (varied endings)

An example of a species classified is:
Class: Pisces
Super-order: Acanthomorpha
Order: Perciformes
Family: Cichlidae
Genus: *Oreochromis*
Subgenus: *Oreochromis (Oreochromis)*
Species: *Oreochromis (Oreochromis) placidus* (Trewavas, 1941)
Subspecies: *Oreochromis (Oreochromis) placidus placidus* (Trewavas, 1941)

Common names

Freshwater fish species are most often known to the public by a common name such as "catfish" or "tilapia". Common names are given to animals by people who encounter them, and are passed on through word of mouth and popular literature. They become ingrained in the local language and, like it, may change with time. Common names are often based on distinctive features of the species, or, as is often the case in southern Africa, on old names introduced from European or indigenous roots, for example "tilapia", derived from the Tswana word "thlape", meaning fish. Little known or obscure species usually do not have a distinct common name, but may be known under broad collective common names. Common names often have restricted local use and are often inconsistently applied to a particular species. The same name may refer to different species in different areas (as in the case of "ghieliemientjie"), or different names may refer to the same species in different places (as in the cas of *Serranochromis robustus,* which is called "nembwe" in Zambia, Botswana, Namibia and Zimbabwe, "tsungwa" in Malawi, and is also known as "robbie" and "yellowbellied bream" in places).

These are some of the problems that limit the broad value of common names. From the scientific point of view there is therefore a need to standardise common names without being too prescriptive or rigid. In this book only one or two common names are given for any one species, usually following the list of standardised common names published by the J.L.B. Smith Institute of Ichthyology. In a few cases an alternative common name is presented and, where common names have not previously been given, a new suggestion is made. Sometimes the common name may be more stable than the scientific name for a while, as in the case of the rainbow trout, which has been subject to several recent taxonomic reviews.

COLLECTION, PRESERVATION AND MEASUREMENT

Opportunities for collecting fishes may arise unexpectedly – as when there is a natural fish-kill caused by cold weather, or when a water body is drying out. Anglers sometimes catch unusual fishes that they do not recognise. Ichthyologists and resource managers collect fishes during their projects and surveys, and voucher specimens should always be preserved and lodged in a recognised collection. Even aquarium pets die sooner or later and, if in good condition, may be worth preserving and lodging in a museum collection. Generally it is illegal to collect fish specimens from private or public waters without a permit. It is necessary always to obtain the permission of the landowner before collecting or fishing from a property.

Specimens can be sent to the J.L.B. Smith Institute of Ichthyology, or to any other natural history museum in southern Africa where freshwater fishes are actively curated and studied at present (addresses given on page 379).

Collection and Preservation
Whole specimens, or parts of specimens, may be collected and preserved. A series of specimens is usually better than a single specimen only, and, if at all possible, the series should include specimens of different sizes and sexes.

After capture, specimens should be handled carefully and restrained from struggling, in order to avoid damage. Without delay they should be preserved, frozen, or at least kept cool and moist. Formalin, obtainable from a pharmacy, is the preferred fixative agent. Smaller specimens may be killed by placing in soda water or directly in 10% formalin. Specimens larger than about 150 mm SL should be injected with 10% formalin, or small incisions into the body cavity and muscles should be made to allow for effective penetration of the preservative. Do not remove the scales, gills, or viscera. Avoid preserving specimens in distorted positions and overcrowding specimens in containers, by maintaining a specimen to preservative ratio of at least 1:4. Specimens should remain in 10% formalin for at least 3 or 4 days, preferably longer, before being transferred to 70% ethyl alcohol or 60% propyl alcohol for permanent storage.

A less suitable alternative fixative for small specimens is 70% ethyl alcohol. Specimens can also be preserved in coarse dry salt or in brine (a supersaturated salt solution), or even in whisky or gin.

Sometimes it is possible only to preserve a part of the specimen, such as its skeleton. In these cases it is useful to take a colour photograph and some basic measurements of the whole specimen for later reference. To prepare a skeleton it is best to remove the viscera and as much flesh as possible from the specimen in the field, and then dry the carcass. Later the remaining flesh can be removed by hot (not boiling) water or by exposing the carcass to insects such as ants or beetles.

Labels
Every sample must be carefully labelled as soon as it is collected. Labels must

be of durable material such as parchment, bond-quality paper or photographic paper, as most ordinary paper or cardboard rapidly disintegrates in liquid. Labels should be written using a soft lead pencil or permanent indian ink. Ball-point and felt-tip pens are not suitable because their inks are soluble and fade in sunlight. The following minimum information should be given: collector's name, locality including place, water body, area and country (co-ordinates if possible), and the date. Labels should be placed in the sample container or securely attached to the specimen.

Fig.29 Method of photographing a fish: (a) camera, (b) photographic tank with restraining sheet of glass, (c) painted background board. Soft natural or subdued flashlight should come from behind and above the camera. Use clean water and ensure that no bubbles are on the restraining glass or tank walls.

Photographing fishes (Fig.29)
After death the colours and natural sheen of fishes fades rapidly. One way to record live colours is by photographing the specimen while it is still alive, or as soon after death as possible. Live specimens can be photographed in their habitat by a skilled photographer, or in an aquarium. Live specimens may also be photographed in a special narrow photographic tank, as illustrated on p.64. The specimen is held by means of an inclined glass plate. Attention should be given to the background of specimen photographs to ensure that the colours are clear: a plain neutral coloured background is best. Bright sunlight and shadows from flash units should also be avoided; soft natural light is most suitable for recording the true colours of fishes.

With freshly killed specimens or specimens too large for a photographic tank it may be necessary to pin out the specimen onto a cork or styrofoam board with its fins erect, and allow it to "set" in this position by painting the fins with formalin, before taking the photograph.

Measuring fishes (Fig.30)
Fishes may be measured by means of dividers, calipers, an ordinary ruler or tape measure, or on a measuring board. Measurements are usually made in millimetres (mm), centimetres (cm) or metres (m), and imply the shortest straight line distance between two points. A few useful measurements of fishes referred to in this book are the following:

Standard length (SL) – the distance from the tip of the snout to the mid-base of the caudal fin. The mid-base of the caudal fin is the mid-point along the vertical line of articulation or flexure of the caudal fin rays. Standard length is

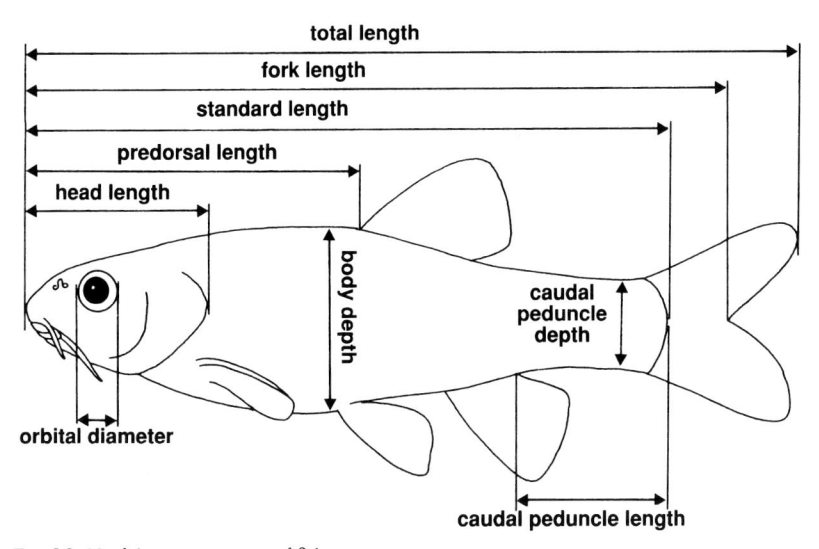

Fig.30 Useful measurements of fishes.

66 COLLECTION, PRESERVATION AND MEASUREMENT

used widely in scientific studies.

Total length (TL) – the distance from the tip of the snout to the furthest tip of the caudal fin.

Fork length (FL) – the distance from the tip of the snout to the end of the mid-caudal rays.

Head length (HL) – taken from the tip of the snout to the furthest bony edge of the operculum.

Body depth (BD) – the greatest vertical distance across the body.

Predorsal length (PDL) - the distance from the tip of the snout to the anterior base of the dorsal fin.

Caudal peduncle length (CPL) – the distance from the base of the last anal fin ray to the mid-base of the caudal fin (see Standard length).

Caudal peduncle depth (CPD) – the least vertical distance of the caudal peduncle.

Orbit or eye diameter (OD) – the greatest horizontal distance across the bony orbit or eye.

Fin spines and rays (Fig.31)

The fins of bony fishes are supported by hard spines and segmented soft rays. In non-spiny-rayed fishes such as the cyprinids, the characins and catfishes, segmented rays may be modified into bony spines. Spines may be simple or serrated along the edges. Soft rays are either simple or branched. In this book the last simple fin ray in the dorsal fin of non-spiny-rayed fishes is termed the primary dorsal ray. The last ray of the dorsal or the anal fin may be divided to the base, in which case it is counted as a single ray.

One of the most reliable ways of telling fish species apart is the fin ray formula. In the fin ray formula spines (whether true spines or modified soft rays)

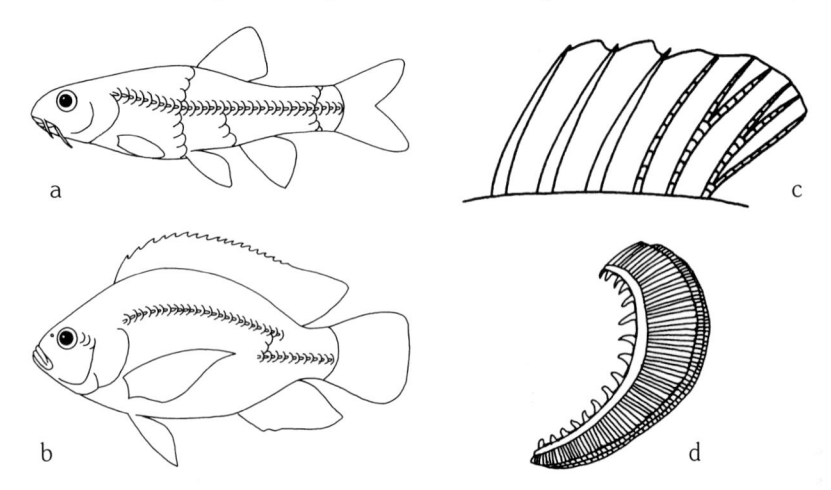

Fig.31 Taking counts of scales (a & b), finrays (c) and gill-rakers (d).

COLLECTION, PRESERVATION AND MEASUREMENT 67

are designated by means of roman capital letters (I, II, III, etc). Simple or unbranched segmented rays are designated by roman lower case letters (i, ii, iii, etc). Branched rays are given by arabic numerals (1,2,3, etc.). The dorsal fin is prefixed D, and the anal fin A (e.g. D III, 8; A iii, 5).

Scale counts (Fig.31)
Lateral scales are counted in linear series along the lateral line row or along an equivalent row if the lateral line is absent. The lateral line count is taken to the last scale over the base of the caudal fin as determined by the articulation or line of flexure of the caudal fin rays. Additional scales present on the caudal fin itself are not counted. Odd or abnormally small scales are generally not included in scale counts. If the lateral line is divided, as in cichlid and anabantid fishes, the lateral line count includes all the pored scales in the upper line and the pored scales in the lower line starting with the scale following that directly below the last one counted in the upper series. Transverse scale counts are taken as scale rows crossing an imaginary vertical line. Scale counts from the base of fins are generally taken from the anterior base of the fin.

Gill rakers (Fig.31)
Gill rakers on the first gill arch (either the total number or the number along the lower limb of the arch only) are counted.

Pharyngeal bones and teeth
The pharyngeal bones and teeth of cyprinid and cichlid fishes are valuable taxonomic characters for certain species. In the case of cichlids the shape and dimensions of the bones as well as the shape of the teeth are considered. In cyprinids the shape of the bones and teeth as well as the number of rows and number of teeth in each row on the pharyngeal bones are used. To take these counts the pharyngeal bones must be dissected from the fish and the surrounding flesh removed, either mechanically or by soaking the bones in an enzyme (trypsin) solution.

Precautions for collectors
Natural water bodies such as rivers and lakes have unpredictable dangers, and should be treated with care and respect. A few common hazards to beware of are:
- Smooth rocks and muddy banks are slippery when wet.
- Flowing water is always unpredictable and strong.
- Bottom surfaces are usually uneven and few water bodies in southern Africa do not contain rusty wire, broken glass or other sharp objects.
- The leaves of many waterside plants like reeds and rushes are dangerously sharp.
- Many waters contain bilharzia and other diseases.
- Water from the veld should always be boiled before drinking, especially in lowland reaches that have passed through occupied lands.

68 COLLECTION, PRESERVATION AND MEASUREMENT

- Crocodiles and hippos are dangerous animals that should never be underestimated.
- Handle dangerous fishes such as the electric catfish and fishes with sharp spines (catfishes and cichlids) with caution and care.
- Formalin is an extremely dangerous chemical and must be handled with care. Avoid inhaling the fumes or direct contact with the skin. Immediately wash from eyes, nose or mouth should accidental contact be made.

Southern African Freshwater Fishes – Introduction and Classification

Categories of fishes in freshwater
Primary freshwater fishes – fishes living in inland waters, with little or no tolerance of saltwater.
Secondary freshwater fishes – fishes relatively tolerant of salt water, but normally living in inland waters.
Marine fishes – fishes tolerant of salt water and normally living in the sea. Marine fishes may be tolerant of low salinity (i.e. less than 35‰).
Estuarine fishes – marine or secondary freshwater fishes normally found living and breeding in estuaries.
Peripheral (marine) fishes – marine fishes frequently living and breeding in inland waters other than estuaries.
Stragglers or sporadic (marine) fishes – marine fishes sometimes found living, but generally not breeding, in inland waters.
Diadromous fishes – fishes that, in the course of their life cycle, regularly migrate between inland waters and the sea, or vice versa.
Alien species – a species not naturally occurring in a defined area but introduced into it from outside that area.
Translocated species – a species transferred by man or via a manmade structure from one river system to another.

Composition of the fauna (Figs 32,33)
How many fish species occur in the continental waters of southern Africa? An exact answer is difficult to give because new discoveries, the introduction of alien species and changes in the taxonomy (for example when what were thought to be two species are shown to be only one species) constantly alter the number. If all the categories of fishes found in continental waters are included, the present assessment, in 1992, is 270 species in 102 genera and 38 families.

About 60% (160) of the species are primary freshwater fishes, mostly cyprinids, characins and catfishes, and 21% (56) are secondary freshwater species, mostly topminnows and cichlids. Thirty-seven peripheral and sporadic marine species are usually found in only the lower reaches of rivers and coastal lakes, and comprise about 14% of all species recorded in freshwaters. Of these marine species 11 (30%, or 4% of the total fauna) are peripheral marine species and 26 (70%, or 10% of the total fauna) are "stragglers" or sporadic marine species. Five diadromous species, migrating between sea and the rivers and back to the sea during the course of their life cycle, occur in the region. These are the four eels (*Anguilla* species) and the freshwater mullet *(Myxus capensis)*.

70 SOUTHERN AFRICAN FRESHWATER FISHES

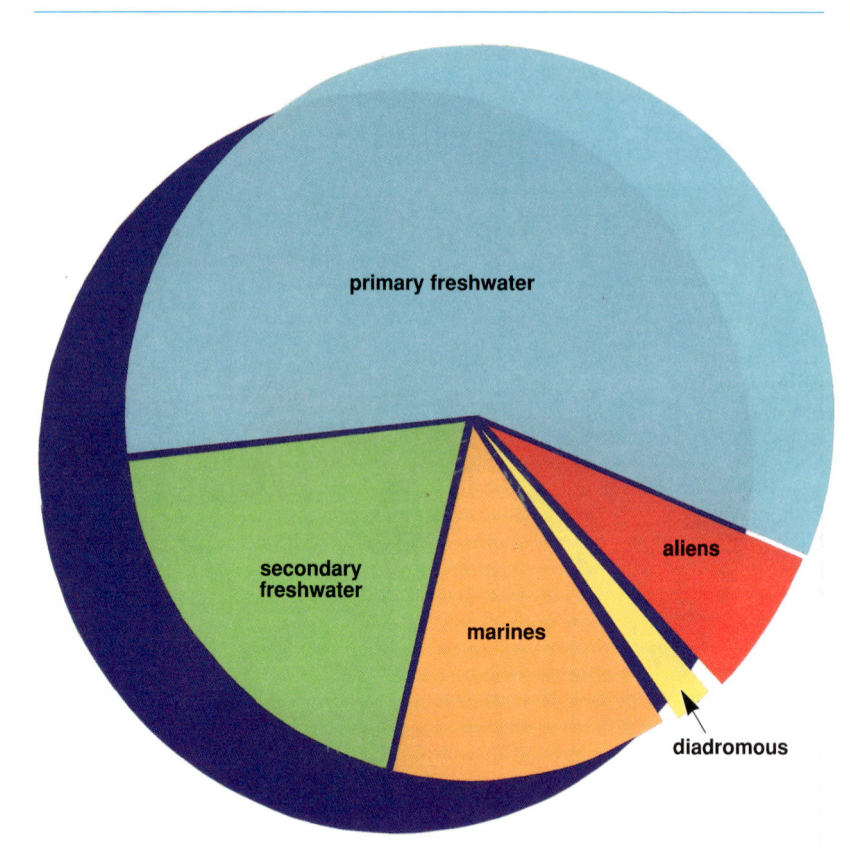

Fig.32 Proportions of different categories of fishes in the southern African fauna.

There are also 18 alien fish species (about 7% of the total fauna), in southern African freshwaters.

Southern Africa covers 16% of the continent, but the freshwater fish fauna comprises less than 10% of the total African freshwater fish fauna. Compared with certain regions in Africa, the southern African fauna is relatively poor. The Zaire river system alone has 700 or more fish species and the larger African Rift lakes – Lakes Malawi, Tanganyika and Victoria – have over 300, 220 and 200 species respectively.

Two families, the cyprinids with about 74 species or 30% of the total, and the cichlids with 33 species or 13% of the total, dominate the fauna. Other important families in terms of numbers of species are the squeakers (Mochokidae) with 17 species, snoutfishes (Mormyridae) with 9, air-breathing catfishes (Clariidae) with 8, annual killifishes (Aplocheilidae) and toothcarps (Cyprinodontidae) each with 7, and the characins with 6. The largest genus by far is *Barbus,* with about 50 species or 20% of the total fauna. However, it is recognised that the genus *Barbus* is composed of several distinct groups of species which, in future, are likely to be allocated to different genera. Other large genera in southern Africa include *Labeo* (12 species), *Clarias* (6), *Chiloglanis* (8 or 9), *Synodontis* (9), *Nothobranchius* (6), *Serranochromis* (13) and *Oreochromis* (7).

Proceeding from north to south there is a decrease in both numbers and diversity of freshwater fishes in southern Africa. Considering only primary and secondary indigenous species, the Zambezi river system has about 134 species, the Limpopo 50, the Phongolo 40 and the Tugela 12. On the west coast the Cunene has 66 species, the Orange 16, the Olifants 10 and the Berg 4. Most southern Cape rivers have only 3 or 4 indigenous freshwater species. There are 20 or more families represented in the Zambezi, 14 in the Limpopo, 5 in the Orange and 3 in the Olifants. The relative proportion of cyprinid fishes increases further south.

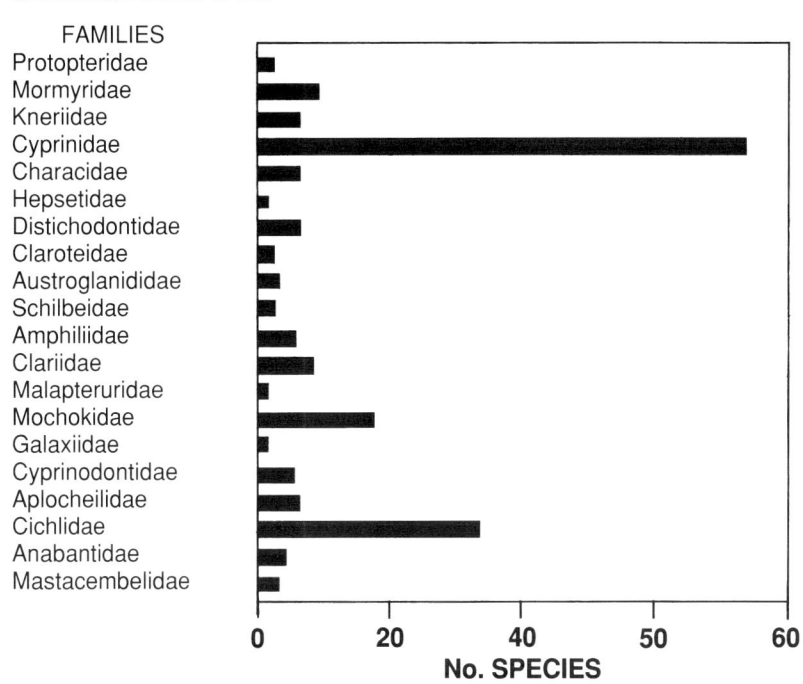

Fig.33 Relative sizes of the indigenous primary and secondary freshwater fish families in southern Africa.

Endemicity

About 61% of the primary and secondary freshwater fishes are endemic to southern Africa (i.e. do not occur naturally beyond this region). The greatest concentration of endemics is in the Cape but others are found throughout the subcontinent. Most endemics are restricted to an area such as the eastern or southern Cape and a number of species occur only in a single river system. The Clanwilliam Olifants River in the south-west Cape Province has 10 indigenous freshwater fish species of which 8 are endemic to that system. The Orange River system has 6 endemic species, some of which have now been translocated to other river systems. The Namaqua barb *(Barbus hospes)* occurs only below the Augrabies Falls, and the Drakensberg minnow *(Pseudobarbus quathlambae)* is restricted to high-altitude tributaries in Lesotho. The Limpopo system has only 2 (4%) endemic species, but 23 (17%) of the 134 species in the Zambezi fauna are endemic to that system.

More than half the freshwater fishes in the Cunene, Okavango or Zambezi systems also occur in immediately adjacent river systems in Central Africa such as the Zaire, the Quanza in Angola and Lake Malawi. Some very widely distributed species in Africa include Cornish Jack *(Mormyrus anguilloides)*, tigerfish *(Hydrocynus vittatus)*, silver robber *(Micralestes acutidens)*, imberi *(Brycinus imberi)*, African pike *(Hepsetus odoe)*, sharptooth catfish *(Clarias gariepinus)*, vundu *(Heterobranchus longifilis)*, electric catfish *(Malapterurus electricus)* and minnows such as straightfin barb *(Barbus paludinosus)* and threespot barb *(Barbus trimaculatus)*.

Alien and translocated species

Man has introduced at least 18 alien species from elsewhere to the subcontinent. Some of the aliens are not widely established or known, but others, like common carp *(Cyprinus carpio),* rainbow trout *(Oncorhynchus mykiss),* brown trout *(Salmo trutta),* largemouth bass *(Micropterus salmoides),* smallmouth bass *(M. dolomieu)* and kapenta or Kariba sardine *(Limnothrissa miodon),* are among the best known of all our freshwater fishes. Early reports indicate that ornamental carp were introduced as early as the 1700s. Common carp were officially introduced to South Africa in the 1850s, brown trout were introduced in 1892 and rainbow trout in 1896. Both species of trout have been widely stocked into mountain streams throughout the southern and eastern sectors of southern Africa. Bass were introduced between 1928 and 1939 and are also well established in many water bodies. These alien sportfishes have provided an important recreational resource, but unfortunately they have also been largely responsible for the decline of some indigenous species, several of which are now considered to be threatened. The conservation authorities and angling bodies are now seeking to find a balance between these conflicting interests.

Several southern African species have been translocated to river systems beyond their natural range, either deliberately as in the case of smallmouth yellowfish *(Barbus aeneus)* and the banded tilapia *(Tilapia sparrmanii),* or inadvertently through canals and pipelines connecting different river basins. Five or more species have been introduced from the Orange to the Great Fish River in the eastern Cape through the Orange–Great Fish canal. The increase in the number of interbasin water transfer systems in southern Africa is resulting in an ever-increasing transfer of fish species from one river system to another.

These immigrant species are a conservation threat because they may compete with and displace, prey on, or interbreed with the resident species. In addition, they may transfer foreign parasites and diseases.

Zonation

Zonation describes the sequence in distribution of species along the length of a river system. Generally only a few small fish species like minnows or knerias occupy the headwater zones of a river where the streams are small and swift. Different species enter and others disappear from the fauna as the river extends downstream, so that the community of the lowland river is generally different from that of the headwaters or other upland reaches, and more diverse.

Good examples of faunal zonation are found in rivers along the Great Escarpment, especially in the eastern Transvaal where the river passes from cooler upland to warmer lowveld climatic conditions. In the Sabi River, for example, the upper reaches are occupied by species such as rosefin barb *(Barbus argenteus)*, orangefin barb *(B. eutaenia)*, shortfin barb *(B. brevipinnis)*, smallscale yellowfish *(B. polylepis)*, Incomati chiselmouth *(Varicorhinus nelspruitensis)*, pennant-tail rock catlet *(Chiloglanis anoterus)*, stargazer and Natal mountain catlets *(Amphilius uranoscopus* and *A. natalensis)*. As the gradient declines near the foot of the escarpment, species such as bulldog *(Marcusenius macrolepidotus)*, silver robber *(Micralestes acutidens)*, largescale yellowfish *(Barbus marequensis)*, three-spot barb *(B. trimaculatus)*, longbeard barb *(B. unitaeniatus)*, red-eye and leaden labeos *(Labeo cylindricus, L. molybdinus)*, barred minnow *(Opsaridium zambezense)*, southern mouthbrooder *(Pseudocrenilabrus philander)* and longfin eel *(Anguilla mossambica)* appear. Over the lowveld reaches down to the Kruger Park and Mozambique, where the river is larger and more slowly flowing, the community includes species such as Churchill *(Petrocephalus catostoma)*, imberi *(Brycinus imberi)*, Hamilton's barb *(B. afrohamiltoni)*, broadstripe barb *(B. annectens)*, bowstripe barb *(B. viviparus)*, east-coast barb *(B. toppini)*, red-eye barb *(B. radiatus)*, red-nose, red-spotted and silver labeos *(Labeo rosae, L. congoro, L. ruddi)*, river sardine *(Mesobola brevianalis)*, tigerfish *(Hydrocynus vittatus)*, sharptooth catfish *(Clarias gariepinus)*, butter barbel *(Schilbe intermedius)*, brown squeaker *(Synodontis zambezensis)*, lowveld rock catlet *(Chiloglanis swierstrai)*, Mozambique tilapia *(Oreochromis mossambicus)*, redbreast tilapia *(Tilapia rendalli)*, lowveld largemouth *(Serranochromis meridianus)*, Madagascar mottled eel *(Anguilla marmorata)* and tank goby *(Glossogobius giuris)*.

The gradient of the river is one factor determining which species of a given community will be present. Some are particularly suited to fast-flowing rivers; others prefer slow-flowing sections and pools. Upland rivers are likely to have steeper gradients than downstream sections, although this is not always the case and much depends on the local landscape. Waterfalls often form distinct barriers to fish distribution. Some notable examples of waterfalls that restrict fish species are the Victoria Falls on the Zambezi, the Chivirira Falls on the Save, the Selawandoma Falls on the Runde, and the Augrabies Falls on the Orange.

Distribution and biogeography (Figs 34,35,36)

Southern African freshwater fishes can be grouped into two geographical categories, a tropical or Zambezian fauna and a temperate fauna. The temperate fauna is further subdivided into the Karoo group and the Cape group.

The Zambezian fauna is the largest group, with about 178 species, or 83% of the primary and secondary freshwater fishes. It is comparatively diverse and includes many fish families that are not part of the temperate fauna. Examples are lungfish, mormyrids, kneriids, characins, several catfish families, topminnows and killifishes as well as cichlids and spiny eels. The number of Zambezian species decreases markedly from north to south and only a few hardy species occur south of the Lake St Lucia area in Natal. Only one species, the Mozambique tilapia *(Oreochromis mossambicus),* occurs naturally further south than the Natal border. Five widespread tropical species occur in the Orange, which is the natural southern boundary for this fauna on the west coast.

The temperate fauna is comparatively small and comprises about 36 species or 17% of the primary and freshwater fishes, but it is entirely endemic. Most (83%) temperate species are cyprinids, but there are also the interesting southern catfishes *(Austroglanis* species) and the two anabantids *(Sandelia* species). The Cape component comprises only 15 species, which are restricted to the rivers of the Cape Fold Mountains, the Amatolas and the Drakensberg. Of special interest are two large cyprinids from the south-west Cape, whitefish *(Barbus andrewi)* and sawfin *(Barbus serra),* as well as the redfin minnows *(Pseudobarbus* species) and Cape galaxias *(Galaxias zebratus).* The distribution of species of the Karoo fauna is centred around the Orange basin. This fauna includes yellowfishes *(Barbus aeneus, B. capensis, B. kimberleyensis, B. natalensis, B. polylepis)* and the *Labeo umbratus* group of labeos, chubbyhead barb *(Barbus anoplus)* and its allies, as well as southern rock catfishes *(Austroglanis* species).

Evolutionary events in the earth's history as well as ecological factors account for the distribution of fishes in southern Africa. Historical events such as the capture of one river by another or a lowering of sea-level due to major climatic changes tend to determine the general pattern of distribution, whereas ecological factors such as temperature refine the pattern and usually determine the presence or absence of species at the local level.

One explanation for freshwater fish distribution in southern Africa is that the fishes entered from further north in Africa, extending southwards in distinct "waves" of invasion. Each wave progressed further southwards during periods when the different river basins were interconnected. Thus the first invasion is thought to have been in the mid-Pliocene (about 2–3 million years ago) and resulted in what is now the Cape and Karoo fauna reaching the Orange and Cape coastal rivers. A second invasion may have occurred during the late

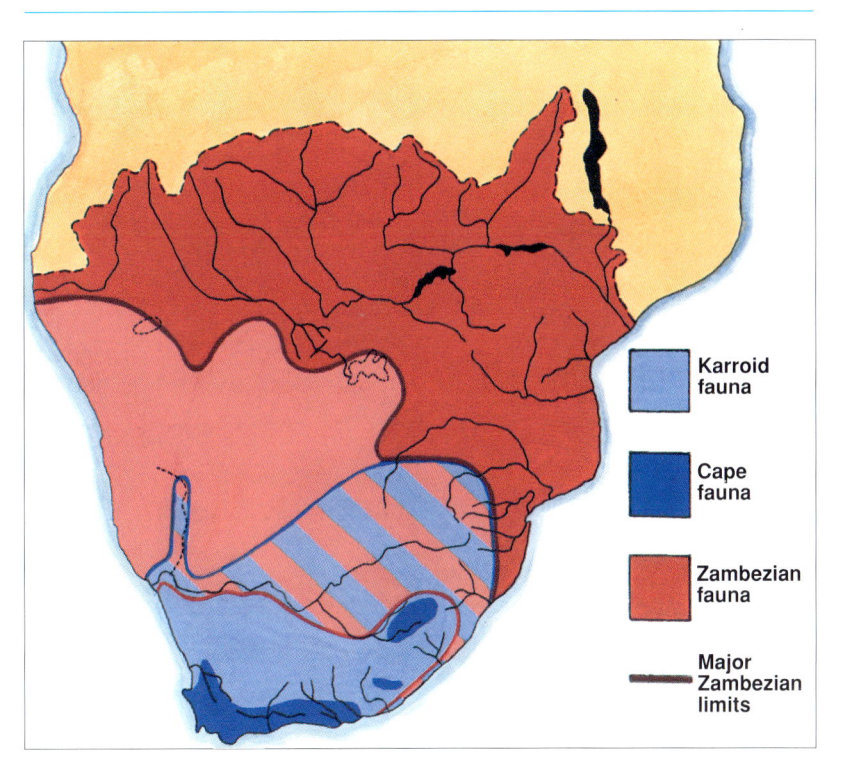

Fig.34 Biogeographical zones of the southern African freshwater fish fauna. There is some overlap between the Zambezian (tropical) fauna and the Karroid or temperate fauna as shown by the cross-banded area.

Pliocene (1,8–2 million years ago) when a connection between the Okavango–upper Zambezi and the Limpopo basin is thought to have existed. During the Pleistocene (less than 1,8 million years ago) an invasion occurred along the coastal region, linking the lower Zambezi and Limpopo basin. Finally, more recent connections between the Orange and the Limpopo basins explain the presence of species common to the two systems.

One problem with the "waves of invasion" theory is that, in the case of the temperate fishes, we do not know for sure which fishes beyond southern Africa they are related to. Therefore we cannot trace their origins and history before the stage at which their ancestors actually reached their present ranges. However, there are a few indications that the temperate fauna has existed in southern Africa for a long period of time. For example, the closest relatives of the Cape galaxias *(Galaxias zebratus)* are found in Australia, New Zealand and South America and it is probably a relic from the time when all these landmasses were connected as the supercontinent Gondwanaland. It has also been suggested that this species may have reached southern Africa through oceanic dispersal.

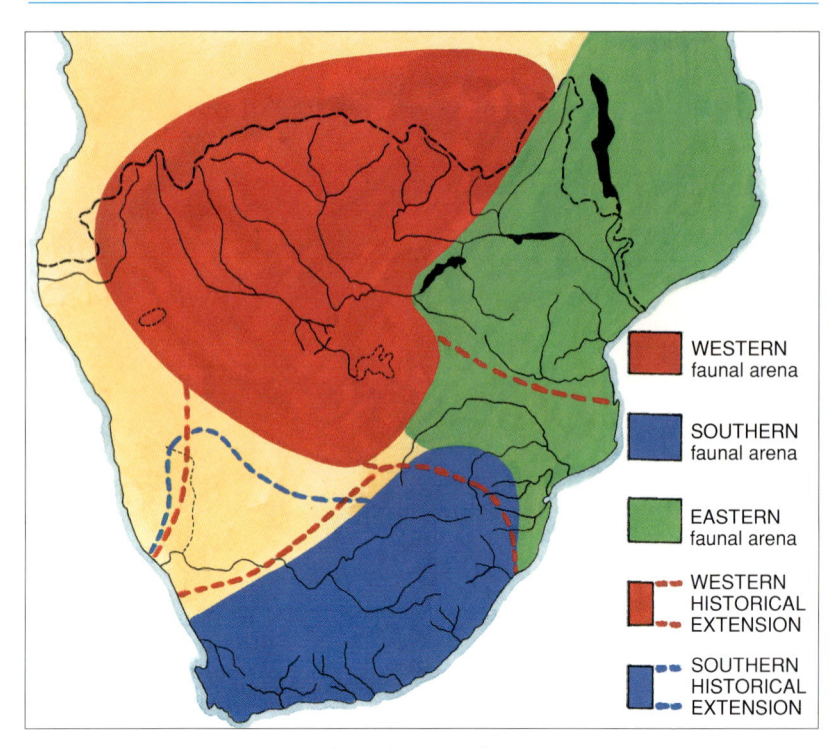

Fig.35 Biogeography: Southern African freshwater fishes are considered to be derived from three evolutionary arenas: a Western arena that includes the Kunene, Okavango, upper Zambezi, and Kafue river systems as well as the upper reaches of certain tributaries of the Zaire river system; an Eastern arena that includes the middle and lower Zambezi and east coastal rivers from the Phongolo to East Africa; and a Southern arena that includes Transvaal tributaries of the Limpopo and systems to the southern tip of the subcontinent. Proposed historical extensions to the Western and Southern arenas are shown.

One study indicated that the closest relatives of the *Labeo umbratus* group of species are certain Asiatic *Labeo* species. Such relationships, if true, suggest that the temperate fauna may even stem from a time before the separation of India about 120 million years ago. So it is difficult to accept that the temperate fauna originated further north in Africa.

Whatever its early origins, this temperate fauna has speciated and evolved to a large extent in southern Africa. The redfin minnows (*Pseudobarbus* species) are a closely related lineage in the rivers draining the Cape Fold Mountains and the high Drakensberg. The pattern of distribution of the species accords with the drainage history and indicates that the lineage has been in these rivers for a long period of time, at least since the late Oligocene some 20 million years ago, and possibly even since the Palaeocene about 60 million years ago. These dates are based on episodes of drainage history linking the Orange River to the

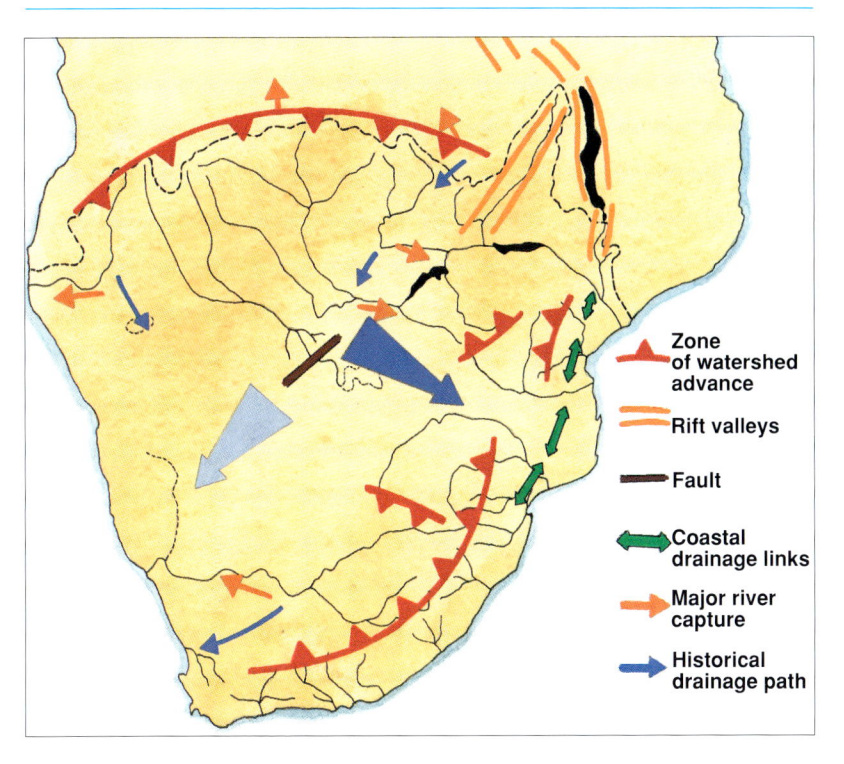

Fig.36 Biogeography: Geomorphological factors affecting drainage patterns and fish distribution transfer in southern Africa: (a) Advancing watersheds e.g. eastern coastal rivers and the Zaire headwaters, capture headwaters of opposing drainage systems. (b) Historical drainage paths are changed by means of major river captures e.g. Orange River, or blocked by geological faults e.g. Okavango River. (c) drainage connections occur across low gradient watersheds during high floods or during periods of sea-level decline e.g. Mozambique and Maputaland coastal areas. (d) Rift valley faulting disrupts historical drainage lines and directs drainages e.g. Lake Malawi and the Shire River.

Olifants system that have been determined by geologists from offshore sediment studies.

The distribution of tropical species provides evidence for past drainage connections between certain basins such as the Okavango–upper Zambezi, and the Limpopo and the Upper Zambezi–Zaire basin. Some of these connections occurred relatively recently and gave rise to fish distributions that correspond to the Pliocene and Pleistocene "invasions" mentioned above. River capture and present-day interconnections of the headwaters of the Zambezi and Zaire systems account for the presence of many species common to these two systems. Nevertheless, 23% of the Zambezi fauna is endemic to that system and the presence of other endemic tropical species in southern Africa, such as several suckermouth catlets (*Chiloglanis* species), indicates that a great deal of speciation and evolution has occurred within southern Africa. Much more information is required about broader distributions and interrelationships of African fishes to obtain a more accurate picture of the origins of the southern African fauna.

Evolutionary relationships (Fig. 37)

The sharks and sawfishes belong together in an early branch of cartilaginous fishes. The lungfishes are the most primitive of the bony fishes found in southern Africa. The mormyrids belong in a distinct lineage without close relatives in southern Africa. Eels and tarpons are considered to be related, largely on account of the fact that they both have a leaf-like (leptocephalus) larva. The clupeids, the family to which the freshwater herrings belong, form a branch by themselves.

The majority of southern African freshwater fishes belong to the Ostariophysi, which includes the Kneriidae in one lineage (the Anotophysi) and the much more diverse Otophysi, or fishes with modified vertebrae (Weberian apparatus) linking the swimbladder to the inner ear, in the other. Although the cyprinids and the characins look much more like one another than either do to the catfishes, this is an example where general similarity and close relationship are not the same. In fact the characins and catfishes are actually more closely related to each other than either of these groups is to the cyprinids.

The Galaxiidae are more closely related to alien trout than to any other African freshwater fish.

The remaining fishes all have true spines in their dorsal and anal fins and belong to the so-called acanthomorph lineage. The Cyprinodontiformes, an order that includes the topminnows, killifishes and live-bearers, are related to the estuarine and sporadic marine atherinids. The pipefishes are in a specialised offshoot from the mainstem leading to the two derived orders of perciform and synbranchiform fishes.

In evolutionary terms the perciform and synbranchiform groups are considered to be more advanced than most other fishes. Taken worldwide, the order Perciformes is the largest and most diverse group of modern fishes and includes 150 families and about 7 800 species. Consequently it is not surprising to find that our knowledge of the interrelationships of different perciform fishes is still often scant and vague. The spiny eels were until recently considered to be perciform fishes, but detailed studies have shown that they belong within the synbranchiform lineage, named for the swamp eels from tropical waters.

Within the southern African freshwater fauna the perciform fishes include the cichlids and the anabantids as well as a host of marine families such as the gobies, sleepers, moonies, mullets and ambassids. The cichlids belong in a lineage that includes several marine families such as the parrotfishes (Scaridae), the wrasses (Labridae) and the surfperches (Embiotocidae). The anabantids are related to Asian freshwater fishes collectively known as "labyrinth fishes" on account of the labyrinth-like air-breathing organ they all possess. These fishes

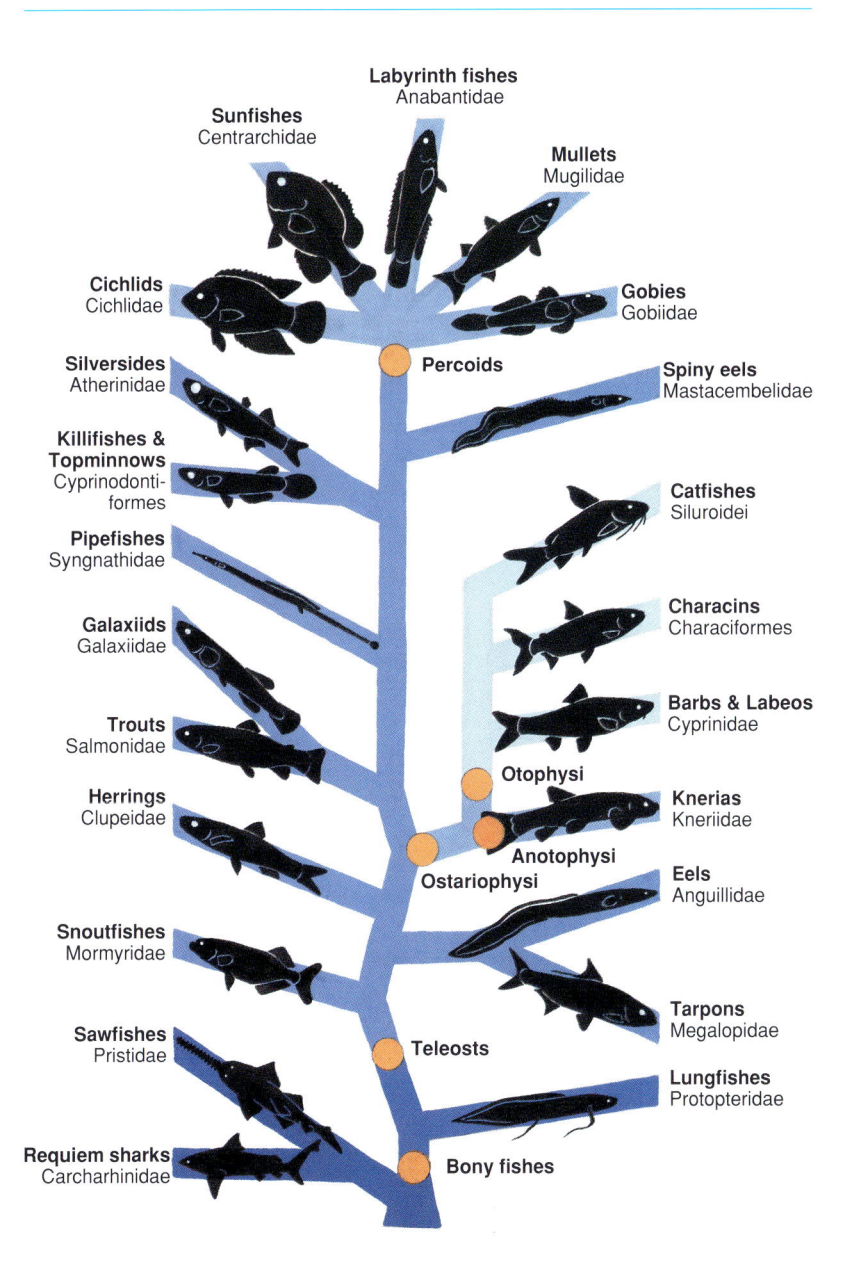

Fig.37 Diagram to show broad relationships between the major groups of southern African freshwater fishes.

include several forms well known to aquarists, such as the gouramis (Osphronemidae, Belontiidae, Helostomatiidae), including the Siamese fighting fish *(Betta splendens)*.

The alien basses, bluegill sunfish (Centrarchidae) and the perch (Percidae) are also part of the very large perciform radiation.

KEY TO FAMILIES

Note: the context of this key is southern African freshwaters. Certain character sets may be broader than given for a particular family beyond this region.

1a	Five pairs of external gill slits	2
1b	Single, or single pair of gill openings	3
2a	Head without extended rostrum, gill slits lateral
	Carcharhinidae (requiem sharks), p.343

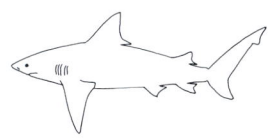

2b	Head with extended rostrum with well-spaced teeth along either edge, gill slits ventral ....**Pristidae (saw sharks), p.345**

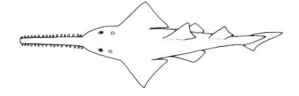

3a	Body without scales, or scales small and not clearly visible	4
3b	Body with clearly visible scales	12
4a	Body slender, elongate and eel-like, length greater than 8 times depth; dorsal, caudal and anal fins united; pelvic fins absent	5
4b	Body not eel-like, length less than 8 times depth, dorsal, caudal and anal fins separated, pelvic fins present	6
5a	Head pointed with fleshy rostral appendage, a series of spines along back
	Mastacembelidae (spiny eels), p.339

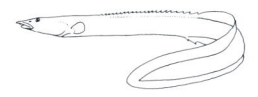

5b	Head without fleshy rostral appendage, no spines along back ....**Anguillidae (freshwater eels), p.104**

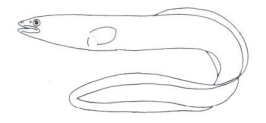

6a	No barbels around mouth	**Galaxiidae (galaxiids), p.258**

6b	Three or four pairs of barbels around mouth	**Siluroidei (catfishes)** 7
7a	Rayed dorsal fin not present, adipose fin present	....
	......................................**Malapteruridae (electric catfishes) p.238**	

7b	Rayed dorsal fin present, adipose fin present or absent	8
8a	Dorsal fin without spine, at least 26–31 dorsal soft rays	....
	......................................**Clariidae (air-breathing catfishes), p.227**	

8b	Dorsal fin with or without spine, less than 10 dorsal soft rays	9
9a	Anal fin with more than 40 soft rays	.....**Schilbeidae (butter catfishes), p.224**

9b	Anal fin with fewer than 15 soft rays	10
10a	Dorsal and pectoral fins without spine, leading pectoral fin ray pectinate (comb-like)	....................................**Amphiliidae (mountain catfishes), p.218**

10b	Dorsal and pectoral fins with spine	11
11a	Mouth terminal, teeth fine, in bands along jaws, barbels simple (unbranched)	....................**Claroteidae (p.211) and Austroglanididae (p.215)**

11b	Mouth inferior, oval or disc-shaped, mandibular teeth in one or two rows, projecting forward, barbels simple or branched	....
	...................................**Mochokidae (squeakers, suckermouth catlets), p.240**	

12a Pectoral and pelvic fins filamentous, caudal fin pointed ....**Protopteridae (African lungfish), p.89**

12b Pectoral and pelvic fins with rays, not filamentous 13
13a Head covered with scales (or bony plates) 22
13b Head naked (without scales)...14
14a Jaws without teeth 15
14b Jaws with teeth 16
15a Mouth inferior, lower lip with hard edge, no barbels; gill slit short, restricted to sides of head; scales very small ....**Kneriidae (knerias), p.112**

15b Mouth variable, barbels present or absent; gill slit extending to ventral side of head; scales variable, seldom very small ....**Cyprinidae (barbs, yellowfishes, labeos), p.117**

16a Gill slits small, restricted to sides of head; scales with reticulated striae; dorsal and/or anal fin with more than 16 soft rays; caudal fin lobes partly or largely covered with scales ....**Mormyridae (snoutfishes), p.92**

16b Gill slits extended to ventral side of head; scales with radial or linear striae; anal fin with less than 16 branched rays 17
17a Scales ctenoid, with fine but separate ctenii (scale teeth); mouth square, inferior with lower jaw closing within lateral (side) plates of upper jaw ....**Distichodontidae (citharines), p.193**

17b Scales cycloid; mouth variable 18

18a Adipose fin present 19
18b Adipose fin absent 21
19a Scales very small; cheeks not bony ....**Salmonidae (trouts), p.260**

19b Scales moderate to large; cheeks with bony plates 20
20a Jaws extended, head pointed; teeth large but uneven in size; dorsal fin behind pelvics ....**Hepsetidae (African pike), p.208**

20b Jaws not extended, head rounded; teeth uni- or multi-cuspidate, evenly reduced in size along jaws ....**Characidae (characins), p.199**

21a Mouth not extending to below eye; keeled bony scutes in ventral midline, scales thin and easily shed ....**Clupeidae (herrings), p.109**

21b Mouth extending to below eye; scales large and robust; last ray of dorsal fin extended, filamentous ....**Megalopidae (tarpons), p.102**

22a Body tubular, encased in bony rings...........**Syngnathidae (pipefishes), p.354**

22b Body not tubular, nor encased in bony rings 23
23a Dorsal and anal fins without spines; dorsal fin placed far back over the anal fin, pelvic fins abdominal ....
.......................**Cyprinodontiformes (killifishes, toothcarps, livebearers), p.266**

23b Dorsal and anal fins with spines and soft rays 24
24a Two entirely separate dorsal fins 25
24b Dorsal fin undivided, spinous section partly or wholly confluent with soft ray section 28
25a Head and body depressed; eyes dorsal; pelvic fins on ventral side, below pectoral fins 26
25b Head and body compressed or fusiform; eyes lateral; pelvic fins on sides of body, behind pectoral fins..27
26a Pelvic fins united to form a disc ....**Gobiidae (gobies), p.364**

26b Pelvic fins closely separated ....**Eleotridae (sleepers), p.361**

27a Anal fin with I, 11–17 rays ....**Atherinidae (silversides), p.350**

27b Anal fin with III, 8–9 rays ....**Mugilidae (mullets), p.351**

28a Body ovoid and compressed; dorsal and anal spines reduced, covered by firm skin; pelvics rudimentary or absent ....**Monodactylidae (moonies), p.358**

28b Body oblong or ellipsoid; dorsal and anal spines well developed, freely depressed and erected; pelvics not rudimentary 29
29a Lateral line in single series 30
29b Lateral line in two separate series 33
30a Dorsal spines XII–XIII, head bones variously serrate...............................
....**Ambassidae (glassies), p.347**

30b Dorsal spines XIII or more, head bones not serrate 31

86 KEY TO FAMILIES

31a Anal spines I–II ....**Percidae (perches), p.289**

31b Anal spines III 32
32a Dorsal spines VIII–IX+I; teeth fine, sharp, in bands along jaws. ....
....**Centrarchidae (sunfishes), p.283**

32b Dorsal spines XI–XII; teeth heterodont, outer anterior pointed and sharp, innermost blunt and molariform ....**Sparidae (seabreams), p.356**

33a Anal spines III–IV; pair of single nostrils ....**Cichlidae (cichlids), p.291**

33b Anal spines VI–IX; pair of double nostrils ....
....**Anabantidae (labyrinth fishes), p.333**

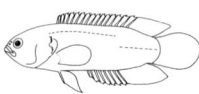

Species accounts

FAMILY PROTOPTERIDAE
African lungfishes

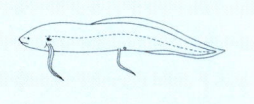

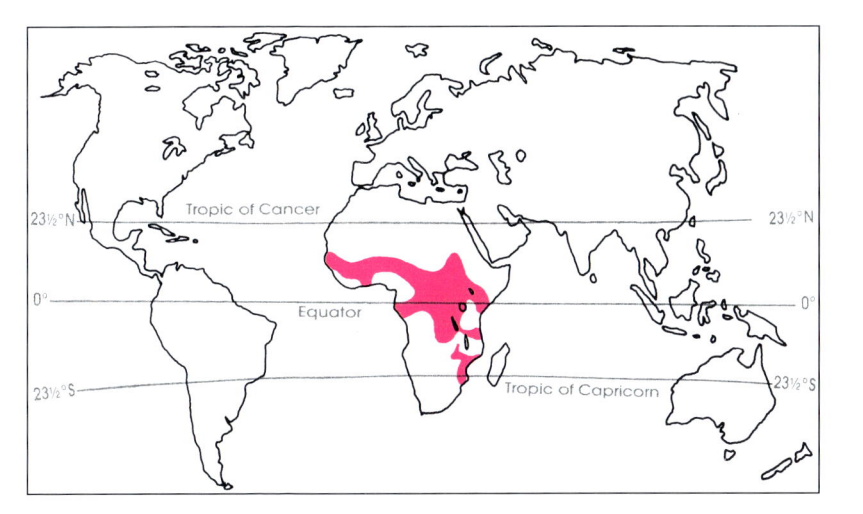

Lungfishes belong to an ancient lineage that traces back in fossil forms to the Lower Devonian Period (400 million years ago). They are related to the coelacanths and possibly represent the nearest living relatives of the ancestor of all four-legged vertebrates. The African family includes a single genus with four species. African lungfishes are related to the South American species (*Lepidosiren paradoxa* – family Lepidosirenidae) and more distantly to the Australian lungfish *Neoceratodus forsteri*, which belongs to the family Ceratodontidae.

Genus *Protopterus* Owen, 1839

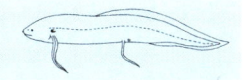

This African genus includes four species, two of which occur in southern Africa. Lungfishes have distinctive elongated tapered bodies and filamentous pectoral and pelvic fins. In southern Africa they are restricted to the tropical reaches of the eastern coastal plain.

KEY TO SPECIES

1a Distance snout to origin of dorsal fin 1,4–1,7 times head length, or 45–56% distance snout to vent ....***P. amphibius* (p.91)**
1b Distance snout to origin of dorsal fin 2–2,4 times head length, or 54–62% distance snout to vent ....***P. annectens* (p.90)**

LUNGFISH

Longvis
Protopterus annectens brieni Poll, 1961

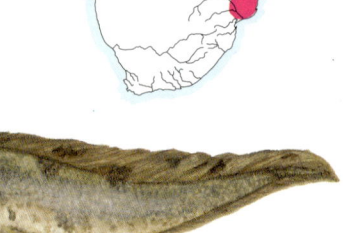

Description Scales soft, cycloid, 40–50 in lateral series. Body elongated and tapered to a point, pectoral and pelvic fins slender and tapered, dorsal and anal fins with soft rays only. Head robust, snake-like, mouth large with sharp teeth, nostrils open under the upper lip, hidden when mouth is closed. Gill chamber openings short, restricted to sides in front of pectoral bases. Small external gills are present above each gill opening. Anus behind pelvic base, offset on side of body. Greyish brown with dark brown spots and blotches, lateral line canals form wavy lines over the head. Attains 600 mm TL.

Distribution Coastal plain of Mozambique from the lower Zambezi to the Incomati, range extends up middle Zambezi valley. Also found in the Zambian Zaire (Lake Bangweulu) area. A northern subspecies (*P. annectens annectens*) occurs across West Africa to the Sudd area of the upper Nile.

Biology and Ecology Lungfish have a lung for breathing air, which enables them to live in poorly oxygenated waters of tropical vleis, pans and swamps. As the water level drops a burrow is formed in soft sediments and a mucous cocoon is secreted. The fish becomes dormant, breathing through a small opening. Aestivation lasts until the habitat is again filled with water, usually after 7–8 months.

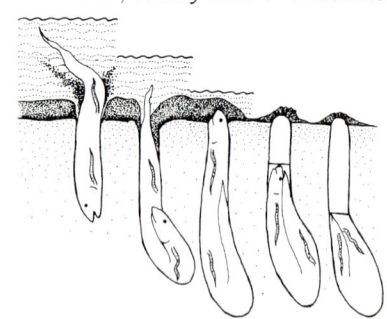

As the water level falls lungfish burrow into the bottom mud to form a cocoon and aestivate through the dry season.

Preys mainly on slow-moving bottom-dwelling creatures such as snails, insects and worms, but also takes fish and amphibians. Prey are sucked into the mouth and repeatedly chewed, ejected and sucked back in. A nest, varying from a simple excavation to a

AFRICAN LUNGFISHES

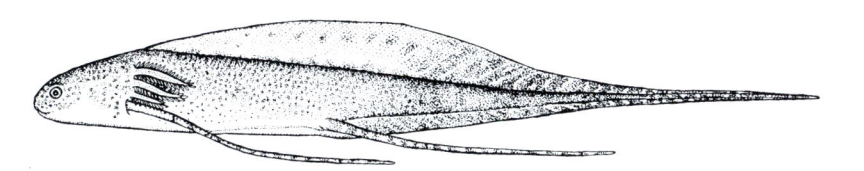

Juvenile lungfish, 32 mm TL.

U-shaped tunnel, is constructed for breeding purposes. The male guards the nest with eggs and young. May live for many years.
Uses Aquarium pet, collected or caught locally for food.
Conservation Vulnerable in South Africa and threatened in Zimbabwe. Has been translocated to additional sites in the Kruger National Park.

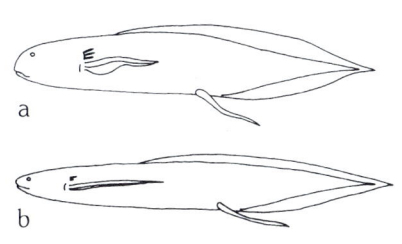

Comparative profiles of (a) east-coast lungfish and (b) lungfish; (c) the anus is offset from the midline.

EAST-COAST LUNGFISH

Ooskus-longvis
Protopterus amphibius (Peters, 1844)

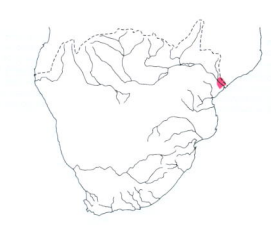

Description As for lungfish but head generally larger (more than 30% distance snout to vent); dorsal fin closer to head (snout to dorsal fin 1,4–1,7 times head length); pectoral fin with broad membranes. Uniform blue- or slaty grey, with small or inconspicuous black spots, belly pale grey, head dark below with white spots or vermiculations. Attains 412 mm TL.
Distribution Coastal lower Zambezi and East Africa.
Note The presence of this species in southern Africa requires confirmation.

92 SNOUTFISHES

FAMILY MORMYRIDAE
Snoutfishes

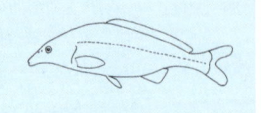

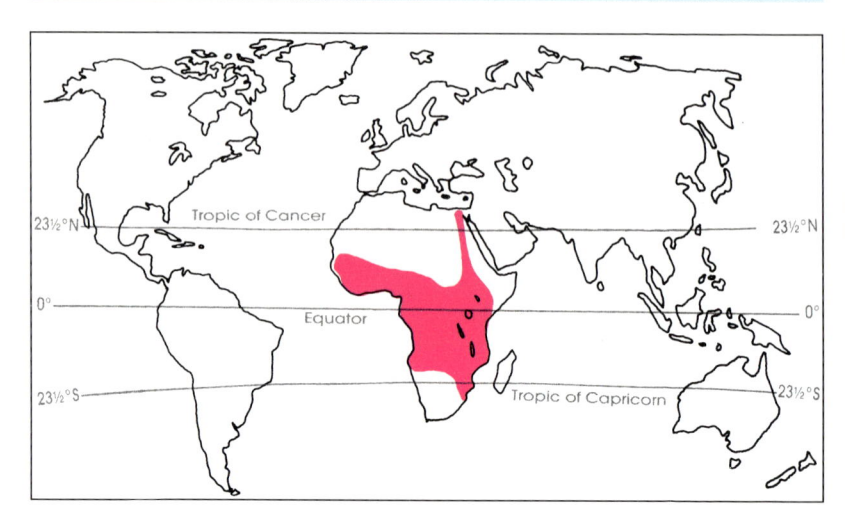

Mormyrids are unusual fishes with a soft body and snout often extended into a proboscis. They are usually active at night and can generate and receive weak electric currents to communicate with one another and to detect predators or prey. Each species has its own "signature discharge" and the sexes of some species also have different discharges. Mormyrids have a large brain – comparable, relative to body weight, to that of humans. Little is known about their breeding biology but certain species have a complex courtship and the male builds a nest and guards the larvae.

The family includes 18 genera and 200 species distributed throughout tropical Africa including the Nile. Their closest relatives are the knifefishes (notopterids) of Africa and south-east Asia and they are more distantly related to the mooneyes (hiodontids) of North America as well as the bony tongues or osteoglossids from South America, Africa and south-east Asia.

KEY TO GENERA AND SPECIES

1a Dorsal fin greater than twice length of anal fin, dorsal origin nearer tip of snout than caudal fin base ....*(Mormyrus)* 2
1b Dorsal fin less than 1,5 times anal fin length, dorsal fin origin nearer caudal fin base than tip of snout 3
2a Snout 3–3,2 times in head length, caudal peduncle more than 4 times in SL, dorsal fin 62–66 rays...................................*Mormyrus lacerda* (p. 95)

2b Snout 2–2,5 times in head length, caudal peduncle less than 4 times in SL, dorsal fin 65–75 rays .... ***Mormyrus longirostris* (p. 95)**
3a Origin of dorsal fin in advance of anal fin, dorsal fin up to 1,5 times length of anal fin. .... ***Hippopotamyrus discorhynchus* (p. 97)**
3b Origin of dorsal fin behind origin of anal fin, dorsal fin shorter than anal fin 4
4a Chin (mental swelling) present 5
4b Chin (mental swelling) absent... 6
5a Chin feebly developed, dorsal fin 19 rays, anal fin 24–26 rays ....
 .... ***Hippopotamyrus ansorgii* (p. 96)**

5b Chin well developed, dorsal fin 23–25 rays, anal fin 28–32 rays ....
 .... ***Marcusenius macrolepidotus* (p. 98)**
6a Head depressed, mouth large, terminal, width subequal to snout length, snout long .... ***Mormyrops anguilloides* (p. 94)**
6b Head compressed, mouth small, subterminal or inferior, snout short 7
7a Mouth inferior, nares close together, dorsal fin 19–24 rays, anal fin with 25–30 rays .... ***Petrocephalus catostoma* (p. 99)**

7b Mouth subterminal, nares widely spaced, dorsal fin 16–18 rays, anal fin 23–25 rays 8
8a Caudal peduncle length 2,5–3 times depth, head rounded ....
 .... ***Pollimyrus castelnaui* (p. 100)**
8b Caudal peduncle length 4 times depth, head concave on top ....
 .... ***Paramormyrops jacksoni* (p. 101)**

Genus *Mormyrops* Müller, 1843

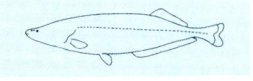

Large fishes with elongate head and body. About 20 species distributed in tropical Africa, one in our area.

CORNISH JACK

Roof-bottelneus
Mormyrops anguilloides (Linnaeus, 1758)

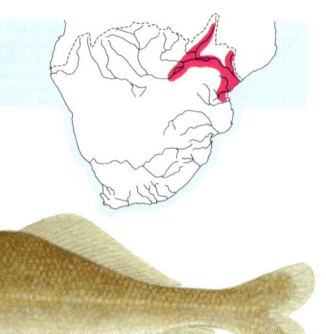

Description D 21–30; A 38–51. Scales small, 85–100 in lateral line. Head and body elongated, median fins set well back, dorsal fin shorter than anal, caudal relatively small, forked with rounded lobes. Head smooth and depressed in front, mouth terminal with small pointed teeth in a single row, eyes small, gill slit restricted to sides, inclined at an angle. Grey above, lighter silvery white below, often with a bronze or yellow sheen. Juveniles are darker, greyish blue or brown. Attains 1,2 m TL, 15 kg. Zimbabwean angling record is 13,75 kg, Malawi 10,87 kg.
Distribution In southern Africa restricted to the middle and lower Zambezi and the Buzi and Pungwe rivers. Also widespread through the Zaire basin and West Africa, the Nile and Lakes Malawi, Tanganyika and Mobuto.
Biology and Ecology Juveniles occur in marginal habitats, adults prefer deep quiet water between boulders and below overhangs, away from strong currents. Also occurs beneath *Salvinia* mats and in river estuaries in Lake Kariba. Juveniles prey on invertebrates, mainly shrimps and insect larvae. Larger individuals (about 170 mm SL) also feed on small cichlids, minnows and labeos. Breeds in summer during the rainy season. Mature females carry 25 000 or more eggs. May live for 8 or more years.
Uses Popular angling species, also taken by spearfishermen.
Notes The name "Cornish Jack" was probably given by early settlers for the resemblance between this fish and the European pike, known as "Jack" in parts of England.

Genus *Mormyrus* Linnaeus, 1758

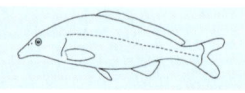

Characterised by the long dorsal fin and relatively short anal fin together with the extended snout (hence "bottlenose"). About 20 species distributed throughout tropical Africa to the Zambezi, two in southern Africa.

SNOUTFISHES

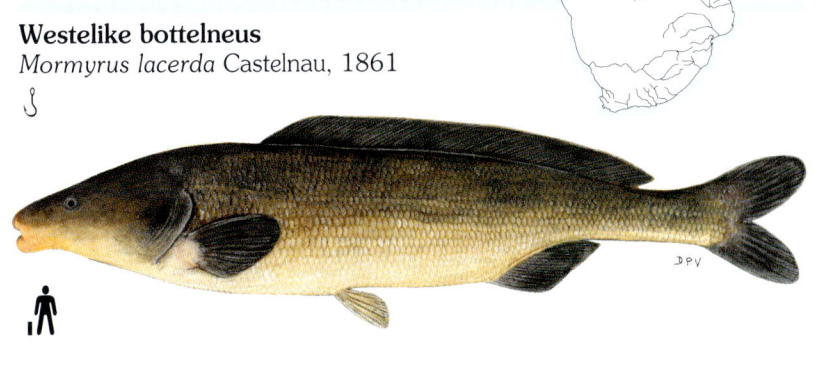

WESTERN BOTTLENOSE

Westelike bottelneus
Mormyrus lacerda Castelnau, 1861

Description D 62–68; A 18–19. Scales in lateral line 80–90. Body moderately elongated and compressed; dorsal fin extended, origin in advance of pelvics, caudal forked with partially scaled, rounded lobes. Head and forebody smoothly decurved, snout extended to about 1/3 of head, tapered; mouth terminal and relatively small, teeth bicuspid, 7–8 in upper jaw, 8–10 in lower, gill slits on sides only. Greyish brown above, lighter below often with yellowish tinge. Attains 500 mm TL, 2 kg. Zimbabwean record is 0,323 kg.
Distribution Cunene, Okavango, upper Zambezi and Kafue systems.
Biology and Ecology Prefers quiet stretches of river channels, deep pools and floodplain lagoons with aquatic vegetation. May form small shoals. Feeds mainly on insect larvae, shrimps, small snails and small fish. Spawns in summer during the rainy season; larger females carry up to 7 000 eggs.
Uses Caught by subsistence fishermen and anglers.

EASTERN BOTTLENOSE

Oostelike bottelneus
Mormyrus longirostris Peters, 1852

Description D 65–75; A 17–19. Scales in lateral series 85–100. Similar to western bottlenose but deeper bodied, forebody and head more strongly decurved, snout longer (2/5–1/2 head length), scales smaller and finer. Females smaller and deeper bodied than males. Mouth terminal, teeth small, bicuspid, 5–7 in upper jaw, 8–12 in lower jaw, gill slits inclined on sides only. Olive grey or brown above, lighter below. Attains 750 mm SL, 10 kg. Zimbabwean angling record 9,973 kg, Malawi 2,0 kg; Zimbabwe spearfishing record 8,25 kg.
Distribution Middle and lower Zambezi, Buzi, Pungwe and lower Save-Runde systems. Also in the Ruvuma and Rufiji rivers in Tanzania, Lakes Malawi and Tanganyika and the Zambian Zaire system.
Biology and Ecology Favours quiet deep water with a soft muddy bottom. Occurs in shoals, feeds on invertebrates, especially insect larvae, shrimps, and snails, occasionally takes fish eggs and small fish. Active mainly at night. Breeds in summer during the rainy season, moving upstream in rivers after flood spates have receded. Females carry 10 000–70 000 eggs. When caught can give a mild shock.
Uses An angling species, caught with worm and small bottom-set hook.

Genus *Hippopotamyrus* Pappenheim, 1906

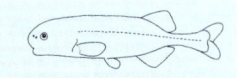

This genus is defined on certain skeletal characteristics. Body moderately elongate, snout short, mental lobe present, dorsal fin shorter or slightly longer than anal. About 15 species are distributed throughout tropical Africa, 2 in southern Africa.

SLENDER STONEBASHER

Slanke klipstamper
Hippopotamyrus ansorgii (Boulenger, 1905)

Description D 18–19; A 24–26. Scales small, 67–72 in lateral series. Body long and slender, compressed; dorsal fin shorter than anal fin, set far back, origin behind origin of anal, caudal fin forked, with rounded lobes. Mouth small, terminal, with small mental lobe, 7 or 8 bicuspid teeth in both jaws. Usually dark brown or black, with vertical bar from dorsal origin. Attains 150 mm SL.

Distribution Cunene, Okavango, upper Zambezi, Buzi and Pungwe rivers. An isolated population occurs in the Ruo River (lower Zambezi system) in Malawi. Also in Cuanza River, Angola.

Biology and Ecology Found in rocky habitats in flowing waters. Feeds on small aquatic invertebrates such as insect larvae.

ZAMBEZI PARROTFISH

Zambezi-papegaaivis
Hippopotamyrus discorhynchus (Peters, 1852)

Description D 30–36; A 23–27. Scales in lateral line 67–70. Body relatively deep, compressed, dorsal fin longer than anal, dorsal origin before anal fin origin, caudal forked, with rounded lobes. Head rounded with blunt snout, mouth with mental lobe, teeth bicuspid, 5–6 in each jaw. Females usually smaller than males, latter distinguished by notch or kink in anal fin. Greyish brown to dark brown, nearly black, lighter below, dark vertical bar sometimes evident between dorsal and anal fins. Attains 310 mm SL, about 1,1 kg. Zimbabwean angling record 0,75 kg.

Distribution Cunene, Okavango, Zambezi, Buzi and Pungwe rivers. Absent from the Kafue River. Also found in the upper Zaire and Lakes Tanganyika and Malawi.

Biology and Ecology Favours large river channels with a soft bottom and fringing vegetation. A nocturnal shoaling species, feeding on bottom-living invertebrates, especially chironomid larvae. Breeds during summer rainy season; females carry up to 5 000 eggs.

Uses Occasionally caught on rod and line.

Genus *Marcusenius* Gill, 1862

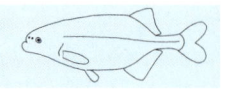

A relatively large genus of about 37 species. Main characters include skeletal features and a well-developed mental lobe on the lower jaw. Widespread in tropical Africa, one species in our area.

BULLDOG

Snawelvis
Marcusenius macrolepidotus (Peters, 1852)

Description D 23–25; A 28–32. Scales in lateral series 50–70, 14–16 rows around caudal peduncle. Body moderately long, with median fins set well back; dorsal fin shorter than and originating behind anal fin. Males with kink in anal fin. Prominent mental lobe on lower jaw. Colour variable, from light golden brown to dark olive or grey with bronze flecks and dark brown blotches. Attains 300 mm SL, 0,5 kg. SA angling record 0,333 kg, Zimbabwe 0,318 kg, Malawi 0,20 kg.

Distribution Widespread and common in the Cunene, Okavango, and Zambezi systems and in east coastal rivers and lakes from the Ruaha (Tanzania) south to the Umhlatuzi in Natal. Also in the upper Zaire.

Biology and Ecology Favours well-vegetated, muddy bottomed marginal habitats of rivers and floodplains. A shoaling species, moving inshore after dark. Feeds on a wide range of invertebrates, especially midge and mayfly larvae and pupae taken from the bottom and off plant stems. Migrations in rivers have been recorded but it is not known if this is for breeding purposes. Breeds in rainy season in shallow, vegetated localities; females carry up to 6 000 eggs. In the Okavango this species is a major prey of large clariid catfish during their annual feeding run in October–November.

Uses Occasionally caught on rod and line. Interesting aquarium subjects.

Genus *Petrocephalus* Marcusen, 1854

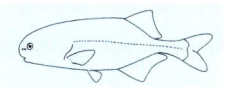

Defined on characteristic skeletal features and unique electroreceptor "rosettes" around the eyes that are not found in other mormyrids. About 20 species are distributed throughout the Afrotropical region, 1 in southern Africa, although a critical comparison of taxonomic characters from different populations has not been made.

CHURCHILL

Stompkoppie
Petrocephalus catostoma (Günther, 1866)

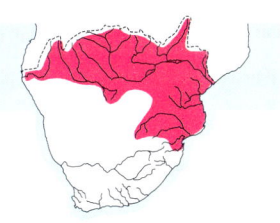

Description D 19–24; A 25–30. Scales in lateral series 35–40, 12–16 rows around caudal peduncle. Body oval, dorsal fin shorter than anal, origin of dorsal slightly behind origin of anal; caudal forked with gently pointed lobes. Males with kink in anal fin. Head smooth, rounded; mouth inferior, short and straight; snout short with nostrils set very close together. Colour variable, from silvery to dark brown with lighter breast and belly regions. Attains 130 mm SL.
Distribution Widespread from the Cunene, Okavango and Zambezi systems to the Phongolo. Also in the Zambian Zaire, Lakes Malawi and Tanganyika and northwards to the Tana River and Lake Victoria in Kenya.
Biology and Ecology Shoals within quiet reaches of rivers and floodplains. Feeds on insect larvae and other small invertebrates. Breeds during summer rainy season, possibly moving upstream to suitable sites. An unconfirmed report claims the males are territorial and build a nest.
Uses A potentially attractive aquarium species. Caught by subsistence fishermen.

Genus *Pollimyrus* Taverne, 1971

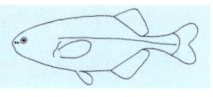

Defined mainly on skeletal characters. About 19 species widely distributed in tropical Africa, 1 species in southern Africa.

DWARF STONEBASHER

Dwerg-klipstamper
Pollimyrus castelnaui (Boulenger, 1911)

Description D 16–18; A 22–26. Scales in lateral series 46–53, 12–14 around caudal peduncle. Body oval; dorsal origin behind origin of anal; caudal forked, lobes rounded. Head rounded, snout short, mouth terminal, nostrils well separated. Mottled dark brown in colour. Attains 70 mm SL.
Distribution Cunene, Okavango, upper Zambezi and Kafue rivers. Also found in northern areas of Lake Malawi.
Biology and Ecology Inhabits dense vegetation along margins of rivers and floodplain lagoons. Biology not studied.
Uses A potentially interesting aquarium species.

Genus *Paramormyrops* Taverne, Thys van den Audenaerde & Heymer 1977

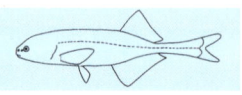

A recently described genus with only two species, one from the upper Zambezi in Angola and another from Gabon. Elongated fishes with a concave head profile.

GHOST STONEBASHER

Spook-klipstamper
Paramormyrops jacksoni (Poll, 1967)

Description D 18; A 23. Scales in lateral series 50, 12 around caudal peduncle. Body long and slender; dorsal fin behind origin of anal, pectorals reach well beyond pelvic bases; caudal peduncle long and slender. Head concave-fronted, mouth subinferior. Mottled dark brown. Attains 52 mm TL.
Distribution Longa River, a tributary of the upper Zambezi in Angola.
Remarks Known only from the type specimen (holotype).

FAMILY MEGALOPIDAE
Tarpons

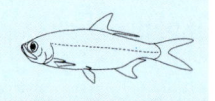

A small family with a single genus and only two species, both found in marine, estuarine and freshwater habitats. Several fossil genera are known. While both species are well-known gamefish the much larger Atlantic tarpon (*Megalops atlanticus*) is renowned for its angling qualities. Like eels, tarpons have leaf-like leptocephalus larvae, and are thus considered to be related.

Genus *Megalops* Lacepède, 1803

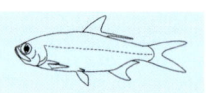

A single species in our area.

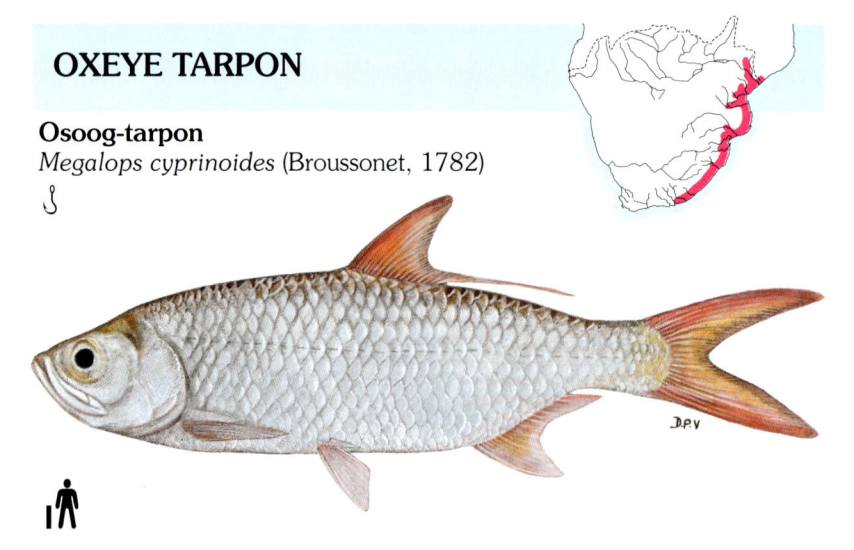

OXEYE TARPON

Osoog-tarpon
Megalops cyprinoides (Broussonet, 1782)

Description D 17–21; A 24–31. Lateral line scales 36–42. Body streamlined and compressed; dorsal fin with last ray extended into a long filament; caudal fin deeply forked. Prominent elongate scales at base of paired fins. Head without scales, eye large, mouth large, reaching to below eye, upper jaw prominent, covers sides of mouth when closed, teeth extremely fine. Attains 1 m TL, usually less than 500 mm in southern African rivers.

Distribution Widespread in tropical and subtropical latitudes of the Indo-Pacific. Extends down the east African coast to as far as Natal, rarely to the eastern Cape. Reported from as far inland as the lower Shire in Malawi, and the Save-Runde junction in Zimbabwe.

Biology and Ecology Found in coastal waters and estuaries, enters rivers. Breeds offshore in the sea, possibly throughout the year. The leptocephalus larvae are found both offshore and inshore and in brackish water. Juveniles have been collected in freshwater but distinct migrations of adults, larvae, or juveniles have not been reported. Juveniles feed on plankton, adults take shrimps, insect larvae and fish. The tarpons are among the few marine fishes known to breathe air, rising regularly to the surface to do so. The swimbladder is modified for this purpose.

Uses An excellent angling species on light tackle or using a fly. In India and the East Indies it is a major aquaculture species.

FAMILY ANGUILLIDAE
Freshwater eels

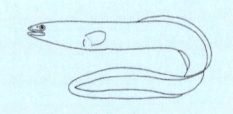

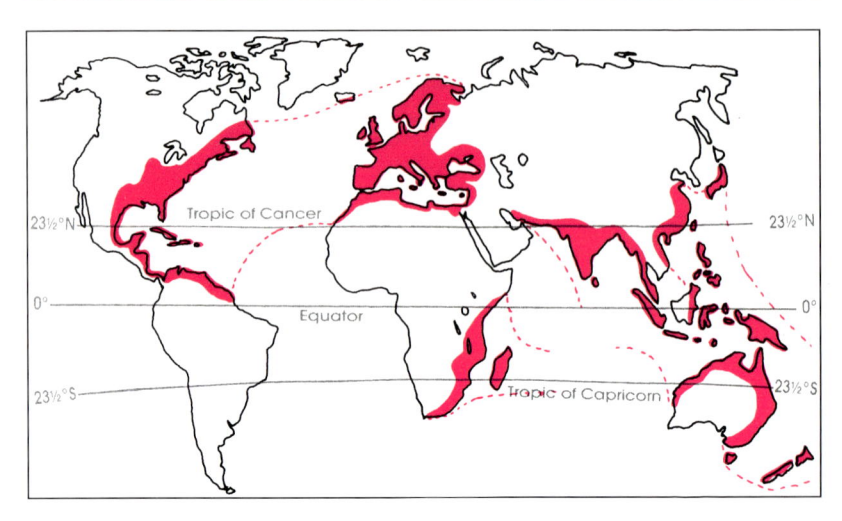

Genus *Anguilla* Schrank, 1798

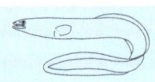

This family comprises a single genus (*Anguilla*) of 16 species of freshwater eels found in several ocean basins, including 4 species from the east and southeast African coast. Eels are typically elongate and sinuous, with soft dorsal and anal fins that join to form the tail. They lack pelvic fins and the scales are minute and embedded so as to be difficult to detect. Their life history is complex. It involves oceanic breeding, a pelagic planktonic larval stage (leptocephalus larvae), migration into estuaries and metamorphosis into a glass eel, at which stage it migrates into freshwater and becomes an elver. Further migration upstream follows and the mature eel finally returns to the sea to breed. Before entering the sea it undergoes a physiomorphological change to the sea-going form (silver eel). The entire cycle takes several years depending on the species. Eels are a valuable food resource and are farmed in Europe and the Far East.

KEY TO SPECIES

1a Body pigmentation plain 2
1b Body pigmentation mottled 3
2a Dorsal fin extending well beyond origin of anal fin, distance between dorsal

fin origin and anal fin origin 9–17% TL..................**A. mossambica (p. 105)**

2b Dorsal fin origin narrowly in advance of anal fin origin, distance between dorsal fin origin and anal fin origin 0–3% TL ....**A. bicolor bicolor (p. 106)**
3a Dorsal fin origin nearer to gill slit than to anus, distance between dorsal fin origin and anal fin origin 16–19% TL......................**A. marmorata (p. 108)**
3b Dorsal fin origin nearer to anus than to gill slit, distance between dorsal fin origin and anal fin origin 7–14% TL.............**A. bengalensis labiata (p. 107)**

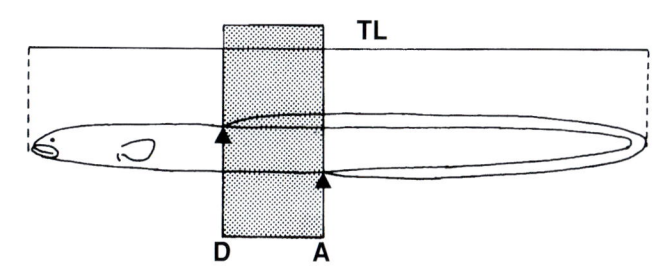

LONGFIN EEL

Geelbek-paling
Anguilla mossambica Peters, 1852

Description Head and body elongated, with thick smooth skin, scales minute and embedded. Dorsal fin origin well in advance of anal fin origin, both joined with caudal. Mouth large, lips thick, teeth fine, forming narrow bands on jaws and palate. Gill slits small, restricted to sides in front of pectoral fins. Olive-brown or grey, lighter below. On maturity prior to

entering the sea the colour changes to dark bronze above and light yellow or silvery below. Attains 1,2 m TL. SA angling record 5,73 kg, Zimbabwe 3,06 kg.
Distribution East coast rivers from Kenya south to Cape Agulhas, also Madagascar and other western Indian Ocean islands. Moves well inland and is the most common species in Natal, the Transkei and the Cape.
Biology and Ecology Glass eels enter the rivers mainly in summer, at night, on high spring tides when the river is flowing strongly. In freshwater the glass eels change into elvers and continue to migrate upstream, ascending natural and man-made barriers. They feed actively and on attaining 25–30 cm TL cease to move upstream and remain in a particular pool or river stretch until fully mature. Small eels prey on insects such as blackfly larvae (*Simulium* species) and other small aquatic invertebrates; adults feed on crabs, frogs and fish. Males are usually smaller than females and remain in freshwater for 8–10 years, females for 15–20 years. On maturity the eyes enlarge, the snout becomes more pointed and body fats increase in preparation for the long return migration to the sea. The gonads only ripen when the eels are at sea. The return migration by the adults to the sea takes place in summer, usually in association with floods or strong river flows after heavy rains.
Uses Angling and aquaculture. Caught mainly at night on baited bottom-set hooks.

SHORTFIN EEL

Kortvin-paling
Anguilla bicolor bicolor McClelland, 1844

Description Dorsal fin origin much closer to anal fin origin than to gill slit, eyes before angle of jaw, teeth bands broad without gaps between teeth rows, vomerine band extending as far back as jaw bands. Dark olive to

bluish brown above, lighter below. Mature adults change to bronzy silver. Attains 800 mm TL.
Distribution Widespread but relatively uncommon along east and south-east African coast and Madagascar. Restricted to lowland (coastal) reaches of river systems.
Biology and Ecology See longfin eel.

AFRICAN MOTTLED EEL

Afrika-bontpaling
Anguilla bengalensis labiata Peters, 1852

Description Typical eel form with dorsal fin origin nearer anus than gill slit, jaw hinge behind eye, teeth forming narrow bands divided by groove, vomerine band with broad base and narrow extension. Yellowish brown, mottled with dark brown or black. A large eel; attains 1,45 m TL and 18 kg or more. SA angling record 20,638 kg, Zimbabwe 18,250 kg, Malawi 6,62 kg.
Distribution Overall, similar to other southern African eels; uncommon south of the Save River. The dominant species in the Zambezi system and farther north in East Africa.
Biology and Ecology Life history similar to that of the longfin eel. Penetrates far inland, surmounting formidable barriers in its upstream migration, including the Kariba and Cahora Bassa dams. Adults prey on fish, including trout in the streams of the eastern highlands of Zimbabwe.
Uses Angling. Strong tackle is required; a baited bottom-set hook at night is the usual method. Because of their large size, agility and strength all eels must be carefully handled on landing.

MADAGASCAR MOTTLED EEL

Madagaskar-bontpaling
Anguilla marmorata Quoy & Gaimard, 1824

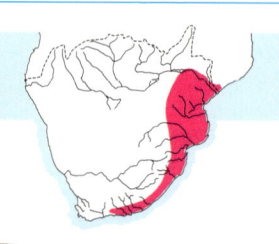

Description Typical eel with dorsal fin origin nearer to gill slit than to anus, distance from dorsal fin to anal 16–19% TL, maxillary toothbands with distinct longitudinal groove. Mottled yellow and dark brown or black. Attains 1,85 m TL and 18 kg. SA angling record 16,363 kg.
Distribution Rivers of Madagascar and adjacent islands and south-east Africa to the eastern Cape. More common south of the Limpopo system.
Biology and Ecology Similar to other eels; inhabits deep rocky pools and is active at night, feeding on wide range of prey, especially crabs, frogs and fish.
Uses Angling species.

FAMILY CLUPEIDAE
Herrings

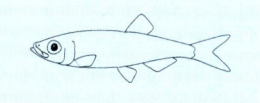

Clupeids are small, silvery, pelagic shoaling fishes of great economic importance. Although most are marine there are about 20 genera and nearly 40 species in African continental waters, including 2 species, 1 introduced by man, in southern Africa.

Genus *Gilchristella* Fowler, 1935

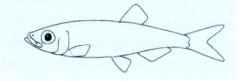

Small compressed fishes restricted to the estuaries and coastal reaches of rivers from the Cape to Natal. Currently a single species is described but at least two forms, possibly different species, are known.

ESTUARINE ROUND-HERRING

Rivier-rondeharing
Gilchristella aestuaria (Gilchrist, 1913)

Description D iii, 11–12; A iii, 17. Scales light and easily shed. Body compressed, fusiform; fins short, pectorals low on body, pelvics before dorsal, anal long-based, caudal forked. Mouth upturned, eyes large. Transparent, with a silvery lateral band. Attains 60 mm SL.

Distribution East coast from Kosi Bay to the southern Cape and as far north as the Olifants River on the west coast.

Biology and Ecology Occurs in estuaries and freshwaters, where it breeds throughout the year with a peak in spring and early summer. Maturity may be attained within the first or second year and an age of up to 5 or 6 years is recorded. Feeds chiefly on zooplankton by filtering or selecting individual organisms from the water column.

Uses A valuable link in the natural foodchain between small crustaceans and larger predatory fishes and birds.

Genus *Limnothrissa* Regan, 1917

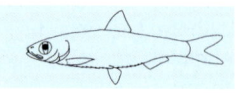

Blade of the upper jaw (maxilla) broad throughout its length, upper jaw teeth very small, front teeth of the lower jaw enlarged, sharply pointed. Keeled scutes in front of and behind the pelvic fins. Two species, one in Lake Tanganyika and one in Lake Mweru. Both species have been translocated to other lakes in Africa, one occurs in our area.

LAKE TANGANYIKA SARDINE (KAPENTA)

Tanjanikameer sardyn (Kapenta)
Limnothrissa miodon (Boulenger, 1906)

Description D iii, 10; A iii, 15. Scales small and thin, easily shed. Body torpedo-shaped with short fins, pectorals low on body, pelvics behind dorsal origin, anal long-based, caudal forked; 13 scutes before pelvics, 9–11 behind. Mouth terminal, lower jaw projecting, lower front teeth large, sharply pointed and curved backward. Transparent with a silvery lateral band. Attains 140 mm SL.
Distribution Introduced from Lake Tanganyika to Lake Kariba in 1967/68, since spread down the middle Zambezi to Lake Cahora Bassa. Also introduced into Lake Kivu.
Biology and Ecology Found throughout Lake Kariba in both inshore habitats and open water to a depth of 20–35 m depending on the thermocline. Forms large shoals which rise in the water column and disperse at night, congregating and descending during the day. Feeds mainly on zooplankton and small

insects, occasionally very small fish. Breeds inshore in protected waters from September to March with peaks in early spring and late summer. The thin transparent juveniles remain inshore, later moving offshore to feed and mature. In Kariba breeds at about 40 mm length or 6–8 months' age and may attain a maximum of about 140 mm TL after 2 years. Most only live for about a year and the bulk of the commercial catch are 30–50 mm TL. An important prey of the tigerfish in Lake Kariba.

Uses A major commercial species in Lake Kariba, where up to 25 000 tonnes per annum may be harvested by boats deploying lift nets with lights at night. Used widely as bait by anglers, especially for tigerfish.

Family Kneriidae
Knerias

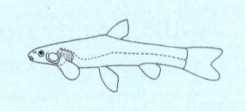

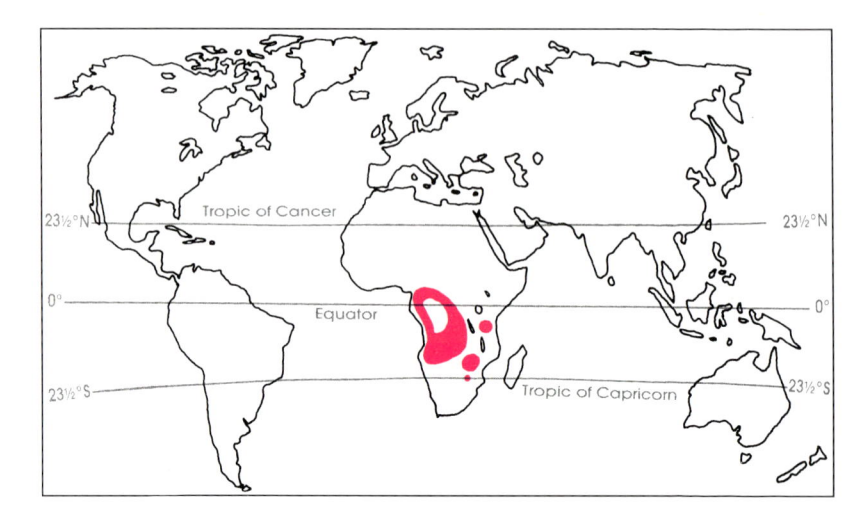

An African family of small stream fishes, mostly occurring around the periphery of the Zaire basin and neighbouring rivers. It is one of several gonorynchiform families that include a few African freshwater fishes, the marine milkfish (*Chanos chanos*) and beaked sandfish (*Gonorynchus gonorynchus*). The nearest relatives of these families are the group known as the Otophysi, which includes cyprinids, characins and siluriform catfishes. When frightened kneriids may secrete an "alarm" pheromone (Schreckstoff) similar to that of cyprinids. Two genera and about 25 species, 5 in our area.

KEY TO GENERA

1a Dorsal fin about equidistant from tip of snout and base of caudal fin, anal fin nearer base of pelvics than base of caudal, males with well-developed contact organ on gill cover and body ....***Kneria*** (p. 113)

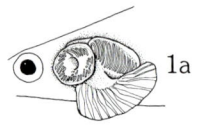

1b Dorsal fin distinctly nearer to caudal fin base than tip of snout, anal fin nearer caudal base than base of pelvics, males without contact organs..............
....***Parakneria*** (p. 115)

Genus *Kneria* Steindachner, 1866

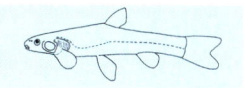

Males of these small, slender "earfishes" develop disc-like contact organs on each gill cover and adjacent body region, used for maintaining contact with the female during mating. They have fine sieve-like gill rakers and a long coiled gut. Three species are currently reported from southern Africa but the taxonomy is uncertain and they are not easily identified.

SOUTHERN KNERIA

Suidelike skulpoortjie
Kneria auriculata (Pellegrin, 1905)

Description D ii–iii, 7; A iii, 6. Scales minute and difficult to count, 80–100 in lateral line. Body slender, dorsal fin nearer base of caudal fin than tip of snout. Head smooth, rounded, mouth ventral, tadpole-like. Lateral line arched behind head to avoid contact organ. Translucent brown with flecks and blotches on upper body, a thin dark mid-lateral line on trunk and caudal peduncle, a dark spot at base of pectoral and pelvic fins. Attains 70 mm TL.
Distribution Upland streams of lower Zambezi, Pungwe, Buzi and Save in Zimbabwe and Mozambique. A relict southern pocket occurs in the Crocodile (Incomati system), Transvaal. Identity of specimens from the Kafue and upper Zambezi requires confirmation.
Biology and ecology Shoals occur in pools of small, clear, silt-free, rocky streams. Reported to breathe air and to climb over damp rocks and up the sides of waterfalls during migrations. Scrapes diatoms, algae and detritus from rock surfaces and also takes small aquatic insects such as mayfly nymphs and midge larvae. Matures after a year; may live for 2 or 3 years. Breeds in spring and summer, larger females bear up to 600 eggs.
Uses Potential aquarium fish.
Conservation Rare in South Africa. Transvaal populations are threatened through habitat destruction and introduced fishes.

CUNENE KNERIA

Kunene skulpoortjie
Kneria maydelli Ladiges & Voelker, 1961

Description D ii–iii, 6–7; A ii–iii, 5–6. Similar to southern kneria, dorsal slightly nearer to tip of snout than to mid-base of caudal. Attains 57 mm SL.
Distribution Cunene system in Angola and Namibia.

NORTHERN KNERIA

Noordelike skulpoortjie
Kneria polli Trewavas, 1936

Description D ii–iii, 7; A iii, 7–8. Similar to southern kneria, dorsal nearer mid-base of caudal than tip of snout. Dark spot not present at base of pelvic fins of type specimens. Attains 70 mm SL.
Distribution Upper reaches of the Cunene, Okavango, and upper Zambezi in Angola and Zambia. Also in headwaters of Angolan coastal rivers.

Genus *Parakneria* Poll, 1965

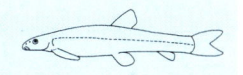

The males of *Parakneria* do not develop contact organs on the head. They are usually more slender than *Kneria*, with more rays in the paired fins, and the origin of the dorsal lies before the pelvics. Twelve species, two from southern Africa.

CUBANGO KNERIA

Cubango-skulpoortjie
Parakneria fortuita Penrith, 1973

Description D iii, 8; A iii, 5. Scales minute, about 100 in lateral line. Body slender, origin of dorsal nearer to caudal base than to snout, origin of anal nearer to caudal base than to pelvics. Head smooth, round in front, flat below, mouth straight, tadpole-like; gill openings form a slit above pectoral fins. Pale yellow-brown with darker blotches on dorsal surface and an irregular broad lateral band, caudal with two broad diagonal bands and a dark triangular basal mark. Attains 57 mm SL.
Distribution Cutato River, a tributary of the Okavango, in Angola.
Biology and Ecology Lives amongst rocks in flowing water. Feeds off diatoms and other algae and detritus scraped from rock surfaces.

GORONGOZA KNERIA

Gorongoza-skulpoortjie
Parakneria mossambica Jubb & Bell-Cross, 1974

Description D iii, 7; A iii, 5–6. Scales minute, 105–120 in lateral series. Body slender, cylindrical; fins short, origin of dorsal above pelvics, nearer caudal base than snout; origin of anal nearer the caudal base than pelvics. Head smooth, rounded in front, flat below; mouth ventral, tadpole-like. Translucent yellow-brown with dark blotches above and along sides. Attains 60 mm SL.

Distribution Tributaries of the Pungwe in the Gorongoza National Park, Mozambique.

FAMILY CYPRINIDAE
Barbs, yellowfishes, labeos

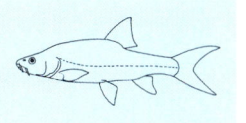

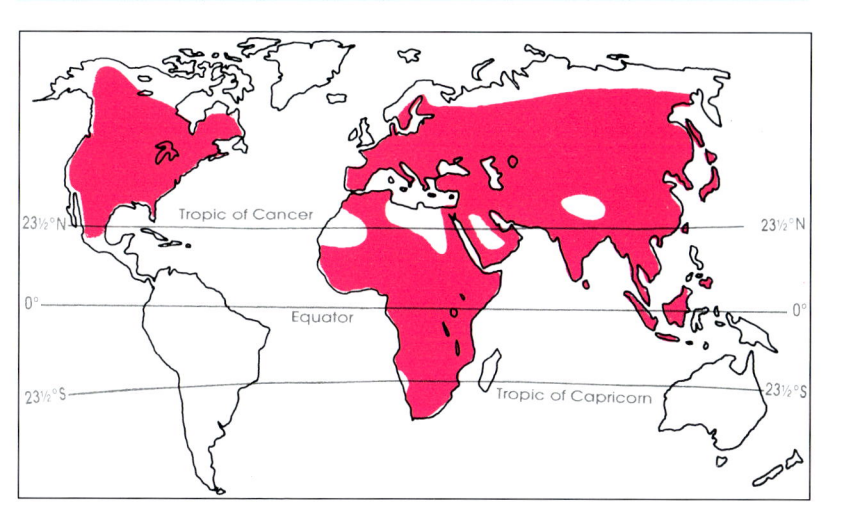

Cyprinids are primary freshwater fishes with a wide range of sizes and shapes, life-history styles and habitat preferences. They lack teeth on the jaws, but have strong pharyngeal (throat) bones with teeth. They lack a true stomach and, especially in detritus and plant feeders such as labeos, the gut may be extended and convoluted. Cyprinids are often strong swimmers and some are distinctly modified to live in strong currents. Males may differ from females by having longer fins, brighter breeding colours and tubercles on the head, body and fins. Many species have characteristic pigment patterns, although it is always necessary to consider the full range of variation of the pattern when identifying species.

An extremely large family with about 275 genera and more than 1 600 species, from Africa, Europe, Asia and North America. In Africa there are at least 24 genera and 475 species and it is the largest family in southern Africa with 7 genera and about 80 species. Certain species are economically important in fisheries, aquaculture, the aquarium trade and angling. Several southern African cyprinids are threatened.

KEY TO GENERA (INDIGENOUS AND INTRODUCED)

1a Eyes well below level of mouth, visible from below, gill rakers fused to form spongy plate..***Hypophthalmichthys* (p. 191)**
1b Eyes above level of mouth; gill rakers separated from each other 2

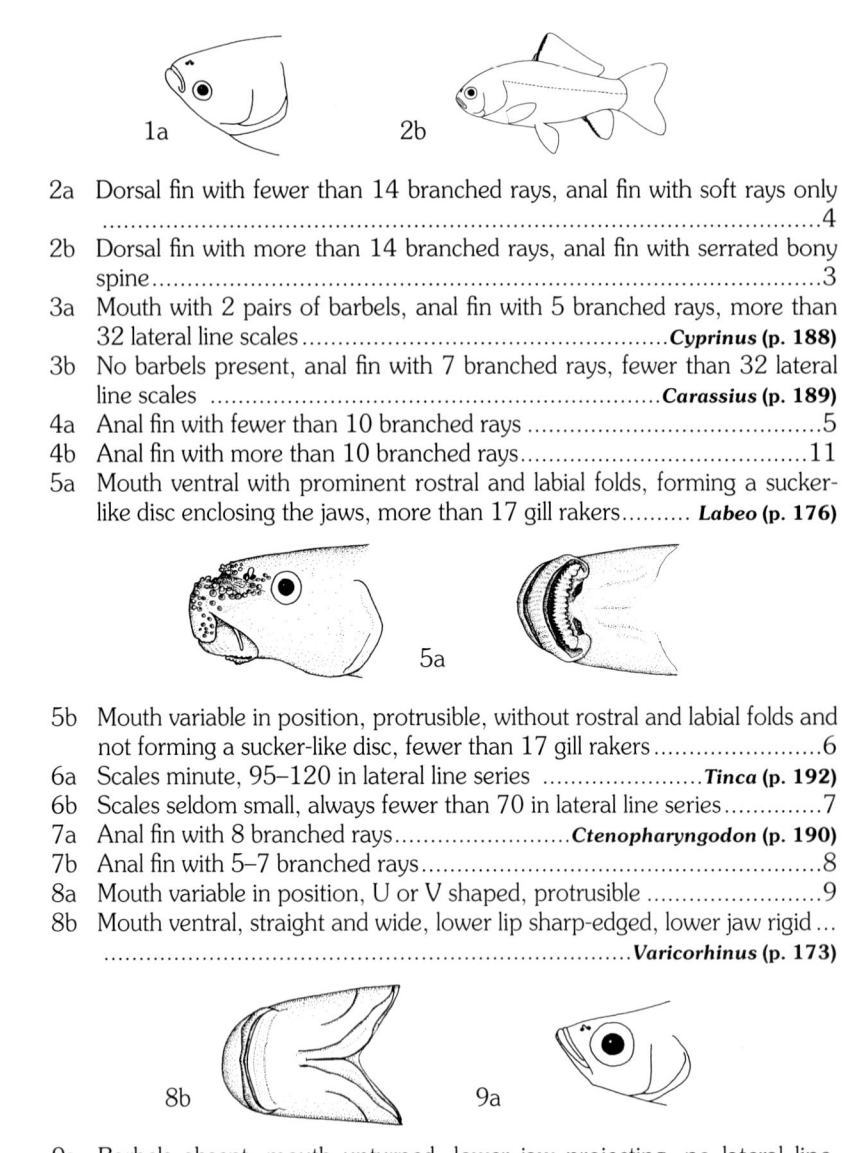

2a Dorsal fin with fewer than 14 branched rays, anal fin with soft rays only 4
2b Dorsal fin with more than 14 branched rays, anal fin with serrated bony spine..3
3a Mouth with 2 pairs of barbels, anal fin with 5 branched rays, more than 32 lateral line scales...*Cyprinus* (p. 188)
3b No barbels present, anal fin with 7 branched rays, fewer than 32 lateral line scales ....*Carassius* (p. 189)
4a Anal fin with fewer than 10 branched rays 5
4b Anal fin with more than 10 branched rays...11
5a Mouth ventral with prominent rostral and labial folds, forming a sucker-like disc enclosing the jaws, more than 17 gill rakers.......... *Labeo* (p. 176)

5b Mouth variable in position, protrusible, without rostral and labial folds and not forming a sucker-like disc, fewer than 17 gill rakers........................6
6a Scales minute, 95–120 in lateral line series ....*Tinca* (p. 192)
6b Scales seldom small, always fewer than 70 in lateral line series.............7
7a Anal fin with 8 branched rays........................*Ctenopharyngodon* (p. 190)
7b Anal fin with 5–7 branched rays..8
8a Mouth variable in position, U or V shaped, protrusible 9
8b Mouth ventral, straight and wide, lower lip sharp-edged, lower jaw rigid ... .*Varicorhinus* (p. 173)

9a Barbels absent, mouth upturned, lower jaw projecting, no lateral line, maximum size 50 mm SL ....*Coptostomabarbus* (p. 149)
9b One or 2 pairs of barbels usually present, mouth terminal or sub-terminal, lower jaw rarely projecting, lateral line complete or incomplete 10
10a Distinctive scarlet patches at the base of all fins, mature males with large conical tubercles on snout and top of head, mouth sub-terminal, mandibular

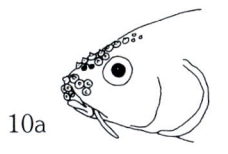

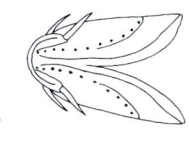

sensory canal absent or extremely short .... *Pseudobarbus* (p. 122)

10a   10a   10b

10b Fins without basal scarlet patches, mature males with or without large conical tubercles on head, mouth variable, mandibular sensory canal not reduced .... ***Barbus*** (p. 128)
11a Dorsal fin with 8–10 branched rays, origin of dorsal fin behind pelvics, in front of origin of anal fin, fewer than 45 lateral line scales........................ .... ***Opsaridium*** (p. 120)
11b Dorsal fin with 7–8 branched rays, origin of dorsal fin above origin of anal fin, 45–59 lateral line scales .... ***Mesobola*** (p. 119)

Bariliins and Neobolins

Bariliins and neobolins are related groups of generally shoaling, streamlined, active swimming predatory species with large mouths. Their anal fin is longer based than that of the African barbine and labeine cyprinids. Bariliins are relatively large fishes and occur in tropical areas of Africa and Asia; the smaller neobolins are entirely African.

Genus *Mesobola* Howes, 1984

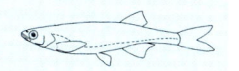

Small sardine-like cyprinids, with the dorsal fin nearer the caudal fin than the tip of the snout, its origin above the origin of the anal fin. Four species, found mainly in central, east and south-east Africa; one in southern Africa.

RIVER SARDINE

Riviersardyn
Mesobola brevianalis (Boulenger, 1908)

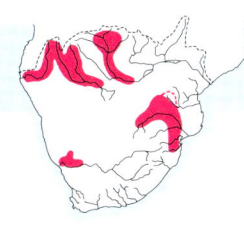

Description D ii, 7–8; A iii, 12–17. Scales small, easily shed, 45–59 in lateral line, which dips sharply down behind pectoral fin and follows a low contour, 16 around caudal peduncle. Body slender and streamlined, dorsal origin above the origin of the anal fin, caudal forked. Eyes large, mouth large and terminal. Breeding males develop tubercles along lower jaw and lower surfaces of head. Translucent silvery white on head and lower body, a silvery band along midbody. Attains about 75 mm SL.
Distribution Cunene, Okavango, upper Zambezi systems and east coastal rivers from the Limpopo to the Umfolozi in northern Natal. An isolated population is found in the Orange below the Augrabies Falls.
Biology and Ecology Occurs in shoals; prefers well-aerated, open water of flowing rivers. Feeds from the water column on planktonic crustaceans and insects such as midges and ants. Attracted to light at night. Breeds in early summer.
Uses Introduced to dams as forage for larger game fish in Zimbabwe.

Genus *Opsaridium* Peters, 1854

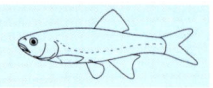

These African bariliins are characterised by vertical bars on the body and sexually mature males with tubercles and an extended anal fin. About nine species; two in southern Africa.

BARRED MINNOW

Balkghieliemientjie
Opsaridium zambezense (Peters, 1852)

Description D iii, 8–10; A iii, 11–13. Scales 40–43 in lateral line, which dips to lower half of body, 14 around caudal peduncle. Body fusiform and streamlined; dorsal origin behind pelvic fins; anal large,

BARBS, YELLOWFISHES, LABEOS

rounded, males with anterior rays extended. Head pointed, eyes large, mouth large, lower jaw extending to below orbit. Silvery with bluish tinge and a series of 9–16 bluish black vertical bars on body, dorsal with sooty black and red membrane, lower head and chest flushed with rose. Attains about 150 mm SL.

Distribution Okavango, Zambezi and east coastal rivers south to the Phongolo; restricted to escarpment and lowveld waters of the more southern rivers. Also southern tributaries of the Zaire system.

Biology and Ecology Favours clear, flowing waters of larger perennial rivers, frequenting pools below rocky rapids. Lives in shoals and feeds on drifting insects and other small organisms. Breeds in summer.

Conservation Rare in South Africa. Threatened chiefly by water abstraction and pollution. Weirs and dams obstruct its movement along rivers.

DWARF SANJIKA

Bandvin-balkghieliemientjie
Opsaridium sp.

Description D ii, 8–9; A iii, 13. Scales 45–49 in lateral line, which dips to lower half of body, 16–17 around caudal peduncle. Body fusiform; dorsal nearer base of caudal than tip of snout, origin behind pelvics, before anal; caudal forked; anal with anterior rays extended. Head pointed, with large terminal mouth, lower jaw extends to below mid-orbit. Pale bluish grey with 11–13 darker upright bars along body, dorsal fin with a distinct black band arching from leading edge to lower hind corner. Males have prominent tubercles on head and fins. Attains 110 mm SL.

Distribution Tributaries of the middle and lower Shire (lower Zambezi) in Malawi. Also in affluent streams of Lake Malawi.

Biology and Ecology Inhabits swift-flowing streams in rocky reaches over clean sand. Feeds on insects and other invertebrates in the drift. Breeds in summer.

Genus *Pseudobarbus* Smith, 1841
Redfin minnows

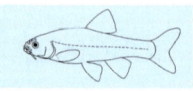

A distinct genus of barbine minnows from the Cape Fold Mountains and the Drakensberg. Adults have bright scarlet patches at the base of the fins. The primary dorsal fin ray is soft and flexible and scales are radiately striated. Male redfins have brighter colours and longer fins than females, and develop large tubercles on the head during the breeding season. The redfins appear to be descendants of an ancient lineage in southern Africa. They are probably related to other endemic southern African minnows such as the chubbyhead and redtail barbs. Redfin minnow populations have declined markedly in recent decades and most species are threatened, including three that are endangered.

KEY TO SPECIES

1a Mouth with two pairs of barbels 2
1b Mouth with one pair of barbels 3
2a Anterior barbels shorter than orbit diameter, visible only in specimens larger than 45 mm SL (Berg River, Verlorenvlei) .... *P. burgi* (p. 123)
2b Anterior barbels greater than orbit diameter, visible in specimens larger than 20 mm SL (Breede, Duivenhoks and Kaffirkuils rivers) .... *P. burchelli* (p. 123)
3a Scales extremely small, more than 60 in lateral line series (alpine tributaries of the Maluti and Drakensberg mountains) .... *P. quathlambae* (p. 127)
3b Scales moderate sized, fewer than 45 in lateral line series 4
4a Scales relatively small, 35–45 in lateral line series, 16–18 rows around caudal peduncle (Groot [Gamtoos] and Gourits systems) .... *P. asper* (p. 125)
4b Scales relatively large, 25–37 in lateral line series, 12–16 rows around caudal peduncle 5
5a Barbels short (less than or equal to orbit diameter), adults with prominent black patches over body, breeding males with few tubercles on head (tributaries of west coast Olifants system) .... *P. phlegethon* (p. 126)
5b Barbels longer than orbit diameter, adults with simple lateral band and midpredorsal stripe or dashes, body relatively slender (body depth 3,8–5,3 in SL), pharyngeal bones with two rows of teeth (mountain tributaries of Gourits and Keurbooms) .... *P. tenuis* (p. 126)
5c Barbels longer than orbit diameter, adults with simple lateral band and (usually) small spots along back on either side of midline in front of dorsal fin, body relatively deep (body depth 3,3–4,4 in SL), pharyngeal bones with three rows of teeth (tributaries of coastal rivers from Algoa Bay to Mossel Bay) .... *P. afer* (p. 124)

BURCHELL'S REDFIN

Burchell se rooivlerkie
Pseudobarbus burchelli Smith, 1841

Description D iii–iv, 7–8; A iii, 5. Lateral line scales 29–39. Body fusiform, moderately deep and rounded; mouth inferior, with 2 pairs of barbels. Mature males with large conical tubercles on head (5–10 on either side of snout). Juveniles and young adults olive brown with scattered spots and blotches, an irregular stripe expanding into a triangle at the base of the tail. Breeding adults deepen to dark olive brown with lighter ventral parts. Attains 135 mm SL.
Distribution Breede River and adjacent systems, south-west Cape.
Biology and Ecology Inhabits pools and deeper flowing stretches of larger tributary streams and mainstreams. Feeds on detritus and small organisms, usually taken from the bottom. Breeds in summer. Fry and juveniles form large shoals, adults occur in small groups.
Conservation Rare. Development of towns, agriculture and industry has reduced and destroyed habitat and populations have been eliminated by introduced predatory fishes.

BERG RIVER REDFIN

Bergrivier-rooivlerkie
Pseudobarbus burgi (Boulenger, 1911)

Description D iii, 7; A iii, 5. Lateral line scales 30–34, 12 around caudal peduncle. Body deep, fusiform; mouth with 2 pairs of barbels, anterior pair very short, only visible in adults; intestine usually long and involuted. Mature males with prominent tubercles on head. Brown above, sil-

BERG RIVER REDFIN (cont.)

very white below, an irregular dark band along body more prominent in juveniles than adults. Attains 120 mm SL.
Distribution Tributaries of the Berg River and Verlorenvlei, south-west Cape. Previously also in the Eerste River.
Biology and Ecology Found in a wide range of habitats from clear mountain streams to deep, still, vegetated pools of lowland rivers. Feeds mainly from the bottom on invertebrates, algae and detritus. Breeds in summer.
Conservation Endangered. Extirpated from much of its former range, extinct in the Eerste River. Decline caused by habitat deterioration and impact of introduced predatory fishes.

EASTERN CAPE REDFIN

Oos-Kaapse rooivlerkie
Pseudobarbus afer (Peters, 1864)

Description D iii, 7; A iii, 5. Scales radiately striate, moderate sized, 32–37 in lateral line. Body fusiform, mouth sub-terminal, single pair of barbels. Ripe males with large conical tubercles on head (3–4 on either side of snout). Olive brown above, silvery or creamy white below, gill cover golden, a narrow dark band along body and irregular series of spots in front of dorsal fin, fins scarlet, especially in breeding males. Attains 110 mm SL.
Distribution Coastal rivers from Algoa Bay to Mossel Bay. Absent from smaller streams of Tsitsikamma and Outeniqua coasts.
Biology and Ecology Prefers clear rocky pools; fry and juveniles occur in large shoals, adults in small groups. Omnivorous, feeding mainly from bottom on algae and small invertebrates. Breeds in summer, spawning in riffles above pools.
Uses An attractive aquarium species.
Conservation Many populations of this species have been eliminated by bass.

SMALLSCALE REDFIN

Kleinskub-rooivlerkie
Pseudobarbus asper (Boulenger, 1911)

Description D iii–iv, 7; A iii, 5. Scales small, 37–40 in lateral line series. Body deep, fusiform; mouth with a single pair of short barbels, intestine long and involuted. Mature males with prominent conical tubercles on head. Brownish above, silvery white below, a dark irregular band along body, scales with dark centres, giving speckled hen appearance. Attains 80 mm SL.
Distribution Groot River (Gamtoos system) and main branches of the Gourits system, southern Cape.
Biology and Ecology Inhabits standing or slow-flowing pools with a soft or rocky bottom. Thrives in dams and tolerates turbid waters. Juveniles occur in large shoals, adults in small groups. Feeds off the substrate on algae and detritus. Breeds in summer, moving into riffle areas to lay eggs.
Uses Suitable cool-water aquarium or pond fish.

FIERY REDFIN

Vurige rooivlerkie
Pseudobarbus phlegethon (Barnard, 1938)

Description D iii, 7; A iii, 5. Lateral line scales 29–37 (35). Body oblong, mouth with one pair of short barbels. Tubercles of breeding males poorly developed but red patches on fins are brilliant. Silvery golden with scattered black spots and blotches, fins with dark bands across rays. The smallest and possibly prettiest redfin minnow. Attains 71 mm SL.

Distribution Tributaries of the Clanwilliam Olifants River, western Cape.
Biology and Ecology Lives in pools and riffles of clear flowing rocky bottomed streams. Feeds off detritus and small bottom-living insects. Breeds in summer; males are territorial.
Conservation Endangered. Habitat destruction and introduced bass have severely depleted populations.

SLENDER REDFIN

Slank rooivlerkie
Pseudobarbus tenuis (Barnard, 1938)

Description D iii, 7; A iii, 5. Lateral line scales 32–37. Body slender, head length greater than body depth, mouth with a single pair of barbels, pharyngeal teeth in 2 rows only, intestine short. Mature males with tubercles on head. Olive brown with silvery cream ventral parts, a dark lateral band on trunk and a dark mid-dorsal line. Attains 80 mm SL.
Distribution Mountain tributaries of the Gourits and Keurbooms systems, southern Cape.
Biology and Ecology Inhabits pools in clear, flowing Fold Mountain streams. Feeds off the substrate on algae, detritus and bottom-living and other invertebrates. Breeds in summer.
Conservation Rare. Populations are threatened by water extraction and alien predators such as bass and trout.

DRAKENSBERG MINNOW (MALUTI MINNOW)

Drakensberg-rooivlerkie (Maluti-rooivlerkie)
Pseudobarbus quathlambae (Barnard, 1938)

Description D iii, 7; A iii, 5. Scales extremely small, 60–72 in lateral line. Body slender, mouth subterminal, with a single pair of short barbels, pharyngeal teeth in 2 rows, intestine short. Males with numerous small conical tubercles on head. Olive or grey-brown to deep blue with silvery white underneath, a dark lateral band on trunk and dark spots or wavy lines on back, adults with base of fins scarlet. Attains 130 mm SL.
Distribution Headwater streams of the Orange in Lesotho. Type locality is the Umkomazana River in Natal, but not recorded there since the 1930s.
Biology and Ecology Inhabits pools and riffles of clear streams. Feeds on aquatic insects. Breeds in summer, laying eggs in crevices and between cobbles and pebbles. Juveniles shoal in larger pools and in side channels. Adults occur alone or in small groups.
Relationships Most closely related to the slender redfin (*P. tenuis*) of the southern Cape.
Note A previous scientific name is

128 BARBS, YELLOWFISHES, LABEOS

Oreodaimon quathlambae.
Conservation Endangered. Habitat restricted and subject to siltation; vulnerable to competition and predation by introduced trout. Protected within Sehlabathebe National Park.

Genus *Barbus* Cuvier & Cloquet, 1816

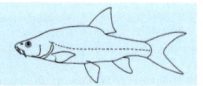

These Old World fishes make up one of the largest fish genera in the world. There are nearly 300 species in Africa and about 50 in southern Africa, making it also the largest genus in our area. Barbs are generally fusiform, with a variable but protrusible mouth and curved pharyngeal bones each with three rows of teeth. The median fins are relatively short, the dorsal with 7–11 branched rays and the anal usually with only 5 branched rays. The lateral line runs along the middle of the caudal peduncle. They range in size from about 20–30 mm SL and 1 g weight to a metre or more in length and many kilograms weight. Smaller species are popular aquarium fishes and the larger ones are fine angling and fisheries targets.

BARBUS: KEY CHARACTERS

A SCALES

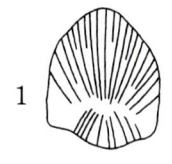

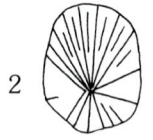

1. Striae parallel – yellowfishes (p.166) and chiselmouths (p.173)
2. Striae radiate – all other barbs

B PRIMARY DORSAL FIN RAY

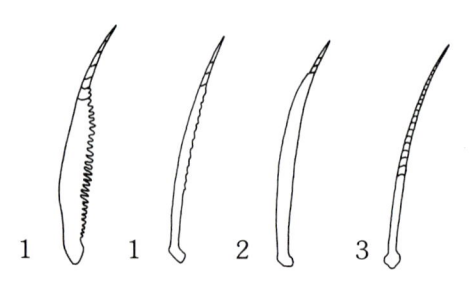

1. Spinous, serrated – sawfin barbs (p.152)
2. Spinous, simple – spinefin barbs (p.150)
3. Flexible, simple – soft-rayed minnows (p.129)

SOFT-RAYED MINNOWS or BARBS

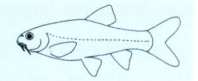

These are commonly observed fishes in streams and other freshwater habitats. Minnows usually occur in shoals and are often well camouflaged from the surface but distinctly marked with stripes, spots and other markings when seen underwater or in aquariums. They are opportunistic feeders on any small creatures, diatoms or detritus, and in turn form a valuable food for larger fish and bird predators. Minnows breed in a variety of ways, in pairs, small groups or large shoals, the males usually developing bright colours, especially shades of gold, yellow or red. Apart from being popular aquarium fishes because of their peaceful natures they are sometimes used for live bait or are stocked as fodder fish in bass and trout dams. Although the relationships of most minnows are not known precisely a few distinct groups of similar and possibly closely related species are recognised here – including the chubbyhead and the goldie barbs.

KEY TO SOFT-RAYED MINNOWS

1a Body (of one or both sexes) without prominent or clearly defined black markings (spots, stripes or bars); usually 7 dorsal branched rays 2
1b Body (of one or both sexes) with prominent or clearly defined black markings (spots, stripes or bars); 8 (rarely 7) dorsal branched rays..................5
2a More than 30 lateral line scales; 14–18 scale rows around caudal peduncle; scales with numerous (more than 15) striae; 3
2b Fewer than 30 lateral line scales; 12 scale rows around caudal peduncle; scales with fewer than 10 striae.........................***Barbus treurensis* (p. 135)**
3a Ripe males with prominent (visible) whitish tubercles on head 4

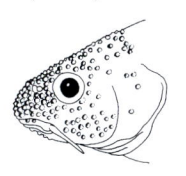

3b Ripe males without prominent (visible) white tubercles on head ....
....***B. anoplus* (p. 132)**
4a One or two pairs of barbels, ripe males golden yellow ....
....***B. motebensis* (p. 134)**
4b Two pairs of barbels, ripe males with orange fins ....***B. gurneyi* (p. 133)**
4c One pair of barbels, ripe males without bright colours on body or fins
....***B. amatolicus* (p. 134)**
5a Body with 12–16 prominent vertical bars ....***B. fasciolatus* (p. 147)**
5b Body without vertical bars; with spots or stripe 6
6a Barbels absent; lateral line absent..7
6b Barbels present; lateral line present (either reduced, interrupted or complete) 8

7a   Mouth upturned; no clear spot at base of caudal fin; mature males without extended fin..***Coptostomabarbus wittei*** (p. 149)

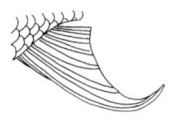

7b   Mouth not upturned; spot at base of caudal fin; mature males with extended sickle-shaped anal fin ....***B. haasianus*** (p. 148)
8a   Barbels very short, usually only posterior pair visible 9
8b   Barbels moderate to well developed 13
9a   Pit-lines on head, dorsum and cheeks, eye red, centres of scales pigmented giving regular scalloped pattern ....***B. radiatus*** (p. 148)

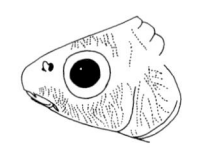

9b   Head without pit-lines; eye silvery or light golden; scale centres not regularly pigmented..10
10a Lateral line incomplete 11
10b Lateral line complete 12
11a Edges of body stripe sharply defined; ocellated spot at caudal fin base
     ....***B. brevidorsalis*** (p. 144)
11b Edges of body stripe diffusely defined; no ocellated spot at caudal fin base
     ....***B. toppini*** (p. 146)
12a Body slender, fins pointed, mid-dorsal black stripe, dashes or spots present..***B. barnardi*** (p. 145)
12b Body short, stocky, fins blunt, no mid-dorsal black stripe, dashes or spots
     ....***B. macrotaenia*** (p. 146)
13a Well-defined stripe (complete or interrupted) from tip of snout to caudal fin base...14
13b Distinct markings (stripe or spots) on body only 15
14a Stripe more or less straight along body, not diverging greatly from lateral line ....***B. thamalakanensis*** (p. 144)

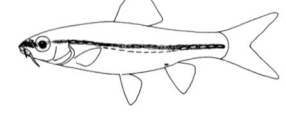

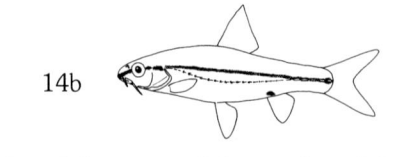

14b Stripe arched, diverging from lateral line over abdomen; lateral line tubules marked with pigment....................................***B. bifrenatus*** (p. 142)

15a Lateral line scales distinctly deeper than adjacent rows, each with dark crescent over anterior side; 10 caudal peduncle scale rows ....***B. bellcrossi*** (p. 137)
15b Lateral line scales not distinctly deeper than adjacent rows; 12 or more caudal peduncle scale rows..16
16a Body with series of spots not joined by pigment band.........................17
16b Body with stripe, dashes or spots joined by pigment band...................18
17a Discrete spots in linear or near linear sequence along body, no thin parallel zigzag bands along lateral body scales; chevron-like pigment along lateral line tubules...***B. lineomaculatus*** (p. 138)
17b Relatively large, diffuse spots in near linear sequence along body; series of thin parallel zigzag bands along lateral body scales; no chevron-like pigment along lateral line tubules...***B. neefi*** (p. 140)
17c Spots fine and irregular; no series of thin parallel zigzag bands along lateral body scales; no chevron-like pigment along lateral line tubules............. ....***B. pallidus*** (p. 140)
18a Barbels relatively short; 3 scales between lateral line and dorsal fin base; body with 3 or 4 spots frequently connected by band of pigment ....***B. annectens/barotseensis*** (pp. 136-7)
18b Barbels relatively long; 4 or 5 scales between lateral line and dorsal fin base; body with black stripe, interrupted dashes or 3 spots 19
19a Body slender, mouth inferior; dorsal fin origin in front of pelvics; chevron-like pigment on lateral line tubules; stripe with diffuse edges ....***B. unitaeniatus*** (p. 141)

19b Body short, mouth terminal or sub-terminal; dorsal fin origin above origin of pelvics; chevron-like pigment on lateral line tubules; body stripe well defined, regular or bulbous ....***B. viviparus*** (p. 143)

19c Body short, mouth terminal or sub-terminal; dorsal fin origin above origin of pelvics; no chevron-like pigment on lateral line tubules; body stripe usually interrupted into dashes ....***B. brevipinnis*** (p. 139)

BARBS, YELLOWFISHES, LABEOS

THE "CHUBBYHEAD GROUP"

The chubbyhead barbs are endemic to the cooler areas of South Africa. The group comprises four species: the chubbyhead, redtail, Marico and Amatola barbs. They differ mainly in the breeding colours and tubercles of the males. Common features include a flexible primary dorsal ray; dorsal iii, 7; anal iii, 5; scales with numerous radiate striae, at least 3 or 4 scales between lateral line and pelvic fin; no distinct pelvic axil scale. Pigmentation is simple, usually an indefinite body stripe and a small spot at the base of the caudal fin. The mouth is small and terminal, with one or two pairs of barbels.

CHUBBYHEAD BARB

Dikkop-ghieliemientjie
Barbus anoplus Weber, 1897

Description D iii, 7; A iii, 5. Scales with numerous radial striations, 33–37 in lateral line series. Primary dorsal ray simple, flexible. Head typically blunt or rounded, mouth small, usually with a single pair of short barbels. Males generally smaller than females, assuming a brilliant golden breeding dress. Females and non-breeding males greyish green above with a small dot at mid-base of caudal fin, males sometimes have a broad dark band along body. Females attain 120 mm SL, males usually less than 100 mm SL.

Distribution Widely distributed from highveld Limpopo to upland Natal, Transkei and the middle and upper Orange basin, including the Karoo. Absent from the lower Orange. Present in larger coastal rivers of the southern and western Cape (Olifants, Gourits, Gamtoos, Sundays and Great Fish) but absent from Cape Fold Mountain streams.

Biology and Ecology Prefers cooler waters, occurring in a wide variety of habitats from small streams to large rivers and lakes. Frequently associates with cover or shelter such as fallen logs, brushwood or marginal vegetation. Breeds during summer, when rivers are swollen after rain. Lays adhesive eggs amongst vegetation. Larvae hatch within 3 days and begin to swim and feed after 6 or 7 days. Reaches maturity after a year; most males live only 2 years, females 2 or 3 years, a few may survive for 4. Omnivorous, feeding on insects, zooplankton, seeds, green algae and diatoms. Preyed on by larger fishes and birds.

Uses Forage fish. Suitable for coolwater aquariums and garden ponds.

REDTAIL BARB

Rooistert-ghieliemientjie
Barbus gurneyi Günther, 1868

Description D iii, 7; A iii, 5. Scales in lateral line 30–34, 12–14 around caudal peduncle. Mouth terminal, with 2 pairs of barbels. Ripe males develop numerous conical tubercles on forehead, snout and lower jaws. Clear brown with dark scale borders, a thin band along body ending in a small distinct spot at base of caudal fin; fins pale yellow, turning orangered in breeding males. Attains 100 mm SL.

Distribution Natal, from the Umtamvuna northwards to the Amatikulu, north of the Tugela basin.

Biology and Ecology Common at altitudes of 300–1 000 m, especially in clear streams of the sandstone belt. Favours pools, where it is frequently the only fish species present apart from eels. It thus represents an important link in the food chain, feeding on aquatic insects and other small invertebrates and falling prey to eels, birds and otters.

Uses Forage fish. Suitable for coolwater aquariums and garden ponds.

134 BARBS, YELLOWFISHES, LABEOS

MARICO BARB

Marico-ghieliemientjie
Barbus motebensis Steindachner, 1894

Description D iii, 7; A iii, 5. Scales in lateral line 32–37, 14 around caudal peduncle. Lateral line incomplete. Mouth small, terminal, usually with 2 pairs of barbels. In colour similar to the chubbyhead barb but breeding males develop tubercles on the snout. Attains 80 mm SL.
Distribution Headwater tributaries of the Marico, Crocodile and Steelpoort branches of the Limpopo system, Transvaal.
Uses Forage fish. Suitable for coolwater aquariums and garden ponds.

AMATOLA BARB

Amatola-ghieliemientjie
Barbus amatolicus Skelton, 1990

BARBS, YELLOWFISHES, LABEOS

Description D iii, 7; A iii, 5. Scales in lateral line 33–37, 16 around caudal peduncle. Mouth with a single pair of long barbels. Breeding males develop prominent tubercles over top and sides of head. Translucent grey, pink or reddish brown, silvery white below, diffuse black band along body. Breeding adults do not turn golden. Attains 70 mm SL.
Distribution Kei and Mbashe systems, Transkei and Border region.
Uses Suitable for cool-water aquariums or garden ponds.

SHORTHEAD BARB

Stompkop-ghieliemientjie
Barbus breviceps Trewavas, 1936

Description D iii, 7; A iii, 5. Scales in lateral series 33, 13 around caudal peduncle. Mouth with two pairs of barbels. Brownish above, silvery white below, an indistinct stripe along side and a small spot at base of caudal fin. Attains 77 mm SL.
Distribution Cunene and Okavango, Angola and Namibia.
Note A little-known species described from the Longa River, Angola. Appears similar to species of the chubbyhead group.

TREUR RIVER BARB

Treurrivier-ghieliemientjie
Barbus treurensis Groenewald, 1958

Description D iii, 7–8; A iii, 5. Scales in lateral line 25–30, 11–12 around caudal peduncle. Mouth with 2 pairs of barbels. Translucent olive brown above, silvery white beneath, a dark band along caudal peduncle and a variable number of dark spots along back and caudal peduncle. Attains 95 mm SL.
Distribution Upper reaches of

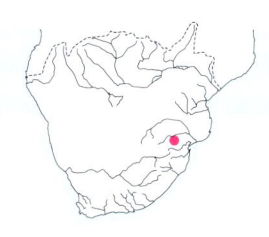

TREUR RIVER BARB (cont.)

Blyde River, Limpopo system, eastern Transvaal. Previously also known from the Treur and Sabie rivers.
Biology and Ecology Inhabits rocky pools and riffles of clear, cool streams. Occurs with the Natal mountain catlet, *Amphilius natalensis*. Feeds on stream insects. Breeds in early summer, with both sexes developing small tubercles on the head. May live for up to 6 years.
Conservation Vulnerable. Reduced to a single population which is protected by a waterfall from invading predatory fishes, especially rainbow trout. This stream is a declared National Heritage Site.

BROADSTRIPED BARB

Breëstreep-ghieliemientjie
Barbus annectens Gilchrist & Thompson, 1917

Description D iii, 7–8; A iii, 5. Scales relatively large, 25–29 in lateral line series, 12 around caudal peduncle, 3 between dorsal fin and lateral line. Mouth with 2 pairs of relatively short barbels (less than orbit). Translucent olive brown with either 3 spots or a broad dark band along the body, silvery white below, a dark spot at base of anal fin. Preserved material

frequently shows 3 spots with the last 2 vaguely connected by a dark band. Attains 75 mm SL.
Distribution East coast rivers from the Zambezi system southwards to the Mkuze in northern Natal. Restricted to the lowveld region south of the Limpopo system.
Biology and Ecology Favours slow-flowing streams with vegetation.
Uses Potential aquarium species.
Relationships Considered to be closely related to or the same as the Barotse barb, *Barbus barotseensis*.

BAROTSE BARB

Barotse-ghieliemientjie
Barbus barotseensis Pellegrin, 1920

Description D iii, 7–8; A iii, 5. Similar to the broadstriped barb but the pigmentation is more consistently in the form of 3 or more distinct spots on the body. Attains 50 mm SL.
Distribution Cunene, Okavango and upper Zambezi systems. Also in southern tributaries of the Zaire system.
Uses Potential aquarium species.
Note Closely related to, possibly the same as the broadstriped barb.

GORGEOUS BARB

Prag-ghieliemientjie
Barbus bellcrossi Jubb, 1964

Description D iii, 7–8; A iii, 5. Scales in lateral line 25–28, 10 around caudal peduncle. Body slender, fins long, pointed; lateral line scales distinctly deeper than adjacent scales. Mouth with 2 pairs of long barbels. Olive brown above, silvery white below, eye red above, fins

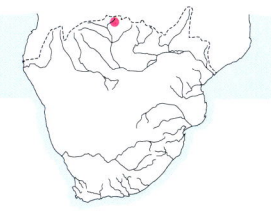

GORGEOUS BARB (cont.)

orange or bright red. Body with 5–6 large spots on sides, spots along mid-dorsal line and at base of dorsal and anal fins, scale borders heavily pigmented, dark vertical bars along base of lateral line scales. Attains 46 mm SL.

Distribution Upper Zambezi headwater zone.
Relationships May be related to species of the tropical subgenus *Clypeobarbus*, named for their deep shield-like midbody scales.
Uses An attractive aquarium species.

LINE-SPOTTED BARB

Lynkol-ghieliemientjie
Barbus lineomaculatus Boulenger, 1903

Description D iii, 8; A iii, 5. Scales in lateral line 26–32, 12 around caudal peduncle. Slender bodied with 2 pairs of long barbels. Translucent brown above, silvery white below, gill cover iridescent gold, lateral line scales with prominent chevron bars; a variable series of dark spots along body, last spot on caudal peduncle straddles lateral line. Attains 75 mm SL.
Distribution Cunene, Okavango, Zambezi and Limpopo systems, common in Zimbabwe and Zambia. Also

widespread in Central and East Africa.
Biology and Ecology Inhabits a wide range of habitats from small streams to large rivers. Moves upstream to spawn in flooded grassy areas.
Uses An attractive aquarium species.

GOLDIE BARBS

Another distinct group of southern African minnows whose relationships with other minnows are not clear. The group comprises three species, the goldie barb (*B. pallidus*), the shortfin barb (*B. brevipinnis*) and the sidespot barb (*B. neefi*). These barbs have a relatively small, compact body, two pairs of barbels, and bright golden male breeding livery. The taxonomy of the group is not yet settled.

SHORTFIN BARB

Kortvin-ghieliemientjie
Barbus brevipinnis Jubb, 1966

Description D iii, 7–8; A iii, 5. Scales in lateral line 27–30, 10–12 around caudal peduncle. Body compact, head short, mouth with 2 pairs of long barbels. Translucent brown with silvery white below, scales with dark pigment along borders creating a mesh-like pattern, a series of irregular dashes or a single stripe along midbody. Breeding males turn bright golden. Attains 45 mm SL.
Distribution Typically found in Sabi-Incomati and Steelpoort-Limpopo systems.
Biology and Ecology Found in headwater streams with vegetation. Feeds on small invertebrates. Breeds in spring and summer.
Uses An attractive aquarium species.
Notes The type specimens from the Merite River have very short barbels and fins. These features are probably caused by environmental factors and are not typical of most populations.

SIDESPOT BARB

Sykol-ghieliemientjie
Barbus neefi Greenwood, 1962

Description D iii, 8; A iii, 5. Scales in lateral line 24–29, 12 around caudal peduncle. Two pairs of long barbels. Dark olive above, golden green on the sides, silvery white below, iridescent gold on the gill cover. Characteristic markings include a variable number of large, dark spots along body, a spot at the base of the pectoral and anal fins, and thin, wavy parallel lines along top and bottom of each scale row. Attains about 70 mm SL.
Distribution Divided distribution, Transvaal tributaries of the Steelpoort-Limpopo and headwaters of the Upper Zambezi, Kafue and southern Zaire systems in Zambia and Zaire.
Uses An attractive aquarium species.

GOLDIE BARB

Goud-ghieliemientjie
Barbus pallidus A. Smith, 1841

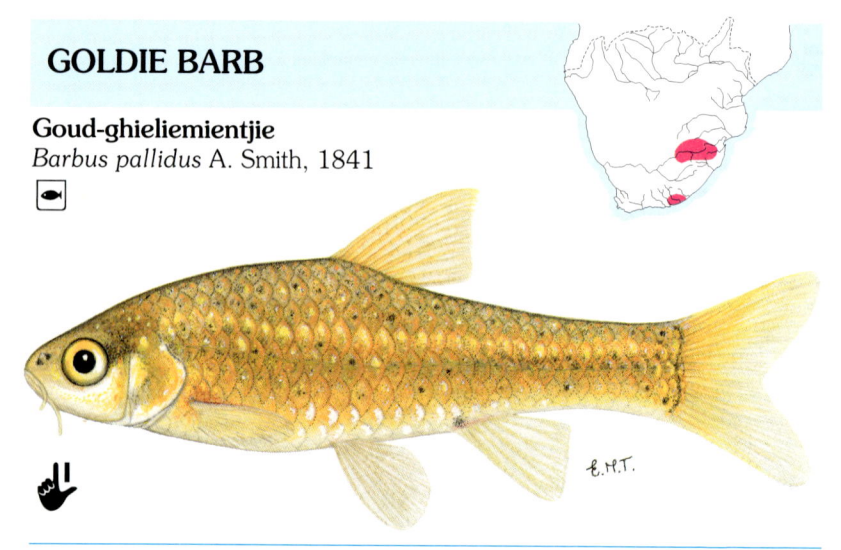

Description D iii, 7–8; A iii, 5. Scales in lateral line 26–30, 12 around caudal peduncle. Lateral line complete or incomplete. Body short, head short, 2 pairs of long barbels. Translucent light brown above, silvery on sides and below, with irregular scattered spots on sides and back and a row of spots above lateral line. Breeding males turn bright golden. Attains 70 mm SL.
Distribution Divided distribution, coastal streams of eastern Cape from the Great Fish to the Krom, also tributaries of the Vaal and Limpopo in Transvaal and the Phongolo and Tugela in Natal.
Biology and Ecology Inhabits pools in clear, rocky streams often with emergent marginal vegetation. Breeds in summer, breeding pairs lay eggs in vegetation.
Uses An attractive aquarium species.

LONGBEARD BARB

Langbaard-ghieliemientjie
Barbus unitaeniatus Günther, 1866

Description D iii, 8; A iii, 5. Scales in lateral line 29–35. Body slender and attenuated; back short, with dorsal fin origin in advance of pelvics. Eyes large, dorso-lateral in position; mouth inferior, with 2 pairs of long barbels. Translucent brown with silvery white below, a characteristic dark lateral stripe and chevron markings on lateral line, dorsal fin tip and trailing edges black. Attains 140 mm SL.
Distribution Widely distributed in southern Africa from the Zambian Zaire system and the Cunene, Okavango and Zambezi south to the Phongolo. Absent from lower Zambezi, Buzi, Pungwe and Save systems.
Biology and Ecology Found in a wide variety of habitats including flowing and standing waters; thrives in dams and lakes. Feeds on aquatic invertebrates and grass seeds. Breeds after rains during summer months.
Uses Suitable aquarium and garden pond fish.

HYPHEN BARB

Skakel-ghieliemientjie
Barbus bifrenatus Fowler, 1935

Description D iii, 8; A iii, 5. Scales in lateral line 28–32, 12 around caudal peduncle. Body slender, 2 pairs of long barbels equal or greater in length than orbit diameter. Translucent brown, silvery white on sides and below; a distinct regular black stripe arcs from tip of snout through eye to end of caudal peduncle, lateral line marked by line of black pigment, a black spot at base of anal fin, dorsal base dark. Certain populations have the black body stripe broken into dashes. Attains 70 mm SL.

Distribution Widespread over northern parts of southern Africa including the Cunene, Okavango, Upper Zambezi, Kafue, Zambian Zaire and Limpopo systems. Isolated populations occur in Malawi and on the eastern shores of Lake St Lucia in Natal.

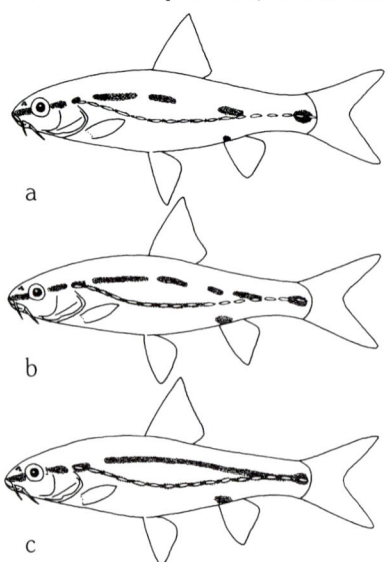

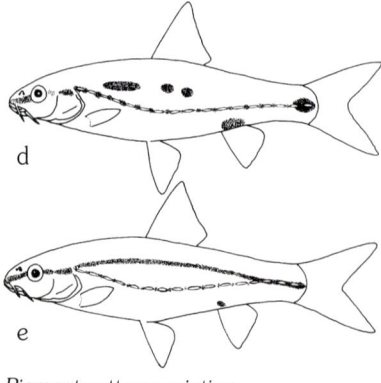

Pigment pattern variation: (a) Chambeshi, (b) Lake Malawi, (c) Transvaal, (d) Quanza (Angola), (e) Okavango

Biology and Ecology Inhabits floodplains, pools and shallow streams with vegetation. Feeds on detritus, algae, seeds and small invertebrates.

Uses: Attractive aquarium fish.
Notes May be confused with bowstripe barb (*B. viviparus*) but distinguished by details of pigmentation.

BOWSTRIPE BARB

Boogstreep-ghieliemientjie
Barbus viviparus Weber, 1897

Description D iii, 8; A iii, 5. Scales in lateral line 26–30, 12 around caudal peduncle. Body slender, 2 pairs of long barbels. Translucent olive brown above, silvery on sides and below; a complete or broken black stripe from behind the head ends as a spot at base of caudal fin; lateral line tubules marked by black chevrons, a dark spot present at base of anal fin. Breeding males turn golden. Attains 70 mm SL.

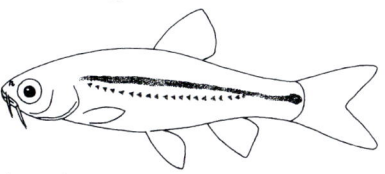

Lateral pigment pattern

Distribution East coastal rivers and freshwater lakes from the Ruvuma (Tanzania-Mozambique border) southwards to the Vungu in southern Natal. Generally confined to lowveld and coastal plain regions but penetrates inland in larger systems such as the Limpopo.

Biology and Ecology Inhabits vegetated pools of streams and rivers and lake margins. Feeds on aquatic insects and other small organisms. Breeds in summer, breeding pairs lay eggs on submerged roots and vegetation. Reaches maturity within a year.

Uses Suitable for aquariums and garden ponds.

Note Distinguished from the hyphen barb (*B. bifrenatus*) by differences in pigmentation: stripe does not extend onto head in *B. viviparus*, but does in the hyphen barb, pigment on lateral line tubules chevron-shaped compared with tubular in hyphen barb.

DWARF BARB

Dwerg-ghieliemientjie
Barbus brevidorsalis Boulenger, 1915

Description D iii, 7; A iii, 5. Scales in lateral series 24–27, 11–14 around caudal peduncle. Lateral line restricted to a few leading scales only. Body short and deep, barbels absent or 1 pair of minute barbels only in largest specimens. A thin black stripe along body ends with a distinct spot at base of caudal fin. Attains 40 mm SL.
Distribution Upper reaches of the Okavango, Zambezi, Kafue and Quanza and southern tributaries of the Zaire system.
Note Formerly known as *Barbus puellus*.

THAMALAKANE BARB

Thamalakane-ghieliemientjie
Barbus thamalakanensis Fowler, 1935

Description D iii, 8; A iii, 5. Scales in lateral line 25–29, 12 around caudal peduncle. Body slender, 2 pairs of long barbels. Translucent brown above, silvery white on sides and below; a regular black stripe passes straight from tip of snout to base of caudal fin, a black spot at base of anal fin. Breeding males turn golden. Attains 40 mm SL.

Distribution Okavango and upper Zambezi.
Biology and Ecology Prefers well-vegetated margins of rivers and lagoons, floodplain pools and backwaters. Feeds on insects and periphyton. Breeds in summer, laying eggs on submerged vegetation.
Uses Attractive aquarium fish.

BLACKBACK BARB

Swartrug-ghieliemientjie
Barbus barnardi Jubb, 1965

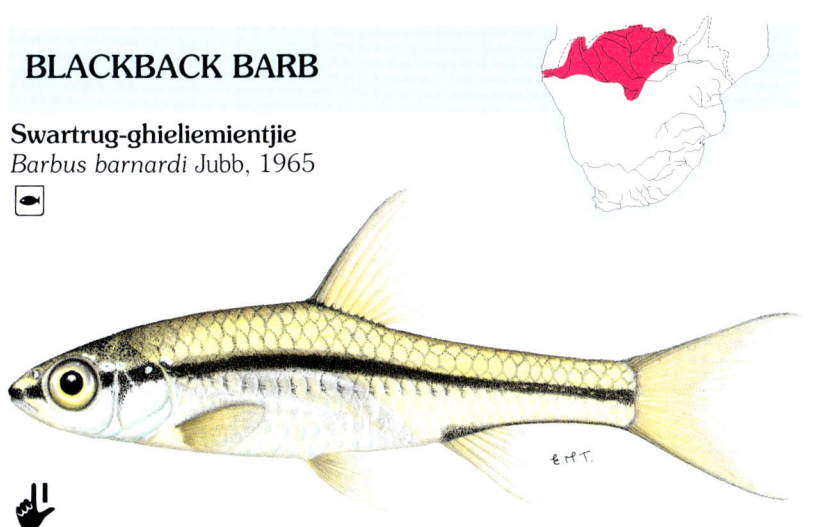

Description D iii, 8; A iii, 5. Scales in lateral line 29–33, 12 around caudal peduncle. Body slender, fusiform, pointed; mouth small, with a single pair of minute barbels. Breeding males with small conical tubercles on the snout. Translucent brown, silver on sides and below, fins pale yellow. A distinctive straight black stripe from tip of snout to caudal base, irregular black spots along midline of back, a black spot at base of anal fin. Attains 70 mm SL.

Distribution Cunene, Okavango, Upper Zambezi, Kafue and Zambian Zaire systems.
Biology and Ecology Lives in shallow, well-vegetated streams, floodplains and marshes. Feeds on small aquatic insects and algae. Breeds in summer, laying eggs amongst vegetation.
Uses Attractive aquarium fish.

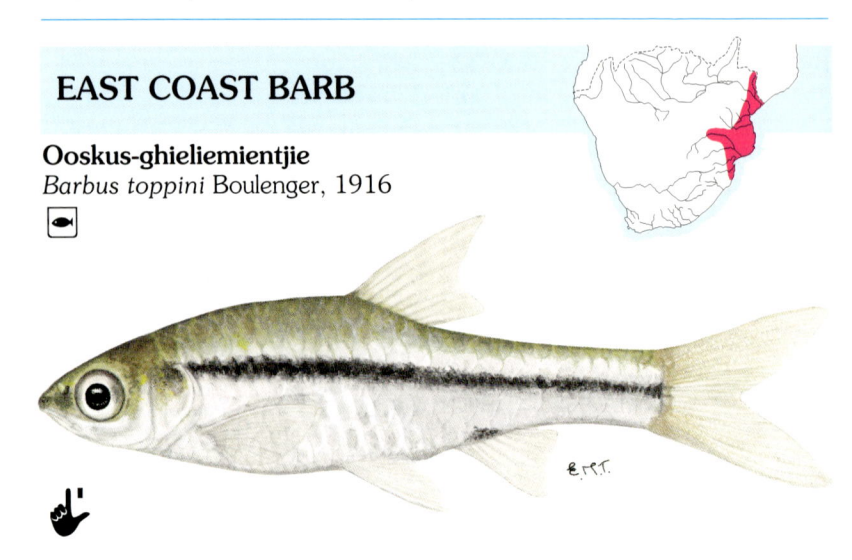

EAST COAST BARB

Ooskus-ghieliemientjie
Barbus toppini Boulenger, 1916

Description D iii, 8; A iii, 5. Scales in lateral series 27–30, lateral line pores on first 8–13 scales only, 12 around caudal peduncle. Mouth small, with a single pair of minute barbels. Translucent olive above, flanks silvery, white below; an irregular black stripe from tip of snout to base of mid-caudal rays, broader and more clearly marked in males. Attains 40 mm SL.

Distribution Lowveld reaches of east coast rivers from Malawi to the Mkuze system, Natal. Also in the Ruaha, Tanzania.
Biology and Ecology Inhabits shallow, well-vegetated streams and pans. Feeds on small aquatic organisms. Breeds in summer, possibly migrating to spawning sites.
Uses Suitable aquarium fish.

BROADBAND BARB

Breëband-ghieliemientjie
Barbus macrotaenia Worthington, 1933

Description D iii, 8; A iii, 5. Scales in lateral line 25–28, 12 around caudal peduncle. Body short, 2 pairs of barbels. Lateral line complete. Breeding males develop tubercles on the snout. Translucent grey, silvery white below, with a straight, broad black stripe from tip of snout to base of caudal fin and a black spot at base of anal fin. Attains 40 mm SL.
Distribution Lower Zambezi, Pungwe River, Lake Malawi.
Biology and Ecology Common in marshy habitats.
Uses Suitable aquarium fish.

BARBS, YELLOWFISHES, LABEOS

BROADBAND BARB (cont.)

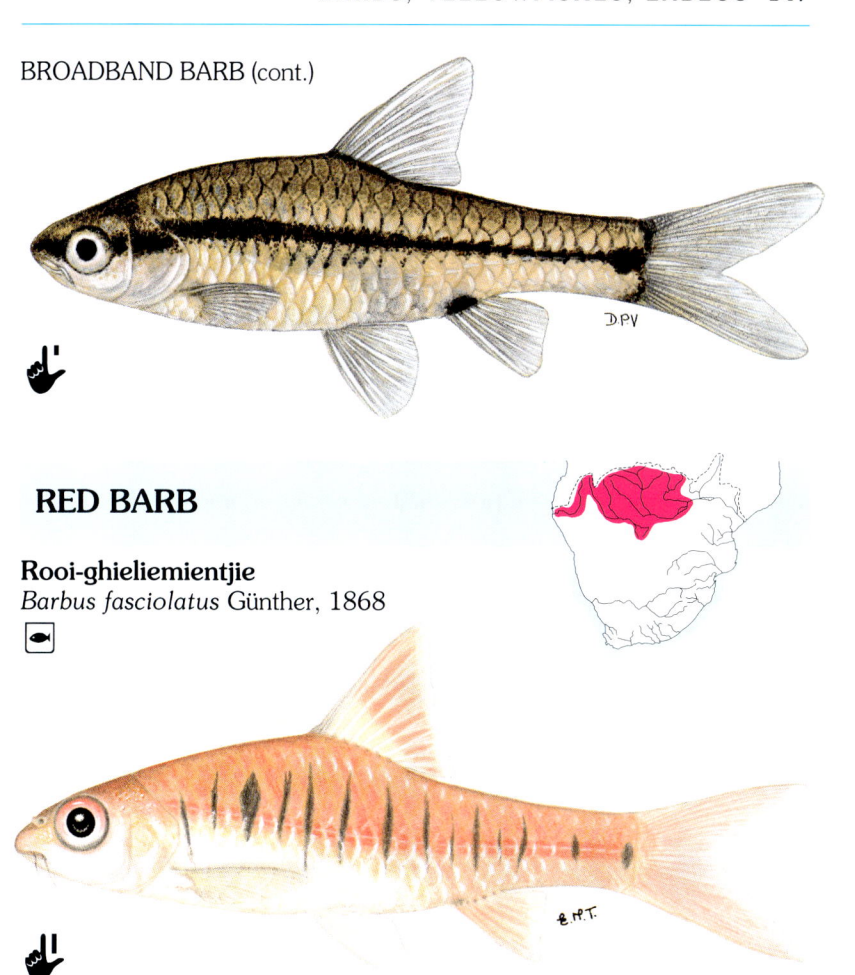

RED BARB

Rooi-ghieliemientjie
Barbus fasciolatus Günther, 1868

Description D iii, 8; A iii, 5. Scales in lateral line 25–30, 12 around caudal peduncle. Body slender, 2 pairs of barbels. Light rose to red, silvery white below, with a series of 10–15 black vertical bars on body, second or third often ovoid and last tending to form a spot at end of caudal peduncle. Attains 60 mm SL.
Distribution Cunene, Okavango, upper and middle Zambezi, Kafue and Zambian Zaire systems.

Biology and Ecology Prefers well-oxygenated but vegetated waters such as floodplain river channels and permanent lagoons. Shy, emerging in subdued light, most active in early morning and late afternoon. Feeds on small organisms, often off plant surfaces.
Uses A very attractive aquarium species.
Note Also called the tiger or barred barb.

148 BARBS, YELLOWFISHES, LABEOS

BEIRA BARB

Beira-ghieliemientjie
Barbus radiatus Peters, 1853

Description D iii, 8; A iii, 5. Scales in lateral line 24–29, 12 around caudal peduncle. Pit lines on top of head and on cheeks a distinctive feature. Mouth with two pairs of very short barbels. Silvery, usually with a straight black band from snout to caudal fin base, dorsal and caudal fins rose red with sooty black edges, eye bright red above. Attains 120 mm SL.
Distribution Widespread in Africa from Uganda southwards, including the Zambian Zaire, Cunene, Okavango, Zambezi and east coast rivers south to the Phongolo system.
Biology and Ecology Favours marshes and marginal vegetation of streams, rivers and lakes. Active in subdued light and at night.
Uses An attractive aquarium fish.
Relationships A member of the subgenus *Enteromius*.

SICKLE-FIN BARB

Sekelvin-ghieliemientjie
Barbus haasianus David, 1936

Description D ii, 8; A ii, 5. Scales small, 35–38 in lateral series. No lateral line, no barbels. Anal fin of mature males extends into a sickle shape. Translucent brown to rosy red (breeding males) with a thin line along midbody ending in a spot at base of caudal; a black triangle on base of dorsal fin, a black spot on base of anal fin. A very small species, attaining 32 mm SL.
Distribution Okavango, upper Zambezi, Kafue, lower Zambezi, Pungwe, Zambian Zaire (Luapula, Lualaba) systems.

BARBS, YELLOWFISHES, LABEOS 149

SICKLE-FIN BARB (cont.)

♂

♀

Biology and Ecology Inhabits swamps and floodplains in well-vegetated habitats.

Uses An attractive aquarium fish.

UPJAW BARB

Boel-ghieliemientjie
Coptostomabarbus wittei David & Poll, 1937

Description D ii, 7; A ii–iii, 5. Scales thin, radiately striate, 26–29 in lateral series, 12 around caudal peduncle. Mouth distinctive, steeply inclined, tongue well developed. No barbels. Eye relatively large. Translucent pink or brown, turning rose red in breeding condition, with a black triangle at base of dorsal fin and a thin, straight mid-lateral stripe. A small species, attaining about 40 mm SL.

Distribution Okavango Delta, upper Zambezi system, Kafue floodplains and floodplains of the Lualaba tributary of the Zaire.

Biology and Ecology Occurs in

150 BARBS, YELLOWFISHES, LABEOS

UPJAW BARB (cont.)

swamps and floodplains in shallow densely vegetated still-water habitats. Eats minute planktonic organisms.
Uses An attractive aquarium fish.

Relationships Probably closely related to the sicklefin barb (*Barbus haasianus*).

SPINEFIN BARBS

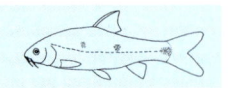

These differ from all other minnows by having the primary dorsal ray spinous but not serrated. Scales are radiately striated. A small group (only 3 species recognised, 2 in our area) of similar species that possibly represents a single polytypic species. Widespread and common in southern and East Africa.

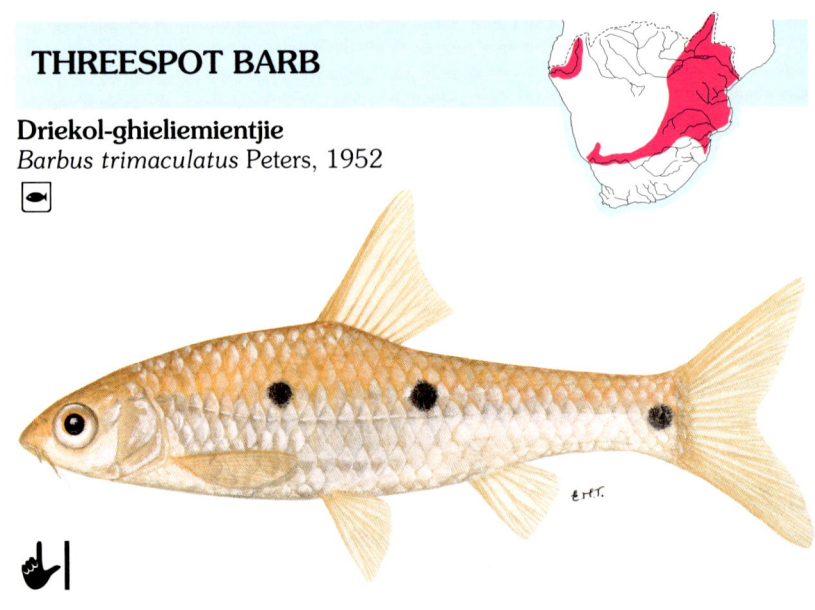

THREESPOT BARB

Driekol-ghieliemientjie
Barbus trimaculatus Peters, 1952

Description D III, 8; A iii, 5. Lateral line scales 31–35, 14 (13–16) around caudal peduncle. Body robust; 2 long barbels. Silvery, tinged with gold when in breeding condition, usually 3 clear black spots on body and base of caudal peduncle. Attains 150 mm SL.
Distribution East coast from Ruvuma, Tanzania, to Umvoti in Natal, also Orange, Cunene and Zambian Zaire systems. Replaced in Okavango, upper Zambezi and Kafue by dashtail barb (*B. poechii*).
Biology and Ecology Hardy, common and found in a wide variety of habitats, especially where vegetation occurs. Eats insects and other small organisms. Breeds in summer, shoals of ripe adults moving upstream in spate after rain. Females produce as many as 8 000 eggs.
Uses Bait for tigerfish. Suitable for ponds and larger aquariums.
Relationships Closely related to the dashtail barb (*B. poechii*) and *Barbus jacksoni* from East Africa.

DASHTAIL BARB

Streepstert-ghieliemientjie
Barbus poechii Steindachner, 1911

Description D III, 8; A iii, 5. Lateral line scales 31–33, 14 around caudal peduncle. Body robust; 2 pairs of barbels. Silvery, olive brown above, prominent black oblong dash on caudal peduncle. Attains 110 mm SL.
Distribution Cunene, Okavango and upper Zambezi systems.
Biology and Ecology Common in riverine and floodplain habitats, frequently in association with the striped robber (*Brycinus lateralis*). These two species are very similar in appearance, suggesting mimicry between them. Feeds on insects and small organisms.
Uses Bait for tigerfish. Suitable for larger aquariums or ponds.
Note Specimens with "shadow" spots, similar to the pattern of the threespot barb, occur frequently. The taxonomic status of this species is therefore uncertain.

SAWFIN BARBS

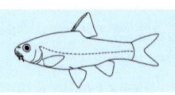

The sawfin barbs are characterised by having a bony, serrated primary dorsal fin ray. About a third of the *Barbus* species in southern Africa are in this group. Some, like the papermouth (*Barbus mattozi*), whitefish (*B. andrewi*) and sawfin (*B. serra*), grow relatively large, but most are minnow-sized and very attractive.

KEY TO SAWFIN BARBS

1a Anal fin with 5 branched rays 3
1b Anal fin with 6–7 branched rays 2
2a Anal fin with 6 branched rays, primary dorsal ray well serrated ....
....*B. calidus* (p. 153)
2b Anal fin with 7 branched rays, primary dorsal ray weakly serrated ....
....*B. erubescens* (p. 154)
3a One or 2 pairs of well-developed barbels 4
3b No barbels, prominent black spot on caudal peduncle................................
....*B. afrovernayi* (p. 157)

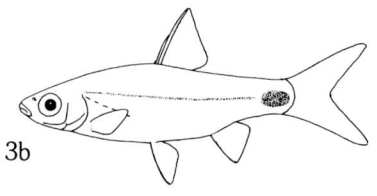

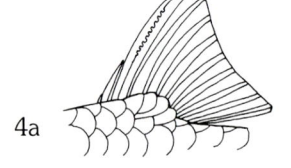

4a Prominent enlarged scales at base of dorsal fin.......................................5
4b No prominent scales at base of dorsal fin..6
5a Head large, rounded, about 3.5 times in SL; horizontal stripe uneven with zigzag edges; mouth to below anterior orbit edge..........*B. miolepis* (p. 155)
5b Head pointed, about 4 times in SL; horizontal stripe usually even, often without zigzag edges; mouth to below anterior orbit edge ....
....*B. eutaenia* (p. 155)
5c Head pointed, about 4 times in SL; horizontal stripe narrow, even; prominent subparallel punctuated stripes above and below midband; mouth small, not reaching to below orbit.........................*B. multilineatus* (p. 156)
6a Dorsal fin origin behind origin of pelvics, inner pelvic fin ray attached to body ....*B. hospes* (p. 157)
6b Dorsal fin origin above pelvics, inner pelvic fin ray free from body...........7
7a One pair of barbels (or anterior pair very short, only visible in large specimens), primary dorsal ray very weakly serrated............*B. trevelyani* (p. 158)
7b Two pairs of barbels 8
8a Lateral line scales 30–36, caudal peduncle 16–18 9

8b Lateral line scales less than 30, caudal peduncle 12–14 10
9a Hind margin of erect dorsal fin perpendicular, caudal peduncle length at least twice depth ....*B. paludinosus* (p. 160)

9a

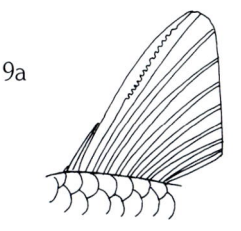

9b Hind margin of erect dorsal fin concave, caudal peduncle length less than twice depth..*B. afrohamiltoni* (p. 162)
10a 12 scales around caudal peduncle 11
10b 14 scales around caudal peduncle, adult fins orange-red ....
....*B. argenteus/choloensis* (p. 159)
11a Spot at base of caudal fin, red or orange-yellow spot on gill cover
....*B. kerstenii* (p. 162)
11b Without spots or characteristic markings ....*B. manicensis* (p. 163)
11c Dark spot at base of caudal fin, spots on body including one on side below dorsal origin..*B. dorsolineatus* (p. 164)

CLANWILLIAM REDFIN

Clanwilliam-rooivlerkie
Barbus calidus Barnard, 1938

Description D IV, 7; A iii, 6. Scales in lateral line 34–39, 16 around caudal peduncle. Body fusiform, dorsal fin placed far back, its origin behind pelvics. Head pointed, eye large, 2 pairs of barbels. Brown above, silvery white below, with a broad dark band along body and irregular dark blotches on back, base of fins scarlet-red. Breeding adults (both sexes) develop

scattered small tubercles over head and back. Attains 82 mm SL.
Distribution Tributaries of the Clanwilliam Olifants, western Cape.
Biology and Ecology Favours large, deep pools in clear streams. Feeds mainly on insects from the surface waters. Breeds in summer, males congregating in a nuptial school over vertical rock surfaces in flowing water.
Conservation Rare, many populations have been reduced or extirpated by introduced alien bass.
Relationships Closely related to the Twee River redfin *Barbus erubescens*.

TWEE RIVER REDFIN

Tweerivier-rooivlerkie
Barbus erubescens Skelton, 1974

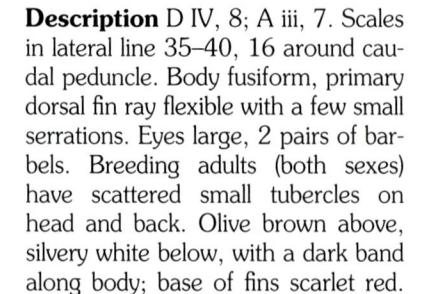

Description D IV, 8; A iii, 7. Scales in lateral line 35–40, 16 around caudal peduncle. Body fusiform, primary dorsal fin ray flexible with a few small serrations. Eyes large, 2 pairs of barbels. Breeding adults (both sexes) have scattered small tubercles on head and back. Olive brown above, silvery white below, with a dark band along body; base of fins scarlet red. Breeding males turn red. Attains 95 mm SL.
Distribution Twee River, tributary of Clanwilliam Olifants system, western Cape.
Biology and Ecology Inhabits pools and deeper flowing stretches, forming schools of similar sized individuals. Juveniles sometimes in mixed schools with the Cape galaxias. Feeds on aquatic and other insects from surface and midwaters. Breeds during summer, males congregating over bottom in flowing water.
Conservation Vulnerable. Threatened by water extraction, agricultural pollution and introduced fishes.

ORANGEFIN BARB

Oranjevlerk-ghieliemientjie
Barbus eutaenia Boulenger, 1904

Description D III, 8; A iii, 5. Scales in lateral line 24–27, 12 around caudal peduncle. Body stocky, fusiform; mouth large, with 2 pairs of barbels. Sheath of large black scales at base of dorsal fin. Olive above, silvery white below, fins yellow or orange, a broad ragged-edged black band from snout through mid-caudal rays, "shadow" bands occur above and below main band in well-marked specimens. Attains 140 mm SL.

Distribution Cunene, Okavango and Zambezi, east coast systems south to the Incomati system, Transvaal. Also in the Cuanza (Angola), the Zaire system and Lake Tanganyika.

Biology and Ecology Prefers clear-flowing waters, usually headwater streams with rocky habitats. Feeds on insects.

Uses An attractive aquarium species.

ZIGZAG BARB

Sigsag-ghieliemientjie
Barbus miolepis Boulenger, 1902

Description D III, 8; A iii, 5. Scales large, 23–26 in lateral line, 12 around caudal peduncle. Robust and deep-bodied, 2 pairs of long barbels. Sheath of enlarged black scales at base of dorsal fin. Olive above, silvery on lower sides and below, fins yellow; a bold black zigzag band along body to end of caudal peduncle, with parallel "shadow" bands above and below main band. Attains 125 mm SL.

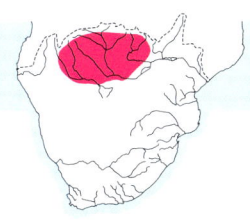

Distribution Okavango, upper Zam-

ZIGZAG BARB (cont.)

bezi, Kafue and Zaire systems.
Uses Suitable for large aquariums.
Relationships Similar to orangefin barb (*B. eutaenia*) but relatively deeper bodied, with larger, more robust head, smaller eye and shorter back. Pigmentation is usually more striking.

COPPERSTRIPE BARB

Koperstreep-ghieliemientjie
Barbus multilineatus Worthington, 1933

Description D III, 7–8; A iii, 5. Scales in lateral line 25–27, 12 around caudal peduncle. Body short, 2 pairs of barbels. Sheath of enlarged scales at base of dorsal fin. Attractive coloration, olive brown above, with silvery sides, dorsal primary ray black, fins yellow, a dark stripe from tip of snout through to base of mid-caudal rays, with a series of 3 clear "shadow" broken bands above and 2 below the main stripe. Breeding males with a bright copper band along body through mid-caudal rays. Attains 45 mm SL.
Distribution Cunene, Okavango, upper and middle Zambezi and Kafue

BARBS, YELLOWFISHES, LABEOS 157

rivers. Also Zambian Zaire (Lake Bangweulu area).
Biology and Ecology Inhabits shallow, well-vegetated water in backwaters, floodplains and river margins.

Uses Attractive aquarium species.
Note Distinguished from juvenile orangefin barbs (*B. eutaenia*) by stronger linear markings and light pigmentation of scales at base of dorsal fin.

SPOTTAIL BARB

Kolstert-ghieliemientjie
Barbus afrovernayi Nichols & Boulton, 1927

Description D III, 7; A iii, 5. Scales 27–33 in lateral series, 12 around caudal peduncle. Lateral line restricted to first 3–7 scales only. Mouth small, upturned, no barbels. Translucent grey-brown with iridescent lilac-yellow stripe along body, silvery below, a large conspicuous black spot on caudal peduncle. Small, attains 45 mm SL.

Distribution Cunene, Okavango, upper Zambezi and Kafue rivers. Also Zaire system.
Biology and ecology Inhabits quiet, well-vegetated waters, where it feeds from the surface or on small invertebrates living on plant surfaces.
Uses Attractive and peaceful in aquariums.

NAMAQUA BARB

Namakwa-ghieliemientjie
Barbus hospes Barnard, 1938

Description D III, 7; A iii, 5. Scales small and obscure, 37–39 in lateral line, 16 around caudal peduncle. Body slender, dorsal fin placed far back, origin behind ventral fins, basal serrations on primary ray point upwards, ventral fins attached along inner rays, caudal peduncle slender,

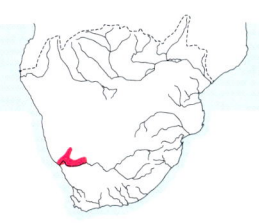

NAMAQUA BARB (cont.)

caudal fin deeply forked. Mouth inferior, with 2 pairs of equal-sized long barbels. Pale silvery or white all over, fins clear. Attains about 75 mm SL.
Distribution Orange River, below Augrabies Falls.
Biology and Ecology Favours open water in the mainstream and backwaters, where it feeds on zooplankton and aquatic insects.
Conservation Rare, but appears to have benefited from the regulated flow of the Orange below the large hydro-electric dams.

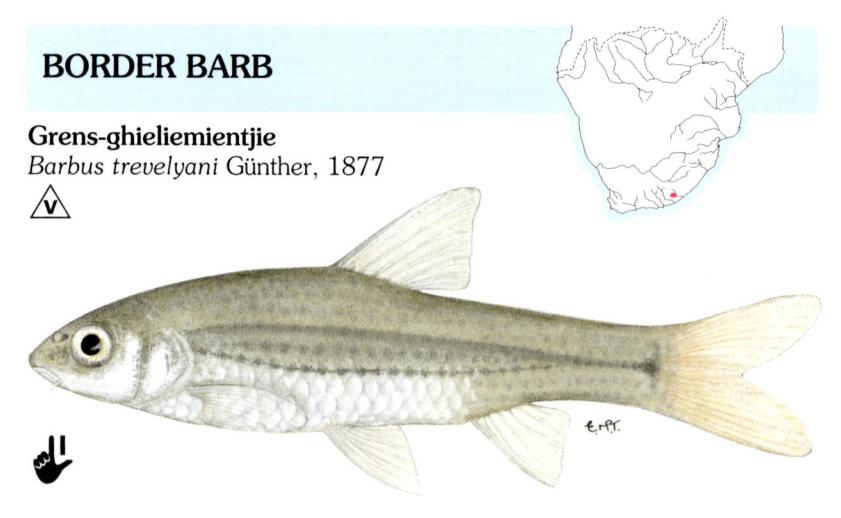

BORDER BARB

Grens-ghieliemientjie
Barbus trevelyani Günther, 1877

Description D III, 7; A iii, 5. Scales in lateral line 33–37, 14 around caudal peduncle. Primary dorsal fin ray with very small serrations only. Mouth with 1 or 2 pairs of short barbels. Breeding adults (both sexes) develop small tubercles on head, males turn golden. Translucent grey-brown, silvery below, with a thin regular black stripe along body ending as a triangular spot at base of caudal fin; lateral line tubules traced with black pigment. Attains 95 mm SL.
Distribution Keiskamma and Buffalo systems in the Ciskei and eastern Cape. Unconfirmed report from the

Nahoon River.
Biology and Ecology Inhabits pools and riffles of clear rocky streams. Feeds on aquatic and terrestrial insects, chiefly mayfly nymphs, as well as seeds and algae. Breeds in spring and early summer.
Conservation Vulnerable. Threatened by siltation, invading riparian plants and alien predators such as trout. Has been bred in captivity.

ROSEFIN BARB

Roosvlerk-ghieliemientjie
Barbus argenteus Günther, 1868

Description D III, 7–8; A iii, 5. Scales 27–32 in lateral line, 14 around caudal peduncle. Two pairs of well-developed barbels. Generally a silvery fish, with light olive dorsal surface, a vague stripe along caudal peduncle, fins orange-red in mature specimens. Attains 190 mm SL.
Distribution Divided distribution, Cuanza and Cunene in Angola, Incomati and Phongolo systems along eastern Transvaal-Natal escarpment.
Biology and ecology Inhabits pools and riffles in clear rocky streams. Feeds on aquatic and adult flying insects and takes trout flies.
Uses Suitable for larger aquariums.
Relationships Similar to, and possibly even the same species as, the silver barb (*B. choloensis*).

SILVER BARB

Silwer-ghieliemientjie
Barbus choloensis Norman, 1925

Description D III, 8; A iii, 5. Scales 28–30 in lateral line, 14 around caudal peduncle. Two pairs of barbels. Silvery with orange tinted fins. Attains 150–200 mm SL.
Distribution Tributaries of the lower

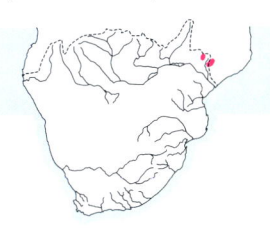

SILVER BARB (cont.)

Shire, lower Zambezi system, Malawi.
Biology and Ecology Prefers running water and rocky habitats.

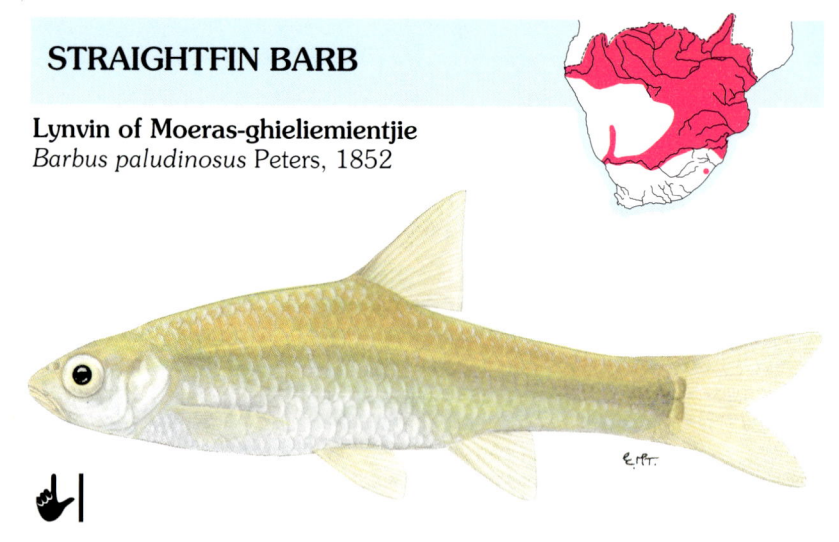

STRAIGHTFIN BARB

Lynvin of Moeras-ghieliemientjie
Barbus paludinosus Peters, 1852

Description D III, 7; A iii, 5. Scales in lateral line 32–36, 16 around caudal peduncle. Primary dorsal fin ray serrated on distal half, hind margin of erect dorsal fin vertical. Head pointed, mouth small, with 2 pairs of short barbels. Plain olive grey or silvery in turbid waters, a thin sideline sometimes present. Females generally attain a larger size than males. Attains 150 mm SL.

Distribution Widespread in east coastal rivers from East Africa south to the Vungu, Natal, and from the southern Zaire tributaries and the Quanza in Angola to the Orange.
Biology and Ecology Hardy, preferring quiet, well-vegetated waters in lakes, swamps and marshes or marginal areas of larger rivers and slow-flowing streams. Feeds on a wide variety of small organisms including

insects, small snails and crustaceans, algae, diatoms and detritus. Spawns amongst vegetation during summer. Females are multiple spawners, laying from 250–800 eggs at 50–60 mm SL to as many as 2 500 eggs at 112 mm SL. Eaten by larger predators such as the sharptooth catfish, tigerfish, largemouth breams (*Serranochromis* species) and birds.

Uses An important component of the "matemba" fishery of Lake Chilwa in Malawi, where they are caught in nets and traps and sun-dried.

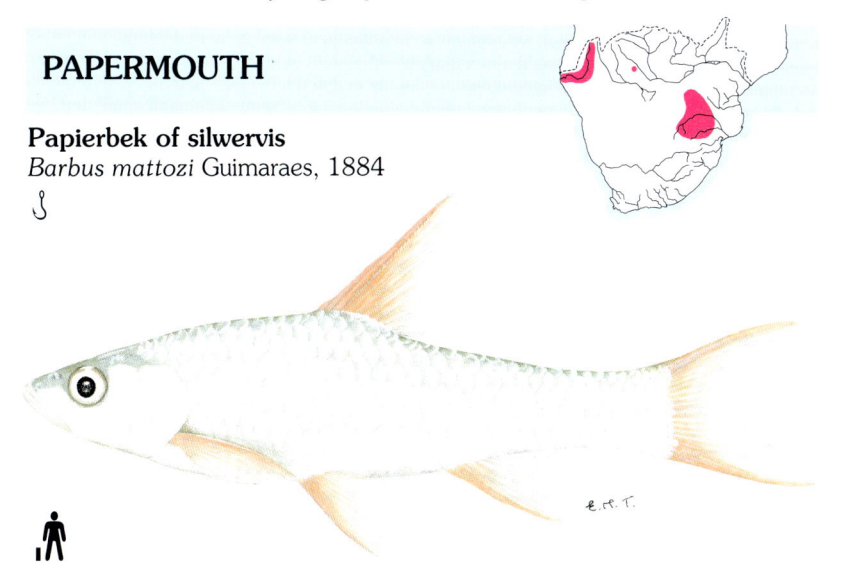

PAPERMOUTH

Papierbek of silwervis
Barbus mattozi Guimaraes, 1884

Description D IV, 8; A iii, 5. Scales in lateral line 29–35, 14 around caudal peduncle. Body fusiform; mouth large, protruding, with 1 or 2 pairs of short barbels. Silvery with orange fins. In Cunene specimens a black bar occurs behind the gill openings. Attains about 400 mm SL. SA angling record 1,355 kg, Zimbabwe 1,304 kg.

Distribution Limpopo system in Zimbabwe and Transvaal and headwater reaches of the Gwai (Zambezi system) in Zimbabwe. Recorded once from the Kwando in Angola (upper Zambezi system). Also in the Quanza and Cunene, Angola.

Biology and Ecology The natural habitat is large pools of cooler perennial rivers; thrives in man-made impoundments. An active predator, initially on small planktonic crustaceans and insects; when larger (over 175 mm SL) small fishes become the main prey. Waterlily seeds are also eaten. Migrates upstream with the first summer flood to spawn. May live for 8 or 9 years; attains maturity after 3 years. Main predators are birds, otters, large catfish and large papermouths.

Uses Larger individuals (over 250 mm SL) are highly regarded as angling targets, smaller specimens are considered a nuisance. Generally unsuitable for handling or keeping in aquariums.

HAMILTON'S BARB

Hamilton se ghieliemientjie
Barbus afrohamiltoni Crass, 1960

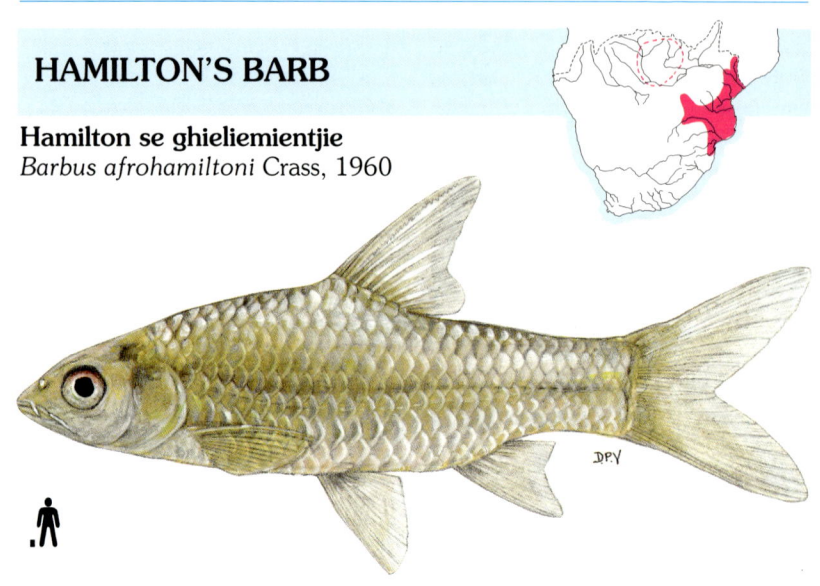

Description D III, 8; A iii, 5. Scales in lateral line 30–34, 16 around caudal peduncle. Relatively deep-bodied, with steep back and deep caudal peduncle. Mouth large, with 2 pairs of barbels. Silvery in life. Attains 175 mm SL.
Distribution Lowveld reaches of tropical east coast rivers from the lower Zambezi to the Phongolo. Also reported in the upper Zambezi, Kafue, Nata and Zambian Zaire (Lake Bangweulu) systems.
Biology and Ecology Prefers placid waters such as pans and large pools. Feeds on insects.
Uses Suitable bait species for tigerfish.

REDSPOT BARB

Rooikol-ghieliemientjie
Barbus kerstenii Peters, 1868

Description D III, 7; A iii, 5. Scales in lateral line 23–27, 12 around caudal peduncle. Fairly deep-bodied; mouth with 2 pairs of barbels. Light brown above, silvery on the sides and below; a bright yellow, orange or red spot on each gill cover. Lateral line pores are marked with black chevrons; a black zigzag stripe ending in a spot at end of caudal peduncle is usually present. Attains 75 mm SL.

Distribution Cunene, Okavango, upper Zambezi, tributaries of the lower Zambezi and the Save-Runde systems. Also widespread in central and East Africa to the Lake Victoria basin.

Biology and Ecology Occurs in mountain streams and along the vegetated fringes of large rivers.

Uses Suited to well-aerated aquariums.

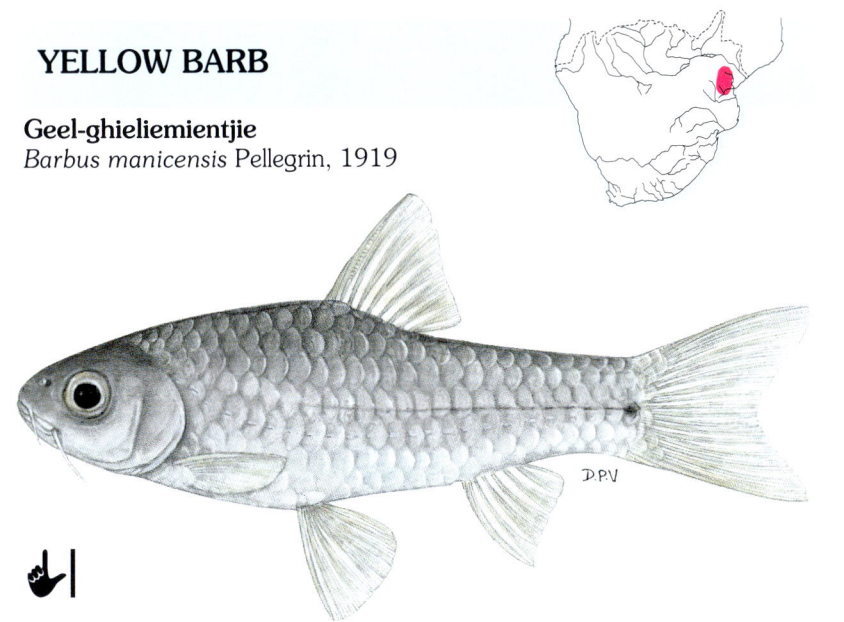

YELLOW BARB

Geel-ghieliemientjie
Barbus manicensis Pellegrin, 1919

Description D III, 7–8; A iii, 5. Scales large, 22–25 in lateral line, 12 around caudal peduncle. Body stout; 2 pairs of barbels. Plain silvery. Attains 150 mm SL.

Distribution Pungwe, Buzi and lower Zambezi in Mozambique. Records from the upper Zambezi, Kafue and Zambian Zaire are unconfirmed.

CUNENE BARB

Kunene-ghieliemientjie
Barbus dorsolineatus Trewavas, 1936

Description D III, 7; A iii, 5. Scales in lateral line 25–28, 11–12 around caudal peduncle. Deep body, short back, large head, 2 pairs of barbels. Colour in life not recorded; pigmentation simple, dark spot on sides below dorsal fin, smaller spots on caudal peduncle. Attains 75 mm SL.
Distribution Upper reaches of the Cunene, Angola. Described from adjacent coastal drainage.

SAWFIN AND WHITEFISH

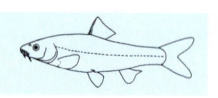

These two large barbines from the south-west Cape belong in a distinct group of their own. They are unlike any other African barbine fishes but are similar to the true European barbels. Characteristic features include radiately striated scales, a serrated primary dorsal fin spine and an elongate, pointed snout. The two Cape species are very similar but the whitefish has six branched rays in the anal fin, the sawfin five.

SAWFIN

Saagvin
Barbus serra Peters, 1864

Description D IV, 8; A iii, 5. Scales 41–44 in lateral line, 20 around caudal peduncle. Primary dorsal fin ray bony and serrated. Snout long and pointed, especially in adults; mouth relatively small, subterminal, 2 pairs

BARBS, YELLOWFISHES, LABEOS

SAWFIN (cont.)

of barbels. Small tubercles cover the head of breeding adults of both sexes. Juveniles silvery with irregular dark blotches. Adults deep olive gold, light cream below. Attains about 500 mm SL, 7 kg. SA angling record 3,04 kg.
Distribution Olifants system, western Cape Province.
Biology and Ecology Favours deep pools and runs of mainstreams, also impounded waters; young occur in smaller tributaries. Breeds in summer, congregating in deep pools below waterfalls and rapids. Feeds on insects and other invertebrates as well as algae and detritus mainly off the bottom, leaving characteristic pockets in sand and gravel beds.
Uses Occasionally caught by anglers..
Conservation Vulnerable. The sawfin population has declined following the introduction of bass, increasing habitat destruction or alteration and the impedence of large dams.

WHITEFISH

Witvis
Barbus andrewi Barnard, 1937

Description D IV, 8; A iii, 6. Scales in lateral line 38–41, 16 around caudal peduncle. Serrations on primary dorsal ray reduce with age. Head with long, pointed snout, mouth subterminal with 2 pairs of barbels. Breeding

adults develop a cover of fine tubercles on the head. Juveniles silvery with irregular dark blotches. Adults deep olive above, sides golden, underparts cream. Attains 600 mm SL. SA angling record 3,407 kg.
Distribution Berg and Breë systems, south-west Cape.
Biology and Ecology Favours deep, rocky pools of larger tributaries and mainstreams and does well in dams such as Voëlvlei and Brandvlei. Feeds on bottom-dwelling invertebrates and algae. Breeds in summer, congregating at the head of large, stony pools or at the base of rapids. Eggs are laid in gravel in flowing water and hatch after about 5 days. Common name probably derives from glint of rolling fish in clear pools.
Uses Occasionally caught by anglers.
Conservation Vulnerable. Threats include introduced bass and habitat destruction through water abstraction and pollution. Has been artificially bred and restocked by conservation authorities.

YELLOWFISHES

These large barbine cyprinids are characteristic of many African rivers and lakes. Unlike minnows, yellowfish grow to a large size and live for many years. They have scales with longitudinal or parallel striae and the primary dorsal fin ray is usually spinous. They are extremely variable in shape and appearance, even within the same population. This is particularly true of the mouth and lips, which may be thin and firm or thick and fleshy. Three forms are recognised, the normal U-shaped mouth with moderate lips, a straight-edged mouth with horny lower lips, and thick, fleshy (rubberlips) lips. Lip development is determined largely by feeding habits and can therefore change from normal to thick depending on habitat and food resources. "Rubberlips" appear to be an adaptation for grubbing between cobbles or loose rocky substrates. A straight mouth with horny lower lip is used for scraping algae from rock surfaces, while a normal mouth is used in a variety of ways, usually grubbing in sandy or soft organic sediments. Yellowfish are popular angling species, giving a good fight on light tackle. They migrate upstream to breed, usually over gravel beds. They have been relatively well studied on account of their large size and economic value. One species, the Clanwilliam yellowfish, is rare and threatened.

KEY TO SPECIES

1a 27–33 scales in lateral line, 12 around caudal peduncle 2
1b 35 or more scales in lateral line 3
2a Dorsal fin longer than head (upper Zambezi, Okavango and Cunene rivers) ....***Barbus codringtonii*** (p. 173)
2b Dorsal fin shorter than head (middle and lower Zambezi to the Phongolo) ....***B. marequensis*** (p. 172)
3a Origin of pelvic fin below or behind origin of dorsal fin, primary dorsal fin

ray flexible, slender, rarely spinous..4
3b Origin of pelvic fin before origin of dorsal fin, primary dorsal fin ray stout, spinous 5
4a Eye pupil level with nostrils, usually 40 lateral line scales, fin membranes dark blue-grey in adults (Limpopo, Incomati and Phongolo systems) ....***B. polylepis* (p. 170)**

4b Eye pupil below level of nostrils, usually 36 lateral line scales, fin membranes not blue-grey in adults (Tugela system to Umtamvuna system, Natal) ....***B. natalensis* (p. 169)**
4c Usually 42 (range 41–45) lateral line scales, 18 around caudal peduncle (Clanwilliam Olifants system) ....***B. capensis* (p. 171)**
5a Distance between orbit and preopercular groove greater than snout length, mouth terminal ....***B. kimberleyensis* (p. 167)**

5b Distance between orbit and preopercular groove subequal or shorter than snout length, mouth subterminal..................................***B. aeneus* (p. 168)**

LARGEMOUTH YELLOWFISH

Grootbek-geelvis
Barbus kimberleyensis Gilchrist & Thompson, 1913

Description D IV, 8–9; A iii, 5. Scales in lateral line 37–45 (usually 42), 16 around caudal peduncle. Dorsal fin above pelvics, unbranched ray bony and spinous; anterior rays of anal fin relatively longer than other rays in adults. Mouth large, terminal, lips thin, 2 pairs of slender barbels; eyes dorso-lateral, not visible from below; snout length equal to or less than eye to preopercular groove. Silvery when young, later olive grey or light olive yellow, anal fin light orange in adults. This is the largest scale-bearing indigenous fish species in southern Africa, with a maximum recorded size of 22,2 kg and 825 mm FL. Females generally reach a greater size and age than males. SA angling record 22,2 kg.

Distribution Vaal-Orange system; generally only found in the larger tributaries and dams, absent from higher reaches in Lesotho and the southern tributaries of the Cape.

Biology and Ecology Adults prefer flowing water in deep channels or below rapids, but the species does well in dams. Primarily a predator, initially taking insects and small crustaceans, but piscivorous above 300 mm FL. Breeds in mid- to late summer over gravel beds in running water. Fecundity increases in larger females to as many as 60 000 ova. The eggs hatch after 2–3 days and larvae begin to feed 3–4 days later. Growth is relatively slow, reaching about 100 mm FL after two years and 300 mm at 5 years. Males mature at 6 years and females at 8 years. Individuals may live for 12 or more years.

Uses A renowned angling species, taking a variety of lures and live bait.

Conservation The largemouth yellowfish is becoming scarce and is being artificially cultured and restocked.

SMALLMOUTH YELLOWFISH

Kleinbek-geelvis
Barbus aeneus (Burchell, 1822)

Description D IV, 7–9; A iii, 5. Scales in lateral line 36–44 (usually 40), 16 around caudal peduncle. Dorsal fin origin behind origin of pelvics, primary dorsal fin ray stout and spinous; anal fin with leading rays extend-

ed in adults. Mouth subterminal to inferior, with 2 pairs of barbels; lips variable, from thin and firm forming a scraping edge to moderate or very thick and fleshy (rubberlips); eyes lateral, visible from below; snout length less than orbit to preopercular groove. Silvery with dark blotches when small, blotches gradually disappear and adults are golden olive-bronze above, cream below, anal fin with orange tinge. Attains about 500 mm FL. SA angling record 7,837 kg.
Taxonomic note *B.aeneus* is the earliest correct name for this species, which was formerly called *Barbus holubi*.
Distribution Natural range Orange-Vaal system; also translocated to larger Cape coastal rivers including the Gourits, Great Fish and the Kei, as well as the Limpopo and Kyle Dam in Zimbabwe.
Biology and Ecology Prefers clear-flowing waters of large rivers with sandy or rocky substrates; also found in large dams. Occurs at higher altitudes and in smaller tributaries than the largemouth yellowfish. Breeds in spring through to midsummer after the first substantial rains of the season. Migrates upstream to spawn over suitable gravel beds. Fecundity increases from about 6 000 eggs at 300 mm FL to about 60 000 eggs at 500 mm FL. Eggs are laid in the gravel and hatch in 3–8 days; after a further 4–6 days larvae begin feeding on microscopic organisms. Larger fishes are broadly omnivorous depending on the available food, with benthic invertebrates, including bivalve molluscs, vegetation, algae and detritus forming the major food of the species. Matures at about 200 mm SL in males and from 240 mm SL in females.
Uses An important angling species.

SCALY

Natalse geelvis
Barbus natalensis Castelnau, 1861

Description D IV, 8–9; A iii, 5. Scales in lateral line 35–39 (usually 36), 14–18 (usually 16) around caudal peduncle. Dorsal fin origin in front of pelvics, primary ray may be flexible (usually in upland fish) or spinous (lowland localities). Mouth extremely variable from straight scraping form to enlarged "rubberlips" form; barbels well developed, as long as or greater than orbit diameter. Colour variable, depending on water clarity and body condition. Fry silvery with irregular dark markings, juveniles lose dark marks but remain silvery. Adults olive above, sides bronze, cream below. Attains 638 mm TL. SA angling record 4,628 kg.

Distribution Natal, widespread from the Mkuze southwards to the Umtamvuna on Transkei border. Translocated to the Save in Zimbabwe.

Biology and Ecology Found in a wide variety of habitats from pools and rapids of clear streams to deep turbid waters of larger rivers and impoundments. Juveniles shoal in large schools in shallow, marginal habitats. The scaly tends to move upstream in summer and retreats downstream in winter. Feeds on various foods from algae and detritus to invertebrates such as crabs and aquatic insect nymphs. Breeds in summer, migrates upstream and spawns over gravel beds. Fecundity is reported as high as 20 000 ova per female. Males mature as yearlings from about 100 mm FL and females as 2 year olds, from about 150 mm FL.

Uses Angling species. The current record has stood since October 1956.

Note The scaly from Natal and the smallscale yellowfish (*B. polylepis*) of Transvaal rivers are very similar but do not occur together.

SMALLSCALE YELLOWFISH

Kleinskub-geelvis
Barbus polylepis Boulenger, 1907

Description D IV, 8; A iii, 5. Scales in lateral line 36–44 (usually 40), 14–18 (usually 16) around caudal peduncle. Primary dorsal ray segmented and flexible, dorsal origin above or before origin of pelvics. Mouth subterminal with variable lips; two pairs of barbels. Both sexes develop small white tubercles on head, upper body scales and anal and dorsal fin

rays. Juveniles silvery with dark spots over body, adults dark olive green above, bronze on the sides and cream below, fins dark grey-green. Attains 460 mm TL, 6,8 kg. SA angling record 6,18 kg.
Distribution Restricted to the southern tributaries of the Limpopo, and the Incomati and Phongolo systems.
Biology and Ecology A cool water species not found below 600 m altitude. Occurs in deep pools and flowing waters of permanent rivers and in dams. Feeds primarily on algae (winter months) and aquatic insects (summer), but also takes mussels, snails, crabs and small fish. Breeds during spring and summer, males maturing at a smaller size (170 mm FL) than females (from 300 mm FL); females grow larger than males.
Uses A popular angling species.

CLANWILLIAM YELLOWFISH

Clanwillam geelvis
Barbus capensis A. Smith, 1841

Description D IV, 9; A iii, 5. Scales in lateral line 40–45 (usually 42), 16–20 (usually 18) around caudal peduncle. Primary dorsal fin ray segmented and flexible, dorsal origin above or slightly in front of origin of pelvics. Lips variable, 2 pairs of barbels. Juveniles silvery with dark blotches, adults golden. Largest size recorded 987 mm TL, 10,66 kg. SA angling record 5,679 kg.
Distribution Clanwilliam Olifants system, western Cape.
Biology and Ecology Favours deep pools and runs of large tributaries and mainstreams as well as impounded waters. An omnivore feeding on algae and aquatic invertebrates such as insects, snails and crabs. Large specimens also take frogs and small fish. Breeds in summer, migrating upstream to spawn over gravel beds.
Uses An excellent angling species.
Conservation Rare. Populations have been affected by the construction of large dams, abstraction of water and the introduction of bass. Now being bred at a specially built hatchery and restocked.

LARGESCALE YELLOWFISH

Grootskub-geelvis
Barbus marequensis A. Smith, 1841

Description D IV, 8–10; A iii, 5. Scales large, 27–33 in lateral line, 12 around caudal peduncle. Dorsal fin in front of origin of pelvics, primary ray flexible, height extremely variable, even within one population. Mouth subterminal, lips extremely variable; two pairs of barbels. Males and females develop small tubercles on top and side of head and on anal fin rays. Colour varies with water clarity from pale olive to bright golden yellow. Juveniles silvery with dark blotches. Attains 470 mm TL, about 6,0 kg. SA angling record 5,75 kg, Zimbabwe 3,4 kg.
Distribution Widely distributed from the middle and lower Zambezi south to the Phongolo system. Larger specimens generally occur in lowveld rivers (below 600 m altitude).
Biology and Ecology Favours flowing waters of perennial rivers. Uncommon in dams. Feeds on a wide variety of food items, primarily algae and aquatic insect larvae; also takes small fishes, snails, freshwater mussels and drifting organisms such as beetles and ants. Breeds in spring and summer, migrating upstream in rain-swollen rivers to spawn in rapids. Males mature at a smaller size (70 mm FL) than females (280 mm FL); females grow larger and live longer. Occurs together with the smallscale yellowfish in many Transvaal rivers.
Uses A minor angling species because of its relatively small size.

UPPER ZAMBEZI YELLOWFISH

Bo-Zambesi-geelvis
Barbus codringtonii Boulenger, 1908

Description D iii–iv, 9–10; A iii, 5. Scales large, 29–32 in lateral line, 12 around caudal peduncle. Primary dorsal ray flexible, dorsal fin relatively tall. Lips variable, frequently thickened (rubberlips); 2 pairs of barbels. Attains 390 mm TL, 3,2 kg.
Distribution Okavango and upper Zambezi systems.
Note Very similar to the largescale yellowfish and may represent the same species.

Genus *Varicorhinus* Rüppel, 1836
CHISELMOUTHS

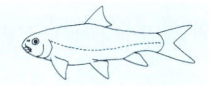

Chiselmouths are very similar to yellowfishes, but have a specialised wide, straight, inferior mouth with a sharp, horny lower lip. Certain yellowfish may develop a similar mouth form but chiselmouths only have a "chisel"-like mouth, which is used for scraping algae and associated growths from the surface of smooth rocks and plants. Scales are longitudinally striated and the primary dorsal ray is flexible. Three species occur in southern Africa.

KEY TO SPECIES

1a 35–41 scales in lateral line, 14 around caudal peduncle ....*V. nelspruitensis* (p. 174)
1b 28–30 scales in lateral line, 12 around caudal peduncle 2
2a 1 pair short barbels, colour demarcated dark above, light below..*V. pungweensis* (p. 175)
2b 2 pairs short barbels, not markedly colour demarcated...*V. nasutus* (p. 174)

SHORTSNOUT CHISELMOUTH

Kortsnoet-beitelbek
Varicorhinus nasutus Gilchrist & Thompson, 1911

Description D iv, 9–10; A iii, 5. Scales longitudinally striated, 28–30 in lateral line, 12 around caudal peduncle. Dorsal fin origin in front of origin of pelvics. Snout short and pointed, mouth inferior, wide with short horny edge to lower jaws; two pairs of short barbels. Silvery or golden olive with a dark spot on caudal peduncle. Attains about 400 mm SL, 3 kg. Zimbabwe angling record 1,95 kg.
Distribution Middle and lower Zambezi, including the Gairezi tributary; Pungwe River in Mozambique.
Biology and Ecology Inhabits rocky reaches of fast-flowing rivers. Feeds on algae and aquatic insects from rocks and other submerged surfaces – including hippos – but also takes drifting food items.
Note Very similar to and sometimes considered to be a form of the largescale yellowfish. It differs superficially in having a shorter snout and generally shorter barbels.

INCOMATI CHISELMOUTH

Inkomati-beitelbek
Varicorhinus nelspruitensis Gilchrist & Thompson, 1911

Description D iv, 8–9; A iii, 5. Scales longitudinally striated, 35–41 in lateral line, 14 (13–16) around caudal peduncle. Primary dorsal ray flexible, dorsal origin in advance of origin of pelvics. Head broad, convex;

BARBS, YELLOWFISHES, LABEOS

INCOMATI CHISELMOUTH (cont.)

mouth wide, inferior, with a straight, horny-edged lower jaw and a single pair of short, flattened barbels. Both sexes develop small white tubercles on head, especially on cheeks and snout, scales and anal fin. Dark olive above, light olive yellow to creamy white below. Attains 320 mm TL.
Distribution Escarpment streams of the Incomati and Phongolo systems, Transvaal and Natal.
Biology and Ecology Favours cool rocky flowing-water habitats. Occurs in schools of up to 50–100 fishes. Scrapes "aufwuchs" and benthic invertebrates from rocks. Breeds in summer.
Uses Occasionally caught by anglers.

PUNGWE CHISELMOUTH

Pungwe-beitelbek
Varicorhinus pungweensis Jubb, 1959

Description D iv, 9–10; A iii, 5. Scales longitudinally striated, 28–30 in lateral line, 12 around caudal peduncle. Primary dorsal ray flexible; origin of dorsal in advance of pelvics. Mouth inferior, wide, with horny scraping lower lip and one pair of very short barbels. Dark olive above,

golden yellow-cream below. Juveniles are grey above, silvery on the sides with a black spot at end of caudal peduncle. Males with prominent white tubercles on the snout, cheeks and scales. Attains 180 mm SL.
Distribution Pungwe-Buzi rivers in Zimbabwe and Mozambique; also the Ruo, tributary to the lower Shire (Zambezi) in Malawi.
Biology and Ecology Favours rocky rapids of cool, clear mountain streams. Scrapes algae and insects from the rocks. Breeds in spring–summer, young found in deep pools below rapids.
Uses Occasionally caught by anglers and subsistence fishermen.

Genus *Labeo* Cuvier, 1817
LABEOS or MUDFISHES

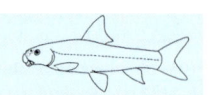

The large genus *Labeo* is widely distributed in Africa and south-east Asia. In Africa there are at least 80 species, most growing to more than 150 mm SL. Labeos are specialised feeders on algae, "aufwuchs" and detritus from the substratum, and have large inferior mouths with well-developed complex lips. They have grinding teeth in the pharynx and a very long, coiled intestine. Most labeos are strong swimmers, frequently adapted for flowing waters. Labeos migrate *en masse* upstream to breed and some have been observed climbing exposed rocky barriers, clinging by means of their mouths and pectoral fins.

KEY TO SPECIES

1a Lateral line scales 43 or more 2
1b Lateral line scales fewer than 43 5
2a Lateral line scales 50 or more 3
2b Lateral line scales 43–50 4
3a Lateral line scales 80 or more .... *L. seeberi* (p. 179)
3b Lateral line scales 53–68 .... *L. umbratus* (p. 177)
4a Dorsal fin branched rays 9 .... *L. rubromaculatus* (p. 179)
4b Dorsal fin branched rays 10–11 .... *L. capensis* (p. 178)
5a Head length about equal to body depth 6
5b Head length clearly less than body depth 7
6a Lateral line scales 34–37, caudal peduncle 14 (12–16), lateral line to dorsal fin 5 rows, dorsal rays iii, 9 (10) .... *L. cylindricus* (p. 184)
6b Lateral line scales 37–38, caudal peduncle 16, lateral line to dorsal fin 5 rows, dorsal rays iii, 10 .... *L. ansorgii* (p. 186)
6c Lateral line scales 38–41, caudal peduncle 18 (17–21), lateral line to dorsal fin 6 rows, dorsal rays iii, 9–10 .... *L. molybdinus* (p. 185)
7a Dorsal rays iii, 9 (10), lateral line scales 40–43, caudal peduncle 18–22 .... *L. ruddi* (p. 182)
7b Dorsal rays iii, 10 or more, lateral line scales 34–40 8
8a Mouth relatively small, lips without transverse plicae, dorsal fin branched rays 11–13, red tubercles on snout 9

BARBS, YELLOWFISHES, LABEOS 177

8b Mouth relatively large, lips with transverse plicae, dorsal fin branched rays 10–11, snout without red tubercles 10
9a Dorsal fin extended, hind edge convex .... *L. altivelis* (p. 180)
9b Dorsal fin relatively low, hind edge concave .... *L. rosae* (p. 181)
10a Dorsal fin hind edge concave .... *L. lunatus* (p. 186)
10b Dorsal fin hind edge straight or convex .... *L. congoro* (p. 183)

LABEO UMBRATUS GROUP

This group comprises four species restricted in distribution to the Orange basin and adjacent river systems. All have relatively small scales, especially *Labeo seeberi*. All tolerate relatively low oxygen concentrations and thrive in dams. Possibly more closely related to Asian labeos than to other African species.

MOGGEL

Moggel
Labeo umbratus (A. Smith, 1841)

Description D iii–iv, 9 (8–10); A iii, 5. Scales small, 53–68 in lateral line, 26–34 around caudal peduncle. Head rounded and fleshy; mouth small, subterminal or inferior, lips variable, with 2 small barbels. Greyish with iridescent pink and cream mottling, off-white below. Attains 500 mm TL. SA angling record 2,853 kg.

Distribution Orange-Vaal system as well as the Gourits, Gamtoos, Sundays, Great Fish and Bushmans systems of the south and south-east Cape coastal regions. Has been translocated to the Keiskamma and Buffalo systems in the eastern Cape as well as the Olifants-Limpopo in the Transvaal.

Biology and Ecology Prefers standing or gently flowing water and thrives in shallow impoundments and farm dams. Feeds on soft sediments and detritus. Breeds after rains in summer, migrating upstream to suitable spawning sites over flooded grassy banks of rivers or within shallow rocky stretches. Fecundity is very high, large females producing as many as 250 000 small eggs. The sticky eggs attach to grass or rocks, hatching after about 40 hours. Newly hatched larvae repeatedly swim to the water surface and are carried by the current into the stream and deeper water. Growth is rapid and the young fish reach about 100 mm SL after a year. After 2–3 years males mature from about 150 mm SL or larger and females at about 250 mm SL. Ages of 5 or 6 years may be attained.

Uses Commercial and subsistence fisheries, especially in dams. Occasional angling species. Used in aquaculture and physiological research.

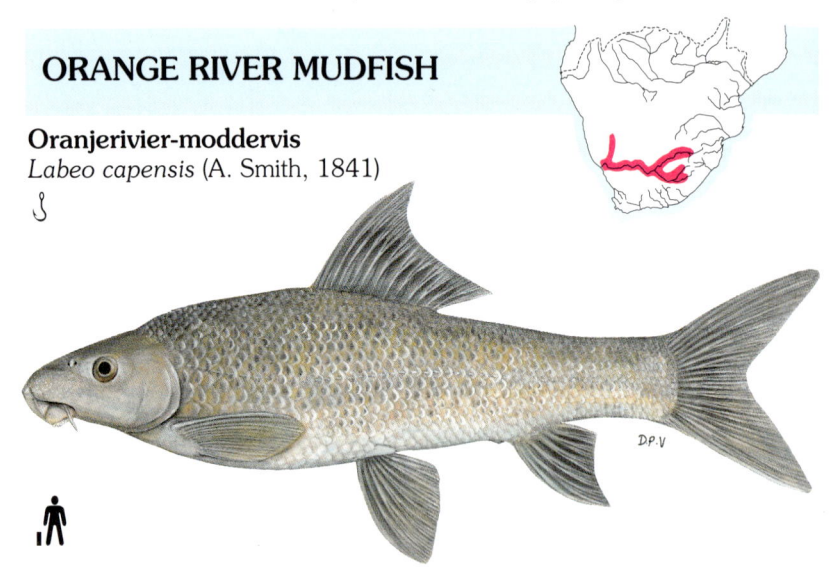

ORANGE RIVER MUDFISH

Oranjerivier-moddervis
Labeo capensis (A. Smith, 1841)

Description D iii, 10–11; A iii, 5. Scales 42–50 in lateral line, 20–22 around caudal peduncle. Fins large and pointed. Head depressed; mouth with papillose outer lips, 2 pairs of slender barbels. Juveniles are slender, adults become deeper bodied with the nape rising steeply behind the head. Smaller specimens silvery grey with white below; adults darker grey, becoming very dark bluish black when spawning. Attains 500 mm TL. SA angling record 3,83 kg.

Distribution Orange-Vaal system.

Biology and Ecology Prefers running waters of large rivers and also does well in large impoundments. Grazes from firm surfaces of rocks and plants. Breeds in summer, gathering in large numbers in shallow rocky rapids where the eggs are laid. Larvae hatch after 3–4 days. Growth is fairly rapid and the young fish reach 80–90 mm SL after a year, maturing from about 220 mm SL (males) to 240 mm SL (females). Ages of 8 or 9 years may be attained.

Uses Occasional angling species.

TUGELA LABEO

Tugela-moddervis
Labeo rubromaculatus Gilchrist & Thompson, 1913

Description D iv, 9–10; A iii, 5. Scales 42–48 in lateral line, 20–24 around caudal peduncle, small and embedded along back in front of dorsal fin and on belly and chest. Head depressed, mouth ventral with papillose outer lips, 2 pairs of short barbels. Juveniles are slender, in larger specimens the nape rises. Juveniles silvery white, adults olive grey with golden brown tinge to scales. Attains 500 mm SL, in excess of 2,7 kg. SA angling record 1,95 kg.

Distribution Widespread in the Tugela system, Natal.

Biology and Ecology Prefers deep pools and slow-flowing river stretches but does occur in rocky rapids. Feeds on green algae, diatoms and detritus. Shoals migrate upstream in spring and summer to breed. Large numbers of small eggs are laid and young are found in shallow backwaters.

Uses Angling. Could be exploited from dams.

CLANWILLIAM SANDFISH

Clanwilliam-sandvis
Labeo seeberi Gilchrist & Thompson, 1911

Description D iv, 9–10; A iii, 5. Scales minute, 77–90 in lateral line, 36–50 around caudal peduncle. Predorsal back scales and those on belly and chest reduced and embedded. Body slender, caudal peduncle nar-

CLANWILLIAM SANDFISH (cont.)

row. Head smooth, snout subequal to postorbit, mouth with well-developed papillose lips, a single pair of barbels. Olive grey with golden tinge, white below. Attains 355 mm SL. SA angling record 0,269 kg.
Distribution Clanwilliam Olifants system, western Cape.
Biology and Ecology Lives in the mainstream and larger tributaries, favours pools and deep runs of the river. Feeds on algae, detritus and small invertebrates by grazing off rocks as well as grubbing in soft sediments. In the clear water of the Olifants this species is frequently observed as silvery flashes as it rolls and twists when feeding. Migrates upstream in masses during spring and summer for breeding.
Uses Occasionally caught by anglers.
Conservation Rare. Numbers have declined due to dams blocking breeding migrations, reduced water flow and impact of introduced fishes.

LABEO NILOTICUS GROUP

This group includes about nine species of small-mouthed labeos, with small tubercles on the snout and generally pale pigmentation. There are three closely related species in southern Africa from east coastal tropical rivers.

MANYAME LABEO

Manyame-moddervis
Labeo altivelis Peters, 1852

Description D iii, 11–13; A iii, 5. Scales 36–39 in lateral line, 16–18 around caudal peduncle. Body relatively deep and compressed; dorsal fin usually very large, with extended rays. Snout with red tubercles, mouth subterminal, lips papillose, a single pair of short barbels. Juveniles silvery with large black spot on caudal peduncle. Adult colour variable but

BARBS, YELLOWFISHES, LABEOS

MANYAME LABEO (cont.)

often very attractive, with bright green base, iridescent pinkish scales, and a bright green band on the body behind the gill cover; silvery white below, fins deep bluish grey. Attains 400 mm TL, about 3,6 kg. Zimbabwean angling record 3,062 kg, Malawi 0,52 kg.

Distribution Middle and lower Zambezi, Pungwe, Buzi and Save systems in Mozambique. Also Zambian Zaire system (Chambeshi–Bangweulu–Luapula).

Biology and Ecology Prefers large rivers but is also found in large lakes and dams. Grazes on algae and "aufwuchs" from rocks. In summer after the onset of rains migrates upstream into tributaries to breed. Lives for up to 9 years.

Uses An important gill-net subsistence fishery target in the middle and lower Zambezi areas. Previously formed part of a large fishery (now collapsed from over-exploitation) in the Luapula, where migrating fish were harvested at barriers, the ripe eggs being processed in a form of caviare. In Zimbabwe this species is an angling and spearfishing target.

REDNOSE LABEO

Rooineus-moddervis
Labeo rosae Steindachner, 1894

Description D iii, 11–12; A iii, 5. Scales 37–40 in lateral line, 16–20 around caudal peduncle. Moderately deep bodied and compressed; dorsal fin with concave hind edge. Head small, mouth with papillose lips, a single pair of short barbels. Colour variable, base colour golden green with silvery pink scales; eye reddish above, snout with red tubercles. Juveniles are

REDNOSE LABEO (cont.)

silvery with a black caudal peduncle spot. Attains 410 mm TL, about 3 kg. SA angling record 3,025 kg.
Distribution Lowveld reaches of the Limpopo, Incomati and Phongolo systems.
Biology and Ecology Prefers sandy stretches of larger perennial and intermittent rivers. Feeds on detritus, algae and small invertebrates. An active fish, leaping at barriers when migrating upstream in swollen rivers to breed in summer. Attains sexual maturity at about 150 mm TL.
Uses An angling species, taken with dough-baited bottom-set line.

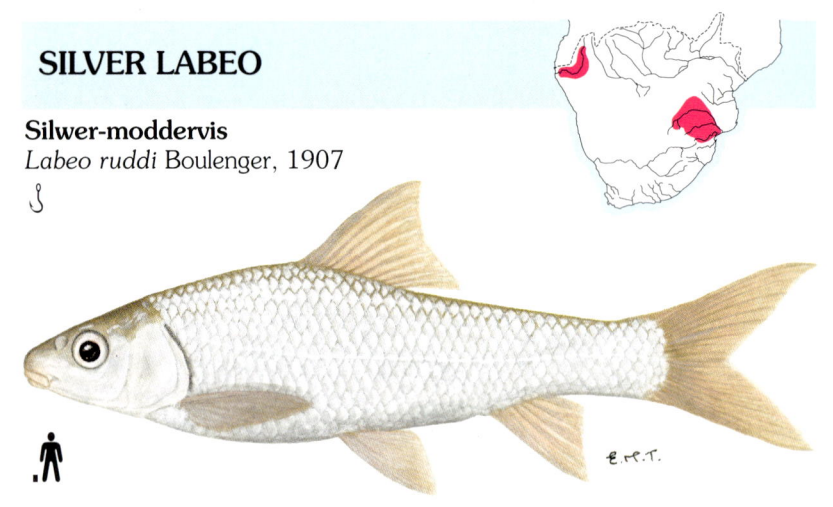

SILVER LABEO

Silwer-moddervis
Labeo ruddi Boulenger, 1907

Description D iii, 9–10; A iii, 5. Scales 40–44 in lateral line, 18–22 around caudal peduncle. Slender bodied, caudal peduncle longer than deep, fins short. Mouth small, lips thin with small papillae, a single pair of short barbels sometimes present. Snout usually without tubercles, if present small and grey or white in colour. Usually plain silvery, juveniles

with a black spot on caudal peduncle. Attains about 300 mm SL, about 1,0 kg. SA angling record 0,92 kg; Zimbabwe 0,474 kg.
Distribution Warmer lowveld reaches of the Limpopo and Incomati systems; also in the Cunene River.

Biology and Ecology Prefers quiet or standing waters of larger rivers. Deep, standing pools with a muddy substrate are typical habitat. Feeds on organic sediments. Moves up rain-swollen rivers to breed.
Uses Occasional angling species.

LABEO COUBIE GROUP

Large labeos widely distributed in Africa, inhabiting rocky, swiftly flowing rivers. About eight species in this group, one from southern Africa.

PURPLE LABEO

Rooiskub-moddervis (Perslyf-moddervis)
Labeo congoro Peters, 1852

Description D iv, 10 (11–12); A iii, 5. Scales 38–40 in lateral line, 16–18 around caudal peduncle. Deep-bodied with a deep caudal peduncle; dorsal fin high, with a straight or convex hind edge. Mouth large and fleshy, with well-developed papillose lips; snout with tubercles. Colour usually dark greenish grey with a purple sheen and a reddish centre to the scales, fins usually dusky black. Attains 415 mm SL, about 7 kg. SA angling record 3,407 kg, Zimbabwe 4,308 kg, Malawi 1,05 kg.
Distribution Warmer lowveld reaches of the middle and lower Zambezi system and east coastal rivers south to the Phongolo system.
Biology and Ecology Inhabits strong-flowing rocky stretches of larg-

er perennial rivers. Largely disappeared from Lake Kariba. Grazes algae and "aufwuchs" from rocks and firm surfaces including the backs of hippos, leaving characteristic tracks. Migrates upstream in swollen rivers to breed.

Uses Caught by subsistence fishermen, previously important in the Kariba area. Regarded by some as an excellent angling species on account of its strong fighting qualities.

LABEO FORSKAHLII GROUP

These are slender, streamlined fishes from fast-flowing waters. They have large fleshy snouts frequently covered in rough star-shaped tubercles and the anus is placed well forward of the anal fin. Probably the largest group of African labeos, with four species in southern Africa.

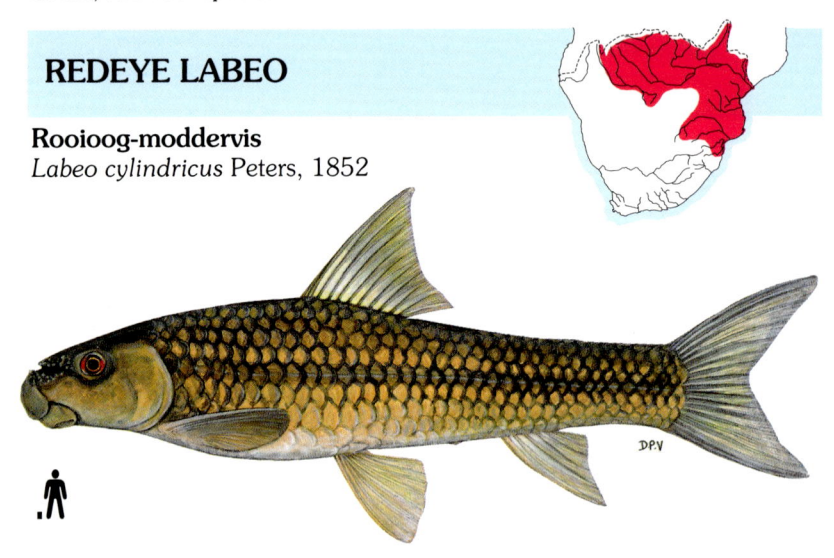

REDEYE LABEO

Rooioog-moddervis
Labeo cylindricus Peters, 1852

Description D iii, 9–10; A iii, 5. Scales 34–37 in lateral line, 14 (12–16) around caudal peduncle, 5 rows between lateral line and dorsal fin. Body cylindrical, head with a prominent stepped snout, usually with rough star-shaped tubercles. Mouth large; outer lips fleshy, inner rims with a horny sharp edge, lower lip papillose; a single pair of barbels. Gill openings restricted to sides of head. Olive to yellow-green with a darker body band, larger specimens usually darker olive grey; eye distinctively red above. Attains 230 mm SL, about 0,9 kg.

Distribution Widespread from East African rivers south through the Zambezi system and east coastal drainages to the Phongolo system in northern Natal. Also reported from the Zambian Zaire and the Lualaba (Zaire basin).

Biology and Ecology Favours

clear, running waters in rocky habitats of small and large rivers, also found in lakes and dams over rocky areas. Occurs in shoals and feeds by grazing algae and "aufwuchs" from the surface of rocks, tree trunks and other firm surfaces, leaving characteristic grazing tracks. Migrates upstream in masses to breed, using the mouth and broad pectoral fins to climb damp surfaces of barrier rocks and weirs.

Uses A useful algal grazer in aquariums. One report suggests that this species "cleans" exposed fungal infections in other fishes.

LEADEN LABEO

Loodvis
Labeo molybdinus Du Plessis, 1963

Description D iii, 9–10; A ii–iii, 5. Scales 38–41 in lateral line, 17–21 around caudal peduncle, 6 rows between lateral line and dorsal fin. Body shape fusiform, snout usually without tubercles. Mouth large, lips fleshy, lower lip papillose, a single pair of small barbels. Greyish brown with iridescent green on upper scales, lighter below. Attains 380 mm SL.- SA angling record 1,685 kg.
Distribution In rivers and lakes from the middle and lower Zambezi south to the Tugela system in Natal, including Lake Sibaya.
Biology and Ecology Appears more suited to deeper waters than the redeye labeo but they do occur together. Favours deep pools, but will enter rapids; grazes algae and "aufwuchs" from firm surfaces. Migrates upstream in rain-swollen rivers to breed.
Uses Occasional angling species; caught by subsistence fishermen.

UPPER ZAMBEZI LABEO

Bo-Zambezi-moddervis
Labeo lunatus Jubb, 1963

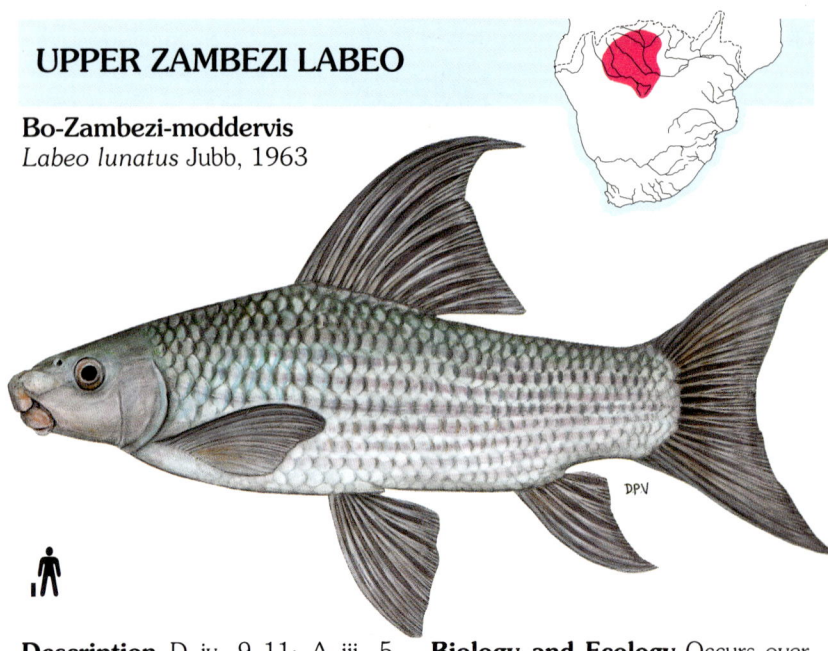

Description D iv, 9–11; A iii, 5. Scales 37–40 in lateral line, 16–20 around caudal peduncle. Body compressed and fusiform, caudal peduncle deep; dorsal fin high and crescentic. Snout with weak tubercles, mouth with fleshy papillose outer lips, sharp-edged horny inner rims. Greenish or silvery grey, scale bases dark grey forming parallel lines along body, fin membranes sooty. Attains 400 mm SL, 2,5 kg.
Distribution Upper Zambezi and Okavango rivers.

Biology and Ecology Occurs over rocks in mainstream and in large soft-bottomed floodplain lagoons. Grazes algae and "aufwuchs" as well as detritus. A shoaling species, breeding in summer, possibly in flooded marginal habitats, as the young fish are caught in large numbers in fish-weirs set across floodwaters receding from floodplains.
Uses Caught by subsistence fishermen in floodplain areas such as the Okavango Delta.

CUNENE LABEO

Kunene-moddervis
Labeo ansorgii Boulenger, 1907

Description D iv, 10; A iii, 5. Scales 35–40 in lateral line, 16–18 around caudal peduncle, 6 from lateral line to dorsal fin. Similar in form to the red-

CUNENE LABEO (cont.)

eye labeo, but slightly more compressed, fins more pointed, scales smaller and eyes larger. Snout with star-shaped tubercles, lips fleshy, lower lip papillose, a single pair of short, flattened barbels. Olive to brown, lighter below, fins sooty. Attains 240 mm SL.
Distribution Cunene and Quanza systems, Angola and Namibia.
Biology and Ecology Prefers flowing water in rocky habitats.

INTRODUCED CYPRINIDS

Several species of European and Asian cyprinids have been introduced successfully into southern Africa. The best known and most widely introduced of these is the common carp. The other species are restricted in distribution in natural waters. Most of them are easily identified on the basis of fin and body features as they are quite different from indigenous species.

KEY TO SPECIES

1a Dorsal and anal fin with strong, serrated leading spine 2
1b Dorsal and anal fin without spine 3
2a Mouth with 2 pairs of barbels, 35–39 lateral line scales (when scales present) .... ***Cyprinus carpio* (p. 188)**

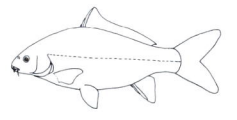

2b Mouth without barbels, 25–31 lateral line scales . ***Carassius auratus* (p. 189)**

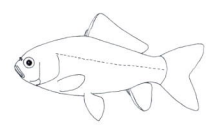

188 BARBS, YELLOWFISHES, LABEOS

3a Scales moderate sized, 37–42 in lateral line..
....***Ctenopharyngodon idella*** (p. 190)

3b Scales minute, 95–120 in lateral line 4
4a Body compressed, eyes low-set, visible from below.................................
....***Hypophthalmichthys molitrix*** (p. 191)

4b Body robust, ovoid; eyes small, not visible from below...***Tinca tinca*** (p. 192)

CARP

Karp
Cyprinus carpio Linnaeus, 1758

Description D III, 17–22; A II–III, 4–5. Scales (when present) 35–39 in lateral line, 14 around caudal peduncle. Three distinct forms are found, those with normal scales (fullscale carp), partly naked with large, scattered scales (mirror carp), and without scales (leather carp). Deep-bodied with a long-based dorsal fin, primary ray of dorsal and anal fins a bony serrated spine. Mouth protrusible, with a single pair of barbels, pharyngeal teeth in 3 rows (1,1,3–3,1,1). Colour variable from olive brown to rich brazen gold, fins dark grey. Attains a large size. World angling record 34,35 kg (France); SA angling record 21,98 kg, Zimbabwe 24,381 kg.

Distribution Widespread throughout southern Africa, but absent from mountain areas and restricted in the warmer tropical areas such as the lowveld. Natural distribution includes Central Asia to the Black Sea and the Danube in Europe. Carp are now established in many countries around the world.

History Early writings indicate that carp were introduced into South Africa in the 1700s, and several importations are reported from the 1800s. The Aischgrund strain was imported in 1955. The Chinese are reputed to have cultured carp for 2 400 years, and the Romans were the first to culture carp in Europe.

Biology and Ecology Hardy and tolerant of a wide variety of conditions but generally favours large water bodies with slow-flowing or standing water and soft bottom sediments. Thrives in farm dams and large turbid rivers. Omnivorous, taking a wide range of plant and animal matter mainly by grubbing in sediments. Breeds in spring and summer, laying sticky eggs in shallow vegetation. Large females are reported to lay in excess of a million eggs. Larvae hatch after 4–8 days and growth is rapid.

Uses A valued aquaculture and angling species. Considered a pest by conservation authorities because of its destructive feeding habits.

GOLDFISH

Goudvis
Carassius auratus (Linnaeus, 1758)

Description D II, 14–20; A II, 5. Scales radiately striated, 26–28 in lateral line, 14–16 around caudal peduncle. Body moderately deep, stocky; dorsal fin long-based, primary ray of dorsal and anal fin bony and serrated. Mouth small, terminal, no barbels. Body shape and fin form extremely varied due to extensive development of domestic varieties. Colour equally variable, wild colour metallic olive-bronze; orange or red with white, black and yellow are the most common domestic colours. Attains about 250 mm SL.

Distribution Feral populations are reported from a few widely scattered localities mostly around larger towns. Known sites include the Cape Flats area, Breë River near Robertson, Baakens River (Port Elizabeth), Grahamstown, Aapies River (Pretoria district), Umsinduzi River (Pietermaritzburg) and the Chinhoyi Caves, Zimbabwe. Natural range uncertain, probably the Far East.

Biology and Ecology Requires a quiet, weedy habitat (as in garden ponds). Omnivorous, feeding primarily on organic sediments, detritus and invertebrates. Lays eggs on submerged vegetation. Long-lived in captivity.

Uses Extremely popular ornamental fish in aquariums and garden ponds. Cultured commercially for the ornamental trade.

GRASS CARP

Graskarp
Ctenopharyngodon idella (Valenciennes, 1844)

Description D iii, 7–8; A iii, 8. Scales 37–42 in lateral line, 16 around caudal peduncle. Body subcylindrical; dorsal fin short, midway between tip of snout and end of caudal peduncle, origin slightly in front of pelvics. Head pointed, mouth terminal; eyes nearer tip of snout than hind margin of head, lateral in position. Body silvery, head and fins dark grey. A large species attaining more than a metre and 45 kg.

Distribution Umgeni above Nagle Dam and farm dams in Natal. Victoria Lake (Germiston) on a tributary of the Vaal, Transvaal. Native to China,

from large temperate rivers draining to the Pacific.
Biology and Ecology Prefers large, slow-flowing or standing water bodies with vegetation. Tolerant of a wide range of temperatures from 0° to 38° C, and salinities to as much as 10 parts per thousand. Feeds primarily on aquatic plants but also takes insects and other invertebrates. Breeds in flowing water of rivers rising in flood, the eggs and larvae floating in the water. Not known to breed in South African rivers. Reported to live for up to 50 years in China.
History First introduced from Malaysia in 1967 and again from Germany in 1975. Cultured and stocked from the Umgeni Hatchery into farm dams in Natal and Transvaal.
Uses Used for weed control in farm dams. Has angling and aquaculture potential. Experiments to produce sterile triploid stock are being carried out for stocking in other areas of southern Africa.

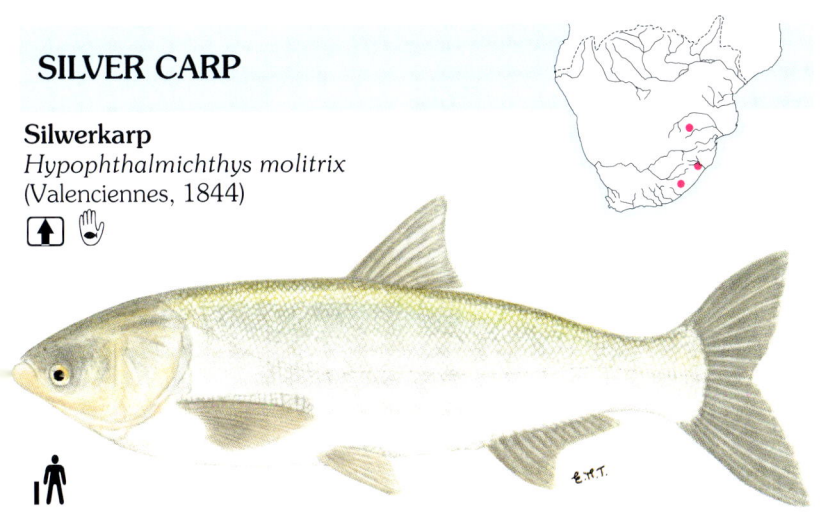

SILVER CARP

Silwerkarp
Hypophthalmichthys molitrix
(Valenciennes, 1844)

Description D iii, 7; A iii, 12. Scales minute, 110–115 in lateral line. Body club-shaped, pelvic fins in front of origin of dorsal. Large head, mouth small, upturned, eyes set low (below the level of the mouth). Gill rakers attached to each other to form a sieve; intestine extended. Attains 1 m TL.
Distribution Restricted to certain hatcheries in Natal, Transvaal and Transkei. Natural range includes the Amur and Yangtze rivers in China and Central Asia.
Biology and Ecology A phytoplankton feeder, requiring standing or slow-flowing conditions such as in impoundments or the backwaters of large rivers. In natural range migrates upstream to breed; eggs and larvae float downstream to floodplain zones. An active species well known for its habit of leaping clear of the water when disturbed.
History First introduced from Israel in 1975.
Uses An important aquaculture species in many places, not yet commercially cultured in southern Africa.

TENCH

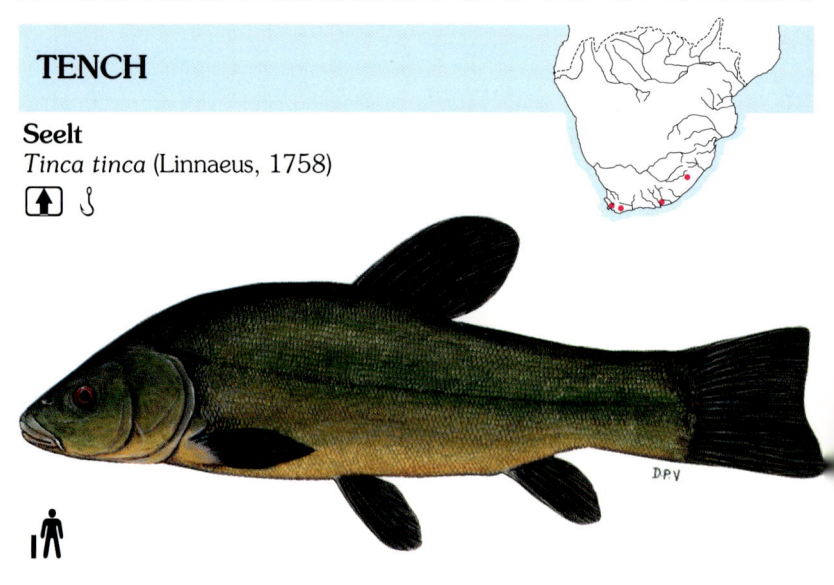

Seelt
Tinca tinca (Linnaeus, 1758)

Description D iii–iv, 8–9; A iii–iv, 6–7. Scales minute, 95–120 in lateral line. Body deep and thickset, fins rounded and fleshy. Second ray of the pelvic fins thickened in mature males. Mouth terminal, protrusible; a single pair of short barbels. Usually slippery on account of mucous secretion. Olive green or coppery brown to almost black, deep yellow underneath, fins black. Attains 640 mm SL, largest recorded in SA 5,791 kg. SA angling record 1,98 kg.
Distribution Established in Breë River and several isolated farm dams in south-west Cape, eastern Cape and Natal. Native distribution is Europe.

Biology and Ecology Prefers deep, well-vegetated water such as in vleis and swamps; tolerant of low oxygen saturations. Omnivorous, feeding from the bottom on a wide variety of invertebrates such as snails and insects. Breeds in shallow water among dense vegetation, laying numerous sticky eggs. After hatching the larvae remain attached to the plants for several days.
History Successfully introduced from England in 1910 after an attempted introduction from Scotland in 1896.
Uses Introduced for angling and later used as a fodder fish for bass. An important food fish in eastern Europe.

CHARACIN FAMILIES

The characins are a large order of strictly freshwater fishes from Africa and South and Central America. Previously they were considered to be most closely related to the cypriniform fishes (carp and their allies), but it is now understood that they are more closely related to the catfishes. Jaws and teeth are notable features of the characins; some, like the tigerfish, are famous – or, like the piranha, notorious – on this account. African characins include four families, nearly 40 genera and over 200 species. Three of the four families, with 12 species, occur in southern Africa.

FAMILY DISTICHODONTIDAE
Citharines

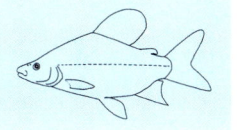

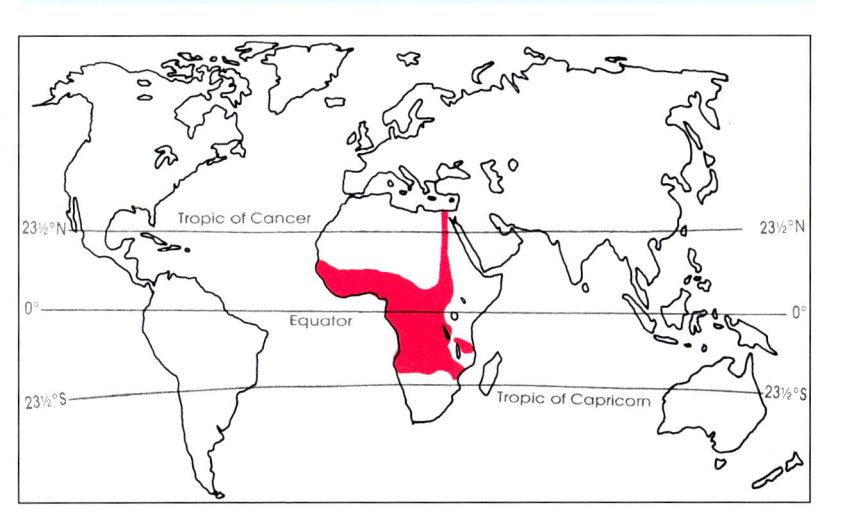

A diverse African family that includes about 17 genera and 90 species. The name "distichodont" refers to the characteristic two rows of teeth of these fishes. They have unusual square-shaped mouths, distinctive ctenoid scales, and many species are attractively marked with bars on the body. Three genera in southern African include comparatively large and very small species.

194 CITHARINES

KEY TO SPECIES

1a Dorsal fin with 23–27 rays, body deep, adults larger than 100 mm SL ....*(Distichodus)* 2
1b Dorsal fin with 12–15 rays, body slender, adults less than 100 mm SL....3
2a Snout extended, mouth terminal, head about 4 times in FL, juveniles with 6–7 dark vertical bars ....*Distichodus mossambicus* (p. 194)
2b Snout short, mouth inferior, head about 5 times in FL, juveniles with 12–16 dark vertical bars................................*Distichodus shenga* (p. 195)
3a Adipose fin present..4
3b Adipose fin absent..........................*Hemigrammocharax machadoi* (p. 196)
4a Body with 8–10 broad bars, lateral line complete, fins long, pectorals reach base of pelvics ....*Nannocharax macropterus* (p. 198)
4b Body with 16–22 bars, lateral line incomplete, fins short, pectorals not reaching base of pelvics ....*Hemigrammocharax multifasciatus* (p. 197)

Genus *Distichodus* Müller & Troschel, 1844

Easily identified on account of their deep compressed bodies, unusual "square" mouths, two even rows of teeth on each jaw, and the ctenoid scales which also cover the adipose fin and most of the caudal fin. A genus of about 20 species of moderately large fishes, two from southern Africa.

NKUPE

Nkupe
Distichodus mossambicus Peters, 1852

CITHARINES

Description D iv, 19–23; A iii–iv, 10–12. Scales ctenoid, 67–70 in lateral line. Body deep and compressed. Adipose fin with scales, caudal deeply forked, largely covered by scales. Head depressed, nape rising steeply with concave predorsal profile, mouth terminal, 2 rows of bicuspid teeth. Adults deep olive, almost black; juveniles silvery, with 6–7 broad vertical dark bars. Attains 570 mm SL. Zimbabwe angling record 7,269 kg, Malawi 5,47 kg.

Distribution Middle and lower Zambezi, Pungwe and Buzi systems.

Biology and Ecology Found only in the mainstream of larger rivers and even in Lake Kariba prefers more riverine habitats. Omnivorous, taking a wide variety of foods including insects, snails, small fish and aquatic plants. Breeds in summer, moving upstream to suitable sites.

Uses A valued, strong fighting angling species. Caught in subsistence fisheries.

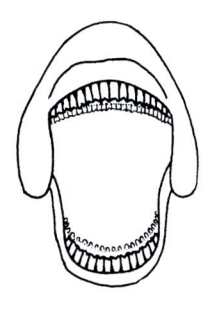

Dental arcade of nkupe

CHESSA

Chessa
Distichodus shenga Peters, 1852

Description D iv, 19–23; A iv, 10–12. Scales ctenoid, 67–70 in lateral line, adipose and caudal fins covered by scales. Lateral line straight. Body deep, compressed, nape rising steeply, with straight or convex pro-

file. Head small, pointed; mouth inferior, with 2 rows of bicuspid teeth. Adults silvery olive with sooty dorsal, anal and caudal fins; pectorals and pelvics yellowish; juveniles silvery, with 12–16 dark vertical bars (usually obscure) and a prominent dark spot at the base of the caudal fin. Attains 500 mm SL. Zimbabwe angling record 6,35 kg, Malawi 1,43 kg.
Distribution Middle and lower Zambezi, Pungwe and Buzi rivers.
Biology and Ecology Favours large rivers, found in shoals over both rock and sand. Omnivorous, prefers algae and plant matter to snails, shrimps and small fish. Breeds in summer during the rainy period, moving upstream to suitable spawning sites.
Uses A valued angling species and good fighter for light tackle. Taken in subsistence fisheries.

Genus *Hemigrammocharax* Pellegrin, 1923

Small, slender fishes with prominent vertical bars along the body and a caudal "eye" spot. The only obvious difference between this and the next genus is that the lateral line is complete in *Nannocharax* and incomplete in *Hemigrammocharax*.

DWARF CITHARINE

Dwerg-sitarien
Hemigrammocharax machadoi Poll, 1967

Description D iii, 10–11; A iii, 8. Scales ctenoid, 34–36 in lateral series, 12 around caudal peduncle. Lateral line incomplete, limited to 8 or 9 scales behind head. Body slender, fins short, no adipose fin. Mouth terminal, 10 slender bicuspid teeth in upper and lower jaws. Translucent, light olive, silvery below, 12–16 irregular bars and a prominent dark "eye" spot at base of caudal fin, caudal fin with 2 or 3 bands, pelvic and anal fins sooty. Males darken

CITHARINES 197

in breeding dress. A small species, attains about 40 mm SL.
Distribution Cunene, Okavango, upper Zambezi and Kafue systems, recently taken from the middle Zambezi above Kariba.
Biology and Ecology Lives in clear, quiet, well-vegetated habitats; common on floodplains and in the Okavango Delta. Feeds by picking periphyton and tiny invertebrates from the stems and leaves of water plants. Breeds in summer.
Uses Attractive and peaceful in aquariums.

MULTIBAR CITHARINE

Veelbalk-sitarien
Hemigrammocharax multifasciatus Boulenger, 1923

Description D iii, 10–12; A iii, 8–9. Scales ctenoid, 40–44 in lateral line, 16 around caudal peduncle. Lateral line incomplete. Body slender, compressed. Head pointed, mouth terminal, eye relatively large. Translucent light olive, 16–25 dark bars and a prominent spot at base of caudal fin. Attains about 45 mm SL.
Distribution Cunene, Okavango, upper Zambezi and Kafue systems. Also in the Zambian Zaire system.
Biology and Ecology Prefers vegetated margins of rivers and oxbow lagoons or shallow lakes. Picks small invertebrates and epiphyton from stems of plants and roots. Breeds in summer.
Uses Attractive and peaceful in aquariums.

Genus *Nannocharax* Günther, 1867

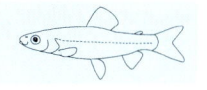

Similar to *Hemigrammocharax*, except that the lateral line is complete. One species in our area.

BROADBAR CITHARINE

Breëbalk-sitarien
Nannocharax macropterus Pellegrin, 1925

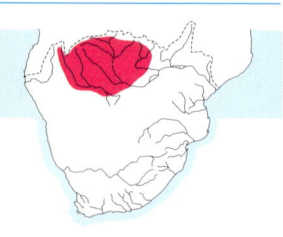

Description D iii, 9–11; A ii, 8. Lateral line complete, scales 40–42, 12 around caudal peduncle. Body slender, fins long and pointed, the pectorals reaching the pelvics, adipose fin present. Head pointed, eyes large, mouth small, terminal. Translucent light olive above, white below, with 8 or 9 large dark blotches merging to form a broad lateral band. Attains 60 mm SL.

Distribution Okavango, upper Zambezi and Kafue, as well as the Kasai (Zaire system).

Biology and Ecology Found in marginal vegetation of large rivers, in flowing water. Picks small insects and other invertebrates from plant surfaces.

Uses Not sufficiently common for aquarium trade.

FAMILY CHARACIDAE
Characins

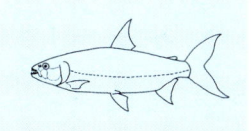

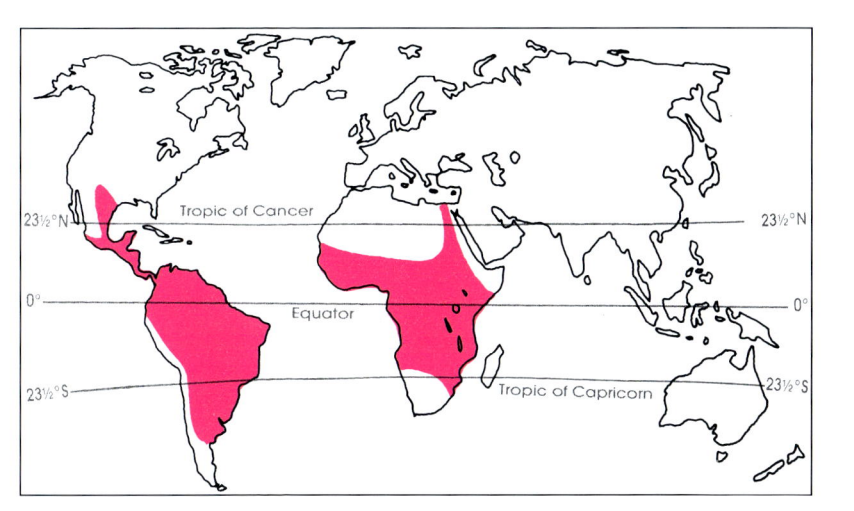

This large family of African and South American freshwater fishes includes many well-known species such as the small, attractive neon tetras and the tigerfishes. The family name is derived from classical Greek meaning "pointed stake" and probably refers to the sharp-pointed teeth of many species. Characins are easily distinguished from the similar shaped cyprinids by having sharp teeth on the jaws and a small adipose fin. Few are of economic importance; most are shiny shoaling species. There are 18 genera and over 100 species of African characins, confined to tropical waters; 5 genera and 6 species in our area.

KEY TO SPECIES

1a Teeth large, canine-like, separated by wide gaps, interlocking and visible when mouth is closed ....*Hydrocynus vittatus* (p. 206)

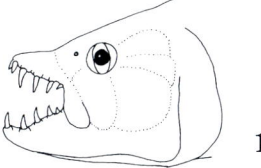

1b Teeth with 3 or more cusps, not visible when mouth is closed 2

2a Oblong black bar across caudal fin base...3
2b No oblong black bar across caudal fin base 4
3a No dark spot behind head; caudal peduncle longer than deep; 5 scales between lateral line and dorsal fin..
....*Brycinus lateralis* (p. 202)
3b Dark spot behind head; body deeper than head length; caudal peduncle deeper than long; 4 scales between lateral line and dorsal fin...................
....*Brycinus imberi* (p. 201)
4a Two small teeth inside outer row on lower jaw, dorsal fin with black tip .....
....*Micralestes acutidens* (p. 203)
4b No teeth inside outer row of lower jaw 5
5a Lateral line complete, black bar along base of anal fin............................
....*Rhabdalestes maunensis* (p. 204)

5b Lateral line incomplete, black bar from base onto anal fin ....
....*Hemigrammopetersius barnardi* (p. 205)

Alestiine characins

The next five species are generalised characins, typically with large eyes, bony cheeks, sharp-pointed multicuspid teeth, large silvery scales, short dorsal fin and long-based, sexually dimorphic anal fin. They are usually shoaling species with omnivorous feeding habits.

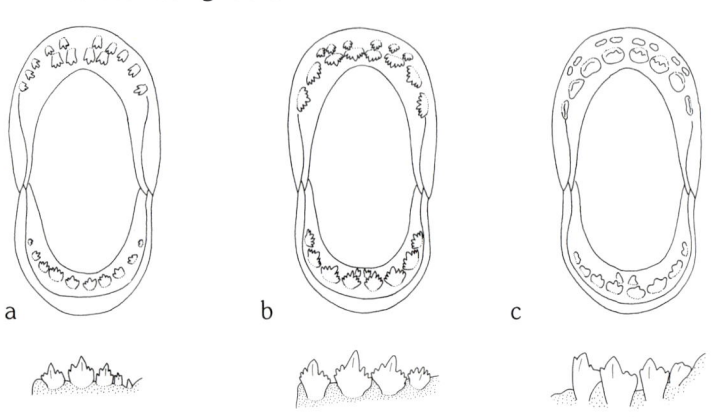

Dental arcade and teeth on lower left jaw of (a) *Rhabdalestes maunensis*, (b) *Micralestes acutidens*, (c) *Brycinus lateralis*.

Genus *Brycinus* Valenciennes, 1849

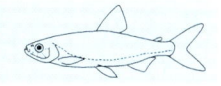

Small to moderate sized shoaling fishes, like miniature tigerfishes, that are swift swimmers and can be a nuisance to anglers, stripping bait from hooks. Frequently used as bait for tigerfish. About 30 species in Africa; 2 in our area.

IMBERI

Imberi
Brycinus imberi (Peters, 1852)

Description D ii, 8; A ii–iii, 14–16. Scales cycloid, radially striated, 23–29 in lateral line, 9–12 around caudal peduncle. Median rays of anal fin extended in males, giving a convex trailing edge to fin; females with straight or slightly concave trailing edge. Body deep, head shorter than body depth; mouth terminal, 2 rows of tricuspid (outer) or multicuspid (inner) teeth. Silvery with yellowish fins, especially the caudal; adipose fin orange, top half of eye orange. Black spot behind head and large dash on caudal base, both markings not always distinct in life. Attains about 180 mm FL; females usually larger than males. SA angling record 0,3 kg, Zimbabwe 0,3 kg, Malawi 0,13 kg.

Distribution East coast rivers from the Phongolo northwards to the Rufigi in Tanzania; absent from the upper Zambezi system. Also widespread in the Zaire system and coastal water bodies of West Africa.

Biology and Ecology Found in a wide variety of habitats including larger rivers and floodplain pans and lagoons. Feeds on aquatic and terrestrial invertebrates, various seeds and plant material as available. Breeds in summer, migrating to spawning sites after rains. Males mature at a smaller size (about 110 mm FL) than females (about 125 mm FL). Lives for up to 5 years. Main predator is the tigerfish.

Uses Bait for tigerfish.

STRIPED ROBBER

Streep-rower
Brycinus lateralis (Boulenger, 1900)

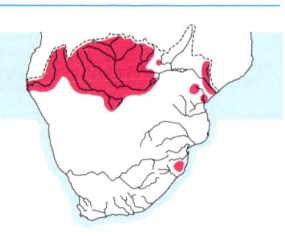

Description D ii, 8; A iii, 15–16. Scales cycloid, radially striate, 30–33 in lateral line, 10–14 around caudal peduncle. Body fusiform, leading rays of anal fin extended in males, forming a rounded edge (edge straight in immatures and females). Head about equal to body depth, mouth terminal, jaws each with 2 rows of sharp tricuspid teeth. Silvery, prominent black caudal dash surrounded by yellow, adipose fin yellow. Attains about 140 mm SL.
Distribution Zambezi system, Okavango, Cunene and Buzi rivers and the St Lucia catchment in Natal. Also known from the Luapula (Zaire system).
Biology and Ecology Shoals in clear, slow-flowing or quiet, well-vegetated waters. Feeds on small aquatic and terrestrial organisms. Moves upstream during rains, possibly to breed. Often found together with the dashtail and the threespot barb and the close similarity of these species suggests mimicry between them.
Uses Bait for tigerfish and largemouth bream. Caught in subsistence fisheries.

Genus *Micralestes* Boulenger, 1899

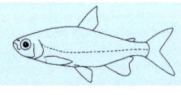

Small silvery characins with distinctive sharp multicuspid teeth, and a pair of teeth behind the outer row on the lower jaw. In Africa about 14 species, one from our area.

SILVER ROBBER

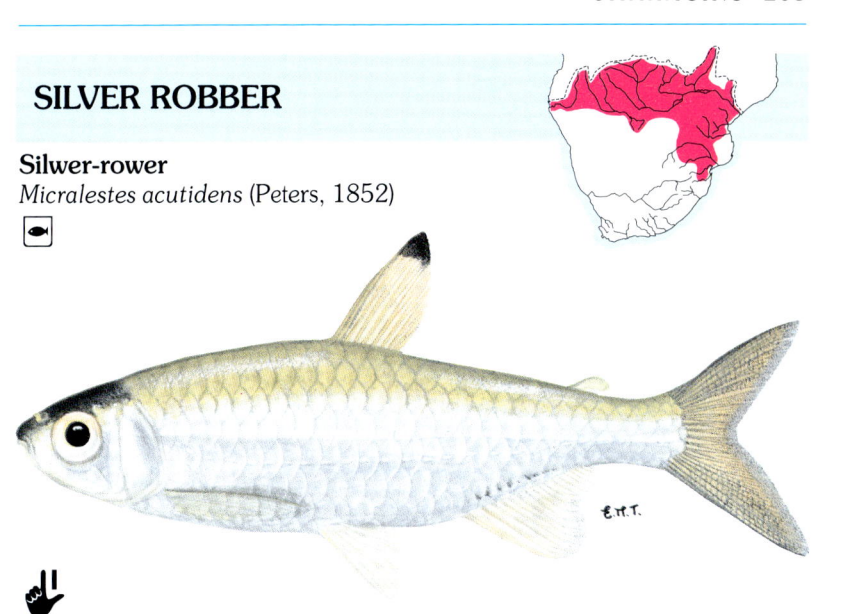

Silwer-rower
Micralestes acutidens (Peters, 1852)

Description D ii, 8; A iii, 14–16. Scales radiately striate, 23–28 in lateral line. Body compressed, fusiform; anal fin of males with expanded trailing edge, females have straight or slightly concave trailing edge. Upper jaw with 2 rows of sharp multicuspidate teeth, 4–6 in outer row, 8 in inner, lower jaw with 8 outer and 2 inner teeth. Silvery with a broad iridescent stripe along body (which preserves as a dark band), fins pale yellow or orange, dorsal fin with a distinctive black tip, anal and pelvic fins with white leading edge. Attains about 80 mm SL.
Distribution Cunene, Okavango, Zambezi and east coast rivers south to the Phongolo. Also widespread throughout the Zaire system.
Biology and Ecology Shoals in clear, flowing or standing, open water. Omnivorous, often feeding from surface waters on winged insects, also takes zooplankton. Mature after a year, lives for about 3 years. A partial spawner, fecundity is moderate, with usually fewer than 700 eggs per female. Shoals migrate upstream after first summer rains; breeds throughout the summer months.
Uses Attractive in larger aquariums. Used as a forage fish and as bait for tigerfish and pike.

Genus *Rhabdalestes* Hoedeman, 1951

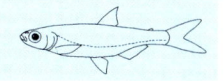

Small, slender characins with sharp multicuspid teeth, two rows in upper jaw, a single row in lower jaw. Leading rays of male anal fin thick and curved, dark bar along base of anal fin. Seven species, one in our area.

SLENDER ROBBER

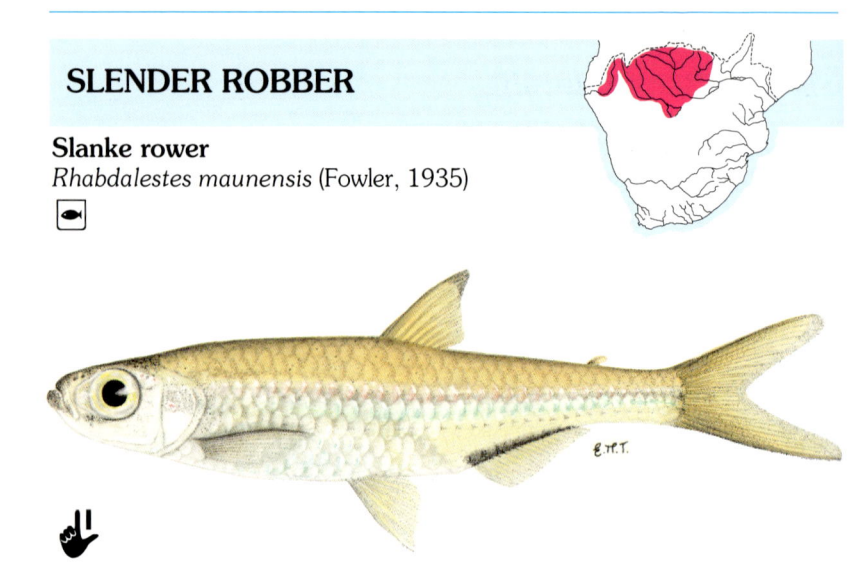

Slanke rower
Rhabdalestes maunensis (Fowler, 1935)

Description D ii, 7–9; A iii, 16–19. Scales in lateral series 33–36, 12–14 around caudal peduncle. Body compressed, more slender than other robbers; fins pointed, in males leading ray of anal fin expanded and recurved, females have a normal fin with a straight or slightly concave trailing edge. Teeth multicuspid, in a single row on both jaws; 6–8 on upper, 8 on lower. Translucent with silvery head and belly, a bluish green iridescent band extends along body, black band along the base of the anal fin is characteristic, adipose fin yellow, caudal fin yellow with black edge. Attains about 60 mm SL.
Distribution Cunene, Okavango, upper Zambezi and Kafue systems. A similar, possibly identical, species (*Rhabdalestes rhodesiensis*) occurs in the Zambian Zaire system (Lakes Bangweulu and Mweru, and Luapula River).
Biology and Ecology Shoals in shallow, vegetated marginal and floodplain habitats. Feeds on small aquatic insects and other invertebrates. A partial spawner, breeding during highwater periods.
Uses Attractive in aquariums.

Genus *Hemigrammopetersius* Pellegrin, 1926

Small African characins similar to *Rhabdalestes* but with an incomplete lateral line. Lower jaw projects beyond upper. Four species, one in our area.

BARNARD'S ROBBER

Barnard se rower
Hemigrammopetersius barnardi (Herre, 1936)

Description D iii, 7–8; A ii, 16–18. Lateral line incomplete, 7–9 tubuled scales, 28–32 scales in lateral series, 12 (rarely 13 or 14) around caudal peduncle. Body compressed, fusiform; in males leading ray of anal fin expanded and recurved, in females fin normal and trailing edge straight. Teeth tricuspid, in a single row on both jaws, 12 on upper, 6–8 on lower. Translucent olive, with silvery head and abdomen and an iridescent green stripe along body; dorsal and caudal fins sooty, with yellow base; a black band above anterior base of anal fin passes across midrays of anal fin. Attains 40 mm SL.

Distribution Lower Zambezi, Pungwe and Buzi systems. Also upper Shire and Lakes Malawi, Chilwa and Chiuta.

Biology and Ecology Shoals in marginal vegetation of rivers and lakes. Feeds on small insects and invertebrates.

Uses A potential aquarium species.

Genus *Hydrocynus* Cuvier, 1816

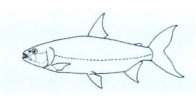

The name *Hydrocynus* means "water dog" and is an apt description for these active, brightly striped, streamlined fishes, with large, sharp, widely spaced, interlocking teeth. The limbs of the lower jaw are hinged together, allowing the gape to expand laterally when striking prey. Tigerfishes are large specialised predators regarded by many as the finest freshwater game fishes in the world. The goliath tigerfish (*Hydrocynus goliath*), found in the Zaire system, is reputed to reach up to 1,5 m length and 50 kg mass. Five species are currently recognised, one occurs in southern Africa.

TIGERFISH

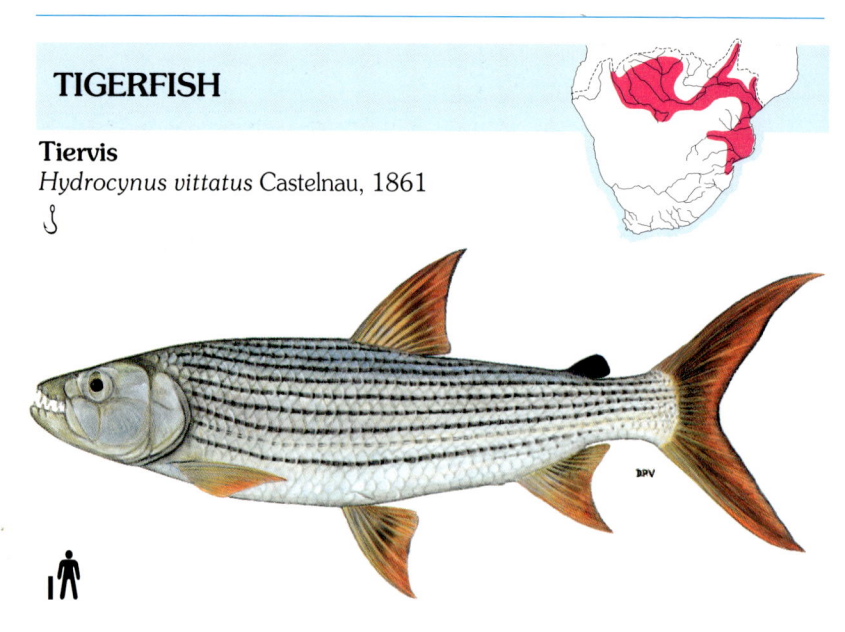

Tiervis
Hydrocynus vittatus Castelnau, 1861

Description D ii, 7–8; A iii, 10–13. Lateral line scales 43–48, 15–16 around caudal peduncle. Body fusiform, fins pointed, caudal deeply forked. Head large with bony cheeks and strong jaws, each with a series of 8 large, protruding, sharply pointed teeth; eyes with vertical adipose sleeves. Juveniles silvery, distinctive parallel stripes begin to show above a size of about 50 mm SL. Adult colour striking, body and head silvery, with bluish sheen on back and a series of parallel longitudinal black stripes; adipose fin black, caudal fin varies from yellow to blood red at full intensity, with black trailing edges; other fins also with yellow to red especially towards their bases; tip and trailing edge of dorsal black. Males and females similar in form, but females grow to above 700 mm FL, males only to about 500 mm FL. SA angling record 5,88 kg, Zimbabwe 15,507 kg, Malawi 7,03 kg.

Distribution Okavango, Zambezi and lowveld reaches of coastal systems south to the Phongolo. Notably absent from Cunene, Kafue, Lake Malawi and the upper Save-Runde. Also in the Zaire, Lake Tanganyika, Rufigi and large Nilo-Sudanian rivers in North and West Africa.

Biology and Ecology All but the largest form roving schools of like-sized fish; aptly described as voracious and fierce. Prefers warm, well-oxygenated water, mainly in larger rivers and lakes, tending to frequent the surface layers where it often falls prey to the swooping African fish eagle. Breeds during summer, adults migrating up- or downstream to suitable spawning sites along flooded river banks and lake shores. Fecundity is extremely high, as many as 780 000 ova in large females of 650–700 mm FL. Spawning may occur at night. Males mature at 2–3 years of age and 300–400 mm FL;

most breeding females exceed 400 mm FL and are generally older fish than the male group. Newly hatched larvae are carried by receding floodwaters to the main water body. Juveniles up to about 30 mm FL are pelagic, staying near surface waters during the day and descending at night. Larger juveniles (30–60 mm FL) change habitat to occupy marginal areas with vegetational cover and later, at a size above 60–80 mm FL, revert to open water habits. Tigerfish attain lengths of 160–200 mm FL in their first year and up to 300 mm FL by the end of the second. Although the sexes have equal growth rates, males mature earlier and suffer higher mortalities so that larger fishes (above 600 mm) are most often females, which live for 8–9 years. Tigerfish are predators throughout life – newly hatched fry less than 10 mm long start feeding on small invertebrates or zooplankton, progressively taking larger plankton and insects and finally fish, becoming exclusive fish feeders above 90–100 mm length. Tooth development keeps pace with the changing diet of young tigerfish: fry of 10–25 mm have conical teeth which are replaced at size 25–35 mm by tricuspid teeth and again by conical teeth at the time when the diet is becoming increasingly piscivorous. Whole sets of teeth are replaced at intervals throughout life, replacement teeth developing in trenches on the jaws below the functional teeth. Prey 40% or more of the size of the attacking tigerfish are taken from the side and then swallowed whole, usually head first. Tigerfish feed on whatever prey is most abundant at a particular time, but slender-bodied shoaling fishes like robbers (*Brycinus* and *Micralestes*), minnows (*Barbus*) and the sardine *Limnothrissa* are favoured. In Lake Kariba the tigerfish were initially mainly found near shore and in river estuaries until the introduction of the Lake Tanganyika sardine or kapenta allowed them to feed in the open waters of the lake.

Uses A major angling gamefish; also an important commercial species in Lake Kariba, with over 184 tonnes taken in 1977.

Conservation Although widespread and still common in certain areas tigerfish have declined in some rivers due to pollution, water extraction and obstructions like weirs and dams that prevent their passage. Tigerfish have not yet been successfully bred in captivity.

Family Hepsetidae
African pike

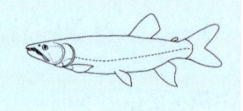

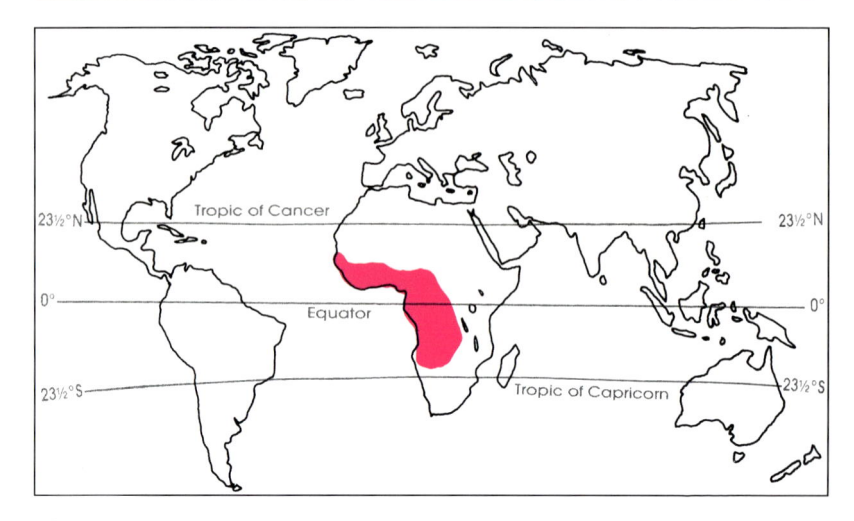

Genus *Hepsetus* Swainson, 1838

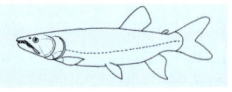

The African pike is easily recognised by its pointed head and crocodile-like jaws. It is a unique, though widespread, element of the African fish fauna and stands alone in its own family. It is most closely related to the South American pike-characins, family Ctenoluciidae.

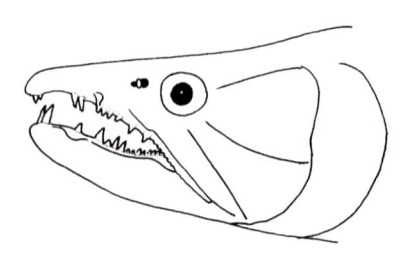

African pike, showing pointed head and sharp canine teeth.

AFRICAN PIKE

Afrika-greepvis
Hepsetus odoe (Bloch, 1794)

Description D ii, 7; A ii, 9. Scales cycloid, 49–58 in lateral line, 24 around caudal peduncle. Body elongate, dorsal and anal fins set well back, caudal forked, adipose fin present. Head pointed, jaws with prominent, unevenly protruding, sharp canine teeth. Breeding fishes develop a fleshy flap on either side of the lower jaw. Basic colour rich brassy olive with dark brown blotches and cream underparts; fins with black spots, adipose fin orange with black spots, 3 brown bands radiate behind eye. Females reach larger size than males. Attains 470 mm FL and about 2 kg. SA angling record 0,805 kg.

Distribution Cunene, Okavango, upper Zambezi and Kafue systems. Also widespread through central Zaire and West Africa to the Senegal River. Notably absent from the Zambian Zaire system and the Great Lakes.

Biology and Ecology Prefers quiet, deep water, as in channels and lagoons of large floodplains. Not usually found with tigerfish, as their habitat and hunting strategies differ. Juveniles and fry inhabit well-vegetated marginal habitats. A top predator, the pike stalks and ambushes prey with a swift, sudden rush. Juveniles prey on small invertebrates and fish; adults eat mostly fish, up to about 30–40% of their own size. Growth is rapid, mature in the second year from about 200 mm FL (males) or 250 mm FL (females). A multiple spawner, breeding over the summer months. Breeding pairs construct a floating foam nest within the shelter of dense marginal vegetation of lagoons, backwaters or protected river channels. The eggs incubate in the nest which is closely guarded and tended by both parents. On hatching, the fry drop to the water surface where they remain suspended beneath the nest until it disintegrates. Relatively short-lived, only 4–5 years.

Uses Excellent angling species on light tackle. Also taken in subsistence fisheries.

CATFISHES (ORDER SILURIFORMES, SUBORDER SILUROIDEI)

The catfishes constitute one of the world's largest groups of fishes with about 31 families, 400 genera and over 2 200 described species. The majority are freshwater forms although two families are primarily marine. Catfishes are most abundant and diverse in South America but also occur in North America, Africa and Eurasia. They usually have a set of three or four pairs of barbels around the mouth, and do not have scales although many species, especially in South America, have bony plates along the body. Many species have a sharp spine in the dorsal and pectoral fins; most also have a large adipose fin behind the rayed dorsal fin. The electric catfishes can generate powerful electric currents. Catfishes range in size from the tiny sand catlets of about 30 mm to the largest of all the species in southern Africa, the vundu (*Heterobranchus longifilis*), reputed to attain well over 55 kg and 1,5 m. Some species are valuable food fishes and the barbel or sharptooth catfish (*Clarias gariepinus*) is a valued aquaculture species in Africa. Many catfishes are popular aquarium species.

Catfishes are most closely related to the gymnotoid fishes (naked-back knifefishes) of South America, a group that includes the so-called electric eel. With the gymnotoids they are most closely related to the characins. Six families with 12 genera and 39 species in our area.

KEY TO FAMILIES

1a No rayed dorsal fin .... *Malapteruridae* (p. 238)
1b Rayed dorsal fin present 2
2a Anal fin long based, more than 20 rays 3
2b Anal fin short based, fewer than 20 rays... 4
3a Dorsal fin without sharp spine, long-based, more than 20 rays................
     ....*Clariidae* (p. 227)
3b Dorsal fin with sharp spine, short-based, fewer than 10 rays...................
     ....*Schilbeidae* (p. 224)
4a Dorsal and pectoral fins without sharp spine, pectoral with pectinate first ray ....*Amphiliidae* (p. 218)

4a

4b Dorsal and pectoral fins with sharp spine..5
5a Mouth more or less terminal in position, lower jaw with broad plate-like toothband .... *Claroteidae* (p.211) and *Austroglanididae* (p. 215)
5b Mouth ventral in position, lower jaw with 1 or 2 rows of protruding teeth
     ....*Mochokidae* (p. 240)

FAMILY CLAROTEIDAE
Claroteid catfishes

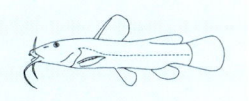

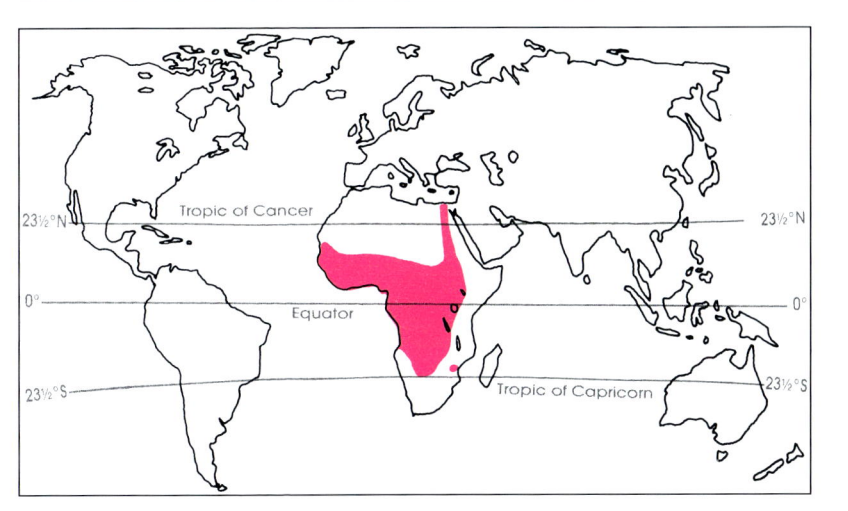

Recently established family of African catfishes that were formerly included in the African–Asian family Bagridae to which they are closely related. Includes two subfamilies and over 90 species in 13 genera, however the generic level classification is still unsettled. Claroteids typically have a large mouth with three or four barbels, a spine each in the dorsal and pectoral fins, a short-rayed dorsal fin and adipose fin and a short-based anal fin. In southern Africa there are two claroteid species.

KEY TO SPECIES OF CLAROTEIDAE AND AUSTROGLANIDIDAE

1a Origin of adipose fin close behind dorsal fin, in advance of origin of anal fin; anterior openings to nostrils on upper lips ....
....*Parauchenoglanis ngamensis* (p. 212)

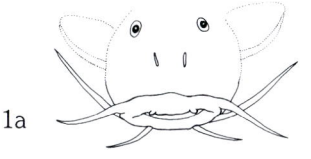

1b Origin of adipose fin distant from dorsal fin, above origin of anal fin; anterior openings to nostrils on snout 2
2a Eye large, with free border, interorbit distance less than twice orbit diame-

ter; nasal barbels longer than posterior naris (opening to nostrils), reaching anterior naris ....*Amarginops hildae* (p. 214)

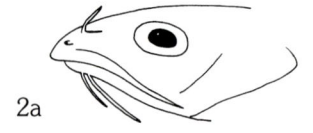

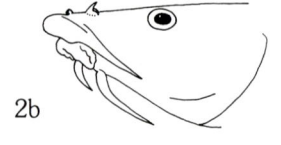

2a 2b

2b Eye moderately small, interorbit distance more than 2,5 times orbit diameter; nasal barbels shorter or equal to posterior naris ....*(Austroglanis)* 3
3a Spine in dorsal and pectoral fins strong and straight, caudal fin forked or emarginate..4
3b Spine in dorsal and pectoral fins relatively weak, curved; caudal fin truncate, humeral process a short stub ....*Austroglanis barnardi* (p. 215)
4a Posterior mandibular barbel opposite gular node, anterior and posterior nostrils equally spaced, caudal fin emarginate.......*Austroglanis gilli* (p. 216)
4b Posterior barbel in advance of gular node, distance between anterior nostrils less than distance between posterior nostrils, caudal fin forked ....*Austroglanis sclateri* (p. 217)

Genus *Parauchenoglanis* Boulenger, 1911

Distinctive African catfishes with relatively large head, tapered snout, fleshy lips with three pairs of barbels, no nasal barbels, and a large adipose fin. About 20 species; 1 in southern Africa.

ZAMBEZI GRUNTER

Zambesi-knorbaber
Parauchenoglanis ngamensis (Boulenger, 1911)

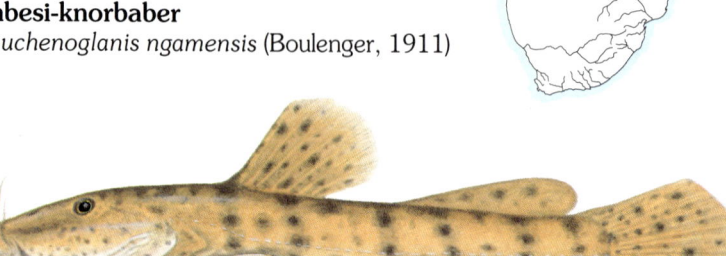

Description D I, 7; A iv–v, 8–9. Dorsal and pectoral fins with a strong spine, dorsal spine smooth, pectoral spines serrated along inner edge only; adipose fin large, extends from behind dorsal to caudal peduncle; caudal rounded. Head large, moderately depressed and pointed; mouth with fleshy lips, fine bristle-like teeth on a small square pad in upper jaw and along lower jaw, and 3 pairs of thick-based barbels of which the outer mandibular is longest; nostrils widely separated, anterior openings small tubes from upper lip, posterior simple slits. Yellow-brown with scattered black spots and 5–7 vertical lines of black spots along body, fins spotted. Attains 380 mm SL.

Distribution Okavango and upper Zambezi systems. Also in the Kasai River, Zaire system.

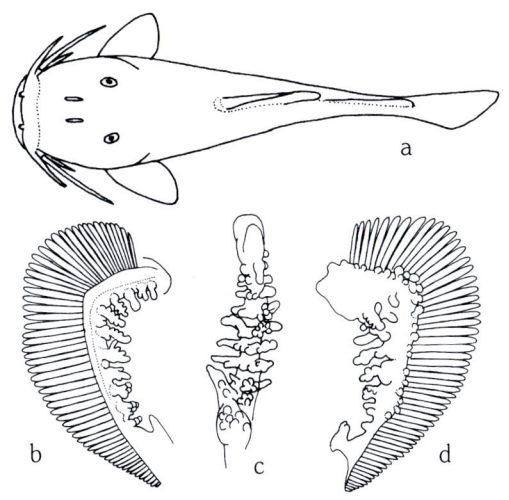

(a) Position of nostrils; right-hand 1st gill arch (b) outside, (c) front, (d) inside.

Biology and Ecology Prefers rocky habitats or marginal vegetation in slow-flowing rivers and lagoons, often sheltering under trees. Feeds on small fishes and invertebrates such as snails, shrimps and insects. Produces relatively few large eggs, suggesting parental care, but no details are known. "Grunts" when removed from the water.

Uses Potential aquarium species.

Genus *Amarginops* Nichols & Griscom, 1917

An African genus, with about 17 species, mostly from Central African rivers, especially the Zaire system. Characterised by large eyes, wide snout, short nasal barbels and short fins. Only one species in southern Africa.

HILDA'S GRUNTER

Buzi-baber
Amarginops hildae (Bell-Cross, 1973)

Description D I, 6; A ii, 7. Dorsal spine without serrations, pectoral spines serrated along inner edge only, adipose fin short, caudal forked. Head flat below with a wide snout; mouth ventral, wide, with a broad band of fine sharp teeth; 4 pairs of slender barbels, including short nasals, maxillaries longest; eyes large, lateral. Olive grey with off-white abdomen. Attains 118 mm SL.
Distribution Lower reaches of Buzi River in Mozambique.
Biology and Ecology Fast-flowing water over rocks with water ferns is the known habitat.
Uses Uncommon, possibly an occasional subsistence catch.

ROCK CATFISHES 215

FAMILY AUSTROGLANIDIDAE
Rock catfishes

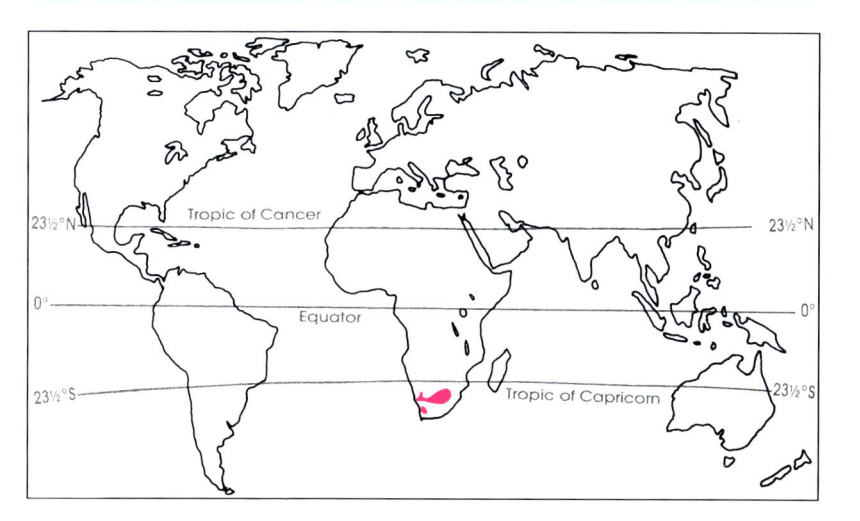

See Key to species of Claroteidae and Austroglanididae on pp. 211–2.

Genus *Austroglanis* Skelton, Risch & De Vos, 1984

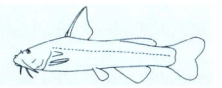

Small riverine catfishes endemic to southern Africa; only three species known. Placement of barbels on lower jaw is characteristic. Relationships are not yet clearly resolved, although they are superficially similar to bagrid catfishes. All three species are threatened and listed in the Red Data Book.

BARNARD'S ROCK CATFISH

Barnard se klipbaber
Austroglanis barnardi (Skelton, 1981)
/E\

Description D I, 6; A iii–vi, 10–13. Fins short, rounded; dorsal with weak spine, pectorals with short curved spine, adipose fin large, caudal truncate. Humeral process stubby. Head depressed, snout broad; three pairs of short barbels (nasals insignificant), mandibulars on ventral side of head.

BARNARD'S ROCK CATFISH (cont.)

Golden brown with dark brown blotches. Attains 75 mm SL.
Distribution Tributaries of Clanwilliam Olifants system, western Cape.
Biology and Ecology Lives among cobbles in clear, flowing water.
Conservation Endangered. Extremely uncommon and threatened by stream channelling, water extraction, sedimentation and introduced bass.

CLANWILLIAM ROCK CATFISH

Clanwilliam-klipbaber
Austroglanis gilli (Barnard, 1943)

Description D I, 6–7; A v–vi, 10–13. Dorsal and pectoral fins pointed, with strong straight spine, adipose moderately large, caudal emarginate. Humeral process pointed. Head depressed, snout broad, mouth subterminal, lips fleshy; 3 pairs of short barbels (nasals insignificant), mandibulars on ventral side of head. Greyish to yellowish brown,

without markings. Attains 127 mm SL.
Distribution Tributaries of the Clanwilliam Olifants system, western Cape.
Biology and Ecology Lives among rocks and cobbles and under banks in clear, flowing streams. Feeds on insects, especially the larvae of caddis and mayflies, and other small invertebrates taken from the bottom.
Conservation Rare. Uncommon and threatened by stream channelling, water extraction, sedimentation and introduced bass.

ROCK CATFISH

Klipbaber
Austroglanis sclateri (Boulenger, 1901)

Description D I, 7–8; A v–vi, 10–13. Dorsal and pectoral fins with a strong spine, dorsal spine smooth, pectoral spines serrated along inner edge only; adipose fin large, caudal forked. Humeral process pointed. Head sloped, flat below, snout rounded; mouth inferior, lips fleshy; 3 pairs of short barbels, mandibulars on ventral side of head. Olive brown with scattered spots over body. Attains 300 mm SL.
Distribution Major tributaries and mainstream, Orange-Vaal system.
Biology and ecology Lives in rocky habitats in flowing water, favouring rapids. Feeds on invertebrates, especially insects, taken from rock surfaces; larger specimens also take small fish.
Uses Rarely caught by anglers.
Conservation Rare–indeterminate. Uncommon, threatened by gross habitat changes caused by construction of weirs and dams, extraction of water, pollution, alluvial mining operations and sedimentation from soil erosion.

FAMILY AMPHILIIDAE
Mountain catfishes

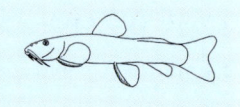

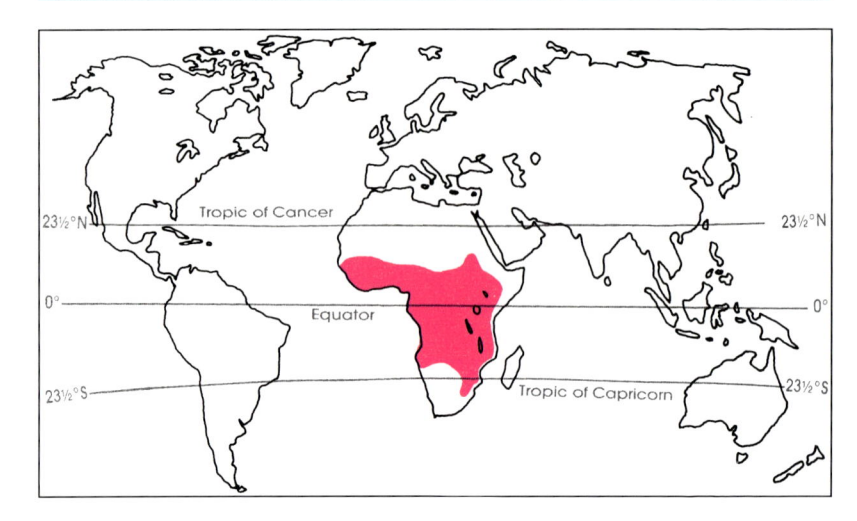

Small African catfishes found mainly in running waters of clear streams and rivers. The family includes soft-bodied mountain catlets as well as several slender armoured species similar to the whiptail catfishes (Loricariidae) from South America. The sand catlets (*Leptoglanis* and *Zaireichthys*) are now placed in this family. In *Amphilius* the primary rays of the pectoral and pelvic fins are broad and pectinate, in *Leptoglanis* each pectoral fin has a barbed spine. The swimbladder is reduced and divided into two spheres, each partly protected by a bony capsule. Nine genera and about 60 species are known, two genera and five species from our area.

Genus *Leptoglanis* Boulenger, 1902
SAND CATLETS

Probably the smallest catfishes in Africa, these attractive little catlets are found living over sandbanks of tropical rivers. They were placed in the Bagridae but research shows that (unlike the Bagridae) their airbladder is encapsulated in bony capsules behind the head, as is that of the mountain catlets (Amphiliidae). Sand catlets differ from other amphiliids by having a spine in the dorsal and pectoral fins. The generic and specific taxonomy of the southern African sand catlets is under revision and several new species are expected.

KEY TO SPECIES

1a Body stout, well marked with pigment blotches, humeral spur short ....*Spotted sand catlet* **(p. 219)**
1b Body slender, pallid, with fine scattered pigment or small clusters (shadows), humeral spur slender and pointed..............*Chobe sand catlet* **(p. 220)**

SPOTTED SAND CATLET

Gevlekte-sandbabertjie
Leptoglanis rotundiceps (Hilgendorf, 1905)

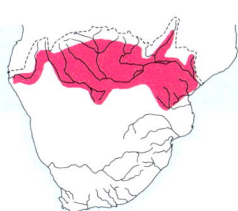

Description D II, 5–7; A iii–iv, 6–7. Lateral line complete (eastern populations) or short, ending at level of origin of pelvic fins. Body stout and tapered, fins rounded to angulate, dorsal spine short, simple; pectoral spine with large barbs along inner edge, adipose elongate, not extending to caudal base, caudal emarginate or truncate. Head short, rounded; eyes dorsal, mouth subterminal with 3 pairs of simple barbels, maxillary barbels each with basal membrane. Humeral spur (process) triangular, short in upper Zambezi population. Transparent to off-white with irregular grey or sooty shadows and a series of oblong dashes along midbody; caudal, anal and pectoral fins with dark bands. Attains 40 mm SL.

Distribution Cunene, Okavango and Zambezi, Pungwe, Busi and Save systems. Also Lake Malawi catchment.

Biology and Ecology Found over sand, usually buried with just eyes protruding. Feeds on minute organisms. Eggs few (12–16) and large (3–5 mm diameter) suggesting possible parental care.

Uses Potentially interesting aquarium species.

Note This species as it currently stands probably represents a complex of several different species.

CHOBE SAND CATLET

Chobe-sandbabertjie
Leptoglanis cf *dorae* (non Poll, 1967)

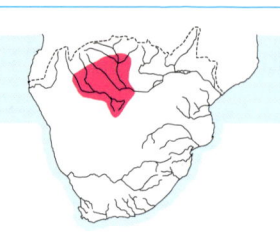

Description D II, 4–5, A iv–vii, 4–7. Lateral line incomplete. Body slender and tapered, fins pointed, dorsal spine simple, pectoral spine with large barbs along inner edge, adipose extends nearly to caudal base, caudal truncate. Head short, rounded eyes dorsal, protruding; mouth subterminal, 3 pairs barbels, maxillaries with well-developed basal membrane. Humeral spur long, slender and pointed. Translucent, very pallid with lightly speckled pigment and small brown patches on body. Attains 25 mm SL.
Distribution Okavango, Kwando, Chobe and upper Zambezi systems.
Biology and Ecology Occurs over fine sand, lying buried with only its eyes protuding.

Genus *Amphilius* Günther, 1864

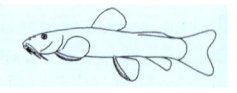

Small, softbodied catlets living in clear, flowing upland streams, usually amongst rocks. Dorsal fin short without a spine, pectorals and pelvics fan-like with pectinate primary rays; head depressed, eyes small, dorsal; a wide, terminal mouth (compare the *Chiloglanis* catlets), with three pairs of barbels. Three species are recognised from southern Africa.

KEY TO SPECIES

1a Caudal peduncle 16–17% SL, caudal peduncle length 1,2–1,3 times caudal peduncle depth, adipose fin confluent with body............................
....*A. laticaudatus* (p. 221)
1b Caudal peduncle 17–21% SL, caudal peduncle length 1,4–2 times caudal peduncle depth, adipose fin confluent with body or with notch behind 2

2a Head length 1,6–2 times distance from head to origin of dorsal fin, adipose fin with notch behind ....A. uranoscopus (p. 223)
2b Head length 1,1–1,3 times distance from head to origin of dorsal fin, adipose fin with notch or confluent with caudal peduncle..........................
....A. natalensis (p. 222)

BROADTAIL MOUNTAIN CATFISH

Breëstert-bergbaber
Amphilius laticaudatus Skelton, 1984

Description D i, 6; A iii, 4–5. Pectoral and pelvic fins broad and fanlike, with pectinate primary rays; adipose fin low and confluent with short, deep caudal peduncle; caudal fin forked, with round lobes. Head depressed, 3,8–4 times in SL, eyes small, dorsal; mouth subterminal, lips fleshy, 3 pairs of barbels, maxillaries reach base of pectoral fins. Mottled brown, creamy white on underparts of head and abdomen. Attains 51 mm SL.

Distribution Buzi system in Mozambique.

Biology and Ecology Inhabits shallow, fast-flowing water over rocks and pebbles.

NATAL MOUNTAIN CATFISH

Natalse bergbaber
Amphilius natalensis Boulenger, 1917

Description D i, 6; A iii, 5–6. Body narrow and slender, caudal peduncle longer than deep, adipose fin either short with a notch behind (Natal populations) or long, low and confluent behind (Transvaal and Zimbabwe); caudal forked. Head depressed, short (4,75–5 times in SL; 1,1–1,3 times distance between head and dorsal fin), narrow, head width less than head length; eyes small, dorsal; mouth subterminal, three pairs of barbels, maxillaries reach pectoral base. Colour variable, usually spotted or mottled brown, sometimes dark brown, nearly black. Attains 125 mm SL.

Distribution Escarpment streams from the Eastern Highlands of Zimbabwe (lower Zambezi) to Natal Drakensberg (Umkomaas system). Also Ruo River in Malawi.

Biology and Ecology Lives among cobbles and rocks in swiftly flowing water. Active at night, feeding on benthic stream invertebrates such as mayfly and midge larvae. Breeds in summer. Preyed on by trout and is now scarce in certain streams.

Uses Attractive curiosity fishes in well-aerated aquariums.

COMMON OR STARGAZER MOUNTAIN CATFISH

Gewone bergbaber
Amphilius uranoscopus (Pfeffer, 1889)

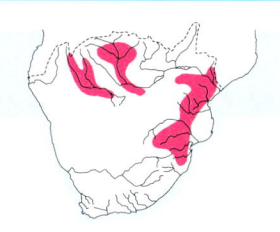

Description D i, 6; A iii, 5–7. Adipose fin short and deep, notched behind; caudal peduncle length about equal to its depth, caudal fin emarginate or shallowly forked. Head longer and broader than that of Natal mountain catlet, length 3,9–4,5 times in Sl., head width equal to or greater than head length. Colour variable, usually yellowish brown or greyish brown, mottled or with dark shadows, blotches or spots. Attains 170 mm TL.

Distribution Okavango and Zambezi systems, east coast rivers south to the Mkuze system in northern Natal. Also widespread in Central and East Africa.

Biology and Ecology Preferred habitat is clear, flowing water in rocky habitats. Feeds on stream insects and other small organisms off rock surfaces. Breeds in summer. Young mountain catlets are easily mistaken for tadpoles. Preyed on by trout and probably eels.

Uses Interesting aquarium subject.

Note *Uranoscopus* refers to the eyes on top of the head, hence "stargazer". It is also a name given to a family and genus of marine fishes with the eyes on top of the head.

FAMILY SCHILBEIDAE
Butter catfishes

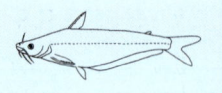

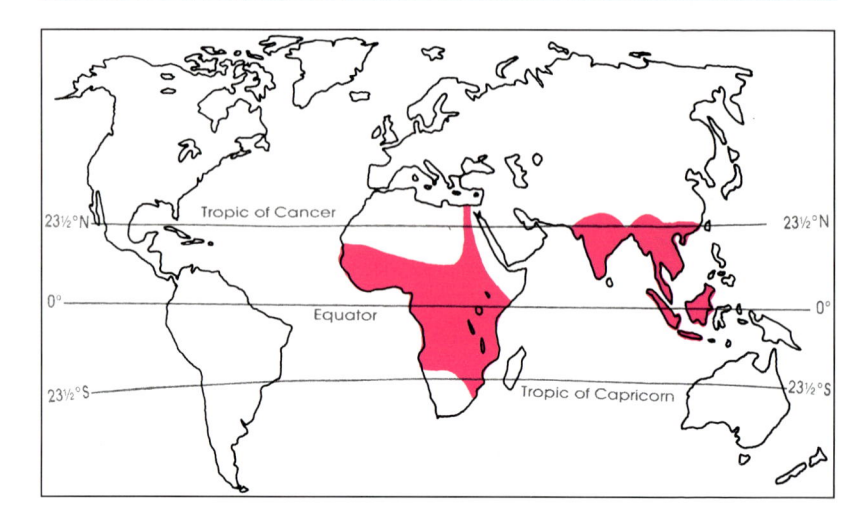

The butterbarbels are shoaling catfishes, swimming in midwater (unlike most other catfishes, which are bottom-dwellers). Their unusual body form – depressed head with large mouth, short deep abdomen and compressed, tapered body with a long anal fin – reflects this midwater lifestyle. Considered good to eat, they are an important fisheries resource and are caught by anglers and subsistence fishermen. Their extremely sharp dorsal and pectoral spines are treated with respect by familiar handlers. Schilbeids occur in Asia and Africa. In Africa there are 5 genera and about 34 species; a single genus occurs in our area.

Genus *Schilbe* Oken, 1817

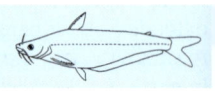

Schilbe now includes two subgenera, *Schilbe* and *Eutropius*, which differ mainly in the absence or presence of a small adipose fin on the back. This is an unreliable character, however, and in some species, including *S. intermedius*, is variously present or absent. The genus includes 22 species in tropical African waters; two species are known from southern Africa.

KEY TO SPECIES

1a Barbels very long, maxillaries and outer mandibulars reaching well beyond base of pectoral fins, underside of head and abdomen covered by pigment (usually distinct, large melanophores)....................**S. yangambianus (p. 226)**
1b Barbels relatively short, maxillaries and outer mandibulars not reaching beyond base of pectoral fins, underside of head and abdomen not covered by pigment ....**S. intermedius (p. 225)**

SILVER CATFISH (BUTTER BARBEL)

Silwerbaber (Botterbaber, Makriel)
Schilbe intermedius Rüppell, 1832

Description D II, 5–6; A iv–v, 47–62. Body elongated, compressed and tapered towards caudal, skin smooth; dorsal and pectoral fins with slender, sharp spines, finely serrated along inner edge; base of anal fin extended but separated from caudal. A small, lobate adipose fin is present in east-coastal populations but absent from Cunene-Okavango and upper Zambezi populations. Head depressed, eyes lateral, mouth terminal, with 4 pairs of thin filamentous barbels, not reaching beyond head. Colour variable depending on water conditions and body condition – in turbid waters usually very light olive or silvery grey with yellow edges; in clear, dark waters dark chocolate mottling is usual; ventral side of head and abdomen is usually clear white with yellow infusions; a large bilateral black blotch behind the head. Juveniles often with 3 broad, dark stripes along the body. Attains about 300 mm SL, 1,3 kg. SA angling record 1,05 kg, Zimbabwe 0,77 kg, Malawi 0,53 kg.

Distribution Cunene, Okavango and Zambezi systems southwards to the Phongolo in northern Zululand. Also widespread throughout tropical Africa including the Nile and West Africa to the Senegal River.

Biology and Ecology Shoals in standing or slowly flowing open water

with emergent or submerged vegetation. Generally more active at night or in subdued light. Feeds from mid- and surface waters on a wide variety of foods including fish, insects, shrimps, snails, plant seeds and fruit. Breeds during rainy season and may be either a single or a multiple spawner in different localities, laying eggs on vegetation. Matures at about 160 mm SL, lives for 6–7 years.
Uses Important subsistence fisheries target. Angling species, but often regarded as a nuisance. Occasionally kept in aquariums but not generally suitable on account of predatory habits.
Note This species was previously known as *Schilbe mystus* and *Eutropius depressirostris*.

YANGAMBI BUTTERBARBEL

Yangambi-botterbaber
Schilbe (Eutropius) yangambianus (Poll, 1954)

Description D II, 5–6; A iv–v, 35–54. Dorsal and pectoral spines long and slender, finely serrated on inner edges; lobate adipose fin present. Head short and rounded, mouth slightly subterminal, with 4 pairs of long filamentous barbels, maxillaries and outer mandibulars reaching beyond base of pectoral fins. Dark chocolate brown with yellowish base colour, a large black blotch on body behind head, underside of head and abdomen pigmented. Attains 132 mm SL.
Distribution Known from a single locality on the upper Zambezi. Also fairly widespread in the Zaire system.
Biology and Ecology Prefers smaller forest streams with rocky bottoms. Feeds mainly on terrestrial and aquatic insects.

FAMILY CLARIIDAE
Air-breathing catfishes

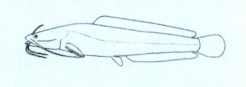

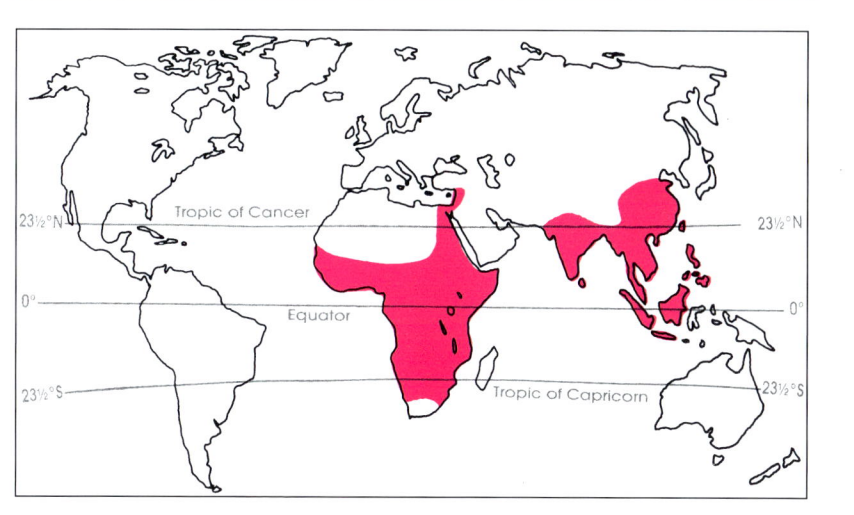

Clariids are African and Asian catfishes well known for their hardiness and ability to breathe air and survive desiccation of the environment. They are easily recognised by their bony, helmetlike head and elongated body with long dorsal and anal fins. The common sharptooth catfish or barbel is extremely widely distributed and is valued in subsistence fisheries, aquaculture and angling. Although species like the vundu attain a very large size, some clariids are relatively small or moderate sized fishes. In Africa fossil records date back to the Miocene and bones of clariids are often found in archaeological middens. The family includes 12 African genera and 74 species, with 3 genera and 8 species in southern Africa.

KEY TO GENERA AND SPECIES

1a Large adipose fin (24–33% SL) present behind rayed dorsal fin
....*Heterobranchus longifilis* (p.236)

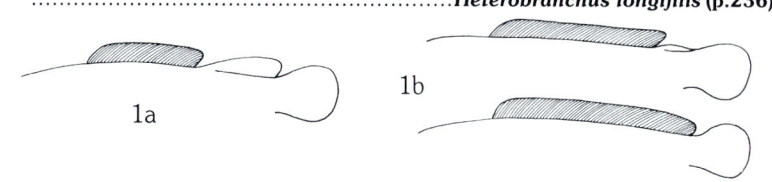

1b Adipose fin lacking or short (6–12,5% SL), rayed dorsal fin extends to over

posterior half of anal fin..2
2a Postorbital margin of head not completely covered with bony plates, bones behind eyes greatly reduced...................***Clariallabes platyprosopos*** (p.235)
2b Postorbital margin of head completely or largely covered with bony plates, bones behind eyes usually not greatly reduced.......................................3
3a Head relatively large, 28–34% SL, short adipose fin present or (usually) short gap between end of rayed dorsal and base of caudal fin present......4
3b Head relatively short, less than 28% SL, rayed dorsal extends to base of caudal fin 5
4a Vomerine toothpad usually a curved band with most teeth sharply pointed, gill rakers on first gill arch numerous, from 24 in small individuals (20–30 mm SL) to more than 100 in large specimens, elongate and close set, no distinct adipose fin present ....***Clarias gariepinus* (p.229)**

4a

4b

4b Vomerine toothpad deep, ovoid or shieldshaped, teeth mostly blunt or granular, gill rakers on first gill arch 18–32, short and widely spaced, distinct adipose fin present....................................***Clarias ngamensis* (p.230)**
5a Head length 25–28% SL, barbels short, less than head length, 8–10 short, well-spaced gill rakers on first gill arch, anal fin origin equidistant from tip of snout and caudal base...***Clarias stappersii* (p.231)**
5b Head length 18,5–24,5% SL, maxillary barbels longer than head, up to 19 gill rakers on first gill arch, origin of anal fin nearer to tip of snout than caudal base 6
6a Pectoral spines barbed along outer edge only, bones behind orbits widely separated...***Clarias liocephalus* (p.232)**
6b Pectoral spines barbed along inner and outer edges, bones behind orbits joined together 7
7a Pigment lacking, eyes vestigial or absent...........***Clarias cavernicola* (p. 234)**
7b Darkly pigmented, eyes well developed ....***Clarias theodorae* (p. 233)**

Genus *Clarias* Scopoli, 1777

Clarias species are easily recognised by their bony head, pectoral fins each with a spine, long-based soft dorsal and anal fins, large mouth with four pairs of barbels, and a chamber above the gills for the accessory air-breathing organ. They are valued food fishes. In Africa 32 species are recognised, 6 occur in southern Africa.

SHARPTOOTH CATFISH

Skerptandbaber (Baber)
Clarias gariepinus (Burchell, 1822)

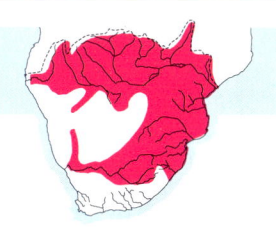

Description D 61–75; A 45–60. Body strongly compressed towards caudal; dorsal fin entirely of soft rays, extends from behind head nearly to base of caudal; pectoral spine with barbs along outer edge only; anal entirely of soft rays, extends from base of anus to base of caudal; caudal rounded. Head large and depressed, heavy boned and completely encased above, eyes small, lateral; mouth large, subterminal, jaws with broad bands of fine, pointed teeth, vomerine band of similar teeth behind upper jaws on palate; 4 pairs of long filamentous barbels, maxillaries longest. First gill arch with numerous (24–110) close set, slender gill rakers, a large chamber above the gill arches is filled with a multi-branched accessory air-breathing organ. Colour varies from almost black to light brown, often marbled in shades of olive green or grey; underparts of head and abdomen white, sometimes with red flush to extremities of fins, especially when spawning. Attains 1,4 m SL, 59 kg. SA angling record 33,3 kg, Zimbabwe 30,845 kg, Malawi 16,1 kg.

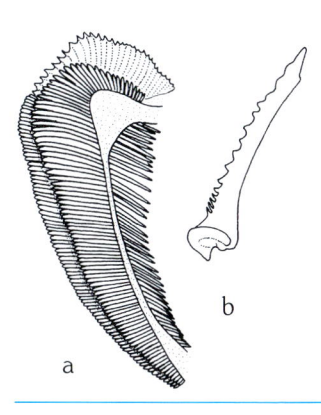

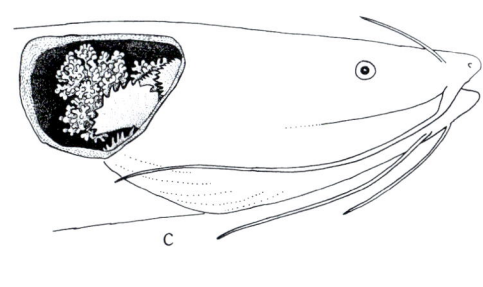

(a) Right-hand 1st gill arch, (b) right-hand pectoral spine, (c) accessory air-breathing organ.

Distribution Probably the most widely distributed fish in Africa, found throughout woodland-savanna zones of the Afrotropical region from the Nile to as far south as the Orange system and the Umtamvuna (east coast). Translocated to the eastern Cape (Sundays, Fish, Keiskamma) and to the southwest Cape (Eerste River and the Cape Flats). Also occurs in Israel, Lebanon and Turkey.

Biology and Ecology Occurs in almost any habitat but favours floodplains, large sluggish rivers, lakes and dams. Can endure harsh conditions such as high turbidity or desiccation and is frequently the last or only inhabitant of diminishing pools of drying rivers or lakes, where it may form burrows. Moves overland under damp conditions if necessary by extending the pectoral spines and crawling. Completely omnivorous – preys, scavenges or grubs on virtually any available organic food source including fish, birds, frogs, small mammals, reptiles, snails, crabs, shrimps, insects, other invertebrates and plant matter such as seeds and fruit, and is even capable of straining fine plankton if necessary. May hunt in packs, herding and trapping smaller fishes. Is preyed on by a wide variety of predators including man, leopards, crocodiles and birds, especially the fish eagle and marabou stork. Breeds in summer after rains, when large numbers of mature fishes migrate to flooded shallow grassy verges of rivers and lakes. Eggs are laid on vegetation and hatch within about 25–40 hours; larvae are free-swimming and feed within 2 or 3 days, remaining inshore within vegetation cover. Growth is rapid, but greatly dependent on local conditions, individuals reaching about 200 mm SL within one year. Growth rate in females declines after about 3 years so that males ultimately reach a larger size. Individuals may mature after a year but most take 2 or more years. Lives for 8 or more years.

Uses An important angling and food fish species.

Conservation A dominant ecological presence where it occurs, so that translocation may threaten native fauna. Strict control over movement from and holding conditions in catfish farms is required.

Relationships A member of the subgenus *Clarias*, closely related to *Clarias anguillaris* from the Nile and West Africa. The widespread species *C. mossambicus* and *C. lazera* have been synonymised with *gariepinus*.

BLUNTTOOTH CATFISH

Stomptandbaber
Clarias ngamensis Castelnau, 1861

Description D 56–62; A 50–58. Distinguished from the sharptooth catfish by having a short adipose fin behind the rayed dorsal and an ovoid vomerine toothplate with granular or blunt teeth. Gill rakers short and

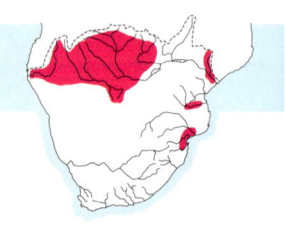

BLUNTTOOTH CATFISH (cont.)

widely spaced, 18–32 on first gill arch. Accessory suprabranchial air-breathing organ well developed. Pectoral spines barbed along outer edge only. Colour variable, grey or dark brown, often marbled, with cream or whitish underside to head and abdomen. Attains about 730 mm TL, 4 kg. Malawi angling record 0,27 kg.
Distribution Cunene, Okavango, upper Zambezi, Kafue, lower Shire (lower Zambezi), Save, Limpopo and Phongolo systems. Also in the Zambian Zaire system and the Cuanza in Angola.
Biology and Ecology Favours vegetated habitats in swamps and riverine floodplains. Often found together with the sharptooth catfish; feeding habits overlap considerably. In the Okavango Delta both species pack hunt together during the annual catfish run. Important foods are molluscs, terrestrial and aquatic insects, shrimps, crabs and fish. Hard-shelled foods such as mussels are crushed before they are swallowed. Breeds during the summer rainy season, large numbers of fishes moving into shallow flooded drainage channels to spawn. Males show a higher growth rate than females and maturity is reached at about 250 mm TL. Lives for 5 or 6 years.
Uses Important in subsistence and commercial floodplain fisheries.
Relationships A member of the subgenus *Dinotopteroides*, most closely related to the West African species *Clarias lamottei*. These species may be more closely related to the genus *Heterobranchus*, including the vundu, than to other *Clarias*.
Note Named after Lake Ngami in Botswana.

BLOTCHED CATFISH

Gevlekte baber
Clarias stappersii Boulenger, 1915

Description D 62–80, A 55–64. Characterised by its large oblong head, relatively short barbels and heavily blotched colour pattern with clearly outlined lateral line. Gill rakers short, widely spaced, 8–10 on first gill arch. Pectoral spines barbed along outer edge, inner barbs reduced. Ori-

BLOTCHED CATFISH (cont.)

gin of anal fin equidistant from tip of snout and base of caudal. Suprabranchial air-breathing organ well developed with platelike branches. Heavily blotched in dark brown and black, lateral line white, head and abdomen off-white below. Attains 410 mm SL.
Distribution Cunene, Okavango, upper Zambezi and Kafue systems. Also in Zambian Zaire system and Kasai, Zaire system.
Biology and Ecology Found in well-vegetated sluggish river channels and floodplain lagoons. Feeds on invertebrates and fish. Breeds during summer rainy season.
Uses Uncommon but taken in subsistence floodplain fisheries.
Relationships Member of the subgenus *Platycephaloides*.

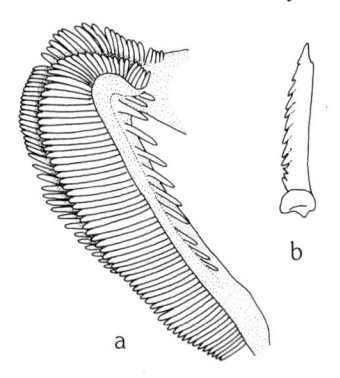

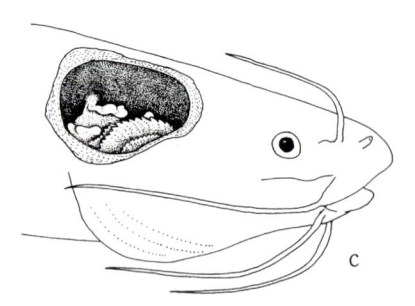

(a) Right-hand 1st gill arch, (b) right-hand pectoral spine, (c) accessory air-breathing organ.

SMOOTHHEAD CATFISH

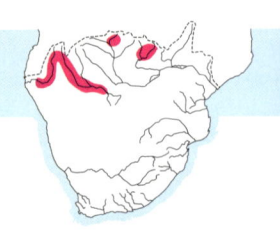

Sagkopbaber
Clarias liocephalus Boulenger, 1898

Description D 67–79, A 51–67. Head short and broad, cheeks behind eyes bulge in adults, bony plates behind eyes separated and notched; mouth terminal, barbels long, maxillaries reach beyond pectoral base. Gill rakers slender, spaced, 8–13 on first gill arch. Suprabranchial organ re-

AIR-BREATHING CATFISHES   233

SMOOTHHEAD CATFISH (cont.)

duced to a peg or simple branched structure. Pectoral spines barbed along outer edge, weakly barbed along inner edge. Either plain or mottled dark brown with head and abdomen light brown below; submarginal band and dark edge to dorsal, anal and caudal fins. Attains 282 mm SL, largest recorded in southern Africa 120 mm SL.
Distribution   Cunene, Okavango, upper Zambezi and Kafue systems. Also from Zambian Zaire through Central African Great Lakes to Lake Victoria region.
Biology and Ecology Little known, taken from rocky habitats in flowing water.
Relationships A member of the subgenus *Brevicephaloides*.
Note *Liocephalus* refers to the smooth head of this species.

SNAKE CATFISH

Slangbaber
Clarias theodorae Weber, 1897

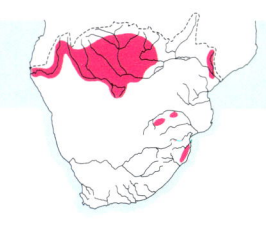

Description D 71–94, A 60–89. Characterised by a relatively small, short head, 4–5 times in SL, long barbels reaching to behind the head, and an elongated slender body with a long anal fin. Gill rakers spaced, 13–19 on first gill arch. Suprabranchial organ reduced, not filling chamber, with thick stubby branches. Pectoral fin spine with barbs along outer and inner edges, origin of anal fin nearer tip of snout than base of caudal. Usually mottled, black or dark brown; lateral line may be marked in white. Attains 350 mm SL.

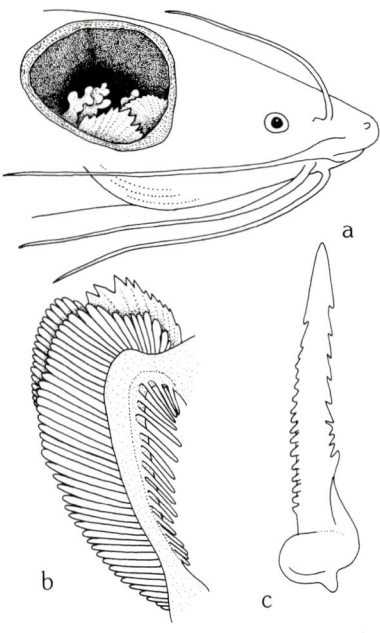

Distribution Cunene, Okavango, upper Zambezi, Kafue, lower Zambezi, Limpopo and coastal systems of northern Natal. Also in the Zaire system, Lake Malawi catchment and the Rufigi River in Tanzania.

Biology and Ecology Prefers dense marginal vegetation or rootstocks along the banks of slow-flowing rivers and floodplain lagoons. Feeds on invertebrates, especially terrestrial and aquatic insects and shrimps, as well as small fish.

Uses Taken in subsistence fisheries. Occasional aquarium pet.

Relationships Member of the subgenus *Anguilloclarias*, close to the cave catfish (*Clarias cavernicola*).

(a) Accessory air-breathing organ, (b) right-hand 1st gill arch, (c) right-hand pectoral spine.

CAVE CATFISH

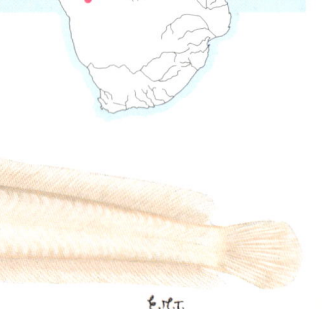

Spelonkbaber
Clarias cavernicola Trewavas, 1936

Description D 64–76, A 51–66. Readily identified by short head, 4–5 times in SL, reduced or absent eyes, long body and complete lack of pigment. Gill rakers short, spaced, 12–15 on first gill arch. Pectoral fin spine barbed along outer and inner edges, anal fin origin nearer tip of

snout than base of caudal. Pale fleshy white with yellowish extremities. Attains 161 mm SL.
Distribution Aigamas Cave, near Otavi, Namibia.
Biology and Ecology Lives over shelves in open, clear water. Feeds on bat droppings, animal carcasses and terrestrial insects that fall into the cave lake.
Conservation Endangered. Major threat is depletion of ground water.
Relationships Member of the subgenus *Anguilloclarias*, close to the snake catfish (*Clarias theodorae*).

Genus *Clariallabes* Boulenger, 1900

Differs from *Clarias* by the absence of bony plates behind the eye. In some species the dorsal and anal fins are united with the caudal fin. An African genus with 15 species, one species in southern Africa.

BROADHEAD CATFISH

Breëkopbaber
Clariallabes platyprosopos Jubb, 1964

Description D 73–82, A 56–63. Characterised by the broad, depressed head with bulging cheeks. Head 4,2–4,8 in SL, barbels long, reaching beyond the head. Suprabranchial organ vestigial or absent. Gill rakers pointed, spaced, 12–13 on first gill arch. Pectoral spine barbed along outer and inner edges. Mottled black or dark brown. Attains

BROADHEAD CATFISH (cont.)

283 mm SL. Zimbabwe angling record 0,128 kg.
Distribution Okavango and upper Zambezi systems.
Biology and Ecology Occurs in rocky rapids of large rivers. Known to feed on fish.
Conservation Rare.
Uses Occasionally caught by anglers.

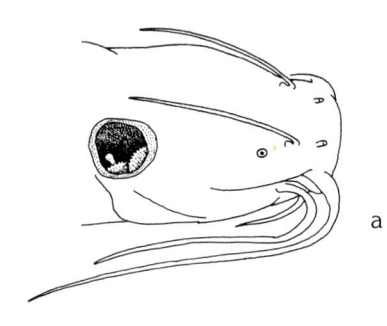

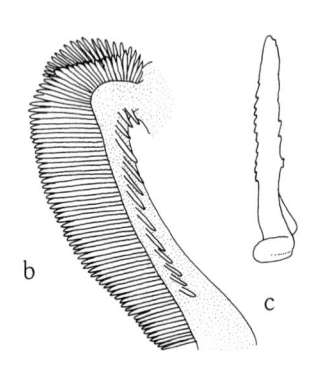

(a) Accessory air-breathing organ, (b) right-hand 1st gill arch, (c) right-hand pectoral spine.

Genus *Heterobranchus* Geoffroy-Saint-Hilaire, 1809

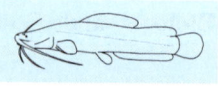

Large African clariids with a prominent adipose fin behind the rayed dorsal fin. Four species, one from southern Africa.

VUNDU

Vundu
Heterobranchus longifilis Valenciennes, 1840

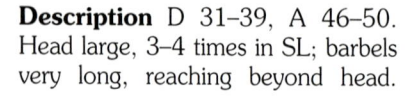

Description D 31–39, A 46–50. Head large, 3–4 times in SL; barbels very long, reaching beyond head. Suprabranchial organ well developed, fills suprabranchial chamber. Gill rakers numerous, 54–84 on first gill

VUNDU (cont.)

arch. Rayed dorsal fin extends to above anterior base of anal; adipose large, extending from rayed dorsal to caudal; anal fin origin nearer caudal fin base than tip of snout. Olive grey or reddish brown, head and abdomen white below. Juveniles have irregular dark blotches or spots, end of adipose fin black, caudal with a black concentric band. Attains 1,17 m SL, about 55 kg. Zimbabwean angling record 50,0 kg, Malawi 29,71 kg.

Distribution Middle and lower Zambezi. Also widespread throughout the Zaire basin to West Africa, including Lakes Tanganyika and Edward and the Nile.

Biology and Ecology Found in large deep rivers within the mainstream or in deep pools and lakes. Most active at night, feeding on any available food, including invertebrates and insects when small, fish and other small vertebrates when large. Scavenges off large carcasses and offal from riverside villages. Breeds in summer during the rainy season, eggs and juveniles being found amoung plant roots in shallow water. Lives for 12 or more years.

Uses An important angling species. Fast-growing hybrids of vundu/sharptooth catfish are being produced for aquaculture.

Note The largest freshwater fish species in southern Africa.

FAMILY MALAPTERURIDAE
Electric catfishes

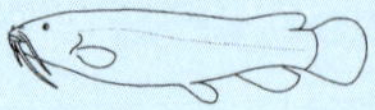

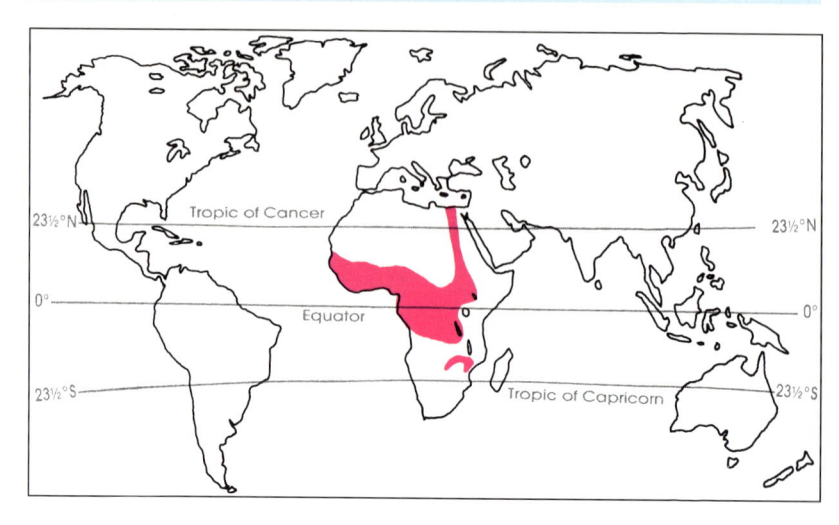

Genus *Malapterurus* Lacepéde, 1803

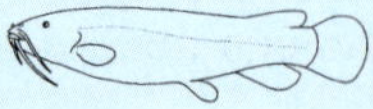

The electric catfishes are both interesting and dangerous creatures, with a rotund, bloated appearance and the ability to deliver a powerful shock. Their electrogenic organ is derived from muscles and covers most of the body. The relationships of electric catfishes are not yet well understood. Widespread in tropical African rivers and lakes. Three species have been described, one in our area.

ELECTRIC CATFISH

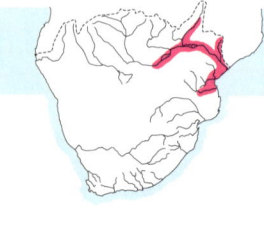

Elektriese baber
Malapterurus electricus (Gmelin, 1789)

Description A 9. No rayed dorsal fin, adipose fin short, pectorals without spines, caudal rounded. Head and body rounded and fleshy, mouth terminal, teeth fine, in broad bands on both jaws, 3 pairs of barbels, outer mandibulars longest, reaching base of pectorals, gill slits short, restricted to

ELECTRIC CATFISH (cont.)

sides. Grey above, off-white below from head to anal fin, irregular black blotches over body, outer edge of caudal yellow. In southern Africa attains 500 mm SL, elsewhere 1,22 m. Zimbabwe angling record 5,33 kg, spearfishing 6,58 kg; Malawi 5,1 kg.

Distribution Middle and lower Zambezi, Pungwe and lower Save. Also throughout the Zaire system to West Africa and the Nile.

Biology and Ecology Lives among rocks or roots; favours sluggish or standing water. Active at night, feeding mainly on fish stunned by electric shocks. The electric organ, capable of generating 300–400 volts, is derived from body muscles, forming a sheath under the skin around the body, and is used for both prey capture and defence. Forms pairs and breeds in excavated cavities or holes. Lives for 10 years or more.

Uses Taken in subsistence fisheries; caught by anglers and divers. Occasional curiosity pets in aquariums.

FAMILY MOCHOKIDAE
Squeakers, suckermouth catlets

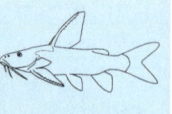

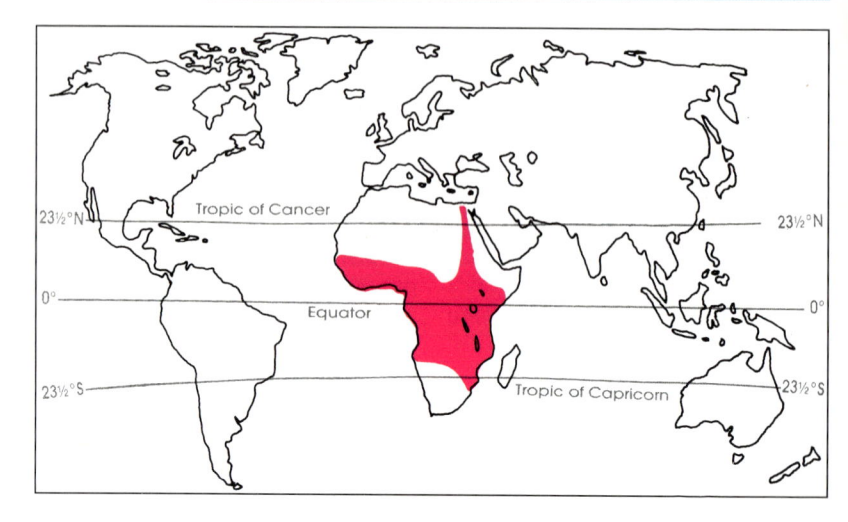

The largest African catfish family with 10 genera and about 170 species. Hallmark features of mochokid catfishes include complex mouths and strong spines in the dorsal and pectoral fins. The identification of mochokid species is often difficult because of the wide variation in characters such as pigment patterns, teeth and barbels. Two distinctly different genera with 17 species occur in southern Africa: the squeakers (*Synodontis*) are moderately large fishes found in slow-flowing vegetated waters, whereas the suckermouth catlets (*Chiloglanis*) are small fishes adapted mainly for life in fast currents.

KEY TO GENERA

1a Head bony, mouth with long barbels, mandibular barbels branched ....*Synodontis* (p. 247)
1b Head depressed, covered by thick skin, mouth forms a disc with short barbels, mandibular barbels not branched........................*Chiloglanis* (p. 240)

Genus *Chiloglanis* Peters, 1868

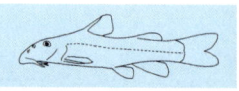

Small catlets usually found in fast-flowing rocky streams or the rapids and rocky stretches of large rivers. The mouth forms a large disc and is used to hold onto rocks or plants in the current. The gill slits are restricted to the sides above the pectoral fin. The genus includes 34 species, 8 from southern Africa; most of these are endemic to the region.

KEY TO SPECIES

1a Dorsal spine serrated ....*C. paratus* (p. 245)
1b Dorsal spine smooth 2
2a Mandibular teeth short, widely spaced, up to 14, width of band 40–50% of width of inside of mouth, maxillary and mandibular barbels long ....
....*C. swierstrai* (p. 247)

2a

2b Mandibular teeth long, widely or narrowly spaced, band width less than 30% of width of inside of mouth...3
3a Mandibular teeth widely spaced, up to 8...4

3a   3b

3b Mandibular teeth closely spaced, up to 12 5
4a Barbels relatively long, caudal fin emarginate ....*C. emarginatus* (p. 243)
4b Barbels relatively short, caudal forked, with large round lobes ....
....*C. bifurcus* (p. 242)
5a Caudal fin forked, skin rough or ridged..6

5a   5b   5b

5b Caudal fin emarginate or pointed, skin smooth.......................................7
6a Eyes relatively large, set close together, interorbit less than twice orbit diameter ....*C. fasciatus* (p. 244)
6b Eyes relatively small, set wide apart, interorbit twice orbit diameter or more
....*C. neumanni* (p. 245)

7a Caudal fin emarginate in adults of both sexes .... *C. pretoriae* (p. 246)
7b Caudal fin pointed in mature males, emarginate in females
....*C. anoterus* (p. 242)

PENNANT-TAILED SUCKERMOUTH (PENNANT-TAILED ROCK CATLET)

Wimpelstert-suierbekkie
Chiloglanis anoterus Crass, 1960

Description D I, 5–6; A iii, 8. Oral disc large, maxillary barbels short, not reaching beyond hind edge of disc, mandibular barbels very short, mandibular toothband narrow, teeth closely gathered, up to 12. Dorsal spine short (half length of fin). Males with conical genital papillum and pennant caudal fin, females with emarginate caudal fin. Dark brown to black with light brown patches and a series of vertical linear spots along back. Attains 90 mm SL.

Distribution Endemic to the escarpment streams of the Phongolo and Incomati systems.
Biology and Ecology Occurs in rocky riffles and rapids. Feeds on insects such as mayfly nymphs and blackfly larvae grazed from rocks. Its spines protect it from predators such as trout. Breeds during the summer; males are generally smaller than females, mature at about 48 mm SL. Probably only lives for 2 or 3 years.
Uses Occasional aquarium species.

INCOMATI SUCKERMOUTH (INCOMATI ROCK CATLET)

Inkomati-suierbekkie
Chiloglanis bifurcus Jubb & Le Roux, 1969

Description D I, 6; A iii, 8. Oral disc large, maxillary barbels reach beyond hind margin of disc, mandibulars short, mandibular teeth long, widely spaced, up to 8. Dorsal spine long, 75–80% length of fin; fins all large,

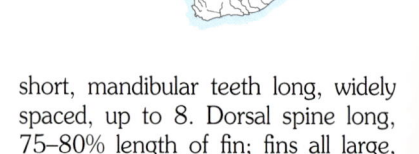

INCOMATI SUCKER-
MOUTH (cont.)

caudal forked with large, rounded lobes. Males with conical genital papillum. Light brown with dark brown shadows, fins yellow with black bands, black spots at the base of either caudal lobe. Attains 68 mm SL.
Distribution Endemic to the Crocodile-Incomati system at altitudes of 900–1 200 m.
Biology and Ecology Occurs in rocky rapids and cascades. Feeds on benthic invertebrates such as mayfly and caddis fly nymphs, blackfly and midge larvae and small snails. Breeds during summer and is a partial spawner.
Conservation Vulnerable. Increasing extraction and regulation of river water as well as pollution threaten this species.

PHONGOLO SUCKERMOUTH (PHONGOLO ROCK CATLET)

Phongolo-suierbekkie
Chiloglanis emarginatus Jubb & Le Roux, 1969

Description D I, 6; A iii, 8. Similar to the Incomati rock catlet but caudal fin is emarginate and barbels longer. Mandibular teeth widely spaced, up to 8. Skin rough, with tiny white warts. Brown with dark brown shadows, lat-

eral line whitish, fins light yellow with black bands and a dark edge to the caudal. Attains 65 mm SL.
Distribution Two areas, tributaries of the Phongolo and Komati-Incomati rivers in South Africa and Swaziland, and the Pungwe and middle and lower Zambezi in Zimbabwe.
Biology and Ecology Occurs in shallow rocky runs and riffles of clear rivers. Feeds on invertebrates such as mayfly nymphs and caddis fly, blackfly or midge larvae grazed from rocks. Breeds in summer.
Conservation Locally rare. Threatened by water extraction, river regulation and sedimentation.

OKAVANGO SUCKERMOUTH (OKAVANGO ROCK CATLET)
Okavango-suierbekkie
Chiloglanis fasciatus Pellegrin, 1936

Description D I, 6; A iii–iv, 7. Body slender and tapered, caudal forked. Head strongly curved, mouth below level of pectoral girdle, barbels moderately long, teeth closely spaced, up to 8. Eyes relatively large, interorbital space less than twice orbit diameter. Translucent white with dark brown shadows on body, dark brown bands across fins. Attains 50 mm SL.
Distribution Okavango and Kwando rivers.
Biology and Ecology Occurs in rocky rapids as well as in fringing vegetation in the mainstream current. Feeds on small invertebrates and algae from the surface of rocks and plants.

NEUMANN'S SUCKERMOUTH (NEUMANN'S ROCK CATLET)

Zambezi-suierbekkie
Chiloglanis neumanni Boulenger, 1911

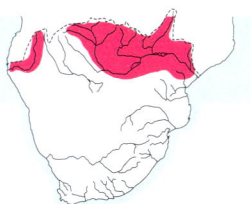

Description D I, 5–6; A iii–iv, 7. Body moderately tapered, dorsal spine with slight outer serrations, its length 80% of fin length, caudal forked. Head robust, barbels moderately long, teeth closely spaced, long, up to 8. Skin rough, with small white warts and ridges. Light brown with black or dark brown shadows, caudal fin with splayed band across either lobe. Attains 65 mm SL.

Distribution Cunene, Zambezi above and below the Victoria Falls, Pungwe and Buzi systems. Also in the Lake Malawi catchment and east coast rivers in Tanzania.

Biology and Ecology Inhabits rocky riffles and rapids as well as pools.

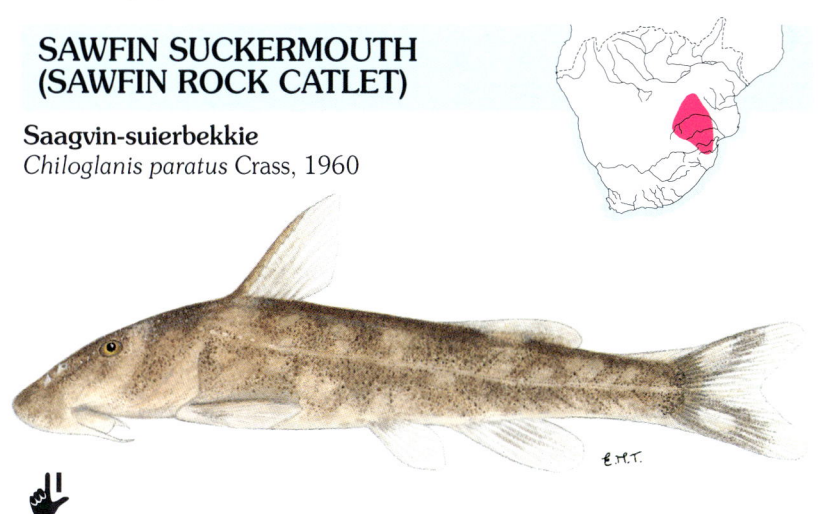

SAWFIN SUCKERMOUTH (SAWFIN ROCK CATLET)

Saagvin-suierbekkie
Chiloglanis paratus Crass, 1960

Description D I, 5–6; A iii, 7–9. The serrated or barbed spines in the dorsal and pectoral fins are hallmarks of this species. Body robust, caudal forked. Head depressed, maxillary barbels moderate, mandibulars very short; teeth closely spaced, up to 12. Skin rough, with small white warts. Dark brown with black shadows, caudal fin with splayed dark brown bands on either lobe. Attains 85 mm SL.

Distribution Phongolo, Incomati and Limpopo rivers.
Biology and Ecology Favours rocky riffles and rapids but may be found in rocky pools of intermittent streams during low water conditions. Migrates into seasonal streams, climbing damp barriers by clinging with the mouth.
Uses Potential aquarium species.

SHORTSPINE SUCKERMOUTH (SHORTSPINE ROCK CATLET)

Kortstekel-suierbekkie
Chiloglanis pretoriae Van der Horst, 1931

Description D I, 5–6; A iii, 7–10. Somewhat variable species, very similar to the pennant-tailed suckermouth. Dorsal fin comparatively small, dorsal spine short, less than 50% fin length, caudal emarginate in both sexes. Head depressed, eyes relatively small; mouth large, with broad premaxillary toothpads, about 12 mandibular teeth in a straight band. Dark brown with small lighter patches on back and distinctive series of vertical linear spots along body, caudal fin with broad splayed black band over either lobe. Attains 65 mm SL.
Distribution Incomati, Limpopo and middle and lower Zambezi, Pungwe and Busi systems.
Biology and Ecology Occurs in shallow rocky reaches, riffles and rapids of permanent rivers. Has a wider altitudinal range than most species, common where it occurs. Feeds on aquatic insects such as mayfly nymphs and caddis fly and blackfly larvae. Breeds during summer, laying eggs between rocks and in gravel.
Uses Potential aquarium species; useful indicator species in river conservation studies.

LOWVELD SUCKERMOUTH (LOWVELD ROCK CATLET)

Laeveldse suierbekkie
Chiloglanis swierstrai Van der Horst, 1931

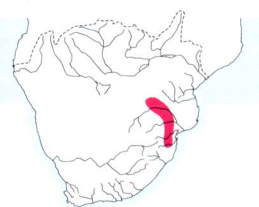

Description D I, 5–6; A iii–iv, 7–10. Body long, slender; dorsal and pectoral spines nearly full length of fin, caudal fin forked. Eyes relatively large and close-set, interorbit 1,5 times orbit diameter; oral disc relatively small, barbels long; up to 14 very short teeth, widely spaced. Brown above with off-white patches, off-white below, lateral line white, black base to caudal fin. Attains 70 mm SL.
Distribution Lowveld and warmer reaches of the Limpopo, Incomati and Phongolo systems.
Biology and Ecology Prefers sandy stretches of flowing rivers where it lives over sandbanks, burying itself in the sand. Feeds on small invertebrates. Breeds in summer.
Uses Potential aquarium species.

Genus *Synodontis* Cuvier, 1816

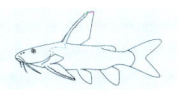

Popularly known as squeakers on account of the sounds they make when removed from the water. Easily recognised by their bony skulls and large sharp dorsal and well-barbed pectoral fin spines which can be locked in place to form a formidable defensive mechanism. Often attractively marked, they are popular aquarium pets but are difficult to identify accurately. A large genus with over 100 species, 9 in southern Africa.

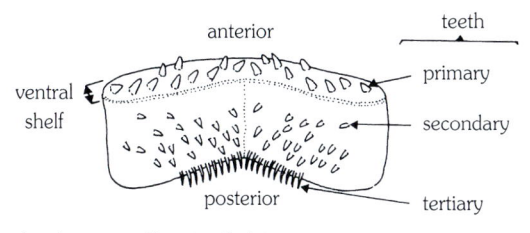

Character of *Synodontis*; premaxillary toothplate.

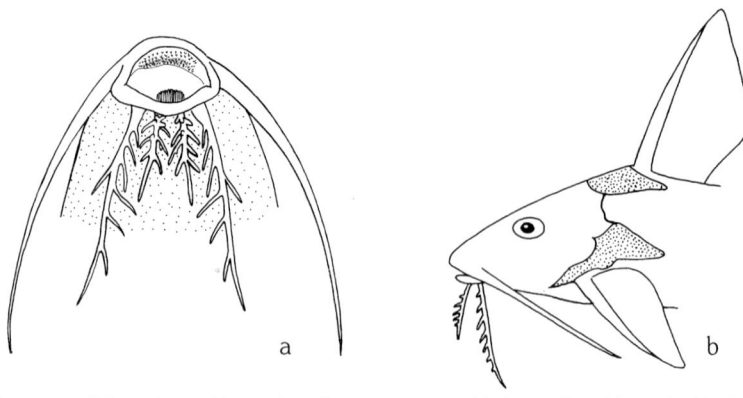

Characters of *Synodontis* (a) mouth with projecting mandibular teeth and branched barbels, (b) strong spines in dorsal and pectoral fins; nuchal plate and humeral process (shaded).

KEY TO SPECIES

1a Humeral process elongated and pointed, outer mandibular barbels with thin, filamentous branches 2
1b Humeral process broad and obtusely pointed with convex margin in adults, outer mandibular barbels with short, thick branches 3
2a Body markings absent or indistinct, or fine widely scattered small spots (smaller than pupil), colour brown or grey, eggs orange or yellow, width of nuchal shield 23–31% head length .... *S. zambezensis* (p. 249)
2b Body with clear spots (larger than pupil), colour olive green, eggs green, nuchal shield width 29–36% head length .... *S. nigromaculatus* (p. 250)
3a Inner mandibular barbels with slender pointed branches; primary and secondary premaxillary teeth not distinctly separated, no distinct ventral shelf to premaxillary toothpad .... *S. woosnami* (p. 252)
3b Inner mandibular barbels with short, blunt branches; primary and secondary premaxillary teeth clearly separated, premaxillary toothpad with ventral shelf 4
4a Snout long, 35–42% predorsal length; mouth below level of pectoral girdle, large (width 53–66% pectoral girdle width), with broad premaxillary toothpad (34–59% pectoral girdle width), ventral shelf of toothpad broad .... *S. macrostoma* (p. 254)
4b Snout moderate, 29–39% predorsal length, mouth at or above level of pectoral girdle, moderate sized (width 34–59% pectoral girdle width), premaxillary toothpad up to 30% pectoral girdle width, ventral shelf of toothpad narrow 5
5a Maxillary barbel with prominent basal membrane (membrane width greater than barbel basal diameter) and prominent papillae along leading edge; anterior rim of mouth with papillae in large specimens ....
.... *S. thamalakanensis* (p. 256)

5b Maxillary barbel with basal membrane absent or narrow (less than barbel basal diameter) and small, closely spaced or no papillae; anterior rim of mouth without papillae 6
6a Tertiary premaxillary teeth numerous (55–170), in 3 or 4 rows, mandibular teeth 25–41 .... **S. vanderwaali (p. 256)**
6b Tertiary premaxillary teeth 12–44, in 1 or 2 rows only, mandibular teeth 12–30 7
7a Maxillary barbels shorter than head, primary premaxillary teeth 9–24 .... **S. leopardinus (p. 255)**
7b Maxillary barbels subequal to or longer than head, primary premaxillary teeth 17–35 8
8a Maxillary barbels with dark basal membrane and finely papillose leading edge .... **S. macrostigma (p. 253)**
8b Maxillary barbels without dark basal membrane, leading edge smooth .... **S. nebulosus (p. 251)**

BROWN SQUEAKER

Bruin skreeubaber
Synodontis zambezensis Peters, 1852

Description D I, 7; A iv–vi, 7–10. Body deep, adipose fin large, caudal forked. Barbels long and slender, mandibular branches filamentous; mandibular teeth 20–40 in single band, no distinction between primary and secondary premaxillary teeth. Humeral process triangular, pointed. Plain olive brown or grey, small spots present or absent. Spotted specimens are more common in populations from the Limpopo, Incomati and Phongolo rivers. Juveniles with albino patches on body are often found. Attains 430 mm SL. SA angling record 0,29 kg, Zimbabwe 0,82 kg, Malawi 0,57 kg.

Distribution Middle and lower Zam-

Right-hand maxillary and branched outer and inner mandibular barbels.

bezi south to the Phongolo system. Absent from upper Save-Runde system.
Biology and Ecology Pools and slow-flowing reaches of perennial and seasonal rivers. Prefers riverine habitats to floodplains. Shelters in holes or crevices or on the underside of logs, frequently in an upside-down position. Active at night, a bottom feeder on detritus and plant matter such as seeds as well as small invertebrates like insects and snails, and will scavenge readily. Breeds in summer during rainy periods.
Uses Taken by anglers but usually considered a nuisance species.
Relationships Close to *S. nigromaculatus* and *S. njassae* from Lake Malawi.

SPOTTED SQUEAKER

Spikkel-skreeubaber
Synodontis nigromaculatus Boulenger, 1905

Description D I, 7; A iv–vi, 7–9. Body deep, caudal forked. Barbels long and slender, with filamentous branches; mandibular teeth 21–43 in a broad band. Humeral process triangular, pointed. Olive green, entire body covered with round black spots about the size of the eye. Eggs are green. Attains 300 mm SL. SA angling record 0,145 kg, Zimbabwe 0,315 kg.
Distribution Okavango and upper Zambezi systems. Also in the Zambian Zaire system, the Kasai River and Lake Tanganyika.
Biology and Ecology Prefers rocks

SQUEAKERS 251

Right-hand maxillary and branched outer and inner mandibular barbels.

or marginal vegetation of flowing

riverine channels to lagoons or backwaters. Feeds on a wide variety of food including detritus, algae and plant material, insects, snails and small fish, and scavenges readily. Breeds during summer rainy season.

Uses Caught by subsistence fishermen.

CLOUDY SQUEAKER

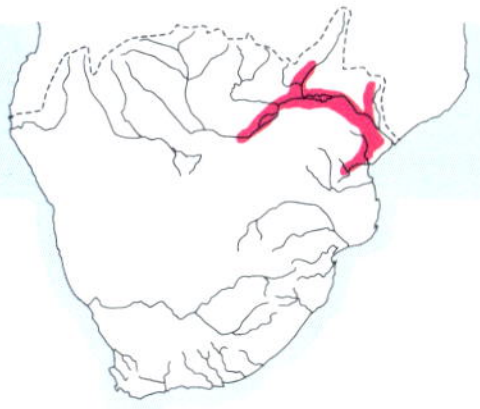

Newelrige skreeubaber
Synodontis nebulosus Peters, 1852

Description D I, 7; A v–vi; 7–9. Body slender, tapered, caudal fin shallowly forked. Mandibular teeth 12–24 in a narrow band; premaxillary toothpad broad, with 24–35 primary teeth on narrow ventral shelf; barbels short, maxillary barbels with smooth leading edge, branches of mandibulars short and stubby. Humeral process pointed, with convex margin in adults. Brown with large dark brown or yellowish brown blotches on body, fins spotted. Attains 150 mm SL.

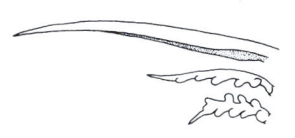

Distribution Middle and lower Zambezi system.

Biology and Ecology Prefers floodplain habitats to riverine ones but does occur in rocky areas where habitats are restricted. Feeds on typical squeaker diet of detritus, algae and benthic invertebrates. Lives for up to 4 or 5 years.

Right-hand maxillary and branched outer and inner mandibular barbels.

UPPER ZAMBEZI SQUEAKER

Bo-Zambezi-skreeubaber
Synodontis woosnami Boulenger, 1911

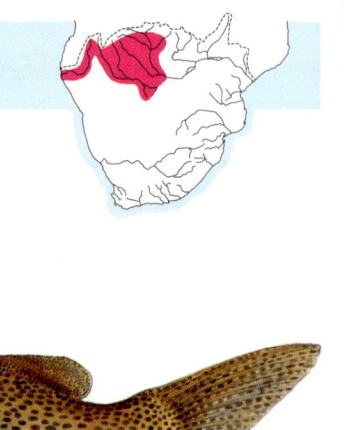

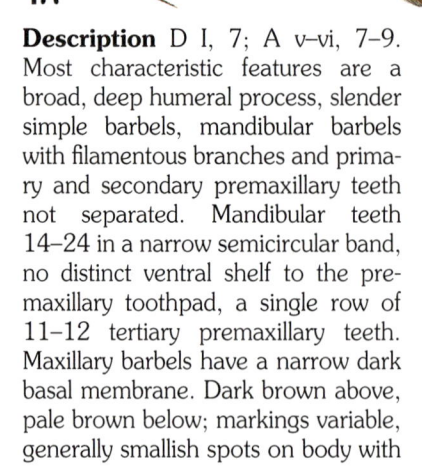

Description D I, 7; A v–vi, 7–9. Most characteristic features are a broad, deep humeral process, slender simple barbels, mandibular barbels with filamentous branches and primary and secondary premaxillary teeth not separated. Mandibular teeth 14–24 in a narrow semicircular band, no distinct ventral shelf to the premaxillary toothpad, a single row of 11–12 tertiary premaxillary teeth. Maxillary barbels have a narrow dark basal membrane. Dark brown above, pale brown below; markings variable, generally smallish spots on body with underside of head and abdomen clear; some individuals with larger spots including oblong markings (more common in Cunene specimens). Attains 205 mm SL.

Distribution Cunene, Okavango and upper Zambezi systems.

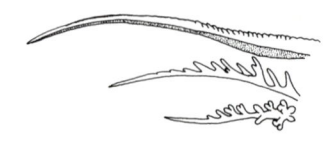

Right-hand maxillary and branched outer and inner mandibular barbels.

LARGESPOT SQUEAKER

Grootvlek-skreeubaber
Synodontis macrostigma Boulenger, 1911

Description D I, 7; A iv–vi, 7–9. Body thickset; caudal fin with shallow fork. Maxillary barbels with dark basal membrane and a papillose leading edge, mandibular barbels with short stubby branches; mandibular teeth 18–27 in a single band, premaxillary toothband with a well-defined ventral shelf, primary and secondary teeth distinct. Humeral process obtusely pointed. Yellowish with characteristic large dark brown or black spots or bars, underparts with smaller spots or plain. Attains 170 mm SL.
Distribution Cunene, Okavango, upper Zambezi and Kafue systems.
Biology and Ecology Prefers slow-flowing and floodplain environments, where it is usually common.

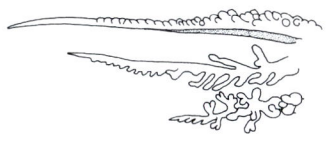

Right-hand maxillary and branched outer and inner mandibular barbels.

LARGEMOUTH SQUEAKER

Grootbek-skreeubaber
Synodontis macrostoma Skelton & White, 1990

Description D I, 6; A v–vi, 7–8. A long snout, large mouth and a distinctive premaxillary toothpad are diagnostic features. Mouth usually below level of pectoral girdle, premaxillary toothpad broad, with broad ventral shelf; primary teeth 22–31, distinct from secondary teeth; mandibular teeth 13–21 in a narrow band. Maxillary barbels simple, without basal membrane; mandibular barbel branches short and stubby. Caudal fin forked. Small spots on head, body with small and large spots, underside clear. Attains 92 mm SL.
Distribution Cunene, Okavango, upper Zambezi and Kafue systems.
Biology and Ecology Possibly favours rocky habitats.

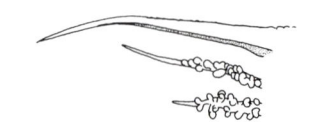

Right-hand maxillary and branched outer and inner mandibular barbels.

LEOPARD SQUEAKER

Luiperdkol-skreeubaber
Synodontis leopardinus Pellegrin, 1914

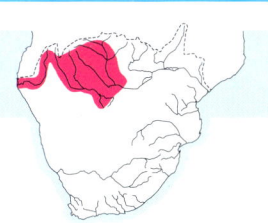

Description D I, 7; A v, 8–10. Head and predorsal with straight profile, sloped about 30°; dorsal fin tall, the spine equal to head length; caudal deeply forked. Mandibular teeth 12–22 in a straight band, premaxillary toothpad with a narrow ventral shelf, primary and secondary teeth distinct, few (12–25) tertiary teeth in a single row. Maxillary barbel smooth or finely papillose, basal membrane narrow, dark; mandibular barbel branches short and thick. Markings variable, usually small spots over entire body, sometimes arranged in clusters; underparts clear or spotted. Attains 196 mm SL. SA angling record 0,32 kg.

Distribution Cunene, Okavango and upper Zambezi.

Biology and Ecology Prefers floodplain drainage rivers and large lagoons.

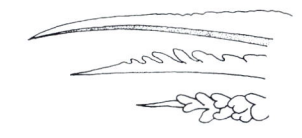

Right-hand maxillary and branched outer and inner mandibular barbels.

BUBBLEBARB SQUEAKER

Borrelbaard-skreeubaber
Synodontis thamalakanensis Fowler, 1935

Description D I, 7; A v–vi, 8–9. Dorsal fin and spine long, longer than head length, caudal forked. Maxillary barbels strongly papillose and with a broad black basal membrane; mandibular teeth 17–28 in a broad band; premaxillary toothpad with a distinct ventral shelf, primary and secondary teeth distinct, tertiary teeth 13–27 in 1 or 2 rows; mandibular barbels with short, stubby branches. Humeral process large and convex. Basic colour off-white with small black spots that tend to merge into wavy stripes. Attains 175 mm SL.

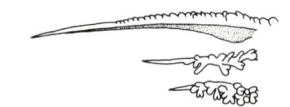

Right-hand maxillary and branched outer and inner mandibular barbels.

Distribution Okavango and upper Zambezi systems.

FINETOOTH SQUEAKER

Fyntand-skreeubaber
Synodontis vanderwaali Skelton & White, 1990

Description D I, 7; A v–vi, 7–9. Dorsal fin spine about equal to head length, caudal forked. Diagnostic features are a large number of mandibular teeth (25–41) in a single row, premaxillary toothpad with a narrow ventral shelf, primary and secondary teeth distinct and a very high number of fine tertiary teeth in several rows across the toothpad. Maxillary barbels

SQUEAKERS

FINETOOTH SQUEAKER (cont.)

simple and long, extending beyond pectoral bases, with narrow dark basal membrane; mandibular barbels with short, stubby branches. Humeral process large and convex. Brown to olive brown, markings variable, usually eye-sized spots or bars merging into a maze-like network. Attains 156 mm SL.

Distribution Cunene, Okavango and upper Zambezi systems.

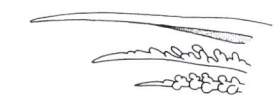

Right-hand maxillary and branched outer and inner mandibular barbels.

FAMILY GALAXIIDAE
Galaxiids

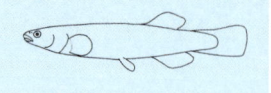

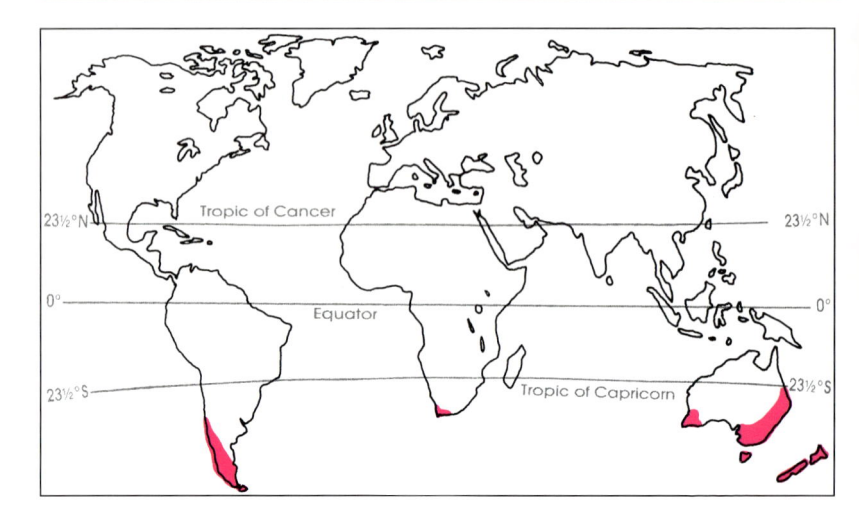

An interesting family of southern hemisphere fishes, related to the whitebaits, icefishes, southern graylings and smelts. These groups are distantly related to the northern salmonids (trouts and salmon). This family includes 6 genera and about 45 species and is most diverse and best represented in Australia and New Zealand. Representatives are also found in South America and one species occurs on the southern tip of Africa. Biogeographers offer two possible explanations for the global distribution of the galaxiids: either they have been distributed with the drifting continents, or they have dispersed with ocean currents.

Genus *Galaxias* Cuvier, 1816

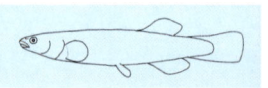

Mostly small fishes, cylindrical in shape and lacking scales, the dorsal fin placed far back. The majority, including the southern African species, are freshwater forms, but some are estuarine and others are diadromous.

CAPE GALAXIAS

Kaapse galaxias
Galaxias zebratus Castelnau, 1861

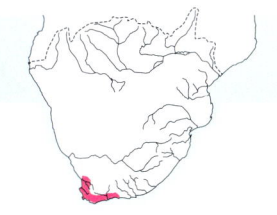

Description D iii–iv, 8–9; A iii–iv, 8–10. Body slender and cylindrical, without scales; dorsal fin placed far back over the anal fin, caudal truncated. Mouth terminal, jaws with teeth, eyes large. Translucent pale brown with or without darker blotches or bars, internal organs visible in living specimens. Attains 75 mm TL.

Distribution Cape coastal streams and rivers from the Keurbooms (south coast) to the Clanwilliam Olifants system (west coast).

Biology and Ecology Occurs in flowing or standing waters but favours gentle currents within shelter of banks near the head of pools. Although small this is an extremely hardy fish and is known to tolerate a wide range of water and temperature conditions. Its small size and cryptic colour enable it to shelter from predators. Feeds on small drifting invertebrates. Matures at about 40 mm, breeding occurs in spring or summer depending on local conditions. One individual was recorded to live for about 10 years in an aquarium.

Uses Suited to cool-water aquariums. A valuable fodder fish for trout.

Relationships Possibly nearest to *Brachygalaxias bullocki* from Chile, South America.

Family Salmonidae
Trouts

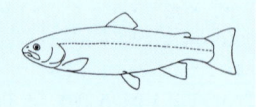

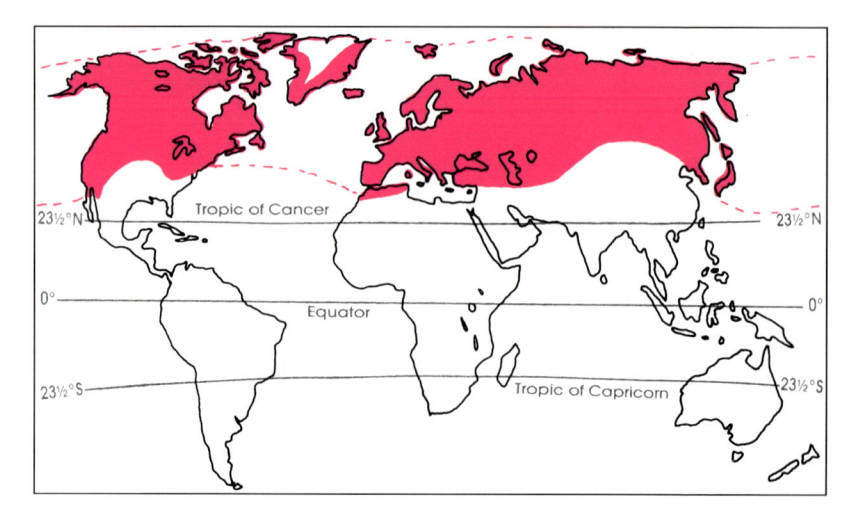

The salmonid family includes charr, trout and salmon, among the best known and most valuable fishes to man. They are naturally distributed in temperate latitudes in the northern hemisphere. All have been introduced to southern Africa in the past but only the trout have survived and flourished. Salmonids are medium to large fishes, with small scales on the body, but not the head, fins with soft rays only, a lobate adipose fin, and large, toothed jaws. All breed in freshwater but some (especially salmon) migrate to sea as juveniles and only return to freshwater as adults in order to breed.

Rainbow and brown trout in South Africa
British colonists in the Cape and Natal realised that in the absence of suitable indigenous angling species, many mountain streams would be suitable waters for the trout. The first reported attempt to import ova was made in 1875, but it was not until 1890 that brown trout ova were successfully imported to Natal from Scotland. After hatching the young trout were stocked into the Mooi, Bushmans and Umgeni rivers. In 1892 brown trout ova were also imported successfully to the Cape, and were hatched in some brewery ponds in Newlands, Cape Town. These efforts prompted the building of hatcheries at Jonkershoek above Stellenbosch, and at Pirie near Kingwilliamstown in the eastern Cape. By 1897 locally bred brown trout were being produced and the first batch of rainbow trout ova were imported. Widespread stocking of suitable rivers followed from these and other importations and both species are now

well established, the rainbow trout being more common. Brook charr were first introduced to the Cape in 1950 from the USA. Until the 1980s trout were bred mainly by nature conservation authorities for sportfishing, but private trout-farming is now a major industry supplying fish for both sportfishing and the table.

Genus *Salmo* Linnaeus, 1758

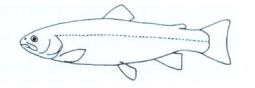

Until recently the genus *Salmo* included both the brown trout and the rainbow trout, but now it is realised that the rainbow trout is more closely related to the so-called "western trouts" and Pacific salmon genus *Oncorhynchus*. The more primitive genus *Salmo* is restricted to European and Asian trout species and the Atlantic salmon. Both brown trout and Atlantic salmon have been introduced to South Africa but only brown trout have survived and established populations.

BROWN TROUT

Bruinforel
Salmo trutta Linnaeus, 1758

Description D iv, 9–11; A iii, 7–8. Streamlined body, large mouth with sharp teeth, very small scales, relatively small fins including a lobate adipose fin and distinctive coloration easily identify brown trout from other species. Eyes moderate sized, jaw extends behind orbit when closed, gill openings large. Lower jaw of mature males becomes large and hooked (called the kype). Colour varies with age and water conditions but hallmark features are large brown and red spots on the sides and upper surfaces of head and body. Dorsal and adipose fins spotted, caudal fin largely without spots, apart from the upper and lower rays. Ground colour varies from silvery brown to yellowish. Mature males tend to darken in colour. Young trout are less spotted and more silvery, with a series of dark greyish vertical bars, known as parr marks, along the body. In South Africa grows to about 750 mm SL and 7,7 kg. SA angling record 3,48 kg, Zimbabwe 3,175 kg, Malawi 0,63 kg.

Distribution Certain streams of the south-west Cape, southern Cape, eastern Cape, the Drakensberg in Natal and Lesotho, and the eastern Transvaal. The natural range is Europe and north-east Africa where populations occur in streams of the Atlas Mountains of Morocco.

Biology and Ecology The essential requirements for brown trout are clear, well-oxygenated cool water, generally less than 21° C, but less than about 16° C for breeding and a maximum of about 25° C for survival). This is usually found in mountain or upland streams, away from occupied, cultivated or overgrazed lands, but may also be in lakes or farm dams in which the catchment is well managed. Generally feeds on aquatic and terrestrial insects, crabs, frogs and small fish if they are available. If necessary, it will even feed on zooplankton such as daphnia. In streams, feeds from the bottom or from drift or the water surface. Breeds in autumn or early winter, with males moving upstream to areas of suitable gravel beds where they establish territories by fighting. Running water is vital. By rapidly beating her body and tail the female excavates a nest or "redd" in the gravel in which the eggs are laid and fertilised. The eggs sink into the gravel and hatch after a period determined largely by temperature, but usually about 3 weeks. The small trout gradually disperse downstream and begin feeding. Growth rate depends on environment and available food but under good conditions brown trout may reach 180 mm after 1 year and 250 mm after 2 years. Trout are territorial and usually found alone in the stream although a particular stretch of habitat may be suitable for holding several individuals. Brown trout mature after 1 or 2 years and, in South Africa, may live for up to 7 years.

Uses A premier sport angling species, cultured for stocking fishing waters.

Genus *Oncorhynchus* Suckly, 1861

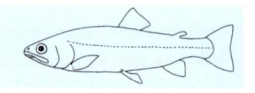

Includes the rainbow and cutthroat trouts as well as six species of Pacific salmon, all from the Pacific Ocean drainages of North America. Differs from *Salmo* in a number of skeletal characters as well as in behavioural and ecological traits.

RAINBOW TROUT

Reënboogforel
Oncorhynchus mykiss (Walbaum, 1792)

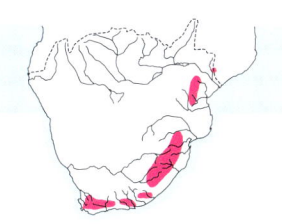

Description D iv, 10–12; A iii, 8–12. Streamlined body with very small scales; dorsal fin in midbody, small lobate adipose fin, caudal shallowly forked. Head rounded, mouth terminal, extending to hind margin of orbit when closed; jaws with sharp teeth, lower jaws of mature males slightly enlarged and hooked. Coloration distinctive, body silvery or light golden with small black spots, dorsal and caudal fins black spotted, adipose fin with black edge and spots, a broad lilac-mauve iridescent band from head to caudal fin. Older males tend to darken. Juveniles have about 10 broad dark grey vertical bars (parr marks) along the body. In North America sea-run or steelhead trout attain 1,22 m and 16,3 kg but in southern Africa a length of about 660 mm and mass of 4,0 kg is very large. South African angling record 5,43 kg, Zimbabwe 3,827 kg, Lesotho 4,224 kg, Malawi 2,16 kg.

Distribution Dams and mountain streams of south-west, southern, eastern, north-eastern Cape, Lesotho, Natal, eastern Transvaal, Swaziland and eastern Zimbabwe. Also high altitude streams of Mount Mulanje in Malawi. Natural range is the rivers of the Pacific coast of North America from northern Mexico to Alaska. Widely introduced in temperate and high-altitude regions throughout the world.

Biology and Ecology Cool (less than 21°C), clear, well-aerated waters are necessary, and cold (less than 15°C) flowing water is essential for breeding. Tends to be slightly more tolerant than brown trout of higher water temperature. Preys as opportunity provides on a wide range of animal foods from small invertebrates including aquatic insects, especially mayfly nymphs, caddis fly and midge larvae, to terrestrial and aerial insects, crabs, frogs and fish. Breeds later in the season than brown trout, from June through to August and even

September. Breeding fish move upstream to suitable gravel beds; the female digs a redd by beating body and tail rapidly on her side over the gravel. Spawning takes place in the redd and usually several redds are built and used by a female before she is spent. The eggs hatch after 4–7 weeks and after a week or so the young are free swimming. Under favourable conditions may grow to 150–180 mm after a year and up to 260 mm after 2 years. Most males mature after a year, females after 2, and the general lifespan is 3 or 4 years, rarely 5 years in southern Africa.

Uses The most important aquaculture species in South Africa; also a top-rated angling gamefish. In recognised trout waters flyfishing only is permitted.

Note For many years, until recently, known as *Salmo gairdneri*.

Genus *Salvelinus* Richardson, 1836

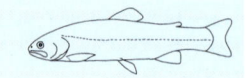

Charrs are a different, more primitive, lineage of the salmonid family, compared to the genus *Salmo* or the more advanced genus *Oncorhynchus*. They generally have even smaller scales than the trout, at least 195 in the lateral line, and in addition the lateral line scales are comparatively smaller than other body scales and of a different shape, appearing to be simple tubes surrounded by skin. They also have 5 infraorbital bones (other salmonids have 6). The genus is holarctic in distribution, across the northern sectors of North America, Asia and Europe; one species in southern Africa, first introduced to the Cape in 1950 from the USA.

BROOK CHARR

Beekforel
Salvelinus fontinalis (Mitchill, 1815)

Description D iii, 9–10; A iii, 7–9. Scales minute, giving leathery appearance to surface; lateral line distinct, straight. Body streamlined, fusiform, fins short, caudal emarginate-truncate. Head with moderately large eye, mouth terminal, upper jaws extend well behind hind edge of orbit when closed, mature males develop a small kype (enlarged hooked jaw). Colour variable, often dark olive brown to reddish brown to mauve; sides with scattered red spots with bluish haloes, dorsal fin with dark brown-black spots. Adult size 200–400 mm SL; reported to reach 860 mm and 6,5 kg in North America. SA angling record 1,035 kg.

Distribution Introduced to streams in the south-west and eastern Cape, Transvaal and Natal. No records have been reported since the 1960s. Native to north-eastern North America.

Biology and Ecology Favours cool, clear, well-aerated waters and breeds over gravel beds in running water. Preferred temperature is up to about 20° C and breeding temperatures are 4–10° C. Diet is similar to that of brown and rainbow trout, with aquatic and terrestrial insects predominating. Breeding behaviour similar to that of trouts – females construct a redd and spawn with a single male. Eggs hatch after 4–6 weeks or more depending on water temperature. Brook charr may attain 7 years in North America.

Uses Introduced for angling purposes in 1950.

Notes Brook charr have been crossed with brown trout to produce the "tiger trout", named for the vermiculated appearance of the hybrid. Brook charr have not been reported for many years from southern Africa and may have died out.

Order Cyprinodontiformes

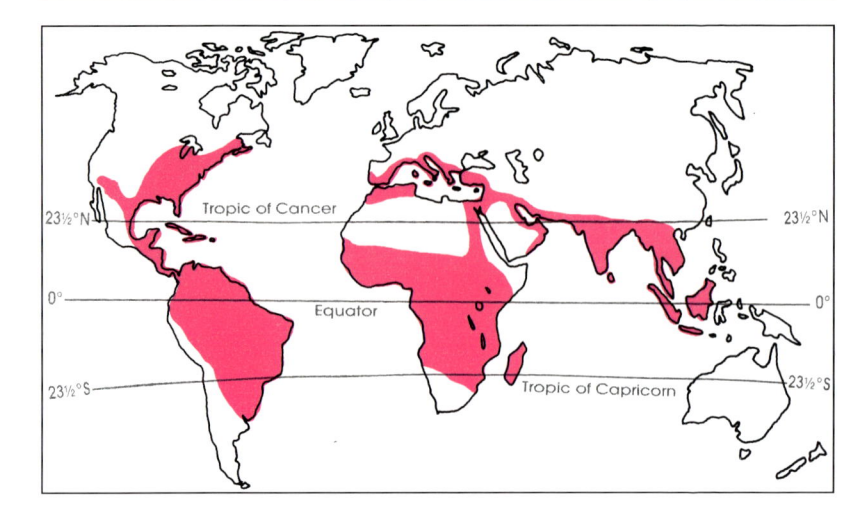

This order includes several families of generally small fishes commonly known as killifishes, topminnows, mosquitofish, rivulins, mollies, swordtails, etc. They are extremely popular aquarium fishes on account of their small size, often attractive colours of the males and hardiness, being easy to keep and breed. They have varied and interesting life histories, some laying eggs and others bearing live young. Distribution is worldwide in tropical continental waters, including both freshwater and brackish or estuarine waters.

FAMILY APLOCHEILIDAE
Annual killifishes

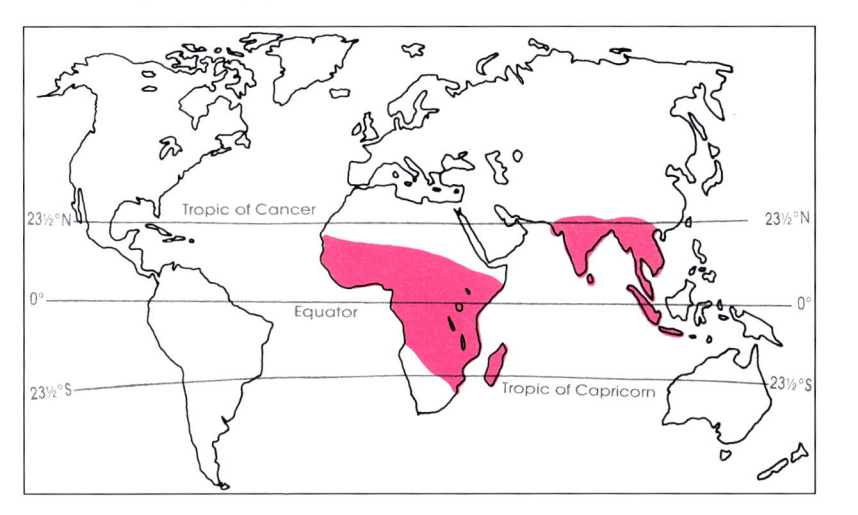

This family comprises six genera of egg-laying killifishes from Africa, Madagascar, India and south-east Asia and includes two genera of very colourful and popular African killifishes.

Genus *Nothobranchius* Peters, 1868

Robust killifishes with large, nearly symmetrical dorsal and anal fins, small pelvic fins and pectoral fins set low on the body. The males grow larger than the females and are brightly coloured. The colour pattern of males is important for the specific identification of these fishes. Known as annual fishes because they usually complete their life cycle within a year, they live in temporary rainpools or riverine floodplains, laying eggs which can endure desiccation. Found in the savanna regions of tropical Africa, the genus includes more than 30 described species, with new species still being discovered. Six species are known from southern Africa.

SPOTTED KILLIFISH

Spikkel-kuilvissie
Nothobranchius orthonotus (Peters, 1844)

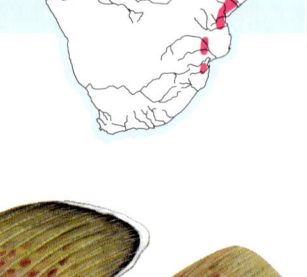

Description D 15–16; A 14–17. Scales in lateral series 27–32. Body robust, dorsal fin far back, opposite the anal fin and generally equal in size, caudal large and rounded or semi-truncate. Head large, covered with scales, mouth dorsal, lower jaw projecting beyond upper jaw. Males have larger dorsal and anal fins than females. Females plain fleshy brown with slight silvery or bluish inflections on the scales and cheeks, fins clear. Red and blue colour forms are recognised in males, but these are probably different expressions of a variable colour pattern. Red spots on the head are diagnostic for the species. The red form has scales with yellow or blue centres and bright red edges, red caudal, pectoral and pelvic fins and red streaks to basal portion of dorsal and anal fins; distal half of dorsal and anal fins green with maroon spots, fin edge brilliant white. In the blue form the red colour is far less accentuated and blue-centred scales are predominant, fins clear green with small red bars and spots, caudal practically clear. Attains 100 mm TL.

Distribution Coastal plain from the lower Zambezi region south to the Mkuze in Natal.

Biology and Ecology Inhabits temporary rainpans and pools, usually without connection to river courses. Lungfish are often the only other fishes in such habitats. Killifish are aggressive predators on insects and aquatic invertebrates. Eggs are laid in the bottom sediments and development is suspended when the water body dries out. The eggs hatch the following rainy season when the pan fills, the fish growing to maturity in a few weeks. Males display to attract ripe females, pair off and spawn, grasping the female by folding over the large dorsal and anal fins. Spawn-

ing occurs daily for an extended period, few eggs are laid at a time. The adults die when the water body dries out.
Uses A popular aquarium species. Used for mosquito larva control.

Conservation Rare in South Africa. Populations are threatened by destruction of pans and by anti-malarial and tsetse fly spraying programmes. Collecting for the aquarium trade is controlled.

BEIRA KILLIFISH

Beira-kuilvissie
Nothobranchius kuhntae (Ahl, 1926)

Description D 14–16; A 13–15. Similar to the spotted killifish in body form, differentiated mainly by the colours of mature males and females. Females pale olive-brown with scattered scales edged with red, scattered red spots on gill cover and cheeks as well as basal regions of dorsal, caudal and anal fins. Males with blue or turquoise centres and red edges to scales, prominent carmine red spots on head and body, caudal brilliant red, sometimes with a thin white edge; dorsal fin pale olive, heavily marked with deep red spots and streaks, edge white; anal fin with pale olive base with deep red spots and bars, membrane deep red, edge white; pectoral and pelvic fins deep red with white edges. Attains 65 mm TL.

Distribution Floodplains of the Pungwe near Beira, Mozambique.

Biology and Ecology Refer to spotted killifish (p. 268).

Uses Aquarium species.

Note Similar to the red form of the spotted killifish and the two species may be synonymous.

TURQUOISE KILLIFISH

Blougroen kuilvissie
Nothobranchius furzeri Jubb, 1971

Description D 14–15; A 14–16. Scales in lateral series 28–30. Similar to spotted killifish in body form. Male coloration distinctive, scale centres turquoise, edged with crimson; dorsal fin and basal portion of caudal and anal fins pale blue with deep red or liver spots and bars, opercular membranes black, edge to dorsal and anal pale blue, caudal with concentric yellow-orange and black bands, pectorals edged with blue, pelvics with deep red markings; female coloration as in spotted killifish. Attains 53 mm TL.
Distribution Pans in Ghona-re-Zhou Game Reserve, south-eastern Zimbabwe.
Biology and Ecology Refer to spotted killifish (p. 268).
Conservation Extremely rare and threatened by habitat destruction and insecticide spraying.

KAFUE KILLIFISH

Kafue-kuilvissie
Nothobranchius kafuensis Wildekamp & Rosenstock, 1989

Description D 16–18; A 16–19. Scales in lateral series 26–31. Similar to spotted killifish in body form, caudal rounded. Male coloration distinctive, scales pale blue with broad red borders, whole fish appears more red than blue, caudal fin variable, either red with light blue and outer black

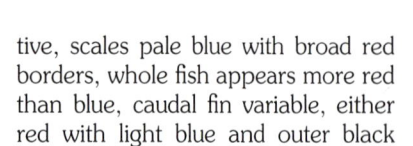

KAFUE KILLIFISH (cont.)

concentric bands, or blue band virtually absent, dorsal fin light blue with red bars and vermiculations, anal fin variable, either predominantly red with a black edge and sometimes a submarginal blue band, or blue with red markings, pectorals reddish towards the base, light blue distally; pelvics light blue; female coloration as in spotted killifish. Variations occur in caudal and anal fin colour patterns, blue band virtually absent in caudal and anal fin of some specimens. Attains 60 mm TL.
Distribution Pans in the Kafue river valley, Zambia.
Biology and Ecology Refer to spotted killifish (p. 268).
Uses Aquarium species.

CAPRIVI KILLIFISH

Gestreepte kuilvissie
Nothobranchius sp.

Description D 16–17; A 16–18. Similar to spotted killifish in body form, caudal rounded. Male coloration distinctive, scales pale blue, edges of certain scales in red, forming irregular series of vertical bands; anal and caudal fins with yellow submarginal band and a black edge, dorsal fin blotched with red and black; female coloration as in spotted killifish. Attains 60 mm TL.
Distribution Pans in Caprivi, Namibia.
Biology and Ecology Refer to spotted killifish (p. 268).
Conservation Endangered. Habitat threatened by road-building and pollution.

RAINBOW KILLIFISH

Reënboog-kuilvissie
Nothobranchius rachovii Ahl, 1926

Description D 14–15; A 15–16. Scales in lateral series 15–26. Body stocky, fins rounded. Male coloration distinctive, head red with turquoise highlights, scales turquoise centred, edged with red, forming irregular red vertical bars, dorsal and anal fins blue with red or deep red markings, edged in white; caudal fin has blue base with red markings, an inner broad orange-red and outer black concentric band; pectoral and pelvic fins pale blue with red base; female coloration as in spotted killifish. Attains 60 mm TL.
Distribution Marshes on the coastal plain near Beira and pans in the Kruger National Park.
Biology and Ecology Refer to spotted killifish (p. 268).
Uses A popular aquarium species.
Conservation Rare in South Africa. Has been translocated to additional sites in the Kruger National Park.

Family Cyprinodontidae
Topminnows

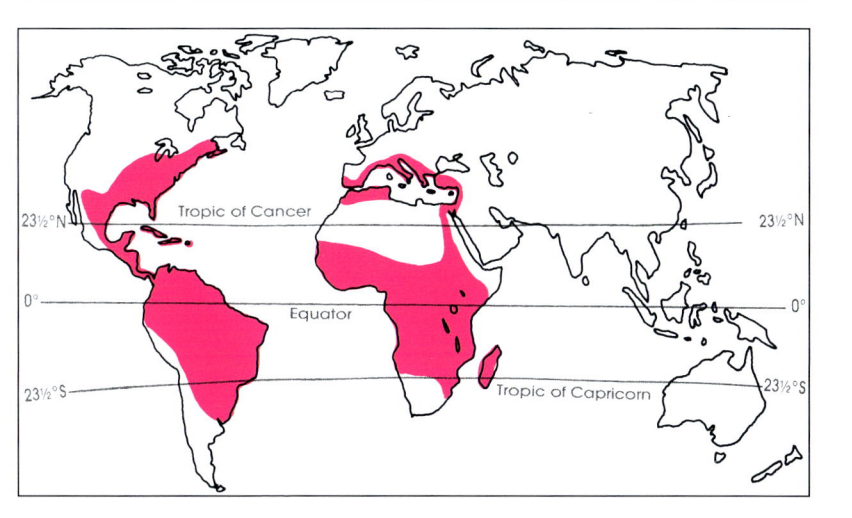

Varied classifications have been proposed for this family. The subfamily Aplocheilichthyinae with about eight or nine genera of African topminnows includes 2 genera from southern Africa. These generally small fishes are named for their habit of living in shallow, weedy habitats and feeding on small creatures from the water surface. The mouth opens upwards and the lateral line system is restricted to the head region where it may form open channels. Although males usually have longer fins and are more colorful than females the difference between males and females is not as pronounced as in the killifishes. Topminnows lay eggs which cannot endure desiccation. Some species are fairly popular aquarium fishes and they are used for mosquito larval control.

Genus *Aplocheilichthys* Bleeker, 1863

There are about 44 species of these small African topminnows. Also known as lampeyes because they have bright iridescent blue or white eyes. Four species are known from southern Africa.

KEY TO SPECIES

1a Scales 23–25 in lateral series, scales clearly outlined in dark pigment, fins barred ....*A. hutereaui* (p. 275)
1b Scales 25 or more in lateral series, scales vaguely or not outlined in dark pigment, fins with light spots or plain 2
2a Body with longitudinal black zigzag stripe....................*A. katangae* (p. 276)
2b Body without longitudinal black zigzag stripe..3
3a Anal finrays 14–15, male dorsal, caudal and anal fins dusky with lemon border..*A. myaposae* (p. 276)
3b Anal finrays 11–14, male dorsal, caudal and anal fins yellow with dark yellow spots and thin black edge ....*A. johnstoni* (p. 274)

JOHNSTON'S TOPMINNOW

Johnston se lampogie
Aplocheilichthys johnstoni Günther, 1893

Description D 6–8; A 11–14. Scales in lateral series 27–29. Body slender, elongated, caudal peduncle length more than twice depth, dorsal fin over posterior anal rays, caudal truncate or semi-truncate. Males more colourful than females, colour translucent yellowish green with light silvery blue iridescence on body scales, sometimes an iridescent blue patch on upper half of gill cover, iris of eye silvery blue, fins clear (females) or yellow with dark yellow spots on the membrane (males), thin black edge to dorsal, caudal and anal fins. Attains about 50 mm TL.

Distribution Cunene, Okavango, upper Zambezi, valley reaches of middle and lower Zambezi, Pungwe and Busi rivers in Mozambique, Limpopo system. Also in the Zambian Zaire system, Kasai-Zaire, Lake Malawi catchment, Lake Rukwa and certain east coastal rivers of Tanzania.

Biology and Ecology Inhabits inshore well-vegetated habitats, often in very shallow water. Prefers standing or gently flowing water as in river backwaters, floodplains and swamps. Usually found in small shoals near the surface. Feeds on small invertebrates such as mosquito larvae and daphnia. A serial spawner, laying eggs which attach to vegetation. When food is abundant breeding occurs daily over an extended period (practically throughout the year in suitable localities). A short mating dance or display is followed by a few eggs being laid at a time. The eggs hatch after 15–20 days and individuals may mature within 5–6 months. Survives for 3–4 years in captivity.

Uses Mosquito control, aquarium species.

MESHSCALED TOPMINNOW

Tralielampogie
Aplocheilichthys hutereaui (Boulenger, 1913)

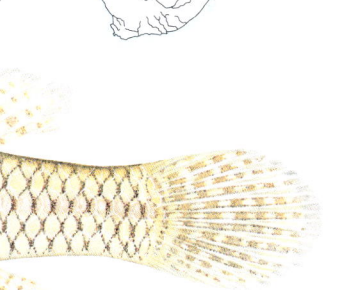

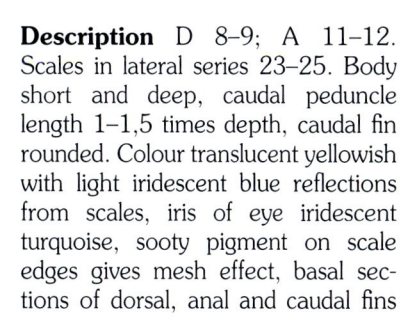

Description D 8–9; A 11–12. Scales in lateral series 23–25. Body short and deep, caudal peduncle length 1–1,5 times depth, caudal fin rounded. Colour translucent yellowish with light iridescent blue reflections from scales, iris of eye iridescent turquoise, sooty pigment on scale edges gives mesh effect, basal sections of dorsal, anal and caudal fins with dark brown blocks. Attains 35 mm TL.

Distribution Okavango, upper Zambezi, lower Shire, Pungwe-Buzi systems near Beira. Also in the Luapula, Zambian Zaire and northern savanna belt of the Zaire system.

Biology and Ecology Strictly a floodplain or marsh-loving species.

Uses Aquarium species.

NATAL TOPMINNOW

Natalse lampogie
Aplocheilichthys myaposae (Boulenger, 1908)

Description D 7–10; A 14–15. Scales in lateral series 27–28. Similar to Johnston's topminnow but tends to have a deeper body and the fin coloration of mature males is distinct: dorsal, caudal and anal fins sooty black with a few yellow spots and a lemon yellow outer edge. Attains 55 mm TL.
Distribution Coastal lakes and rivers in Maputaland, Natal, from Kosi system south to the Umlalazi near Richards Bay.
Biology and Ecology Inhabits inshore vegetated areas of lakes and well-vegetated streams. Feeds on aquatic insects, such as mosquito larvae, and algae. A serial spawner, laying eggs on vegetation.
Uses Potential mosquito control agent; aquarium species.

STRIPED TOPMINNOW

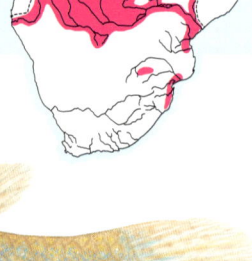

Streeplampogie
Aplocheilichthys katangae (Boulenger, 1912)

Description D 8–10; A 14–15. Scales in lateral series 25–28. Moderately deep bodied with distinctive zigzag black band along the body. Abdomen and lower head white, iris, upper gill cover and scattered mid-body scales iridescent blue-turquoise, fins clear or light yellow. Attains 50 mm TL.
Distribution Cunene, Okavango, Zambezi and Mozambique coastal plain south to Richards Bay area in Maputaland, Natal. Also in the Lufira, Luapula and Zambian Zaire systems.
Biology and Ecology Found in dense marginal vegetation of streams and rivers, uncommon in floodplains. Feeds on insect larvae, daphnia and other small invertebrates. Typical serial spawner, laying eggs on vegetation.
Uses Aquarium species and mosquito control agent.

Genus *Hypsopanchax* Myers, 1924

Very similar to *Aplocheilichthys* topminnows but have a deeper body. Six species, one in southern Africa.

SOUTHERN DEEPBODY

Suidelike dieplyf-kuilvissie
Hypsopanchax jubbi Poll & Lambert, 1965

Description D 10–11; A 16–18. Scales in lateral series 27–28. Hatchet-shaped body of adults distinctive. Males have extended fins and a relatively deeper caudal peduncle than females. Light olive brown with green-blue reflections, the abdomen whitish; dorsal, anal and caudal fins are pale olive green, pectorals and pelvics tinged with orange. Attains 55 mm TL.
Distribution Headwaters of the upper Zambezi and Kasai systems.
Biology and Ecology Taken from small, forested streams with rocky substrate.

FAMILY POECILIIDAE
Live-bearers

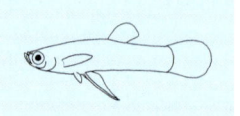

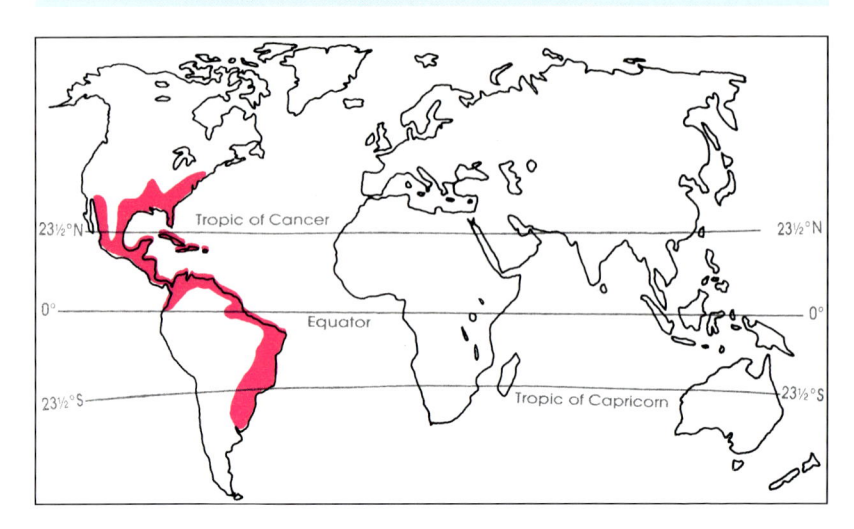

Introduced to southern Africa from Central and South America, these fishes are locally unique for bearing live young. The male anal fin is modified to form a gonopodium or intromittent organ. Many live-bearers are popular aquarium species and it is mainly from released stock that species have become established in natural waters.

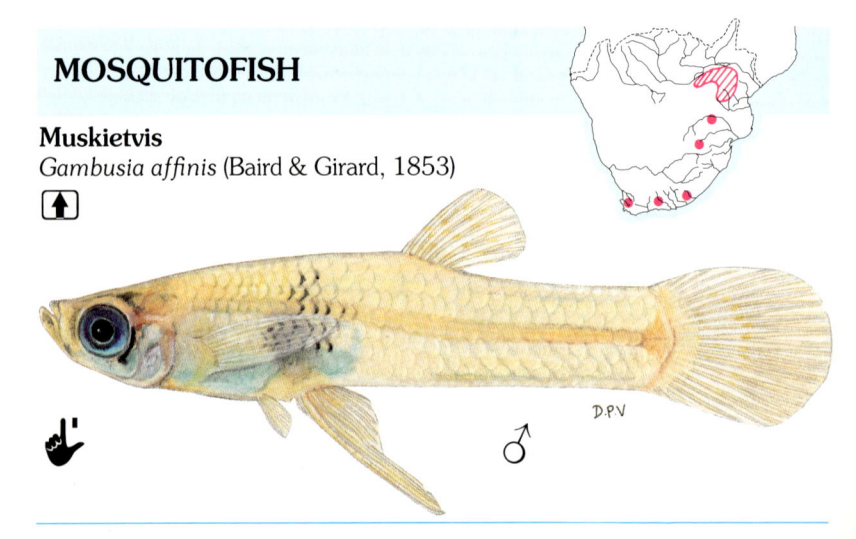

MOSQUITOFISH

Muskietvis
Gambusia affinis (Baird & Girard, 1853)

LIVE-BEARERS

MOSQUITOFISH (cont.)

Description D 6–8; A 9–10. Scales in lateral series 29–30. Head flattened above, mouth upturned, caudal peduncle long, caudal fin rounded. Males slender with anal fin greatly modified and far forward on the body. Female abdomen deep, rounded, anal fin short. Both sexes plain translucent light brown, sometimes with small black spots and iridescent blue reflections, gill cover metallic silvery gold, abdomen silvery, fins clear or lightly marked with dusky spots. A black spot above the vent of the gravid female is typical. Attains 35 mm TL (males) and 60 mm TL (females).

Distribution Scattered isolated populations reported from south-west and southern Cape, Transvaal and Zimbabwe. Natural distribution is Gulf of Mexico drainages of North America from Mexico to Alabama.

Biology and Ecology Requires standing water usually with plant cover. Tolerant of a wide range of water temperature (4–38° C) and salinities from fresh to higher than seawater. Feeds on small live organisms including mosquito larvae and fish larvae. Also known to nip fish fins. Eggs are fertilised internally and fully developed young fish are born.

History and Conservation Introduced before 1936 by aquarists but later bred and distributed by Cape Inland Fisheries Department as a mosquito control agent and forage for bass. Introduced widely to tropical and subtropical countries for mosquito control but has proved to be an aggressive invader species capable of restricting other fish populations by preying on fish larvae.

SPOTTAIL MOSQUITOFISH

Kolstert-muskietvis
Phalloceros caudimaculatus (Hensel, 1868)

Description D 7–8; A 9–10. Scales in lateral series 28–30. Very similar to mosquitofish, male gonopodium long, hooked. Colour translucent olive brown, dark spot at beginning of caudal peduncle, iridescent blue

SPOTTAIL MOSQUITOFISH (cont.)

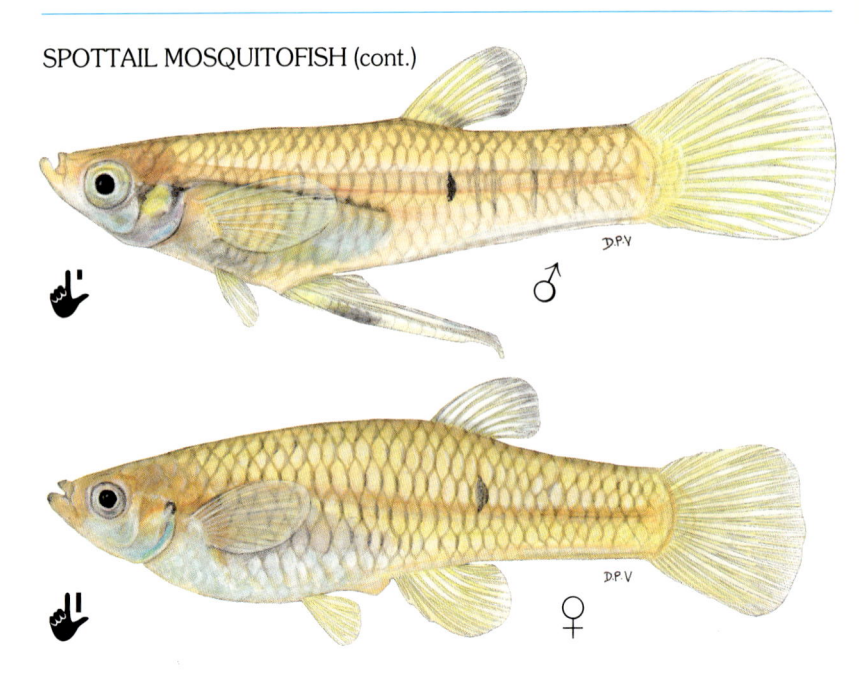

reflection on gill cover; male dorsal fin with sooty edge. Some individuals have scattered black spots over the body. Attains 35 mm (male) or 60 mm (female) TL.
Distribution A single feral population in a tributary of the Ruo, Malawi.

Native range southern Brazil to Paraguay.
Biology and Ecology Feeds on small live aquatic insects and invertebrates but less aggressive than the common mosquitofish. Broods may comprise as many as 50 individuals.

GUPPY

Guppie (Miljoenvis)
Poecilia reticulata Peters, 1859

Description D 7–8; A 8–9. Scales in lateral series 26–28. Females have typical rounded abdomen and caudal fin and the slender male a well-developed gonopodium, long caudal peduncle and variable tail fin. Male colour is extremely variable, often spectacular, in combinations of iridescent red, blue, turquoise and yellow; black spots and stripes often present. Wild colours tend to be less gaudy. Gravid females have a dark spot above the vent. Males attain 30 mm TL, females 60 mm TL.

LIVE-BEARERS

GUPPY (cont.)

♂ ♀

Distribution Feral populations reported from coastal reaches of Natal rivers from Durban southwards, as well as in the Kuruman Eye and Lake Otjikoto in Namibia. Natural distribution north-eastern South America and Caribbean islands.
Biology and Ecology Has a wide tolerance of salinity but does require fairly warm temperatures (optimally 23–24° C) and quiet vegetated water for survival. Feeds on daphnia, mosquito larvae and small worms. Breeds easily, females giving birth to batches of live young.
History and Conservation First introduced and released in 1912 in Transvaal and Natal rivers for mosquito control. However, most feral populations are from aquarium releases, an illegal and potentially harmful practice.

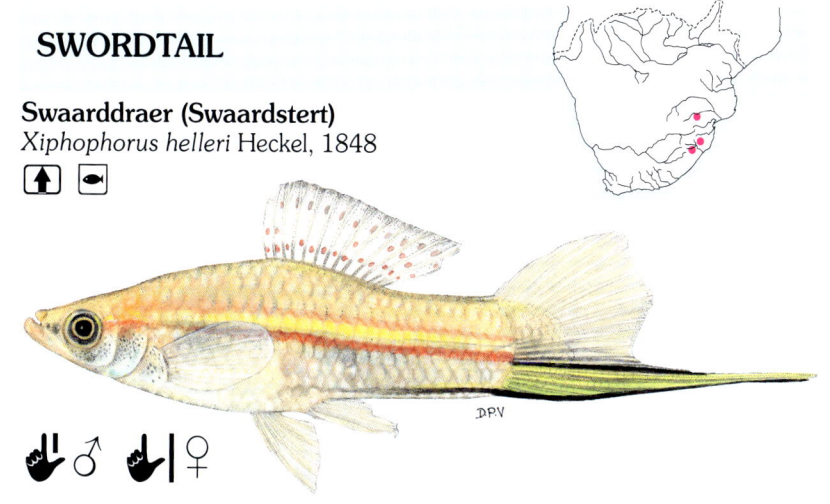

SWORDTAIL

Swaarddraer (Swaardstert)
Xiphophorus helleri Heckel, 1848

♂ ♀

Description D 11–14; A 8–10. Scales in lateral series 26–30. Characterised by the relatively long dorsal fin, the male gonopodium and elongated lower rays of the male caudal fin (the sword). Colour variable; common aquarium variety is orange-red with a black-outlined sword, wild colour is a light translucent brown along back, bright green orange-bor-

dered body stripe and a bright green black-bordered sword. Females may be similar in colour but less intense than males. Males attain 80 mm TL (without sword), females 120 mm TL.
Distribution Feral populations reported from Natal and eastern Transvaal as well as in Lake Otjikoto, Namibia. Natural distribution is on the Atlantic slope of southern Mexico and Honduras.
Biology and Ecology Hardy and tolerant but requires warm temperatures (20–26° C) and quiet water to breed. Feeds on small aquatic invertebrates. Females may produce several broods from a single mating. Can undergo sex change, large females changing into males.
History and Conservation Feral populations are derived from aquarium releases and were first reported in 1974. This fairly large and robust live-bearer may prey on fish larvae and damage indigenous fish populations.

SPINY-RAYED FISHES

Most living fishes belong to lineages that are considered to be more highly evolved than the species already described, and differ fundamentally in body form by having the dorsal and anal fins composed of a series of true spines and soft rays. Other notable differences are: the pelvic fins are farther forward on the body, the pectoral fins are on the sides of the body and orientated in a vertical plane, the upper jaw is bordered by the premaxilla alone, the swimbladder does not have a connecting duct to the alimentary canal, and there is never an adipose fin. Most spiny-rayed fishes are marine species; comparatively few occur in freshwater.

FAMILY CENTRARCHIDAE
Basses and sunfishes

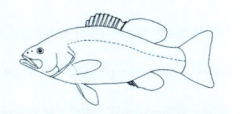

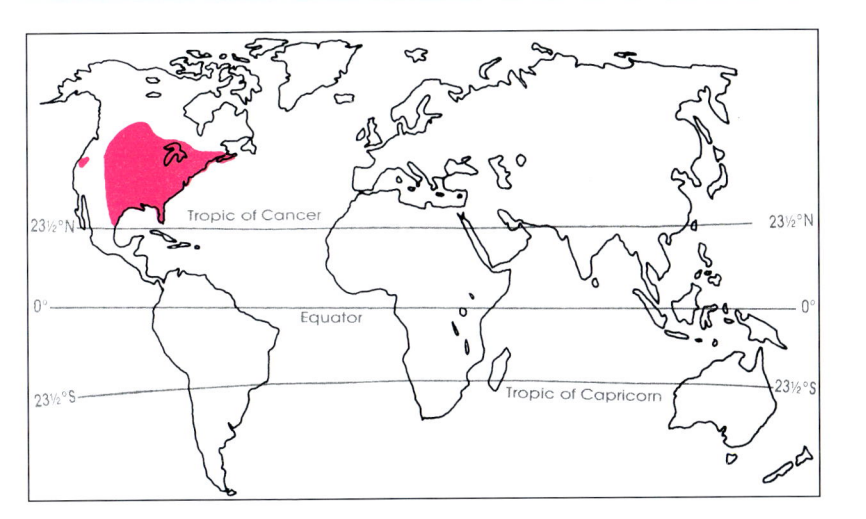

A North American fish family that includes the freshwater basses and sunfishes. The local species were introduced to southern Africa between 1928 and 1939 to complement trout as gamefish in rivers and dams. The family is part of the large percoid group of fishes in which the dorsal and anal fins have a series of spines and soft rays and the pelvic fins are advanced on the body. Four species are established in southern Africa.

KEY TO SPECIES

1a Deep bodied, body depth about half SL; less than 40 lateral line scales
....***Lepomis macrochirus*** (p. 284)
1b Body elongated, body depth about one third SL; more than 60 lateral line scales...2
2a Hind margin of jaw extends well beyond hind border of eye (mouth closed), membrane of spinous and soft-rayed sections of dorsal fin deeply cleft to body ....***Micropterus salmoides*** (p. 286)

2b Hind margin of jaw extends to hind border of eye (mouth closed), membrane of spinous and soft-rayed sections of dorsal fin shallowly cleft 3
3a 11 scale rows between lateral line and first dorsal fin spine, no spotted pigmentation on flanks below lateral line, scales cycloid ....
....***Micropterus dolomieu*** (p. 287)
3b 8 scale rows between lateral line and first dorsal fin spine, spotted pigmentation on flanks below lateral line, scales ctenoid......................................
....***Micropterus punctulatus*** (p. 288)

Genus *Lepomis* Rafinesque, 1819

A deep body and distinct lobe on the upper gill cover are characteristic features of this genus. One species, the bluegill, introduced in 1938 as a fodder species for bass, is now established in many streams and dams.

BLUEGILL SUNFISH

Blouwang-sonvis
Lepomis macrochirus Rafinesque, 1819

Description D IX–X, 10–11; A III, 10–12. Lateral line single and complete, 40–44 scales. Body deep and rounded, dorsal fin deep, spinous and soft-rayed sections continuous, caudal emarginate. Head profile steep, mouth small, eyes large, gill cover with a large black projection on upper corner. Colour variable depending on habitat and condition, usually an iridescent green-blue with vague vertical bands along body, median fins sooty black, pectorals with a yellowish tinge. In breeding males the chest

BLUEGILL SUNFISH (cont.)

turns orange. Attains about 200 mm SL, SA angling record 1,12 kg.
Distribution Cape coastal drainages, middle reaches of rivers in Natal, sparsely in the south-eastern and eastern Transvaal, north-eastern Orange Free State. Uncommon in Zimbabwe and Namibia. Natural distribution is in eastern and central North America.
Biology and Ecology Prefers quiet well-vegetated waters in both river and dams. Preys on invertebrates and small fish. Breeds in summer, males constructing a saucer-shaped nest by fanning clear the substrate; eggs are adhesive and are guarded by the male. Several nests of different individuals may be constructed in the same area. Lives for 10 or more years.
Uses Introduced as a fodder fish for bass. A minor angling species in some areas.
Conservation Bluegills are considered to be a pest as they tend to overpopulate waters, preying on indigenous species, and are not top-rated angling fishes.

Genus *Micropterus* Lacepède, 1802

The freshwater basses are among the most popular freshwater gamefishes. Introduced from 1928 to 1939, they quickly became established in natural waters. In some areas they have caused extensive damage to indigenous fish species and, while still very popular as angling species, are considered to be a conservation problem in certain natural waters. Three species are established in southern Africa.

LARGEMOUTH BASS

Grootbek-baars
Micropterus salmoides (Lacepède, 1802)

Description D VIII–IX+I, 12–13; A III, 9–11. Lateral line complete, 58–69 scales, 6–8 between lateral line and first dorsal spine, no scales on base of dorsal or anal fins. Mouth large, extending well beyond hind margin of orbit when closed, small caniniform teeth in bands on jaws. Dorsal fin membrane deeply cleft between spinous and soft-rayed sections, caudal fin emarginate. Olive green above, light green on flanks, lower half of head and abdomen white; a connected series of short, dark olive green vertical bars forms an irregular band along body, 2 or 3 broad olive stripes radiate behind eye. Attains about 600 mm TL, SA angling record 4,575 kg, Zimbabwe 5,15 kg, Malawi 2,81 kg, world 10,09 kg.
Distribution Widespread throughout Cape coastal drainages, Natal midlands and Transvaal. Also in Malawi, Namibia and Zimbabwe. Natural distribution is in central and eastern North America from the Gulf of Mexico to southern Canada.
Biology and Ecology Favours clear, standing or slow-flowing waters with submerged and floating vegetation. Does well in farm dams. Fairly tolerant of temperatures from below 10° C to as high as 32° C. Primarily piscivorous but will take virtually any animal food it encounters and can handle, including crabs, frogs, snakes and even small mammals. Young bass feed primarily on insects and start taking fish from about 50 mm size. Breeds in spring (October–November) once water temperatures reach about 18° C. Males construct a nest over any firm substrate, including vegetation, fanning the area clear of silt. After egg laying the male guards the nest and newly hatched larvae, which form a shoal until they reach about 25 mm in length. Growth depends on food availability but year-old fish may attain 100–200 mm. May mature after a year and individuals live for 10–12 years.
Uses A very popular, major freshwa-

ter gamefish species. Several sponsored bass fishing tournaments occur annually.
History Introduced to the Cape from stock bred in The Netherlands in 1928. A southern subspecies, known as Florida bass (*M. salmoides floridianus*), was introduced to Natal in 1980.
Note Identification of Florida bass from ordinary largemouth bass is not possible on external characteristics. This may be done by counting the pyloric caecae: ordinary largemouth have 18–29, Florida bass 30–47.

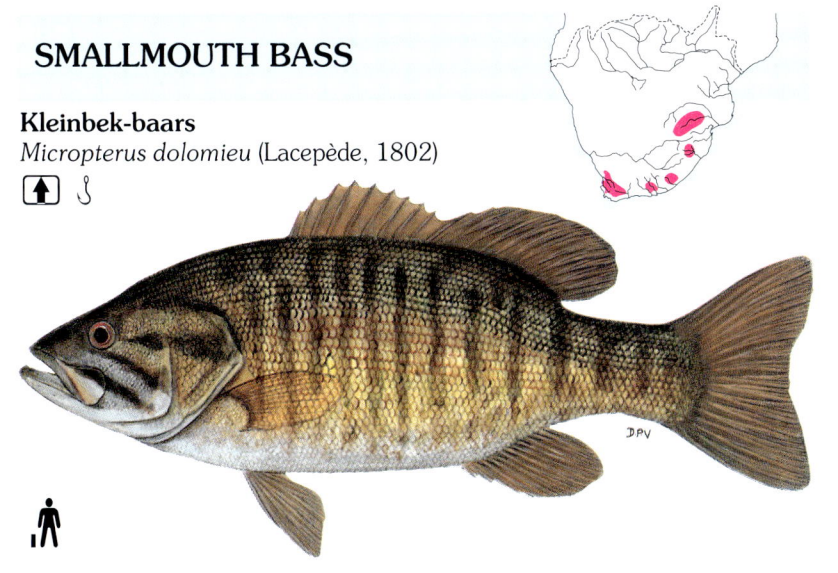

SMALLMOUTH BASS

Kleinbek-baars
Micropterus dolomieu (Lacepède, 1802)

Description D IX+I, 12–14; A III, 9–11. Lateral line complete, 68–81 scales, 11 between lateral line and first dorsal spine, base of soft dorsal and anal fins with scales. Upper jaw, when closed, reaches to line through middle of eye. Membrane of spinous and soft dorsal fin indented but broadly connected. Olive green with a bronze tinge; deep olive vertical bars and radiating bars behind eye are characteristic, fins deep olive-black, underside of head and abdomen greyish white. Juveniles ("bannertails") with yellow and black banded caudal fin. Attains about 550 mm SL. SA angling record 2,8 kg, world 5,41 kg.

Distribution Certain rivers of southwest and eastern Cape, Natal and Transvaal. Natural distribution is eastern central North America.
Biology and Ecology Favours flowing waters and has done well over loose, rocky substrates. Breeds in spring and early summer when temperatures reach about 16° C. Males construct a nest by clearing the substrate and tend the eggs and larvae until about 20 mm size. The "bannertails" feed on insects and crabs and later on small fish. Adults are primarily piscivorous but crabs are also taken regularly. Lives for up to 15 years.
Uses An excellent angling species on

light tackle.
History and Conservation Introduced to South Africa in 1937 to enhance river fishing below the trout zone and to control indigenous fish species like whitefish and scaleys. Very successful in south-west Cape rivers, where it impacted heavily on indigenous species. For this reason smallmouth bass is no longer produced or stocked by nature conservation authorities.

SPOTTED BASS

Spikkel-baars
Micropterus punctulatus (Rafinesque, 1819)

Description D X, 12–13; A III, 10. Lateral line complete, 60–75 scales, 8 between lateral line and first dorsal spine, membrane of spinous and soft-rayed dorsal fins deeply indented, scales on basal membranes of soft dorsal and anal fins. Closed upper jaw reaches to level of hind border of orbit. Deep olive above, with yellowish flanks and a mid-lateral series of deep olive diamond-shaped bars joined to form a band; lower body scales dusky, forming a linear pattern of spots. Attains about 600 mm TL. SA angling record 2,04 kg, world 4,19 kg.
Distribution Introduced to the Cape and Natal. Surviving populations reported from certain eastern Cape and Natal rivers. Natural range is southern central North America.
Biology and Ecology Prefers slightly turbid waters of slow- flowing rivers and dams. Preys on insects, crabs, frogs and fish. Breeds in early summer, males clearing a nest in shallow water and tending the eggs and larvae.
Uses An angling species.
History Introduced in 1939, mainly for stocking turbid waters. Appears to be the least successful bass species in South Africa but it is possible that catches are being misidentified.

Family Percidae
Perches

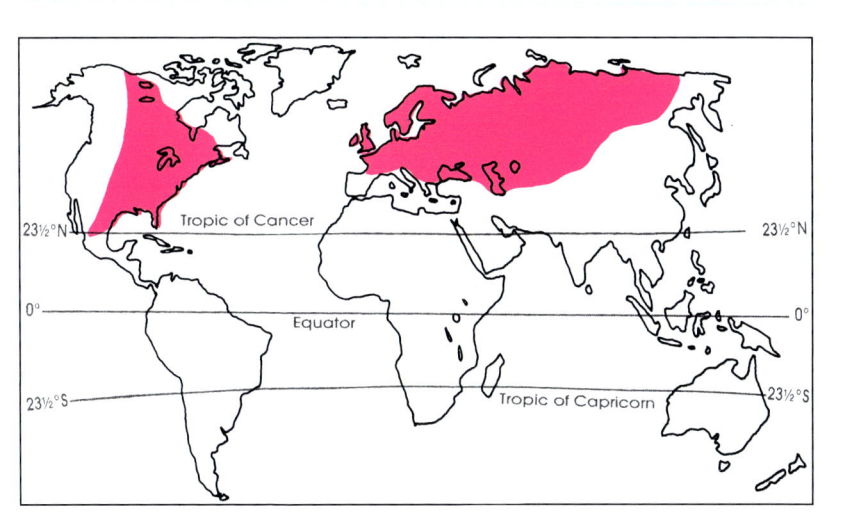

Genus *Perca* Linnaeus, 1758

A northern hemisphere family of freshwater fishes with one species introduced to southern Africa. Easily recognised by their separate spiny and soft-rayed dorsal fins. Perch are not well established like the basses and bluegill, but occasional surviving populations are encountered.

PERCH

Europese baars
Perca fluviatilis Linnaeus, 1758

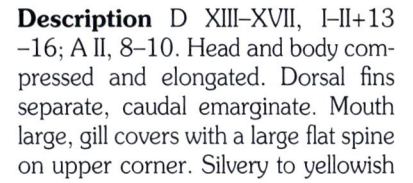

Description D XIII–XVII, I–II+13–16; A II, 8–10. Head and body compressed and elongated. Dorsal fins separate, caudal emarginate. Mouth large, gill covers with a large flat spine on upper corner. Silvery to yellowish green, white below, 6 or more dark vertical bars on body, spiny dorsal fin with a dark patch at rear end, pelvic and anal fins orange. Attains 600 mm TL. Reported to reach 4,75 kg in Europe and 10,4 kg in Australia. SA

PERCH (cont.)

angling record 1,305 kg.
Distribution Isolated vleis or dams in the south-west Cape, eastern Cape and southern Transvaal. Natural range is Europe and northern Asia.
Biology and Ecology A cold-water species, favouring lakes and dams or slow-flowing rivers. Moves in shoals, preying on insects, crabs and fish. Breeds in shallow water, the unguarded eggs attached in strings to roots or vegetation.
Uses Angling species.
History First imported in 1896 and again in 1915. Stocked into suitable localities in 1926.

FAMILY CICHLIDAE
Cichlids

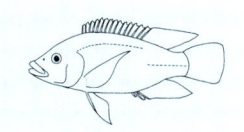

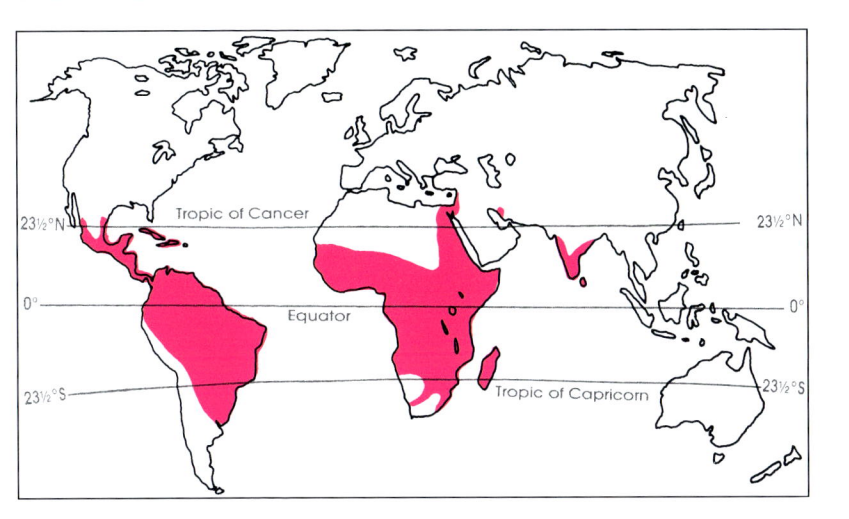

A very large family of fresh and brackish water fishes found in Africa, South and Central America, Madagascar, the Levant, parts of Arabia and India. Many species are extremely important food fishes and others are attractive and biologically interesting aquarium subjects. Cichlids are scientifically important in such fields as evolution, behaviour and physiology. They are most closely related to the marine families Labridae (wrasses), Embiotocidae (surfperches) and Pomacentridae (damselfishes).

Typical features of cichlids are scales on the head and body, the dorsal and anal fins each composed of spinous and soft-rayed sections, pelvic fins in a thoracic position, each comprising a spine and five branched rays, a divided lateral line, and a single nostril opening on either side of the snout. Colour and behaviour are often important taxonomic features. The breeding styles of cichlids usually involve pair-formation, nest building and the guarding of eggs and young. In many species one of the parents, usually the female, picks up the eggs and incubates them and the embryos in the mouth (mouthbrooding).

Within our area, in broad terms, there are two main lineages, the tilapiines, which are chiefly plant or sediment feeders, and the haplochromines, which tend to be predators. The young of tilapiines have a dark eye-spot at the base of the soft dorsal fin, called the "tilapia spot". Adult haplochromines usually have a series of clear spots or ocelli, often called "egg spots" or "egg dummies", on the anal fin. A function of these dummies is to assist the fertilisation of the eggs by enticing the female, when gathering the eggs in her mouth, to the genital region of the male who then releases the milt.

This is the largest fish family in Africa with about 870 species described and many more still to be described. They are especially abundant in the African Great Lakes. In southern Africa there are 8 genera and 41 species. A simple key to cichlid genera is not always practical as many pertinent features are internal, skeletal or behavioural. To facilitate identification, similar or related species or genera have been grouped and briefly introduced. The groups are "riverine haplochromines" (pp. 293–304), sargos (pp. 304–311), serranos (pp. 311–318) and tilapiines (pp. 319–332).

KEY TO GENERA

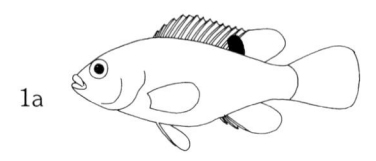

1a Teeth fine, closely set, gill rakers simple; juveniles with distinct black spot on soft dorsal ("tilapia spot") 2

1b Teeth coarse, gill rakers stout, spatulate or branched; juveniles without black spot on soft dorsal 3

2a Adults with "tilapia spot", less than 12 gill rakers on lower limb of first gill arch, substrate spawners and guarders ....***Tilapia* (p. 319)**

2b Adults without "tilapia spot", more than 14 gill rakers on lower limb of first gill arch, mouthbrooders..***Oreochromis* (p. 324)**

3a Chest scales very small, abruptly reduced in size 4

3b Chest scales gradually reduced in size..5

4a Caudal rounded, males without anal fin spots or ocelli, more than 9 posterior upper lateral line scales separated from dorsal base by only $1^{1}/_{2}$ scales ....***Orthochromis* (p. 295)**

4b Caudal truncate, males with prominent anal fin ocelli, less than 9 posterior upper lateral line scales separated from dorsal base by only $1^{1}/_{2}$ scales ....***Thoracochromis* (p. 302)**

5a Caudal fin rounded, anal fin of males with orange tip, no egg spots or ocelli ....***Pseudocrenilabrus* (p. 295)**

5b Caudal truncate, anal fin of males without orange tip, with or without egg spots or ocelli 6

6a Body with 4–5 pronounced black vertical bars, anal fin of males without egg spots or ocelli ....**Hemichromis (p. 294)**
6b Body without 4–5 pronounced black vertical bars, anal fin of males with egg spots or ocelli 7

6b

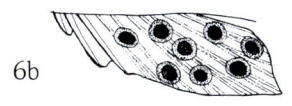

7a Single scale row between orbit and preopercular groove, pharyngeal bones robust, median pharyngeal teeth stout, molariform................................8

7a   7b   7b

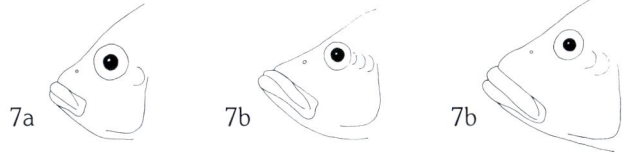

7b Two or more rows of scales between orbit and preopercular groove, pharyngeal bones slender, median pharyngeal teeth moderately large, not molariform 9
8a Last 2 or 3 pored scales in the upper lateral line series separated from the dorsal fin base by not less than 2 scales of approximately equal size ....
....***Sargochromis* (p. 304)**
8b Last 5 to 7 pored scales in the upper lateral line series separated from the dorsal fin base by one large and one small scale ..***Pharyngochromis* (p. 300)**
9a Mouth very large, when closed maxilla extends to or beyond vertical through anterior orbit, teeth unicuspid ....
....***Serranochromis* (p. 311)**
9b Mouth moderately large, when closed maxilla not extending to vertical through anterior orbit, teeth bi- and unicuspid ....***Chetia* (p. 297)**

a   b   c

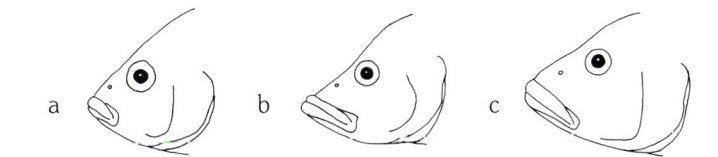

Mouth shapes: (a) *Sargochromis*, (b) *Serranochromis*, (c) *Chetia*

"Riverine haplochromines"

About 7 different, not necessarily closely related genera are included in this grouping. Most of these species are small or moderate-sized cichlids with ellipsoid-shaped bodies, moderately large mouths with unicuspid or bicuspid teeth. All, except *Hemichromis*, are mouthbrooders, the males in breeding dress are brightly coloured and most have anal fin ocelli or egg spots.

Genus *Hemichromis* Peters, 1858

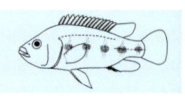

A distinct African lineage of bright coloured, bold predators. They are substrate spawning brood guarders. The species occur mostly in tropical forest habitats in West and Central Africa and are absent from East Africa. Eleven species, one in our area.

BANDED JEWELFISH

Balk-juweelvis
Hemichromis elongatus (Guichenot, 1859)

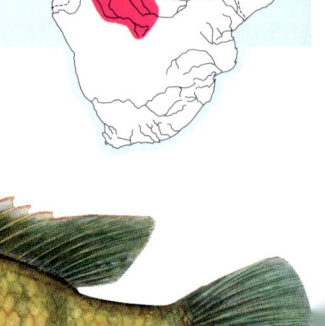

Description D XIII–XV, 11–13; A III, 8–10. Lateral line scales 28–32. Body robust, depth about equal to head length, pectoral fin short. Two distinctive enlarged conical teeth in front of upper jaw. Colour striking and attractive, body dark olive above to bright green on sides and scarlet red below, scales on sides highlighted and iridescent, upper gill cover with conspicuous red and black spots, fins deep sooty olive, tips of dorsal fin red, pelvics black, 5 black diamond-shaped vertical bars along body, with shadow bars between them, an oblique black band on the head passes through the eye. Attains about 190 mm TL.

Distribution Okavango and upper Zambezi systems. Also widespread through the Zaire basin to tropical West Africa.

Biology and Ecology Occurs in littoral riverine habitats and permanent floodplain lagoons with clear water. Preys on shrimps, insects and small fishes. A nesting substrate spawner, breeding in the early summer. The parents guard the nest and larvae.

Uses Occasional aquarium fish. Small numbers taken by subsistence fishermen.

RIVERINE HAPPIES

Genus *Orthochromis* Greenwood, 1954

Sometimes described as "goby-like" on account of their slender body and sharply decurved head profile. The chest and ventral abdominal scales are abruptly smaller than the lateral body scales. Four species, one in our area.

CUNENE DWARF HAPPY

Kunene dwerg-bekbroeier
Orthochromis machadoi (Poll, 1967)

Description D XV–XVII, 9–11; A III, 7–9. Scales in lateral line 29–33, chest scales distinctly smaller than body scales. Body tapered, moderately elongated, caudal fin rounded or subtruncate. Mouth small, horizontal. Body with 10–12 broad vertical mesh-like bars, a dark upright dash at base of caudal fin, dark bars from eye to mouth and from eye across top of gill cover, soft dorsal and caudal fins with dark spots. Breeding males turn bright red. Attains 65 mm SL.
Distribution Cunene system, Namibia and Angola.
Biology and Ecology Little known, a female mouthbrooder.
Uses Potential aquarium fish.

Genus *Pseudocrenilabrus* Fowler, 1934

The rounded caudal fin and orange tip to the anal fin (of males) are distinctive features. These small aggressive cichlids are mouthbrooders. Three species, one in our area.

SOUTHERN MOUTHBROODER

Suidelike mondbroeier
Pseudocrenilabrus philander (Weber, 1897)

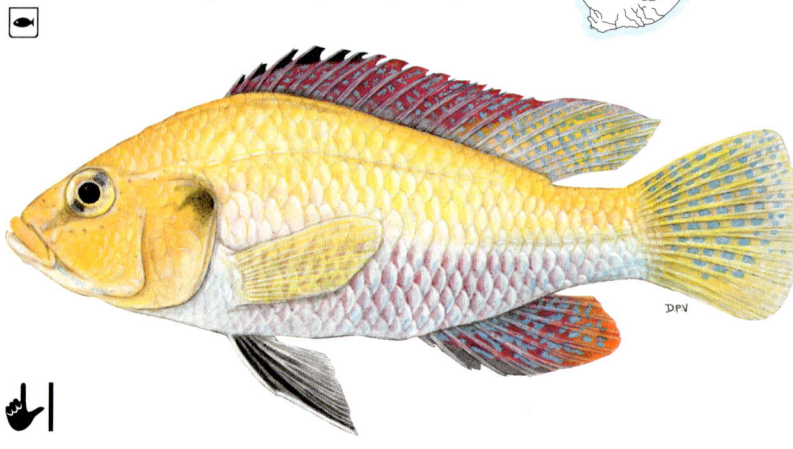

Description D XIII–XVI, 9–11; A III, 7–9. Lateral line scales 27–30, chest scales not sharply differentiated from body scales. Body stout, caudal rounded. Mouth small, horizontal. Females are light brown with black vertical bars and light yellowish fins. Male colours differ with locality; body usually a mesh of iridescent light blue and yellow, with an oblique bar through the eye and iridescent blue lower jaw; dorsal fin has a red tip, black submarginal band and iridescent blue blocks, pelvics black, caudal and anal fins have iridescent blue and red blocks, anal with orange tip; colours are accentuated during breeding. Attains 130 mm TL.

Distribution From the Orange and southern Natal northwards throughout the region. Extends to southern Zaire tributaries and Lake Malawi.

Biology and Ecology Occurs in a wide variety of habitats from flowing waters to lakes and isolated sinkholes; usually favours vegetated zones. Preys on insects, shrimps and even small fish. Breeds from early spring to late summer; males establish and defend a territory, construct a simple cleared nest and attract ripe females. Eggs are laid in the nest, fertilised and collected by the female. She withdraws to a quiet nursery area and broods the eggs, larvae and juveniles until they are able to fend for themselves. Several broods may be raised in a season. Lives for 4–5 years.

Uses Aquarium species. Used for behavioural and evolutionary research.

Conservation Isolated populations in springs and sinkholes threatened by introduced fishes, habitat change and insecticide pollution.

Genus *Chetia* Trewavas, 1961

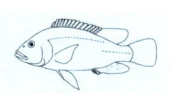

Defined partly on skeletal characters, they resemble the largemouth breams (*Serranochromis*), but juveniles have bicuspid and conical teeth. Four species, 3 in our area.

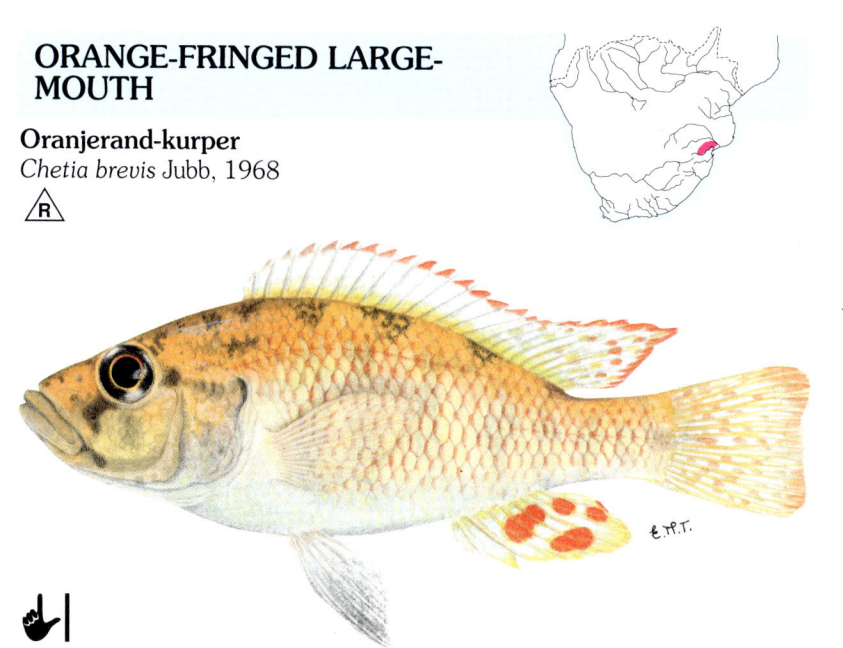

ORANGE-FRINGED LARGEMOUTH

Oranjerand-kurper
Chetia brevis Jubb, 1968

Description D XIV–XV, 10–12; A III, 7–9. Scales ctenoid, 32–34 in lateral line series, cheek scales small and numerous. Body moderately slender, caudal fin truncate. Head large, mouth large, inclined; teeth small, pointed, in 2 rows; 9–10 well-spaced, stout gill rakers. Olive brown, flanks light turquoise, scales with brick-red bases, abdomen whitish, 8–9 dark vertical bars on body, dorsal fin with orange spots and tips, caudal with dark orange blocks and orange tips, male anal fin with 2 rows of large orange spots. Attains 150 mm TL.

Distribution Komati-Incomati system, eastern Transvaal and coastal lakes in Mozambique.

Biology and Ecology Favours pools or standing water, thrives in impoundments. Feeds on aquatic insects and small fish. A mouthbrooder, the female carries the eggs and larvae.

Conservation Rare, threatened by pollution and water extraction. Translocated to dams in the Kruger National Park; construction of dams has been beneficial.

CANARY KURPER

Kanariekurper
Chetia flaviventris Trewavas, 1961

Description D XV, 11–12; A III, 9–10. Scales cycloid, 34 in lateral line, cheek scales small and numerous. Body moderately slender, caudal fin truncate. Mouth inclined, jaws with 2 rows of conical and bicuspid teeth. Olive brown above, silvery to white on sides and abdomen, scales with orange-red base, mature males with bright yellow chest, a series of about 6–7 vertical sooty bars on body, membranes of dorsal and caudal fin with rows of dark brown spots. Male anal fin with orange spots surrounded by yellow. Attains about 200 mm TL. SA angling record 0,815 kg.

Distribution Tributaries of the Limpopo in Transvaal and Zimbabwe.

Biology and Ecology Found in larger intermittent tributaries, favours standing or slow-flowing pools and thrives in impounded waters. Preys on invertebrates and small fish. Breeds in summer, the female mouthbrooding the eggs and larvae.

Uses A minor angling species, often a nuisance but popular with novices and young anglers.

ANGOLAN HAPPY

Angola-happie
Chetia welwitschi (Boulenger, 1898)

Description D XIV–XV, 11–12; A III, 9. Lateral line scales 31–34. Mouth moderately large, teeth conical, 9–11 stout gill rakers on first arch. Colour not known, anal fin of males with large ocelli. Attains 147 mm SL.

Distribution Cunene River and a tributary of the Luangwe-Zaire system, Angola.
Note Known only from a few museum specimens, further specimens are required for study.

Genus *Astatotilapia* Pellegrin, 1903

Features of this genus are that males have few large anal fin ocelli, the chest scales are not markedly smaller or different from the lower body scales and the teeth are mostly bicuspid. About 9 species, mostly from East Africa, one species in our area.

EASTERN HAPPY

Oostelike happie
Astatotilapia calliptera (Günther, 1893)

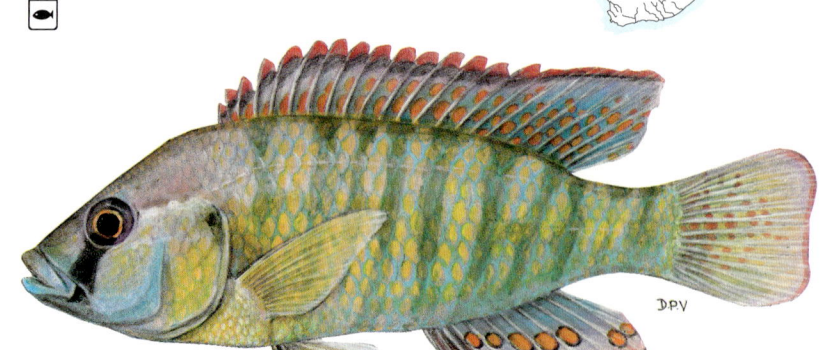

Description D XIII–XV, 9–10; A III, 7–8. Lateral line scales 29–33. Body moderately slender, mouth short, teeth small, mostly bicuspid, in 3–5 rows along jaws, eye large. Gill rakers short, widely spaced, 7–9 on first arch. Olive green, with 8–9 deep olive vertical bars; a dark bar from eye to corner of mouth; mid-lateral scales with blue borders and yellow-orange centres; lower head blue; dorsal fin sooty, with yellow-orange spots and red tips; caudal dirty yellow, with dark orange spots; anal sooty at the base, with yellow outer parts and large bright orange egg-spots. Breeding males are striking, with bright blue head and lower hind body and caudal peduncle, a bright yellow abdomen, large bright orange egg-spots and blue-and-red-flushed dorsal and anal fins. Attains 110 mm TL.

Distribution Lower Zambezi, Pungwe, Buzi and lower Save systems. Also in Lake Malawi catchment.

Biology and Ecology Occurs in a wide variety of riverine and marshy habitats.

Uses Potential aquarium species.

Genus *Pharyngochromis* Greenwood, 1979

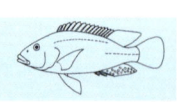

Similar to *Chetia* but characterised by having a stout pharyngeal bone with coarse molariform or submolariform teeth. Males have numerous bright egg-spots on the anal fin. The only species of this genus occurs in southern Africa.

ZAMBEZI HAPPY

Zambesi-happie
Pharyngochromis acuticeps (Steindachner, 1866)

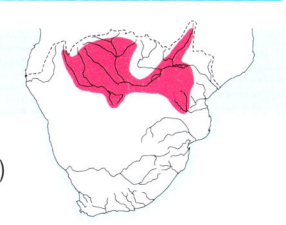

Description D XIV–XVI, 10–13; A III, 7–10. Lateral line scales 31–36, cheek scales 4–5 rows. Body robust, caudal fin truncate. Head large, mouth horizontal or slightly oblique, conical and bicuspid teeth in 3 rows. Gill rakers 7–12, stout and T-shaped. Brown with black bars and iridescent green infusions, body scales with deep red centres; dorsal fin with sooty band, orange-red tips and sooty orange spots especially on soft-rayed section, caudal fin with dark brown spots and anal fin with orange-red margin and a variable number of clear orange egg-spots. Chest of breeding males dark sooty-grey. Attains 220 mm TL, usually less than 100 mm TL.

Distribution Okavango, Zambezi system, upper Save-Runde in Zimbabwe.

Biology and Ecology Found in a wide range of habitats in association with cover such as plants or tree roots. Preys on insects, shrimps and small fish, also eggs and larvae of nesting fishes. Preyed on by cormorants and darters in dams. A female mouthbrooder, breeding in summer. Lives for 3 or 4 years.

Uses Potential aquarium fish.

Genus *Thoracochromis* Greenwood, 1979

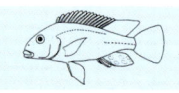

The scales on the chest are abruptly smaller than those on the sides. The males have bright egg-spots without clear borders on the anal fin. Seventeen or more species, widespread in north-east, east and southern Africa, two species from our area.

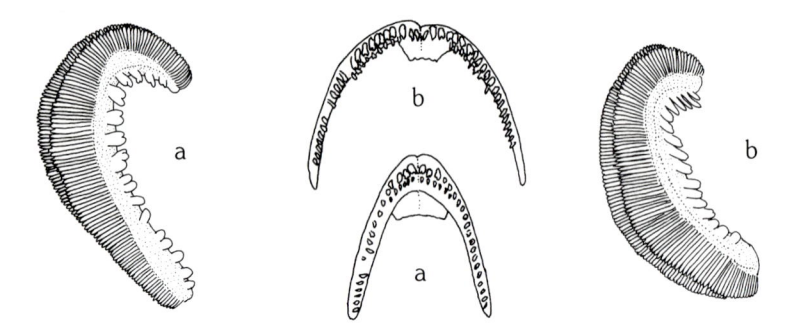

Gill arches and jaws: (a) *Thoracochromis albolabris*, (b) *T. buysi*.

THICKLIPPED HAPPY

Dikbek-happie
Thoracochromis albolabris (Trewavas & Thys van den Audenaerde, 1969)

Description D XIV–XVI, 10–12; A III, 7–9. Lateral line with 32–35 scales, 4–6 rows between lateral line and first dorsal spine, chest scales markedly small. Body moderately slender, depth about equal to head

length, caudal fin truncate. Head pointed, mouth horizontal, with variable but often thick lips, upper jaws with V-shaped gape, 11–17 gill rakers. Males with bright blue cheeks, body infused with yellow, flank scales with orange centres. Dorsal fin bluish with orange spots, a light blue submarginal band and orange-red lappets, caudal spots deep maroon, caudal edges orange-red, anal fin yellow with orange egg-spots and orange edges, pelvics yellow. Attains 150 mm TL.
Distribution Cunene system in Namibia and Angola.
Biology and Ecology Favours rocky habitats.

NAMIB HAPPY

Namib-happie
Thoracochromis buysi (Penrith, 1970)

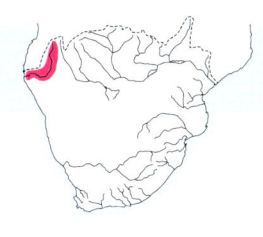

Description D XIV–XVII, 10–13; A III, 7–9. Lateral line scales 32–36, chest scales markedly small. Body moderately deep, caudal truncate. Head broad, eyes large; mouth short, horizontal, teeth bicuspid in 3 rows, upper jaws with wide U-shaped gape; 9–10 short gill rakers. Males with greenish yellow flanks, bright yellow cheeks and bright blue preorbits and lips. Dorsal fin sooty blue with orange spots along membranes, a whitish submarginal band and orange-red lappets and margins, caudal light blue with orange spots and reddish edges, anal sooty with scattered orange surrounded by yellow egg-spots, pelvics sooty. Attains 140 mm TL.
Distribution Cunene system, Namibia and Angola.
Biology and Ecology Favours sandy habitats with vegetation.

Genus *Sargochromis* Regan, 1920
SARGOS

Fairly large, stout-bodied haplochromines, with moderate sized mouths, feeding mainly on snails, freshwater mussels and crustacea. They are mostly characterised by robust pharyngeal bones with rounded, molar-like teeth. The females mouthbrood the eggs and larvae, and the species are of importance to floodplain fisheries. As in other cichlid groups, the differences between the species are sometimes obscure externally and therefore not easy to identify positively. This is particularly true of the juveniles of these sargos. There are seven species in southern Africa.

KEY TO SARGOS

1a Head and predorsal profile straight or gently convex, mouth inclined less than 40° 2
1b Head and predorsal profile concave, mouth inclined 45–55° ....
.... *S. carlottae* (p. 305)
2a Preorbital depth 25–29% head length .... *S. greenwoodi* (p. 308)
2b Preorbital depth 16–24% head length 3
3a Body depth less than 35% SL, mouth inclined less than 20° ....
.... *S. gracilis* (p. 310)
3b Body depth greater than 35% SL, mouth inclined more than 20° 4
4a Head profile steep, greater than 40°, ventral profile of head rounded, mouth inclined 35–45°, pharyngeal bones robust, pharyngeal teeth molariform .... *S. giardi* (p. 307)
4b Head profile less than 40°, ventral head profile straight, mouth inclined 20–35°, pharyngeal teeth in median rows only molariform ....
.... *S. codringtonii* (p. 306) (Okavango/Upper Zambezi), *S. coulteri* (p. 310) (Cunene), *S. mortimeri* (p. 309) (Kafue).

RAINBOW HAPPY

Reënboog-happie
Sargochromis carlottae (Boulenger, 1905)

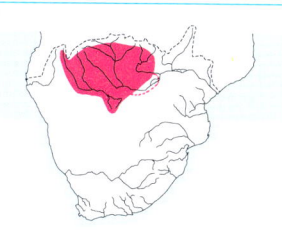

Description D XIV–XVI, 11–13; A III, 9–11. Lateral line scales 28–32. Body depth greater than head length, caudal fin rounded. In adults the head has a distinctly concave profile, cheek relatively short, less than 1,5 times orbit diameter; teeth conical, in 2 or 3 rows, median pharyngeal teeth moderately enlarged and molariform. Juveniles silvery green with dark grey centres to the body scales and about 8 vertical body bars, fins greyish green with deep grey spots and sooty margins. Adults are olive green with dark-bordered scales giving a mesh effect, fins deep olive with sooty pink spots in rows along the membranes; anal fin spots pink-orange, the pelvics sooty. Attains about 260 mm TL, 1,4 kg. Zimbabwe angling record 0,192 kg.

Distribution Okavango, upper Zambezi and Kafue systems. Also in Lake Kariba; introduced to impoundments in middle Zambezi catchment.

Biology and Ecology Prefers deeper permanent floodplain channels and lagoons, with sandy bottom and vegetation. Feeds on aquatic insects, crustacea and snails. A female mouthbrooder; males construct a nest where the eggs are initially laid. Lives for 5 or 6 years, matures after 1 or 2 years at about 100–120 mm.

Uses Subsistence and commercial fisheries; angling target. Useful snail control agent.

GREEN HAPPY

Groen-happie
Sargochromis codringtonii (Boulenger, 1908)

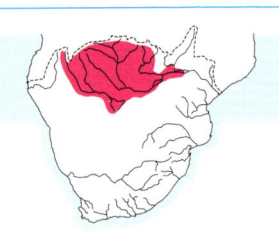

Description D XIII–XVI, 11–16; A III, 9–10. Lateral line scales 28–33. Body deep, greater than head length; caudal sub-truncate. Head with straight profile, deep cheek and snout (preorbit), mouth slightly inclined, teeth conical, in 2 rows, median pharyngeal teeth molariform. Juveniles and non-breeding adults grey to olive green, with rusty red spots at the base of body scales. Breeding males dark olive green to black, Kafue population with yellowish underparts, dorsal and anal fins with red margins, dorsal and caudal fins with deep red or maroon spots; light red spots on the anal. Attains 290 mm TL. Zimbabwe angling record 2,21 kg.
Distribution Okavango, upper Zambezi, Lake Kariba and Kafue systems.
Biology and Ecology Prefers deep, quiet water, slow-flowing channels and floodplain lagoons. Feeds on waterlily seeds, small snails, bivalves and aquatic insects. A female mouthbrooder, breeds in summer, probably spawning twice in the season. Males mature at about 150 mm SL, females at 125–150 mm SL. Lives for 6 or 7 years.
Uses Subsistence and commercial fisheries, angling target, and a snail control agent.

PINK HAPPY

Ligroos-happie
Sargochromis giardi (Pellegrin, 1903)

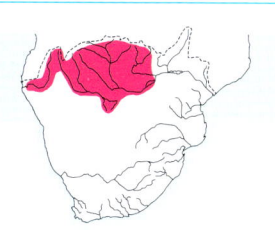

Description D XIV–XVI, 12–15; A III, 9–11. Lateral line scales 29–34. Robust, deep body and large head with a typical steep convex profile are characteristic. Mouth inclined, teeth stout, conical, in 2 rows. Pharyngeal bones robust, pharyngeal teeth enlarged and molariform. Juveniles olive green with yellowish chest, deep greenish black fins and 6–7 dark vertical bars. Adults, greyish green head and dorsal surface, flanks and underparts creamy yellow, fins dark grey with red margins and dark red spots, anal fin with rows of bright yellow orange-centred ocelli along the membranes. Largest specimens come from upper Zambezi floodplains, attains 480 mm TL, about 2,9 kg. Zimbabwe angling record 1,98 kg.

Distribution Cunene, Okavango, upper Zambezi and Kafue systems and Lake Kariba.

Biology and Ecology Prefers deep main river channels and floodplain lagoons with sandy bottoms. Feeds primarily on snails, bivalves and insect larvae. Breeds in early summer, a female mouthbrooder. Nests consist of clear round patches 20–30 cm within dense vegetation in about 3 m water depth. Matures after 2–3 years at about 150–180 mm TL in Liambezi and at 225–300 mm in upper Zambezi; lives for 6 or 7 years.

Uses Important in subsistence and commercial fisheries; angling target. A useful snail control agent.

GREENWOOD'S HAPPY

Greenwood se happie
Sargochromis greenwoodi (Bell-Cross, 1975)

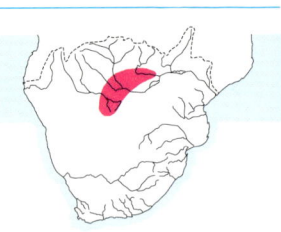

Description D XIV–XVI, 12–14; A III, 8–10. Lateral line scales 29–31. Body deepest at hind margin of head, caudal truncate. Head profile straight, cheeks and preorbital length deep, latter twice orbit diameter, mouth inclined. Pharyngeal bones slender, pharyngeal teeth slender, median row enlarged. Olive green with 2 black bands, one along midbody, the other above upper lateral line; fins dark greyish green, lower caudal with red flush. Male dorsal fin with red edges and dark grey spots on membrane, anal fin with yellow margin and rows of yellow-orange ocelli. In breeding dress males have deep maroon flush on head and forebody. Attains 300 mm SL.

Distribution Okavango, upper Zambezi and Kafue systems.

Biology and Ecology Uncommon, preferring still or slow-flowing water and dense vegetation. Feeds primarily on insects, small snails and other invertebrates and occasionally small fish. A female mouthbrooder, breeding in summer.

Uses Subsistence fisheries, angling target.

MORTIMER'S HAPPY

Mortimer se happie
Sargochromis mortimeri (Bell-Cross, 1975)

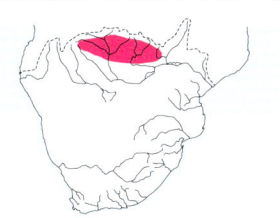

Description D XIV–XVI, 11–14; A III, 8–10. Lateral line scales 30–34. Deep bodied, caudal sub-truncate. Head large, mouth inclined, pharyngeal bone moderately robust with molariform teeth on median rows. Basic pigment pattern consists of a black opercular spot, 2 horizontal bands and 5–9 vertical bars. Juveniles light green. Adults olive green with rust spots at base of body scales, fins with dark grey to purple spots, anal fin grey with orange extremities and rows of orange egg-spots on the membranes. Males have a red margin and orange spots on the dorsal fin, rows of pink egg-spots with orange centres on the anal fin. Attains 277 mm SL.

Distribution Headwater reaches of the upper Zambezi, Kafue and Luangwa (middle Zambezi) systems in Zambia.

Biology and Ecology Occurs in a variety of habitats and dams. Feeds on insects, snails and plants. Breeds in spring and early summer; males construct a sandscrape nest in shallow water, females mouthbrood the eggs and larvae.

Uses Subsistence fisheries.

CUNENE HAPPY

Kunene-happie
Sargochromis coulteri (Bell-Cross, 1975)

Description D XIV–XVI, 11–13; A III, 8–9. Lateral line scales 30–31. Deep bodied, caudal sub-truncate. Head large, mouth inclined, two rows of conical teeth in jaws, pharyngeal bones with molariform teeth in median rows. Juveniles pale to olive green, fins with dark spots. Adults olive green with grey-green fins tinged with red, rust red spots at base of body scales. Males have red spots on fin membranes, forming egg-spots on anal fin, pelvic fin sooty. Attains 216 mm SL.
Distribution Cunene system, Namibia and Angola.

SLENDER HAPPY

Slanke-happie
Sargochromis gracilis Greenwood, 1984

Description D XV, 13; A III, 10. Lateral line scales 34. Head more gently sloping than in other sargos, mouth slightly inclined, teeth bicuspid, pharyngeal teeth not enlarged or molariform. Maximum recorded size 118 mm SL.
Distribution Cutato River, a tributary of the Okavango in Angola. Recently recorded from the Cunene.

SLENDER HAPPY (cont.)

Note Known only from a few museum specimens. Colour illustrated taken from a Cunene specimen. The taxonomy of this species is currently under review and it is likely to be placed in another genus in the near future.

Genus *Serranochromis* Regan, 1920
SERRANOS OR LARGEMOUTH BREAMS

The serranos or largemouth breams are a distinct group of large predatory cichlids found in the rivers of tropical southern and central Africa. They are easily recognised by their large mouths with conical teeth, the high number of scale rows on the cheeks, the relatively high number of soft rays in the dorsal fin and often by numerous bright egg-spots (ocelli) on the anal fin. All are mouthbrooders. They are popular angling species and are important in the floodplain fisheries. Ten species; seven in southern Africa.

KEY TO SPECIES

1a Length of pectoral fin 33–40% SL ....*S. longimanus* (p. 315)
1b Length of pectoral fin less than 33% SL..2
2a Lateral line scales 39–41, dorsal spines 17–18..........*S. thumbergi* (p. 318)
2b Lateral line scales fewer than 39, dorsal spines 14–16 3
3a Teeth in outer row of upper jaw small (more than 50), closely set 4
3b Teeth in outer row of upper jaw large (fewer than 50), wide spaced 6
4a Dorsal soft rays fewer than 14................................*S. meridianus* (p. 314)
4b Dorsal soft rays 14 or more 5
5a Head markedly compressed (narrow), with distinct spots and wavy bars (vermiculations) ....*S. angusticeps* (p. 313)

312 SERRANOS

5b Head moderately compressed, without spots or vermiculations ....
....*S. altus* (p. 312)
6a Pectoral fin 19–24% SL, a dark band along midbody ...*S. robustus* (p. 317)
6b Pectoral fin 23,5–29% SL, vertical bars on body.*S. macrocephalus* (p. 316)

HUMPBACK LARGEMOUTH

Kromkop-grootbek
Serranochromis altus Winemiller & Kelso-Winemiller, 1990

Description D XV–XVI, 15–18; A III, 11–13. Lateral line scales 37–39. Body very deep, caudal fin sub-truncate. Head profile with characteristic deep kink, mouth large and extremely protrusible; teeth conical, close set in 4–6 rows on jaws. Predominantly olive brown with silvery flanks, scales with brown centres giving chequered appearance, head plain, dark spots on fins, dorsal and anal with yellow or orange margins (soft dorsal and caudal fin pink-red in immatures and females), anal fin yellowish with rows of large pink egg-spots. Attains 410 mm SL, about 2 kg.
Distribution Okavango, upper Zambezi and Kafue systems.
Biology and Ecology Found inshore off marginal vegetation of main river channels or deep connected lagoons. Preys primarily on fish, especially mormyrids and butter barbels; more active at night. Breeds in early summer before rains.
Note Previously confused with the thinface largemouth.

THINFACE LARGEMOUTH

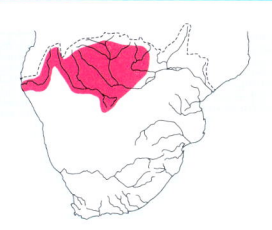

Smalkop-grootbek
Serranochromis angusticeps (Boulenger, 1907)

Description D XIII–XVI, 14–17; A III, 11–13. Lateral line scales 36–39. Head and body greatly compressed, mouth very large, inclined 40–55°, with relatively fine conical teeth. Head and body of both sexes with distinctive red spots and vermiculations. Mature males have bright yellow head, caudal and dorsal fins blue-grey with dark brown spots and a yellowish anal fin with orange-centred cream egg-spots. Attains about 410 mm SL. Zimbabwe angling record 2,195 kg.

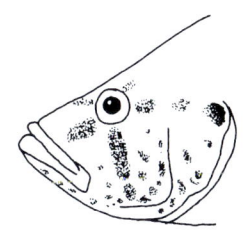

Distribution Cunene, Okavango, upper Zambezi, Kafue and Zambian Zaire systems. Possibly also coastal rivers north of the Cunene in Angola.

Biology and Ecology Prefers lagoons and quiet backwaters with dense vegetation. Its thin profile facilitates stalking and ambushing of small fishes such as robbers (*Brycinus* and *Micralestes*) and barbs on which it preys. Breeds throughout the summer, individual females probably spawning twice a year. Males clear small sandy nests among vegetation in 1–3 m. Growth is rapid, matures after 1 or 2 years at about 175 mm (females) and 250 mm (males). Lives for 8 or 9 years.

Uses A popular angling target. Important for subsistence and commercial fisheries.

Note Until recently the thinface and

humpback largemouths were considered to be a single species, the "spotted" (thinface) individuals as females and "unspotted" (humpbacks) as males. The Zimbabwe angling record may have been a humpback.

LOWVELD LARGEMOUTH

Laeveld-kurper
Serranochromis meridianus Jubb, 1967

Description D XIV–XV, 13–15; A III, 8–10. Lateral line scales 34–36. Body compressed, becoming deep in larger specimens; caudal sub-truncate. Head profile straight or concave in larger individuals, mouth large, jaws set with fine conical teeth. Juveniles brown above, silvery on sides and below with black vertical bars and reddish centres to scales, dark reddish black spots on dorsal, caudal and anal fins. Adults olive brown to yellow with yellowish fins and dark red spots. Male dorsal fin edged with yellow, anal fin with numerous orange egg-spots. Attains 310 mm SL, about 1,2 kg.
Distribution Sabi-Sand tributary of Incomati system, coastal lakes of southern Mozambique and Maputaland.
Biology and Ecology Prefers standing or slow-flowing pools with marginal vegetation, thrives in impounded waters. Preys on small fish, insects and other invertebrates, including snails. The male clears a small nest and attracts the female with a quivering display. Eggs are laid in several bouts and fertilised before being collected by the female. Individuals may breed more than once in a season.

Conservation Rare. Threatened by depleted water supplies, sedimentation, pollution and invasive plants. Translocated to impoundments in the Kruger National Park.
Uses Angling target.

LONGFIN LARGEMOUTH

Langvin-grootbek
Serranochromis longimanus (Boulenger, 1911)

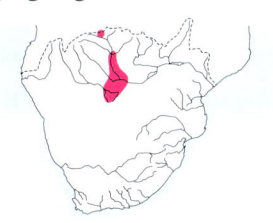

Description D XIV-XV, 13–14; A III, 9–10. Lateral line scales 35. Pectoral fins exceptionally long, 33–40% SL. Head acutely pointed, mouth large, inclined, with 1 or 2 rows of sharp, conical teeth. Colour distinctive, background silvery white, head with large black blotches, 5-6 broad black bars on body, fins sooty with light spots. Anal fin of males with dark red egg-spots, pectorals black. Attains 300 mm TL.
Distribution Okavango Delta, and upper Zambezi floodplains.
Biology and Ecology Very uncommon, occurs in permanent floodplain lagoons and backwaters. Active at night, preying on small fish and insects such as dragonfly nymphs.

PURPLEFACE LARGEMOUTH

Perskop-grootbek
Serranochromis macrocephalus (Boulenger, 1899)

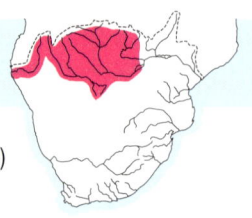

Description D XIV–XVI, 13–15; A III, 9–11. Lateral line scales 34–37. Straight head profile, large mouth with large well-spaced conical teeth and stocky build are characteristic. Pectoral fins relatively long, 23–29% SL. Colour variable, vertical body bars usually evident, females olive brown or yellow with greyish black body bars and fins; males with red flush to soft dorsal, caudal and anal fins. When breeding the males become dark olive with a deep purple flush over the sides and top of head, and the anal egg-spots become creamy pink. Attains 350 mm SL, about 1,5 kg. SA angling record 2,13 kg, Zimbabwe 0,482 kg.
Distribution Cunene, Okavango, upper Zambezi and Kafue systems, Lake Kariba. Also southern tributaries of the Zaire system.
Biology and Ecology Common in a broad range of habitats from mainstream margins to floodplain channels and lagoons. Preys on insects and small fish, including mormyrids and barbs, which are taken near the bottom. Breeds in spring and early summer at low water before the annual floods arrive. Relatively few large eggs are laid and mouthbrooded. Matures after 1–2 years, lives for 5–6 years.
Uses Angling target, important component of subsistence and commercial fisheries.

NEMBWE (TSUNGWA)

Olyfkurper
Serranochromis robustus (Günther, 1864)

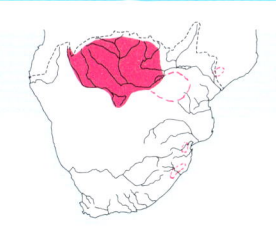

Description D XV–XVI, 13–15; A III, 10–11. Lateral line scales 36–39. Heavy-set robust body, especially of larger specimens, is characteristic; pectoral fins relatively short, 19–23% SL. Mouth large, with large well-spaced conical teeth. Olive to bright green, with a deep olive band along midbody; fins olive, with yellow-orange margins, anal fin of males with orange egg-spots. Two sub-species are described mainly on the basis of male breeding colours: *S. robustus robustus* from Malawi lacks the deep yellow chest and underparts of *S. robustus jallae* from the Okavango-upper Zambezi area, where mature males are rich yellow from the chin to the abdomen, anal fin also flushed with yellow. Attains about 450 mm SL, about 3,5 kg, but one specimen was reported to weigh 6,123 kg. SA angling record 2,0 kg, Zimbabwe 3,24 kg, Malawi 2,25 kg.

Distribution Lake Malawi and the upper Shire River. Translocated to upper Ruo River in Malawi and also to Swaziland. *S. robustus jallae* occurs in the Okavango, upper Zambezi, Kafue and Zambian Zaire systems. Translocated to Lake Kariba and throughout Zimbabwe as well as Natal.

Biology and Ecology Larger specimens prefer deep main channels and permanent lagoons, whereas smaller fishes occur mainly in lagoons and secondary channels. Preys on fish; juveniles most often eat minnows but squeakers are favoured by adults. Breeds in summer, nesting along vegetated fringes of mainstreams.

Uses A major angling target with bass-like qualities. Valuable commer-

cial and subsistence fishery species. for this species in Malawi.
Note Tsungwa is the common name

BROWNSPOT LARGEMOUTH

Bruinkol-grootbek
Serranochromis thumbergi (Castelnau, 1861)

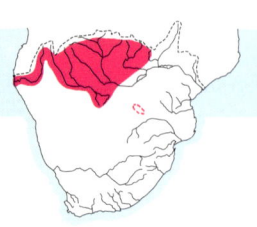

Description D XVII–XVIII, 13–16; A III, 9–12. Lateral line scales 39–41. Body relatively elongated, high dorsal spine counts and lateral line scales distinctive, caudal truncate or emarginate. Teeth conical, relatively small and close-set, 3 rows in upper jaw. Black lateral band usually evident except in large females in breeding dress. Females greyish brown, fins bluish grey with light blue margins. Males olive brown, with rust red centres to body scales; lower head and abdomen light creamy yellow, pelvics yellow, dorsal and caudal fin olive with yellow margins, anal fin sooty yellow with orange egg-spots. Attains 330 mm TL, about 1,2 kg. SA angling record 0,215 kg.
Distribution Cunene, Okavango, upper Zambezi and Kafue systems. Also in Lufira-Lualaba and Zambian Zaire systems.
Biology and Ecology Occurs in floodplain channels and lagoons, favouring open water. Preys on insects, shrimps, crabs and fish. Breeds in typical *Serranochromis* fashion.
Uses Angling target. Component of subsistence fisheries.

TILAPIINES

A major branch of African cichlid fishes; generally deep-bodied, with a mainly vegetarian diet that is reflected in their small notched teeth, fine pharyngeal teeth and extended intestines. Tilapiines are characterised by certain skeletal and other features, most notably that a bulge (apophysis) on the base of the skull is part of the parasphenoid bone only, that the lachrymal bone (preorbital) has five pores for the lateral line, and that a clear black spot is present at the

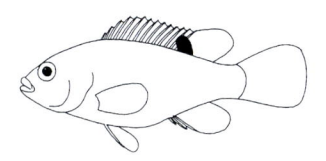

"Tilapia spot"

base of the soft dorsal fin ("tilapia spot"), at least in juveniles. Some genera are substrate spawners (*Tilapia*), others are mouthbrooders (*Oreochromis*). Fine table fish of long-standing value to man, some are popular angling targets, and many are of great value in aquaculture as well as commercial and subsistence fisheries. The natural distribution of the tilapiines is tropical Africa and the Levant (near-Middle East), but certain species have been introduced to tropical and warm temperate areas around the world.

Genus *Tilapia* A. Smith, 1840

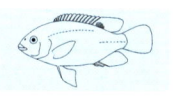

At one stage this genus included all the tilapiine species in southern Africa but now it is restricted to the substrate spawning species. Species of *Tilapia* do not show marked differences between the sexes, but a firm pair-bond relationship is formed between spawning fishes and both parents guard and tend the brood. *Tilapia* tend to feed on coarser foods and are usually smaller than *Oreochromis* species. Adults retain the distinctive "tilapia spot". Thirty species, four in southern Africa.

KEY TO SPECIES

1a Dorsal spines 12–14 (usually 13) colour varied............***T. guinasana* (p. 321)**
1b Dorsal spines 13–16 (usually 14 or more), colour regular, with distinct vertical bars on body..2
2a Dorsal spines 14–16 (usually 15 or 16), dorsal soft rays 12–13, body with 5–7 broad vertical bars, pelvics lightly pigmented............***T. rendalli* (p. 323)**
2b Dorsal spines 13–15, usually 14, dorsal soft rays 9–12, body with 8–9 vertical bars, pelvics heavily pigmented..3

3a Caudal fin truncate, not clearly marked with black blocks ....
....*T. sparrmanii* (p. 320)
3b Caudal fin rounded, clearly marked with black blocks ....*T. ruweti* (p. 322)

BANDED TILAPIA

Vleikurper
Tilapia sparrmanii A. Smith, 1840

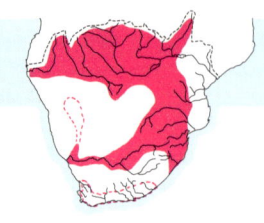

Description D XIII–XV, 9–11; A III, 9–10. Lateral line scales 27–29. Body shape variable, usually moderately deep; ovoid, straight or concave predorsal profile; caudal fin truncate. Mouth small, teeth fine, bicuspid, in 3 rows; 9–12 short, well-spaced gill rakers on first arch. Colour variable, predominantly deep olive green with 8–9 dark vertical bars on body, 2 bars between the eyes, and a well-developed "tilapia spot", a dark spot on gill cover surrounded by iridescent green or blue scales, iridescent blue along the lower jaw. Breeding males have a bright red margin to the dorsal and caudal fin and a grey-black throat and chest. Juveniles with characteristic light "bubbles" behind the tilapia mark on the soft dorsal fin. Attains about 230 mm SL. SA angling record 0,445 kg, Zimbabwe 0,54 kg.

Distribution From the Orange River and Natal south coast northwards to upper reaches of southern Zaire tributaries, Lake Malawi and the Zambezi system. Extensively translocated south of the Orange in the Cape.

Biology and Ecology Tolerant of a wide range of habitats but prefers quiet or standing waters with submerged or emergent vegetation. An omnivore, feeding on available foods including algae, soft plants, small

invertebrates such as insects, and even small fish. Males construct a simple saucer-shaped nest in which eggs are guarded and tended by both parents. The eggs or larvae may be moved by the parents to alternative nests. Newly hatched larvae attach to the substrate by head glands but wriggle constantly for aeration. After 7–8 days the fry are free swimming but remain in a shoal guarded by the parents for several weeks.
Uses Distributed as a forage fish for bass. Common component of subsistence fisheries. Occasional angling target.
Note The distribution of species suggests it is more restricted by high (above 32° C) than low temperatures.

OTJIKOTO TILAPIA

Otjikoto-kurper
Tilapia guinasana Trewavas, 1936

Description D XII–XIV, 10–11; A III, 8–10. Lateral line scales 27–28. Similar to *T. sparrmanii* but generally with fewer dorsal spines and different colours. Coloration unusually variable, from individuals in olive green with dark vertical bars and red streaked fins to others uniform black or vividly particoloured in white, blue, yellow and black. A black throat, abdomen and anal fin are characteristic of breeding individuals. Attains 140 mm TL.
Distribution Naturally endemic to Lake Guinas, Namibia. Translocated to Lake Otjikoto and several reservoirs in Namibia.
Biology and Ecology Lake Guinas is an open sinkhole lake, 120 m across and more than 100 m deep.

Although the fishes may occur in the middle of the lake, they generally congregate, breed and feed from the near-vertical shores. Food is primarily diatoms and algae. Narrow shelves are used for breeding, territories are established and defended, eggs are guarded and tended by both parents.

Conservation Endangered. Use and depletion of local groundwater resources and the potential impact of introduced fishes seriously threaten the species' long-term survival.
Uses Attractive aquarium species. Valuable for evolutionary studies.

OKAVANGO TILAPIA

Okavango-kurper
Tilapia ruweti (Poll & Thys van den Audenaerde, 1965)

Description D XIV–XV, 10–12; A III, 8–9. Lateral line scales 27–29. Body shape more ellipsoid than other southern African *Tilapia* species, caudal rounded, mouth small. Colour variable, body olive or bright iridescent green with 8–9 olive-mauve vertical bars, head with iridescent green and blue (mauve in breeding males), fins mauve or yellowish, the soft dorsal, anal and caudal fins distinctly spotted; margin of dorsal fin a thin tricoloured (blue, white and red) band; pelvics sooty. Breeding females turn dark greenish black. Juveniles may be recognised by ellipsoid shape, spotted caudal fin, sooty pelvic fins and body bars. Attains 104 mm TL.
Distribution Okavango Delta, upper Zambezi, southern tributaries of the Zaire system.
Biology and Ecology Found in swamps and floodplain habitats, especially enriched pans and well-vegetated shallow littoral margins of drainage rivers. Feeds on detritus,

soft plants and insect larvae. Males establish a territory and attract a ripe female to form a pair bond. Females construct a saucer-shaped nest in which eggs are laid and fertilised then tended mainly by the female while the male guards the territory. The eggs and larvae are periodically moved to alternative brood pits excavated by the female.

Uses Attractive aquarium species.

REDBREAST TILAPIA

Rooiborskurper
Tilapia rendalli (Boulenger, 1896)

Description D XIV–XVI, 12–13; A III, 9–10. Lateral line scales 28–32. Body typically deep, head profile convex, mouth protruding with prominent bicuspid teeth. Mature specimens olive green to brown, often with scattered blue scales; 5–7 dark olive broad vertical bars on body, a clear tilapia spot and a bright red throat and chest; the extremities of the soft dorsal, anal and lower half of the caudal fin vary from yellow to red. Juveniles are recognised by the rounded head, beak-like mouth, the few broad body bands, pelvics without pigment, and barred pattern of soft dorsal fin. Attains about 400 mm TL, 2 kg. SA angling record 1,845 kg, Zimbabwe 1,616 kg, Malawi 1,03 kg.

Distribution Cunene, Okavango, Zambezi system, east coastal rivers south to the Phongolo and coastal lakes to Lake Sibaya. Also occurs in estuaries in Mozambique and Natal. Translocated throughout Natal and Transvaal interior. Also in the eastern Zaire basin (Lualaba) and Zambian Zaire, Lakes Tanganyika and Malawi.

Biology and Ecology Tolerant of a wide range of temperatures (11–37° C) and salinity to 19 parts per thousand. Prefers quiet, well-vegetated water along river littorals or backwaters, floodplains and swamps. Feeds mainly on waterplants and algae but also takes aquatic invertebrates and even small fish. Breeding pairs clear the vegetation in shallow water to form a nest about 0,5–1,2 m across and excavate several tunnel-like brood chambers in which the eggs and larvae are protected. Juveniles up to about 15 mm SL remain within the brood chambers. Several broods are raised each summer. Lives for up to 7 years.

Uses A popular angling species, valued in aquaculture and fisheries. Used for weed control in dams.

Note Two subspecies have been named (northern redbreast tilapia, *T. rendalli rendalli*; southern redbreast tilapia *T. rendalli swierstrai*), but recent work does not support this division.

Genus *Oreochromis* Günther, 1889

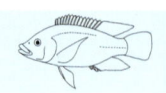

From Africa and the Levant, *Oreochromis* are relatively large, deep-bodied, mouthbrooding cichlids, economically important to man. They are generally tolerant of wide temperature and salinity ranges, and the Mozambique tilapia (*O. mossambicus*) is able to live and breed in both fresh- and seawater. They have fine teeth in several rows on the jaws, fine pharyngeal teeth, a high number of gill rakers, and long intestines. These features are particularly suited for grazing diatoms, algae and detritus. The genus includes 33 species, chiefly from tropical, East and southern Africa. In southern Africa there are six indigenous and two introduced species.

KEY TO SPECIES

1a Usually 3 anal spines..3
1b Usually 4 anal spines ....*O. placidus* (p. 328) or *O. shiranus* (p. 329)
2a Gill rakers on lower limb of first arch 17–20 3
2b Gill rakers on lower limb of first arch 20–27 4
3a Breeding males with white throat, enlarged jaws ....
...................(Lower Zambezi and east coast systems) *O. mossambicus* (p. 325)
3b Breeding males with dark throat, jaws not enlarged ....
................................(Lake Kariba and middle Zambezi) *O. mortimeri* (p. 326)
4a Caudal fin with prominent vertical stripes .... *O. niloticus* (p. 330)
4b Caudal fin without prominent stripes............................*O. aureus* (p. 330)
5a Juveniles and non-breeding adults with 3 spots on body, breeding males blue and silver with red-tinged fins, throat black, male genital papilla simple
.... *O. andersonii* (p. 327)
5b Juveniles and non-breeding adults without 3 body spots, head greenish with dark spots and vermiculations, genital papilla with tassles..................
....*O. macrochir* (p. 331)

MOZAMBIQUE TILAPIA

Bloukurper
Oreochromis mossambicus (Peters, 1852)

♂ in breeding dress

Pharyngeal bone

Description D XV–XVII, 10–13; A III, 9–12. Lateral line scales 30–32. Body moderately deep, caudal truncate. Head profile straight in juveniles and females, concave in mature males; jaws with 3–5 rows slender teeth, bicuspid in outer row, jaws of older males become enlarged and teeth project forward. Gill rakers 16–20 on lower limb of 1st arch. Juveniles silvery, with 6–7 vertical bars, 3 spots along flanks. Adults silvery olive to deep blue-grey, dorsal and caudal fins with red margins. Breeding males turn deep greyish black with white lower head and throat. Attains about 400 mm SL. SA angling record 3,265 kg, Zimbabwe 2,181 kg, Malawi 0,64 kg.

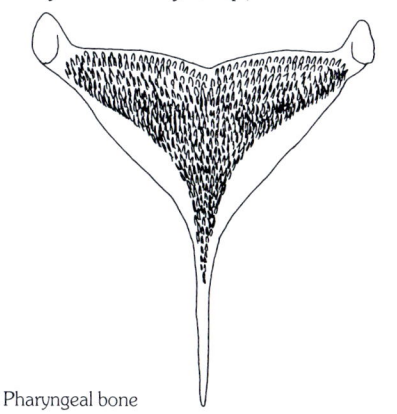

Distribution East coastal rivers from

the lower Zambezi system south to the Bushmans system, eastern Cape Province. South of the Phongolo system, naturally confined to closed estuaries and coastal reaches of rivers. Widely dispersed beyond this range to inland regions and to the south-west and west coastal rivers including the lower Orange and rivers of Namibia. Introduced to tropical and warm temperate localities throughout the world.

Biology and Ecology Occurs in all but fast-flowing waters; thrives in standing waters. Tolerant of fresh, brackish or marine waters and even higher salinity concentrations. Survives lower temperatures (below about 15° C) in brackish or marine waters. Prefers warm temperatures (above 22° C) but tolerates to about 42° C. Feeds on algae, especially diatoms, and detritus, but large individuals may take insects and other invertebrates. Breeds in summer, females raising multiple broods every 3–4 weeks during a season. Males construct a saucer-shaped nest on sandy bottoms; the female mouthbroods the eggs, larvae and small fry. Juveniles shoal in shallow water. Grows rapidly and may mature and breed within a year, but is prone to stunting under adverse or crowded conditions.

Uses Widely used in aquaculture and commercial and subsistence fisheries. A valued angling species. Used extensively in biological, physiological and behavioural research.

KARIBA TILAPIA

Kariba-kurper
Oreochromis mortimeri (Trewavas, 1966)

Description D XVI–XVII, 10–13; A III, 10–12. Lateral line scales 30–32. Body form very similar to that of *O. mossambicus*; the main difference is in the male breeding colours – in *O. mortimeri* the body is iridescent olive blue or bronze with the throat dusky green or black. Mature males develop a concave head profile. Attains 430 mm SL (550 mm TL), about 4 kg. Zimbabwe angling record 3,43 kg.
Distribution Middle Zambezi system including the Luangwa tributary.
Biology and Ecology Thrives in impounded and quiet waters of large rivers. Feeds on algae, especially diatoms, and detritus as well as plants, insects and zooplankton. Breeds practically throughout the year, individual females producing several broods. Nest is saucer-shaped with a raised central mound.
Uses An important commercial and angling species.

THREESPOT TILAPIA

Driekolkurper
Oreochromis andersonii (Castelnau, 1861)

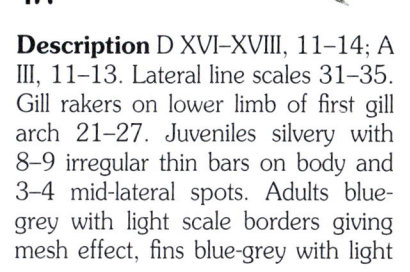

Description D XVI–XVIII, 11–14; A III, 11–13. Lateral line scales 31–35. Gill rakers on lower limb of first gill arch 21–27. Juveniles silvery with 8–9 irregular thin bars on body and 3–4 mid-lateral spots. Adults blue-grey with light scale borders giving mesh effect, fins blue-grey with light spots on soft dorsal and anal, margins of dorsal and anal bright red. Breeding males blue-black with silvery mesh, maroon flush on top of head, outer dorsal and caudal fins intense red. Attains about 450 mm TL, about 3,2 kg. SA angling record 1,97 kg, Zimbabwe 3,09 kg.

Distribution Cunene, Okavango, upper Zambezi and Kafue systems. Occasionally recorded from the middle Zambezi.
Biology and Ecology Hardy, tolerating fresh and brackish water, preferring slow-flowing or standing water such as in pools, backwaters and floodplain lagoons. Adults occupy deep open waters, juveniles remain inshore among vegetation. Feeds on detritus, diatoms and zooplankton. Males excavate large saucer-shaped nests, females mouthbrood the eggs, larvae and fry. Multiple broods are raised during the warmer months. Lives for 7–8 years.
Uses Valued in aquaculture and fisheries, also a popular angling species.

BLACK TILAPIA

Swartkurper
Oreochromis placidus (Trewavas, 1941)

Description D XVI–XVIII, 10–13; A (III) IV, 8–11. Lateral line scales 30–32. Deep bodied with straight predorsal profile, mature males with concave profile, extended soft dorsal and anal fins. Gill rakers on lower limb of first gill arch 16–20. Juveniles silvery with 8–9 faint vertical bars; soft dorsal, anal and caudal fins with dark streaks and light spots. Adults olive brown above, silvery below, with sooty grey head and fins; red margin to dorsal fin. Breeding males sooty grey with black throat and fins and black markings on the head. Attains 300 mm SL. Malawi angling record 1,1 kg.
Distribution Coastal plain from lower Zambezi southwards to the Mkuze in Zululand. Elsewhere, east

coast rivers north to the Lukuledi in Tanzania.
Biology and Ecology Little known. Found in well-vegetated, sheltered habitats along the margins of mainstreams, in floodplain lagoons and coastal lakes.
Uses Taken by floodplain fishermen and anglers.
Note Frequently found together with *O. mossambicus*. Apart from differences in colours of breeding males and anal fin spines, *O. placidus* is deeper bodied, has a deeper caudal peduncle and coarser pharyngeal teeth than *O. mossambicus*.

SHIRE TILAPIA

Shire-kurper
Oreochromis shiranus (Boulenger, 1896)

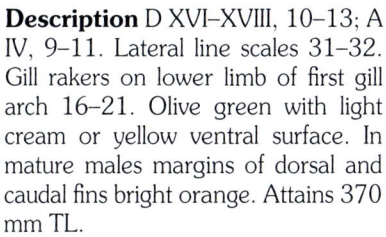

Description D XVI–XVIII, 10–13; A IV, 9–11. Lateral line scales 31–32. Gill rakers on lower limb of first gill arch 16–21. Olive green with light cream or yellow ventral surface. In mature males margins of dorsal and caudal fins bright orange. Attains 370 mm TL.
Distribution Occasionally found in the lower Shire, lower Zambezi system, Malawi. Also in Lake Malawi basin, upper Shire and Lakes Chilwa and Chiuta.
Biology and Ecology Occurs in reedy lagoons and marshes as well as in sheltered rootstocks along shores of rivers. Feeds on algae, plants and phytoplankton. Breeds during summer, males constructing a 50–90 cm diameter, basin-shaped nest in sandy or muddy areas. Females mouthbrood the eggs and young until they reach about 10 mm TL.
Uses A valued subsistence and commercial fisheries species.

NILE TILAPIA

Nylkurper
Oreochromis niloticus (Linnaeus, 1758)

Description D XVI–XVIII, 12–14; A III, 9–11. Lateral line scales 30–34. Gill rakers on lower limb of first gill arch 20–26. Caudal fin distinctly striped. Breeding males with red flush to head, lower body, dorsal and caudal fins. Attains about 400 mm TL.
Distribution Cape Flats area, southwest Cape, Natal and Kariba basin in Zimbabwe. Natural range includes the Nile basin, Rift Valley lakes and certain West African rivers.
History Introduced before 1955 from Israel for aquaculture and as a fodder fish.

ISRAELI TILAPIA

Israelse kurper
Oreochromis aureus (Steindachner, 1864)

Description D XV–XVI, 12–15; A III, 9–11. Lateral line scales 30–33. Gill rakers on lower limb of first gill arch 18–26. Caudal fin with pinkish red extremities, breeding males with bright blue head and blue-black chin

ISRAELI TILAPIA (cont.)

and throat. Attains about 300 mm TL. SA angling record 1,86 kg.
Distribution Cape Flats area, southwest Cape and Natal. Natural range includes Israel, lower Nile, Lake Chad, Niger and Senegal rivers.
History Possibly introduced as early as 1910 for aquaculture. Further introductions made more recently.

GREENHEAD TILAPIA

Groenkop-kurper
Oreochromis macrochir (Boulenger, 1912)

Description D XV–XVII, 11–14; A III, 9–12. Lateral line scales 31–32. Head profile steep, rounded; pectoral fins very long, body deep. Gill rakers on lower limb of first gill arch 20–26. Juveniles silvery, with 8–9 thin straight vertical bars on body and yellowish fins. Adults olive to bright green above, greyish flanks and fins, black spots and marks on head, dorsal fin with yellow margin and green spots on soft membranes. Breeding males (generally larger than females) bright green on head and upper body and have a prominent white, tassel-like genital papilla. Attains about 400 mm TL. Zimbabwe angling record 2,6 kg.
Distribution Cunene, Okavango, upper Zambezi and Kafue rivers, as well as Lake Kariba and the Busi River (possibly by translocation). Introduced to Shashi-Limpopo system. Also in Zambian Zaire system

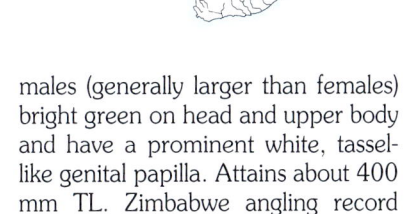

GREENHEAD TILAPIA (cont.)

and southern tributaries of the Zaire. Dispersed widely by man in Zambia and Zimbabwe.
Biology and Ecology Found in quiet waters along river margins and backwaters, in floodplain habitats and impoundments. Feeds mainly on microscopic foods such as algae, especially diatoms, and detritus, taken from the bottom. Juveniles live close inshore in shallow water and feed more on zooplankton and insect larvae. Females mouthbrood eggs, larvae and small fry. Breeds in summer, the males constructing a saucer and mound type nest in shallow water; several nests are often grouped into an arena. In some areas the central mound is star-shaped.
Uses Valued fisheries, aquaculture and angling species.

FAMILY ANABANTIDAE
Labyrinth fishes

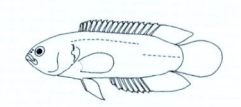

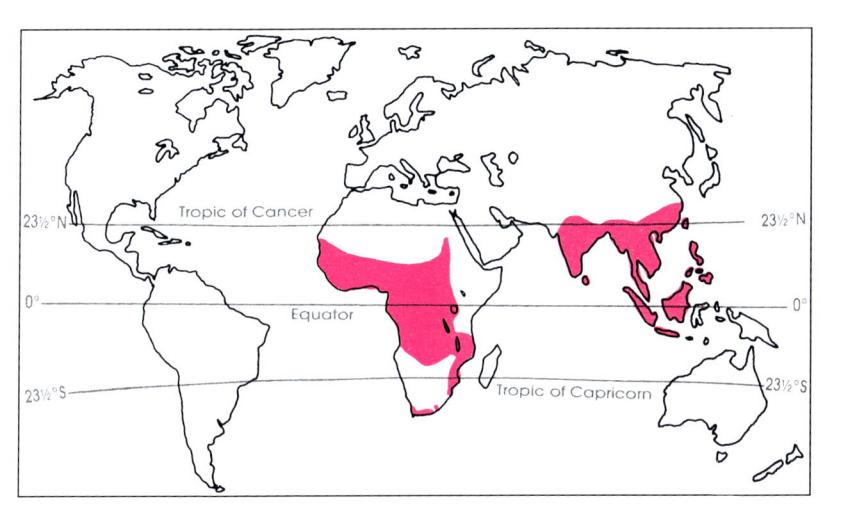

One of the "labyrinth" fish families, well known to aquarists as the familiar gouramis, Siamese fighting fishes and paradise fishes. These fishes have accessory air-breathing organs (the labyrinth) within chambers above the gills, made necessary by the fact that most species live in tropical swamps and streams where low oxygen levels often occur. As in cichlids, the lateral line of anabantids is divided into two sections, but they are easily recognised amongst the spiny-rayed freshwater fishes in southern Africa by a high number of anal fin spines. The anabantid family includes three genera, two from Africa (both present in southern Africa) and one (*Anabas*, the climbing perch) from Asia.

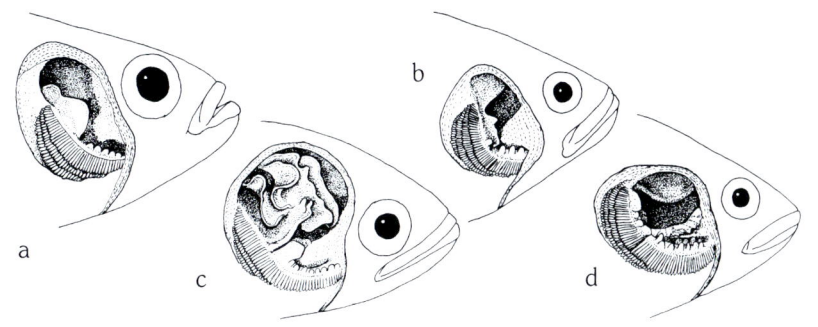

Accessory air-breathing organs: (a) *Ctenopoma intermedium*, (b) *Sandelia capensis*, (c) *C. multispine*, (d) *S. bainsii*.

KEY TO GENERA AND SPECIES

1a Edge of gill cover with spines or serrations ....(*Ctenopoma*) 2

1b Edge of gill cover without spines or serrations........................(*Sandelia*) 3
2a Edge of gill cover with prominent spines, single median pore between the eyes..*Ctenopoma multispine* (p. 336)

2b Edge of gill cover with few spines, two median pores between the eyes ....*Ctenopoma intermedium* (p. 335)
3a Dorsal spine XII–XIV, 3–4 scale rows between lateral line and first dorsal ray, no small scales along bases of dorsal and anal fins, black markings on head and body usually pronounced ....*Sandelia capensis* (p. 338)
3b Dorsal fin spines XV–XVII, 6–7 scale rows between first dorsal spine and lateral line, small scales along bases of dorsal and anal fins, no pronounced black markings on body ....*Sandelia bainsii* (p. 337)

Genus *Ctenopoma* Peters, 1844

Small or moderate sized, sombre-coloured fishes found in tropical African swamps. They have well-developed air-breathing organs and some are known to leave the water and move overland during damp or wet weather. Species belong to two distinct breeding guilds, bubble-nest builders and egg-scatterers. About 20 species, 2 in southern Africa.

BLACKSPOT CLIMBING PERCH

Swartkol-kurper
Ctenopoma intermedium (Pellegrin, 1920)

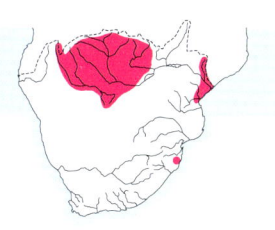

Description D XV–XVI, 8–9; A VIII–IX, 8–9. Lateral line scales 25–30. Body slender, ellipsoid; abdomen short, pelvics far forward, caudal rounded. Head pointed, with eyes far forward; mouth small, with sharp, conical teeth. Usually dark brown or black, head with dark bars radiating from eye, 7–13 dark vertical bars along body and a black spot at base of caudal fin, lappets of dorsal and anal fins white. Breeding males turn very dark. Attains 55 mm SL.
Distribution Okavango, upper and lower Zambezi and Kafue rivers, and the St Lucia basin, Natal. Also in the southern tributaries of the Zaire system.
Biology and Ecology Occurs in dense marginal vegetation of rivers, lakes, lagoons and channels of swamps and floodplains. Preys on insects and other small organisms. Males build a bubble nest on the water surface under which spawning takes place; the eggs float and are stowed in the nest and guarded by the male.
Uses Interesting aquarium species.
Conservation Extremely rare in South Africa, its shallow water habitat making it susceptible to aerial spraying of insecticides.

MANYSPINED CLIMBING PERCH

Stekelrige kurper
Ctenopoma multispine Peters, 1844

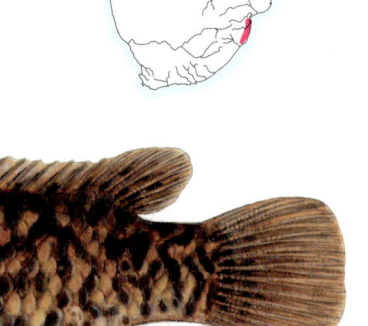

Description D XVI–XIX, 8–9; A VIII–IX, 8–10. Scales ctenoid and coarse, 30–32 in lateral line; head completely scaled, edge of gill cover with undulating series of strong spines, cheek scales of mature males also develop visible spines along free edges. Body elongated, eyes far forward, with a single median lateral line pore between them; mouth terminal, lips thin, teeth sharp, conical. Well-developed air-breathing organ in chamber above gills. Spines of dorsal and caudal fins fairly short, caudal rounded. Brown with irregular dark brown or black bars and spots. Attains 135 mm SL.
Distribution Okavango, upper and lower Zambezi, Kafue, and rivers of coastal Mozambique and northern Natal. Also in the Quanza (Angola) and southern tributaries of the Zaire system.
Biology and Ecology Occurs in vegetated riverine backwaters, floodplain lagoons, swamps and isolated pans. Preys on any suitably small creature, including insects, shrimps and small fish. Well camouflaged; hunts by slowly stalking prey. May congregate in groups to breed; the eggs are scattered around and not guarded. Can endure warm stagnant waters and is known to leave the water and move overland to alternative sites in wet weather or at night.
Uses An interesting aquarium species. Used as bait for sea fishing in Zululand.
Notes Features in folk tales relating to "rains" of fishes, on account of its air-breathing habit and terrestrial movements.

Genus *Sandelia* Castelnau, 1861

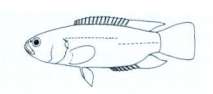

Includes two species in Cape coastal rivers, well isolated from *Ctenopoma* species in tropical waters. *Sandelia* have a smooth (non-spinous) edge to the lower half of the gill cover and a reduced, non-functional air-breathing organ.

EASTERN CAPE ROCKY

Oos-Kaapse kurper
Sandelia bainsii Castelnau, 1861

Description D XV–XVI, 9–10; A VII–VIII, 9–10. Scales in lateral line 30–32, lateral line divided, 22 around caudal peduncle. Scales largest over sides, markedly smaller over upper and lower body and forming a sheath for dorsal and anal fins. Breeding males develop visible ctenii on cheek scales. Body moderately long, head pointed, caudal fin truncate, ragged. Eyes forward on head, mouth large, teeth sharp, conical. Gill cover with 2 spines separated by a deep membrane-covered notch. Olive or grey-brown with scattered black flecks and spots, a dark grey bar behind the eye; fins sometimes pale yellow, with a thin black edge. Attains 260 mm SL. SA angling record 0,13 kg.
Distribution Buffalo, Keiskamma, Great Fish and Kowie systems, eastern Cape.
Biology and Ecology Occurs in rocky streams, favouring marginal habitats where the current is slow. A stalking predator on insects, crabs and small fish. Breeds in summer, but is not a nest builder or brood guarder.
Conservation Vulnerable. Threatened by habitat deterioration, water extraction and introduced predators such as bass and sharptooth catfish.

CAPE KURPER

Kaapse kurper
Sandelia capensis (Cuvier, 1831)

Description D XII–XIV, 8–10; A VI–VIII, 8–11. Scales in lateral line 26–30, lateral line divided, 18 around caudal peduncle. Scales generally even-sized over body, slightly smaller along dorsal and anal fin bases. Spear-shaped with bluntly pointed head, caudal fin truncate. Eyes far forward, gill cover without spines, notch covered by black membrane. Yellow or golden brown with black spots and wavy bands, head with black stripes radiating from eyes, membrane of spinous dorsal and anal fins black. Breeding males turn dark brown or black. Attains about 200 mm SL.
Distribution Southern and south-western Cape coastal rivers from the Coega (Algoa Bay) to the Cape Flats and north to the Verlorenvlei. Introduced into the Clanwilliam Olifants system.
Biology and Ecology Hardy, lives in a wide variety of habitats, favouring quiet or slow-flowing water and plant or root cover. Preys on insects and other invertebrates and small fish. Breeds in summer; males defend a breeding territory and guard the eggs, which are scattered and stick to the bottom.
Uses Aquarium species.
Conservation Many populations have declined and are threatened by habitat destruction and predation from introduced bass.

# FAMILY MASTACEMBELIDAE
Spiny eels

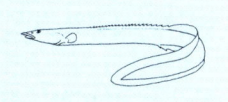

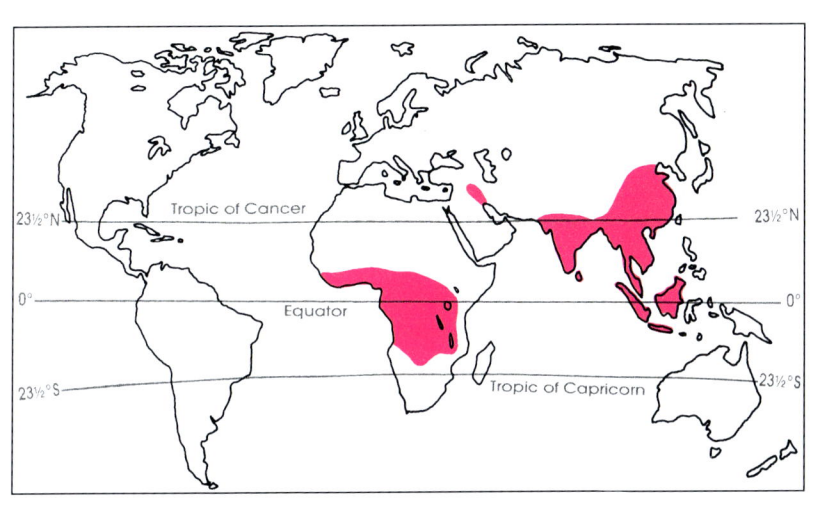

Slender, eel-like fishes with a peculiar rostral appendage and a series of separate spines along the back in front of the soft dorsal fin. Spiny eels are found in a variety of freshwater habitats in tropical Africa and Asia. They are regarded as highly advanced fishes that are most closely related to the synbranchoid swamp eels. In Africa there are 2 genera and about 43 species.

Genus *Aethiomastacembelus* Travers, 1988

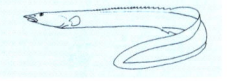

African spiny eels, found in tropical rivers in West and Central Africa. The dorsal fin consists of 15–34 independent spines and a long soft-rayed section that is joined to the caudal and anal fins. The first dorsal spine is well advanced on body. Head with pointed fleshy snout, pelvic fins absent. Favoured habitats are crevices in rocks or amongst densely tangled rootstock or submerged vegetation. About 18 or 19 species, 3 from southern Africa.

KEY TO SPECIES

1a	Dorsal spines 22–26	*A. vanderwaali* (p. 341)
1b	Dorsal spines 27–33	2
2a	Upper Zambezi	*A. frenatus* (p. 340)
2b	Shire, lower Zambezi	*A. shiranus* (p. 340)

LONGTAIL SPINY EEL

Langstert-stekelpaling
Aethiomastacembelus frenatus (Boulenger, 1901)

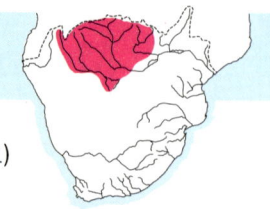

Description D XXVII–XXXIV, 69–81; A II, 66–83. Body slender, eel-like; head and tail pointed. Snout extended into a trilobed appendage; lips large, fleshy. Brown, with a fine reticulated pattern more marked over the tail section, where it may form ocelli. Attains 310 mm TL.
Distribution Okavango, upper Zambezi and Kafue systems. Also in Central African systems, including the Lufira-Zaire and the basins of Lakes Victoria and Tanganyika.
Biology and Ecology Lives in vegetation along the margins of flowing rivers; also found in rocky crevices. Feeds on insects and small invertebrates.
Uses Potential aquarium species.
Note Similar to and possibly the same species as the Shire spiny eel.

SHIRE SPINY EEL

Shire-stekelpaling
Aethiomastacembelus shiranus (Günther, 1896)

Description D XXVII–XXIX, 65–70; A II, 85–90. Similar in form and colour to the longtail spiny eel. Attains 260 mm TL.
Distribution Lake Malawi and upper Shire; reported from lower Shire.
Biology and ecology See longtail spiny eel.

SPINY EELS 341

SHIRE SPINY EEL (cont.)

OCELLATED SPINY EEL

Kolvin-stekelpaling
Aethiomastacembelus vanderwaali (Skelton, 1976)

Description D XXII–XXVI, 64–75; A II, 64–79. Similar in form to long-tail spiny eel, but with fewer dorsal spines, larger head and usually more striking colour. Colour pattern mottled and varied from olive brown to dark brown or black, with yellowish interstices and fins and a prominent series of ocelli along tail section. Attains 180 mm TL.
Distribution Okavango and upper Zambezi systems.
Biology and Ecology Found in rocky rapids, living in crevices. Feeds on insects taken from rocks.
Uses Potential aquarium species.
Conservation Rare.

COASTAL AND ESTUARINE SPECIES THAT MAY OCCUR IN FRESHWATERS

Fish communities in the lower reaches of many rivers often include species of genera or families that are more usually found in estuaries or inshore coastal waters. However certain of these species occur regularly and may even breed in freshwaters. The more commonly encountered species only are presented here.

FAMILY CARCHARHINIDAE
Requiem sharks

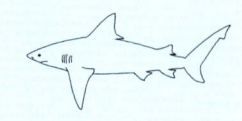

Mostly large streamlined predatory sharks with sharp serrated teeth suitable for dismembering large prey. Nearly all species are live-bearing. Distributed worldwide in tropical and temperate waters. Most species occur in coastal and offshore waters, a few entering estuaries and even freshwaters.

Genus *Carcharhinus* Blainville, 1816

The largest genus of sharks with about 29 species; one species in southern African freshwaters.

BULL SHARK

Bulhaai
Carcharhinus leucas (Valenciennes, 1839)

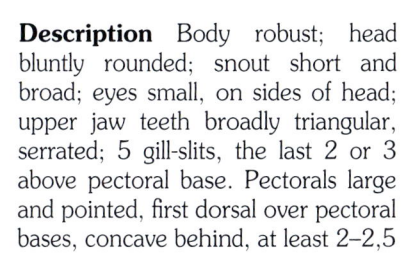

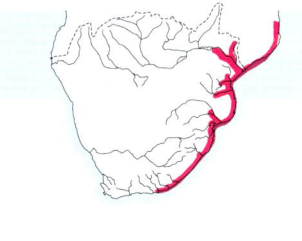

Description Body robust; head bluntly rounded; snout short and broad; eyes small, on sides of head; upper jaw teeth broadly triangular, serrated; 5 gill-slits, the last 2 or 3 above pectoral base. Pectorals large and pointed, first dorsal over pectoral bases, concave behind, at least 2–2,5 times height of second dorsal; caudal with well-developed lobes, upper lobe longer than lower, tip with lobelet. Grey, lighter ventrally with a pale horizontal band on flank. Attains 3,2 m TL. SA rock and shore angling record 304 kg.

Distribution East coast south to the

BULL SHARK (cont.)

eastern Cape. Penetrates the Zambezi to Cahora Bassa and the Lower Shire in Malawi. Reported inland as far as the Kruger National Park boundary in the Limpopo and to Makane's Pont on the Phongolo. Widespread in the tropics and subtropics.

Biology and Ecology Enters estuaries and rivers, proceeding far inland in suitable rivers; also found in lakes and lagoons with coastal connections. Feeds on a wide variety of prey including fish, crustaceans, turtles and dead or live marine and terrestrial mammals. Known to attack humans. From 3 to 13 pups are born in summer.

Uses Frequently caught by anglers. Flesh is edible.

Conservation Numbers of this species have been reduced by shark nets, while large dams on major rivers and reduced river flow may restrict incursions.

Note Also known as the Zambezi shark.

FAMILY PRISTIDAE
Sawfishes

Shark-like rays with the snout extended to form a blade lined with sharp teeth. Pectoral fins expanded forwards onto the head and gill slits on the underside of the body. Adults of some species reach huge sizes (up to 6 m). One or two genera are recognised, with about six species. Distributed worldwide in coastal waters including estuaries and rivers.

Genus *Pristis* Linck, 1790

Three species occur in our area but only one has been recorded from any river in the region.

SMALLTOOTH SAWFISH

Kleintand-saagvis
Pristis microdon Latham, 1794

Description Body shark-like, head and forebody depressed, caudal region compressed. Saw relatively short and broad, length 5 times width of base in mature specimens, 17–22 widely spaced teeth on either side. Mouth ventral, straight, numerous small teeth in bands. Gill slits underneath, behind origin of pectorals. Pectorals large, triangular, extending onto the sides of the head; 2 dorsals, origin of first dorsal well in front of origin of pelvics; anal absent, caudal with distinct lower lobe. Olive above, dirty cream below. Attains 4,6 m TL.
Distribution East coast to as far south as Port Alfred, eastern Cape. Has been caught as far inland as the lower Shire in Malawi, at the Save-Runde junction in Zimbabwe and at

Makane's Pont on the Phongolo in Zululand. Widespread in the tropical and subtropical inshore waters of the Indo-Pacific, Mediterranean and Atlantic.

Biology and Ecology Favours shallow inshore waters and enters estuaries and large rivers. Favours sandy or muddy bottoms, and feeds on benthic animals and small schooling fishes. The saw is used for grubbing and attacking prey as well as for defence. Ovoviviparous, producing 15–20 embryos.

Uses Caught in demersal fisheries with nets, longlines and bottom trawls. Saws sold as tourist souvenirs.

FAMILY AMBASSIDAE
Glassies

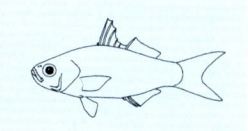

Genus *Ambassis* Cuvier, 1828

Small fishes of tropical estuaries, occasionally entering the lower reaches of rivers. Known as "glassies" on account of their transparent appearance. Recognised by small size, compressed body, transparency, tall strong spines of the dorsal fin and relatively deep separation of the spinous and soft dorsal fin. The serrated ridges of the head are useful taxonomic features. Includes about 24 species from estuaries and rivers of the Indo-Pacific; 3 occur in southern Africa.

KEY TO SPECIES

1a Lateral line interrupted, rostral spine below anterior nostril......................
....*A. gymnocephalus* (p. 347)
1b Lateral line complete, no exposed rostral spine......................................2
2a Preopercle ridge smooth except for 3–4 posterior spines, predorsal scales 9–11...*A. natalensis* (p. 348)
2b Preopercle ridge completely serrate, predorsal scales 14–18 ....
....*A. productus* (p. 349)

BALD GLASSY

Kaalkop-glasvis
Ambassis gymnocephalus (Lacepède, 1801)

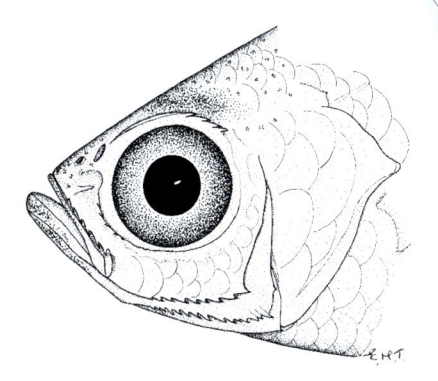

Description D VI–VII/I, 8–10; A III, 8–10. Scales in lateral line 27–29. Identified by the rostral spine and interrupted lateral line. Attains 100 mm SL.
Distribution Coastal lakes and estuaries in Mozambique and Natal southwards to Algoa Bay. Also in inshore tropical waters of the Indian Ocean.
Biology and Ecology Tolerant of freshwater only within a narrow temperature range (23–26° C). Feeds mainly on crustaceans, but also takes small fishes, fish eggs and larvae in estuaries.

SLENDER GLASSY

Slanke glasvis
Ambassis natalensis Gilchrist & Thompson, 1908

Description D VII/I, 9–11; A III, 9–11. Scales in lateral line 27–29. Smooth preopercular ridge with few posterior spines is typical. Attains 90 mm SL.
Distribution East coast from Natal south to Algoa Bay.
Biology and Ecology Tolerant of freshwater within a temperature range of 19–27° C. In summer feeds mainly in early evening and late morning and in winter during both day and night on crustaceans as well as insects (aquatic and terrestrial) and fish.

LONGSPINE GLASSY

Langstekel-glasvis
Ambassis productus Guichenot, 1866

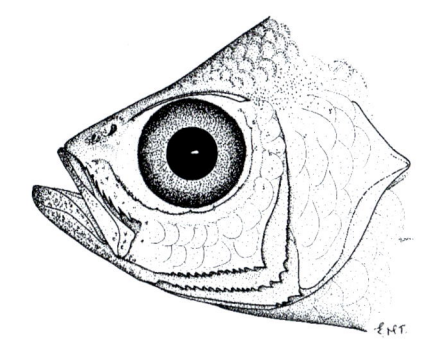

Description D VII/I, 9–10; A III, 9–11. Scales in lateral line 28–29. Preopercular ridge completely serrated. Attains 150 mm SL.
Distribution Madagascar and east coast south to Umtata River.
Biology and Ecology Tolerant of freshwater over a wide range of temperature (7–32° C) and tends to be more tolerant of lower temperatures in water of low salinity (2 parts per thousand) than in sea water (35 parts per thousand). Feeds mainly at night on crustaceans, fish fry and larvae and insects.

Family Atherinidae
Silversides

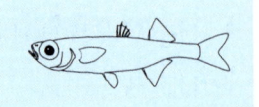

Small silvery fishes with a divided dorsal fin, the first spinous, the second with one spine and soft rays. A bright silvery band along the body gives the common name of "silversides". Large schools occur in estuaries and lower reaches of rivers. One species is usually taken from freshwater habitats in southern Africa.

Genus *Atherina* Linnaeus, 1758

Five species known, one from our area.

CAPE SILVERSIDE

Kaapse spierinkie
Atherina breviceps Valenciennes, 1835

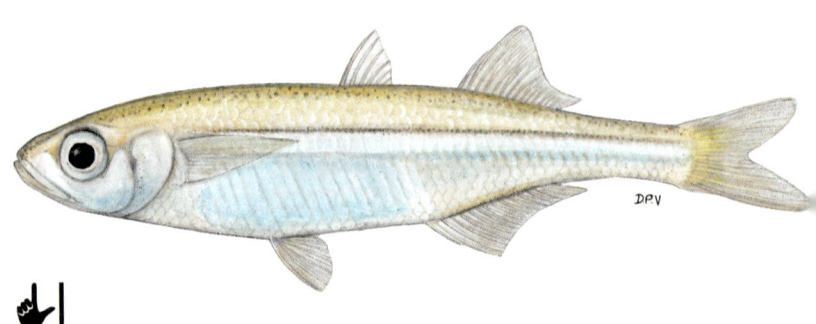

Description D V–VIII+I, 11–15; A I, 15–18. Mid-lateral scales 44–50. Translucent, dark above, bright silvery lateral band. Attains 110 mm SL.
Distribution Estuaries and coastal lakes from northern Natal around to Lüderitz, Namibia.

Biology and Ecology At smaller sizes filter-feeds on small items like phytoplankton and rotifers. Above about 35 mm TL feeds mainly on crustaceans especially amphipods taken from the water body and off the bottom. A valuable prey of predatory fishes and birds.

FAMILY MUGILIDAE
Mullets

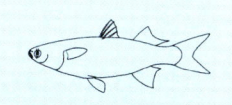

An economically important family of coastal, estuarine and freshwater fishes distributed worldwide in tropical and temperate waters. Recognised by their spear-shaped body, with widely separated dorsal fins (the first with four spines), depressed head and mouth with small loosely attached teeth. There is no lateral line on the body. Three species in three genera recorded from southern African freshwaters.

KEY TO SPECIES

1a Adipose eyelids well developed..............................*Mugil cephalus* (p. 351)
1b Adipose eyelids absent or feeble 2
2a Maxilla end concealed when mouth shut, 43–44 scales in lateral series......
    ....*Myxus capensis* (p. 352)
2b Maxilla end exposed when mouth shut, 33–35 scales in lateral series ....
    ....*Liza macrolepis* (p. 353)

Genus *Mugil* Linnaeus, 1758

Well-developed adipose eyelids are a notable feature distinguishing this genus from other mullets in our freshwaters. Several species worldwide, one in our area.

FLATHEAD MULLET

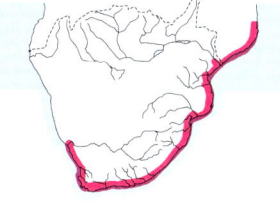

Platkop-harder
Mugil cephalus Linnaeus, 1758

Description D IV+I, 6–8; A III, 8. Scales in lateral series 39–42. The adipose eyelids of this species are a distinctive feature. Origin of anal fin opposite or nearly opposite origin of second dorsal fin. Attains 600 mm FL. SA angling records: freshwater 3,05 kg; rock and surf 3,9 kg; craft at sea 4,5 kg.
Distribution Coastal rivers throughout southern Africa. Worldwide in coastal, estuarine and freshwaters of tropical or warm-temperate zones.
Biology and Ecology Tolerates a wide range of salinity from freshwater to above sea-water concentrations.

FLATHEAD MULLET (cont.)

Breeds at sea near the mouths of estuaries during the winter; juveniles enter estuaries and, to a lesser extent, rivers, mainly during the winter months. They remain for one or two years and mature before moving out to breed. Feeds on algae, especially diatoms, and other tiny organisms from the bottom. Renowned for its jumping abilities.

Uses A valuable food fish, caught by netting and extensively cultured in ponds in certain countries.

Genus *Myxus* Günther, 1861

The absence of adipose eyelids and a pointed scale at the base of the pectoral fins distinguish this species from other mullets in our freshwaters. Several species, one in our area.

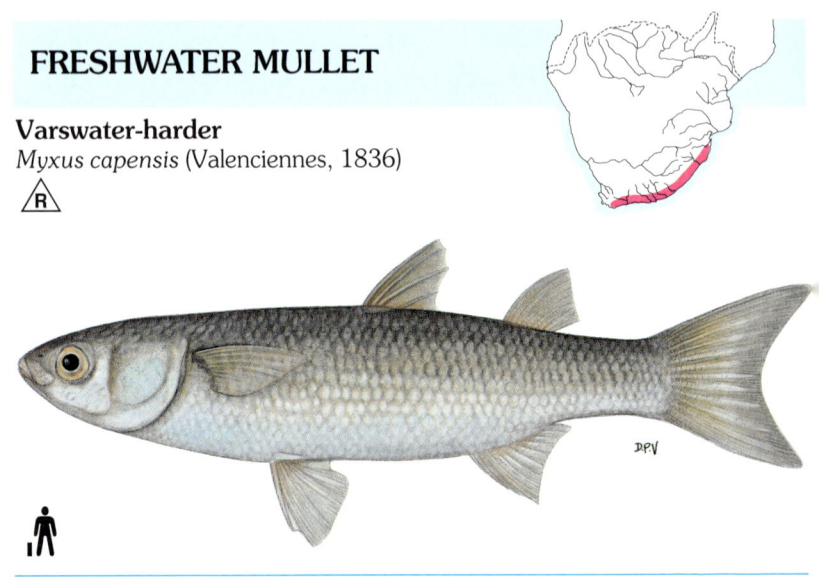

FRESHWATER MULLET

Varswater-harder
Myxus capensis (Valenciennes, 1836)

Description D IV+I, 8; A III, 9. Scales in lateral series 43–45. Adipose eyelids rudimentary, just visible in adults. Upper jaw (maxilla) mostly hidden when mouth closed. Origin of anal fin in advance of origin of second dorsal fin. Silvery grey. Attains nearly 450 mm FL.
Distribution East coastal estuaries and rivers from the Breë River to Kosi Bay. Endemic to southern Africa.
Biology and Ecology More common in Cape rivers than other mullet species, and may occur further than 100 km inland. Breeds at sea, throughout the year, juveniles move into estuaries and enter rivers usually in late winter or early spring. Males remain in freshwater for up to 4 years, females for up to 7 years. Fishes return first to the estuaries before maturing sexually prior to breeding.
Conservation Rare. Dams and weirs obstructing free passage into rivers have caused a decline in populations.

Genus *Liza* Jordan & Swain, 1884

Adipose eyelid rudimentary, pointed scale at the base of the pectoral fins and large scales are features of the one species of this genus in our freshwaters.

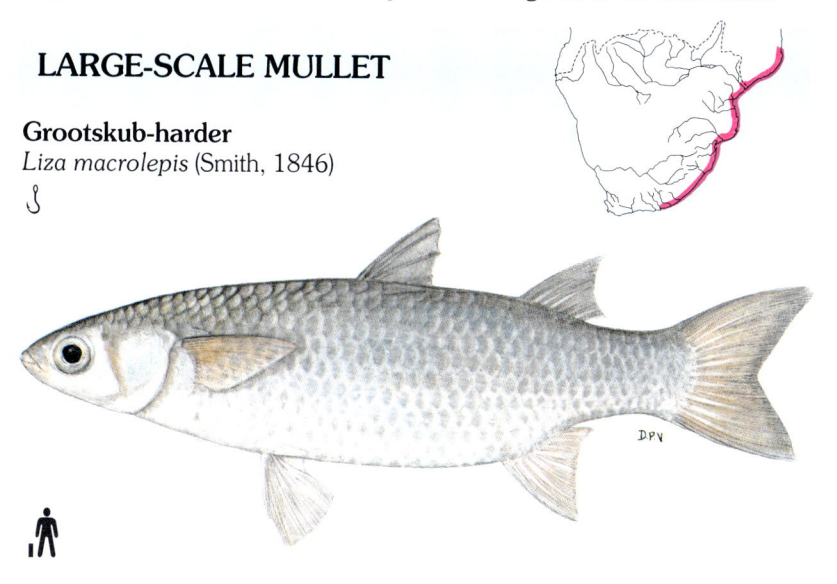

LARGE-SCALE MULLET

Grootskub-harder
Liza macrolepis (Smith, 1846)

Description D IV+I, 8; A III, 9. Scales in lateral series 33–35. No adipose eyelids. Upper jaw (maxilla) exposed when mouth shut. Origin of anal fin in advance of origin of second dorsal fin. Attains 350 mm FL.
Distribution East coast south to eastern Cape, most abundant in Mozambique and northern Natal. Also in Indo-West Pacific.
Biology and Ecology Feeds on diatoms grubbed out of bottom sand.

Family Syngnathidae
Pipefishes

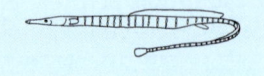

Seahorses and pipefishes are unusual fishes with their bodies encased in a series of bony rings. Seahorses are restricted to marine and estuarine environments but some pipefishes also occur in freshwater. Males incubate the eggs in an abdominal pouch. Distributed worldwide in all but polar seas. About 200 species of pipefishes are known; only 2 are recorded from freshwaters in southern Africa.

Genus *Microphis* Kaup, 1853

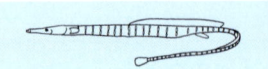

Estuarine and freshwater pipefishes of the Indo-Pacific region. Males with brood-pouch plates. Twenty-one species, two from the freshwaters of our area.

FRESHWATER PIPEFISH

Varswater-pypvis
Microphis fluviatilis (Peters, 1852)

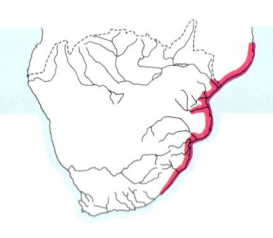

Description D 60–69, A 4. Rings (18–20)+(21–23). Anal ring about midway along length of fish. Male brood-pouch abdominal, without protective membranous folds. Bluish green to yellowish brown with fine black streaks. Attains 210 mm TL.
Distribution East coast south to Transkei. Also recorded from Kenya and Madagascar.
Biology and Ecology Found in quiet water amongst vegetation. Probably feeds on minute invertebrate organisms. Male broods eggs and larvae in abdominal pouch.
Uses Interesting aquarium subjects.

SHORT-TAIL PIPEFISH

Kortstert-pypvis
Microphis brachyurus (Bleeker, 1853)

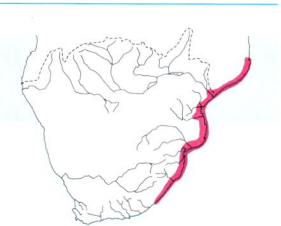

Description D 37–54, A 4. Rings (17–22)+(20–26). Anal ring nearer end of caudal fin than head. Yellowish brown. Attains 215 mm TL.

Distribution East coast from Kenya south to Natal area. Also Madagascar and Mauritius.

Family Sparidae
Seabreams

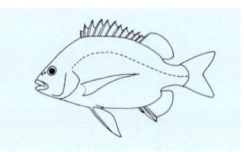

This family includes several well-known marine angling species. One species is recorded sporadically from freshwaters in southern Africa. Diagnostic features include the mouthform, with the maxilla fitting into a groove on the premaxilla and large canine teeth at the front of the jaws, a single lateral line and an undivided dorsal fin.

Genus *Acanthopagrus* Peters, 1852

Described as "rodent-like" fishes on account of the manner in which they dart in and out to nibble baited hooks. One species recorded from our freshwaters.

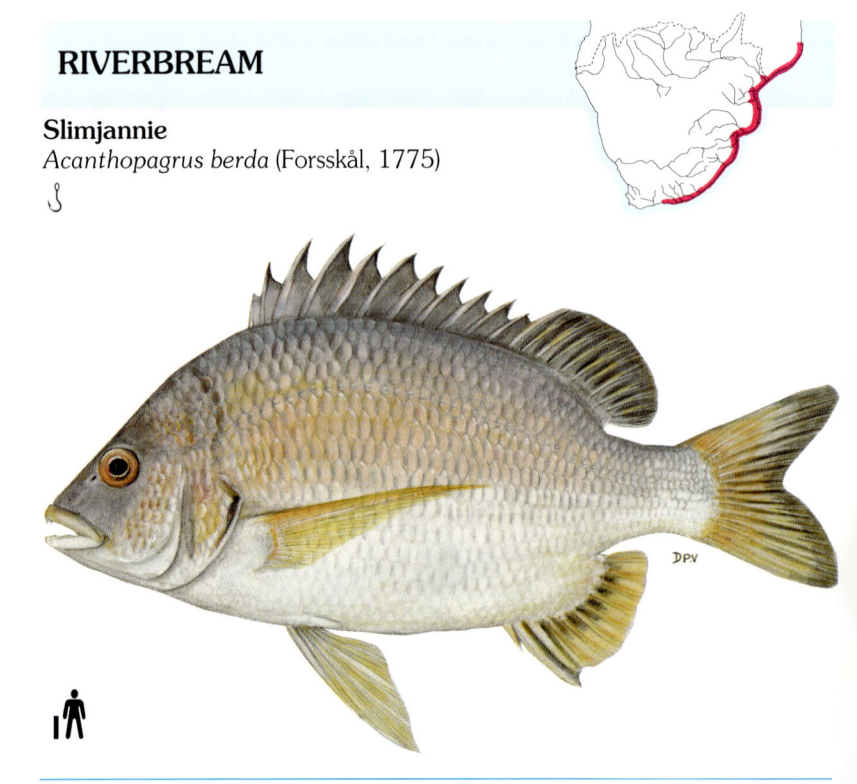

RIVERBREAM

Slimjannie
Acanthopagrus berda (Forsskål, 1775)

Description D XI–XII, 10–13; A III, 8–9. Lateral line scales 43–47. Incisors 4–6 in upper jaw, 6–8 in lower jaw. Deep bodied with forked caudal fin. Silvery grey to black, with a black patch behind upper gill cover. Attains 750 mm FL.
Distribution East coast south to Knysna area. Also in tropical Indo-Pacific.
Biology and Ecology Common in estuaries, relatively uncommon in freshwaters. Feeds on a wide variety of polychaete worms, mussels, shrimps, crabs and small fish. Breeds in winter at sea.
Uses Popular angling species.

FAMILY MONODACTYLIDAE
Moonies

Genus *Monodactylus* Lacepède, 1801

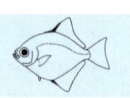

A small family of distinctive deep-bodied fishes common in estuaries, with juveniles frequently entering freshwater reaches of rivers. One genus and two species in southern Africa.

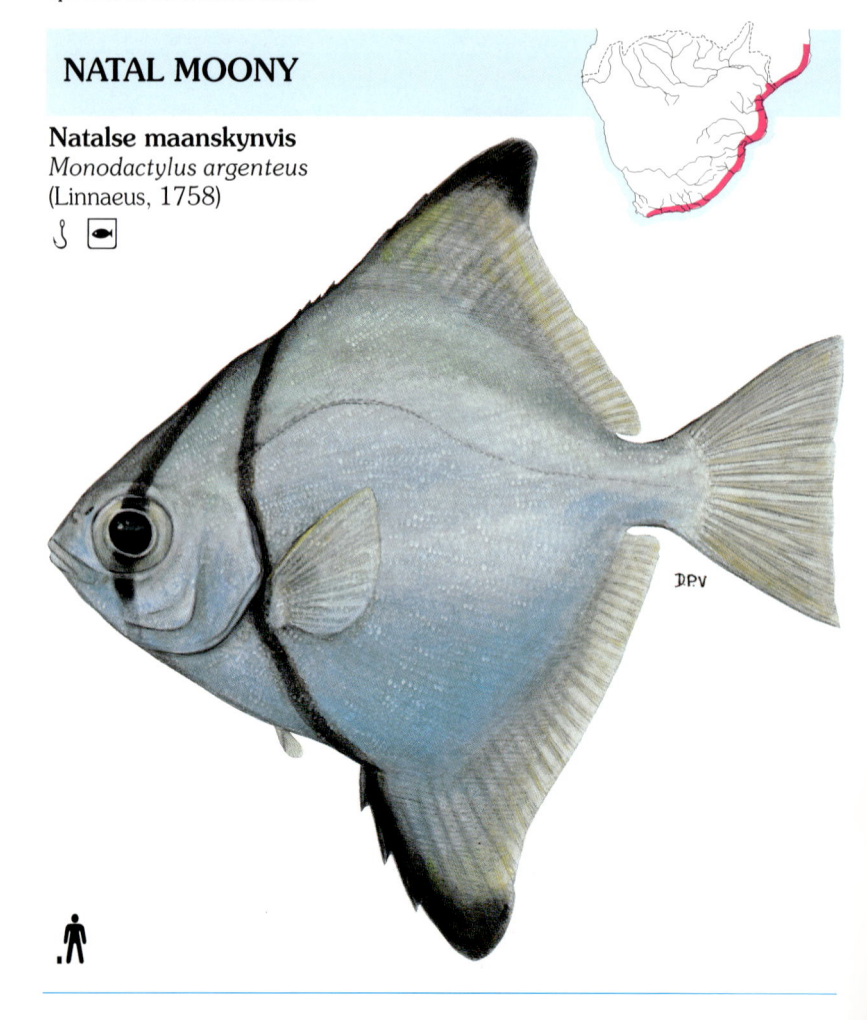

NATAL MOONY

Natalse maanskynvis
Monodactylus argenteus
(Linnaeus, 1758)

Description D VIII, 27–30; A III, 27–30. Scales small, 52–58 in lateral line, scales over base of dorsal and anal fins. Body diamond-shaped, depth 1,2–1,6 in SL. Maxilla width 3,4–5 in orbit diameter. Pelvic fins small or absent. Adults silvery with blackish tips to anterior dorsal and anal fins. Juveniles with 2 dark bars, one through the eye and the second behind the head. Attains 250 mm FL.
Distribution East coast south to the Breë River. Also in the Red Sea and Indo-West Pacific.
Biology and Ecology Occurs in large schools, often frequenting vegetation. Usually only juveniles enter freshwater. Feeds on a wide variety of invertebrates such as small shrimps and crabs taken from the bottom.
Uses Occasional aquarium species, best kept in a shoal. Minor angling interest.

CAPE MOONY

Kaapse maanskynvis
Monodactylus falciformis Lacepède, 1801

Description D VIII, 25–30; A III, 25–29. Scales small, 51–58 in lateral line. Body ovoid, depth 1,5–2 in SL. Maxilla width 2,7–3,7 in orbit diameter. Pelvic fins small or absent. Adults silvery, with blackish tips to anterior dorsal and anal fins. Juveniles with 11–12 dark wavy vertical bars. Attains 310 mm FL.
Distribution East coast south to False Bay. Also western Indian Ocean and the Red Sea.

Family Eleotridae
Sleepers

Bottom-living fishes with two separated dorsal fins, similar to gobies but pelvic fins not united to form a disc. A fairly large family of about 150 species widely distributed in shallow coastal waters, estuaries and sometimes freshwaters. Three species have been recorded from freshwaters in southern Africa.

Genus *Eleotris* Schneider, 1801

A worldwide genus of fresh and estuarine waters. Two species from our freshwaters.

DUSKY SLEEPER

Donker slaper
Eleotris fusca (Schneider, 1801)

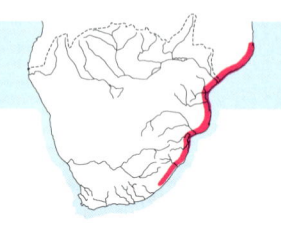

Description D VI+I, 8; A I, 8. Scales in lateral series 57–65. Head depressed, mouth large, reaching to below middle of eye, cheek scaled to below eye. Dark brown to black, with a series of horizontal lines along body. Attains 260 mm TL.
Distribution East coast south to Transkei. Also tropical Indo-West Pacific.
Biology and Ecology Commonly found under logs and rootstocks in muddy reaches of estuaries and mangrove swamps and freshwater streams leading into coastal lagoons.

BROADHEAD SLEEPER

Breëkop-slaper
Eleotris melanosoma Bleeker, 1852

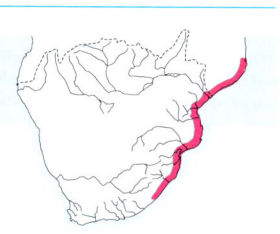

Description D VI+I, 8; A I, 8. Scales in lateral series 46–56. Head depressed, mouth large, reaching to below rear half of eye; cheek scales not below eye. Dark brown to black, sometimes with horizontal lines along body. Attains 170 mm TL.
Distribution East coast south to Transkei. Also tropical Indo-West Pacific.
Biology and Ecology A secretive species that inhabits the muddy reaches of estuaries and mangrove swamps, sometimes penetrating into freshwaters.

Genus *Hypseleotris* Gill, 1863

Whereas most sleepers are bottom dwellers, species of this genus spend most of their time off the bottom in the water column. About 15 species, one from our area.

GOLDEN SLEEPER

Goue slaper
Hypseleotris dayi Smith, 1950

Description D VI+I, 8; A I, 9. Scales in lateral series 24–25. Head compressed, cheeks scaled. Caudal fin truncate. Translucent with golden sheen, iridescent blue-green gill covers, a dark spot at base of caudal and a stripe through eye, extending as a broad dark horizontal band along the body. The dark body band tends to disappear from preserved specimens. Attains 77 mm TL.
Distribution Natal coast north to Kosi Bay.
Biology and Ecology Favours shallow vegetated margins of freshwater streams entering estuaries. In captivity feeds readily on mosquito and other insect larvae.
Uses Attractive in aquariums.
Conservation Rare. Threatened by coastal development and destruction of habitat through farming, industrial and urban activities.

Family Gobiidae
Gobies

Gobies form one of the largest fish families, with over 200 genera and about 2 000 species. Though they are found primarily in inshore marine habitats, there are also many estuarine and freshwater species. Gobies are bottom dwellers, their pelvic fins united into a disc. Several species are recorded from freshwaters in southern Africa.

Genus *Awaous* Valenciennes, 1837

A large depressed head with a convex profile distinguishes the one species in our area.

FRESHWATER GOBY

Varswater-dikkop
Awaous aeneofuscus (Peters, 1852)

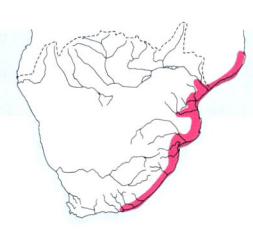

Description D VI+I, 9–11; A I, 10–11. Scales in lateral series 50–62. Head depressed, with a convex profile; mouth sub-terminal, larger in males than females, cheeks and gill covers not scaled. Caudal fin rounded. Brown or greenish brown with darker brown blotches and wavy stripes, 2 dark stripes leading forward from eyes, dark spots on tail. Attains 260 mm TL.
Distribution East coast rivers and estuaries south to Algoa Bay.
Biology and Ecology Found in pools and running water, usually over sandy bottoms into which it may bury itself with only the head and eyes exposed. Preys on invertebrates.

Genus *Croilia* Smith, 1955

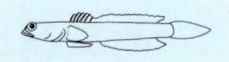

A single species in this genus of scaleless, burrowing gobies.

BURROWING GOBY

Grawende dikkop
Croilia mossambica Smith, 1955

Description D VI, 11–12; A 12. Scales absent. Head and body compressed and elongated, snout steeply sloping, eyes large and projecting. Dorsal fin separated or partly connected by membrane, caudal pointed. Translucent, with brown spots on dorsal fin and head. Caudal fin of males with vertical bars, females with a single horizontal bar on the lower edge. Attains 64 mm TL.
Distribution Coastal lakes and estuaries in Natal and southern Mozambique.
Biology and Ecology Lives in burrows excavated in clean sand, often in association with the sandprawn *Callianassa kraussi*. Feeds on small bottom-living invertebrates. Breeds throughout summer, males are territorial.
Conservation Rare. Threatened by human disturbance and siltation of estuaries.

Genus *Glossogobius* Gill, 1862

Gobies with a depressed head and relatively long snout, large mouths and a bilobed tongue. Found in estuaries and freshwaters, about 20 species, 2 from freshwaters in our area.

RIVER GOBY

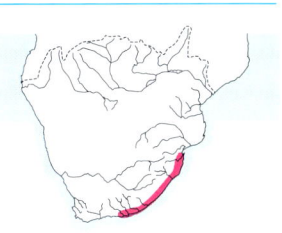

Rivier-dikkop
Glossogobius callidus (Smith, 1937)

Description D VI+I, 8–10; A I, 7–9. Scales in lateral series 28–32. Nape partially naked (without scales), predorsal scales 0–13. Head depressed, snout elongate, caudal fin pointed. Translucent brown with black X-spots along sides, black spot on hind membrane of first dorsal fin, soft dorsal with black and yellow spots and bars. Attains 120 mm TL.

Distribution East coast rivers from Mozambique south to the Kromme River (St Francis Bay).
Biology and Ecology Lives in pools on the bottom amongst cover such as cobbles or vegetation. Feeds on bottom-living insects and small invertebrates. Breeds in early summer; eggs are oval.

TANK GOBY

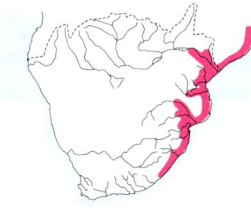

Tenk-dikkop
Glossogobius giuris (Hamilton-Buchanan, 1822)

Description D VI+I, 9; A I, 8. Scales in lateral series 29–33. Nape with visible scales, 15–19 predorsal scales. Head depressed, mouth large, lower jaw projecting. Caudal fin bluntly or sharply pointed. Translucent brown with dark brown or black spots and blotches along back and forming a series along midbody, dorsal fin with black spots. Attains about 400 mm TL. SA angling record 0,195 kg.
Distribution East coast rivers and estuaries south to Transkei. Also throughout the Indo-West Pacific. May occur hundreds of kilometres inland in larger rivers.
Biology and Ecology Inhabits quiet, usually sandy, zones of streams and backwater habitats and floodplain pans. Juveniles feed on bottom-living invertebrates; larger individuals prey on fish and tadpoles. Breeds in freshwater and estuaries in summer.
Uses Caught by subsistence fishermen and anglers.

Genus *Redigobius* Herre, 1927

Small gobies with compressed heads. Males have larger mouths than females. Numerous species, one from freshwaters in our area.

CHECKED GOBY

Blokkies-dikkop
Redigobius dewaali (Weber, 1897)

Description D VI+I, 7–8; A I, 5–7. Scales in lateral series 25–29. Body moderately deep, tail rounded. Head compressed, eyes large, mouth large, reaching below eye (females) or beyond eye (males). Translucent olive brown with dark brown or black bars and spots, including a double spot at base of the caudal fin; first dorsal fin with a large blue (black on preservation) spot near hind edge. Attains 42 mm SL.

Distribution East coast rivers and estuaries from the Limpopo south to Southern Natal; isolated records around Knysna, and recently taken from the Kariega estuary in the eastern Cape.

Biology and Ecology Occurs in clear, vegetated littoral habitats in floodplain pans, lakes and estuaries. Preys on small crustaceans and insect larvae. Breeds in summer.

Conservation Rare. Threatened by deterioration of riverine and estuarine habitats.

Genus *Silhouettea* Smith, 1959

Small, sand-dwelling gobies. Five species, one from freshwaters in our area.

SIBAYI GOBY

Sibayi-dikkop
Silhouettea sibayi Farquharson, 1970

Description D VI+I, 11; A I, 13. Scales in lateral series 24–25. No scales on head and chest. Body slender, elongate; head depressed. First dorsal fin of males tall and pointed, caudal rounded. Pale and translucent with brown and red flecks, oblique rows of spots on body; first dorsal fin of males sooty, with white vertical stripe. Attains 40 mm SL.

Distribution Lake Sibayi and Kosi Bay, northern Natal.

Biology and Ecology Lives over sand in shallow littoral areas to about 20 m depth. Buries body in sand, uses first dorsal fin for display and possibly as a lure to attract prey.

Conservation Rare. Threatened by restricted distribution and increasing human pressure on the environment.

GLOSSARY

Aestivate – to exist in a dormant state during a hot, dry period.
Abdominal – pertaining to the belly or body cavity region.
Acanthomorpha – a large branch of more advanced fishes that includes all the spiny-rayed fishes and other related groups.
Adipose eyelid – transparent tissue partly covering the eye.
Adipose fin – a fleshy fin without rays, on the dorsum behind the rayed dorsal fin. An adipose fin may be small, leaf-like, and narrowly attached to the body, or a large fleshy lobe broadly attached to the body.
Airbladder – see swimbladder.
Algae – simple aquatic plants without roots; freshwater algae are either single cells or strands of cells that may form dense mats.
Alien species – a species not naturally occurring in a defined area but introduced into that area from elsewhere.
Alimentary canal – the gut tract from the mouth to the anus.
Anadromous – migrating upstream from the sea or a lake into rivers to breed (see **diadromous**, **catadromous**, **potamodromous**).
Anal – refers to the anus or vent.
Anal fin – ventral median fin behind the anus.
Annulus – a growth zone formed on scales, otoliths and bones each year, often in late winter.
Anotophysi – a division of ostariophysan fishes which comprises only the order Gonorhynchiformes and is the sister-group lineage to the Otophysi (fishes with a Weberian apparatus).
Anterior – near or towards the front of; the front section.
Anus – the hind opening of the intestine (vent).
Axillary scale – an elongated pointed scale in the axil or junction between the fin and body.

Barbel – a slender tentacle or filamentous projection on the jaws or head, used mainly as an organ of taste and touch.
Benthic – on or near the bottom.
Branched ray – a divided, segmented fin ray.
Branchial – pertaining to the gills.
Branchial arches – gill arches.
Branchiostegal ray – bony rays supporting the membrane along the bottom and hind edge of the gill cover. The membrane serves to close off the gill chamber during respiration.
Buccal – pertaining to the mouth or cheek.

Caecum (pl. caeca) – a blind sac, usually from the alimentary canal.
Canine – pointed conical teeth.
Carnivorous – flesh eating.
Cartilage – smooth skeletal tissue; gristle.
Casque – helmet-like structure.
Catadromous – migrating downstream from rivers to a lake or the sea in order to breed (see also anadromous, diadromous, potamodromous).
Caudal fin – tail fin.
Caudal peduncle – the body section from behind the anal fin to the base of the caudal (tail) fin.
Clasper – elongated lobe of the pelvic fins of males of certain sharks and rays, used as a copulatory organ when mating.
Classification – the arrangement of objects or organisms sorted into different classes or groups.
Cloaca – a pit-like chamber that contains the anus and urogenital openings of cartilaginous fishes.
Common name – an informal vernacular name for an animal; it may differ from place to place.
Compressed – flattened from side to side.
Crepuscular – active at dawn and dusk (see **nocturnal, diurnal**).
Crustacean – an invertebrate organism with a segmented body, a hard outer skeleton and paired jointed limbs (e.g. crab, shrimp).
Ctenoid scale – scale with small tooth-like projections (ctenii) along the outer edge.
Cusp – a projection or raised point on the surface of a tooth.
Cycloid scale – scale with a smooth outer edge.

Deciduous – easily dislodged.
Dentary – largest tooth-bearing bone in each half of the lower jaw.
Dentition – the arrangement of the teeth.
Depressed – flattened from top to bottom.
Derived – an advanced state or condition evolved from a more primitive one.
Dermal – pertaining to the skin.
Diadromous – migrating between the sea and freshwater.
Distal – furthest away from.
Diurnal – pertaining to the daylight hours.
Dorsal (dorsum) – pertaining to the uppermost surface (opposite to ventral).

Ear organ – a structure that develops on each gill cover and shoulder of male knerias during the breeding season, used to grasp the female during mating.
Ecology – study of the relationships between living organisms and their environment.
Ecoregion – a region of relative ecological similarity.
Ecosystem – a dynamic interacting system of organisms and their environment.

Egg-spot or **Egg-dummy** – a discrete egg-like colored spot on the anal fin of cichlid fishes (see also **ocellus**).
Electric organ – a specialised organ of certain fishes for the generation of electricity; the organ is derived from muscle tissue.
Electrogenic – capable of generating electric impulses.
Electroreceptor – organ for receiving electric impulses.
Emarginate – slightly indented edge.
Embryo – the developing organism either within the egg envelope or hatched, and which is dependant on the egg yolk for nourishment.
Endangered – the conservation status of a species threatened with extinction and whose survival is unlikely if the causal factors of the threat continue operating.
Endemic – native to, or occurring naturally in a particular place; used especially for organisms with a restricted range.
Epiphyte – a plant which lives on the surface of other plants.
Euryhaline – tolerant of a wide range of salinities.

Falcate – sickle-shaped, curved with pointed tips.
Family – a taxonomic category which includes one or more genera, has the distinct Latinised suffix -idae (e.g. Cyprinidae).
Fauna – the assemblage of animals in a particular area.
Fecundity – reproductive potential of an organism; the number of eggs produced per individual at any particular time of spawning.
Filamentous – thin and thread-like.
Fin – an appendage of a fish.
Fish ladder – see fish passway.
Fish passway, **fishway** or **fish ladder** – a structure allowing fish to overcome a barrier by swimming or leaping. Man-made fishways often form a series of connected chambers along a sloping channel, up or down which the fishes swim.
Fork length – the length of a fish measured from the tip of the snout to the tip of the mid-caudal rays.
Fry – a lay term for a newly hatched juvenile fish.
Fusiform – spindle-shaped; broadest in the middle and tapered at both ends.

Gasbladder – see swimbladder, airbladder.
Genital papilla – a projection behind the anus that carries the external opening or pore of the reproductive system.
Genus – a taxonomic category that includes one or more species descended from a single common ancestor.
Gills – the breathing organs of fishes consisting of vascularised filaments attached to the gill arches.
Gill arch – a slender bony arch within the pharynx (throat) of a fish supporting the gill filaments. Normally there are four or five pairs of gill arches.
Gill chamber – the space behind the gill arches for the gills.

Gill cover (opercle) – a hinged cover to the gill chamber on each side of the head; formed from a overlapping series of platelike bones.
Gill opening – the opening of the gill chamber at the posterior or hind end of the gill covers, through which water is exhaled.
Gill rakers – projections, often in an outer and inner series, along the anterior edge of each gill arch, which serve to sieve the water passing between the gill arches.
Gill slit – one of a series of openings of the gill chambers of cartilaginous fishes.
Gonads – the internal reproductive organs (either testes or ovaries).
Gular – pertaining to the throat.

Habitat – the place where an organism lives.
Herbivorous – feeding on plants.
Holotype – the sole or designated name-bearing specimen or part of a specimen from which a species or subspecies is first described.
Hypurals – blade-like bones of the caudal skeleton, with which the caudal fin rays articulate.
Hybrid – the offspring produced by parents each of a different species.

Ichthyology – the scientific study of fishes.
Inferior – below or underneath, opposite of superior.
Invertebrate – an animal that has no internal backbone or spinal column.
Isthmus – the narrow bridge of flesh between the lower jaw and the chest, often separating the gill openings.

Juvenile – young organism essentially similar to the adult form.

Keel – a narrow hard ridge.
Kype – the prominent hooked jaws of mature male trout and salmons.

Larva (pl. larvae) – a developing organism after hatching from the egg, which has begun to feed itself and is not solely dependant on egg yolk for nourishment.
Lateral – on the side of.
Lateral line – a sensory system consisting of sensory cells within tubular canals with pores (openings) to the surface, extending over the head and along the body of a fish.
Leptocephalus (pl. leptocephali) – a slender, leaf-like larva of eels and tarpons. The leptocephalus changes radically (metamorphoses) into the typical body form of the juvenile fish.
Littoral – at or near the shore of a lake (or sea).
Lobe – a rounded flattened extension or projection.
Lunate – crescent-shaped, like a crescent moon.

Maxilla (pl. maxillae) – a bone of the upper jaw.
Maxillary – pertaining to the maxilla or upper jaw.
Median – lying in the midline.
Melanophore – cell containing black pigment.
Metamorphosis – complete change in body form from one life history stage to another.
Migration – coordinated movement of animals from one place to another.
Mimic – one animal resembling the form of another, in order to obtain some benefit or advantage.
Mode (-al) – the value or number of most common frequency.
Molar (molariform) – tooth with a smooth, flattened or rounded surface for grinding.
Mollusc – an invertebrate animal of the phylum Mollusca, including snails, mussels, clams, octopods and squids.
Monophyletic – lineage of species with a single common ancestor.
Morphology – the study of shape and form; the form of an organism.

Nape – the dorsal part of the body immediately behind the head.
Naris (pl. nares) – nostril, opening to nasal chamber.
Niche – that part of the environment which provides an organism with the necessary conditions for its existence; or the role of an organism in its environment.
Nocturnal – pertaining to the night hours.
Nuchal – body region behind the head.
Nuptial – pertaining to breeding.

Ocellus (pl. ocelli) – an eye-like spot, a spot surrounded by a clear ring.
Oesophagus – part of the gut or alimentary canal between the pharynx and the stomach.
Omnivorous – feeding on a wide variety of foods including plants and animals.
Opercle – see **gill cover**.
Operculum (pl. opercula) – the principal bone in the gill cover.
Orbit – the bony eye socket.
Ostariophysi – a Superorder category of bony fishes that includes two major divisions or lineages, the Otophysi (fishes with a Weberian apparatus) and the Anotophysi (i.e. the order Gonorhynchiformes).
Otolith – calcareous ear-stone in the inner ear of bony fishes.
Otophysi – a division or lineage of ostariophysan fishes the members of which all have a Weberian apparatus. It is the sister group of the Anotophysi and includes the Cypriniformes (carps, minnows and allies), the Characiformes (tigerfish and allies) and the Siluriformes (catfishes and gymnotoids).
Oviparous – producing eggs that are fertilised, develop and hatch after being laid.

Palate – the roof of the mouth.
Papilla (pl. papillae) – a small fleshy projection.
Parr – juvenile trout and salmon still showing dark marks (parr marks) along the body.
Pan – depression in the earth's surface without an outlet, which is periodically but temporarily filled with water (Afrikaans).
Pectoral fin – paired fins located closely behind the head.
Peduncle – a stalk or stem-like base (see caudal peduncle).
Pelagic – living near the surface in open water.
Pelvic fin – a paired fin located on the ventral side of the body below or behind the pectoral fin and in front of the anal fin.
Periphyton – plants and animals living on the submerged parts of aquatic plants.
Pharynx (pharyngeal) – the throat or hind region of the mouth, surrounded by the gill arches.
Phylogeny (phylogenetic) – genealogical relationships of species and higher taxa through time.
Piscivorous – feeding primarily on fish.
Plankton – minute organisms drifting in the water column.
Plica (pl. -ae) – small ridge or fold of skin.
Posterior – behind, at or near the rear end of.
Potamodromous – migrating in freshwaters.
Predator – an animal that kills and eats other animals.
Predorsal – that part of the head and body in front of the dorsal fin.
Premaxilla (pl. -ae) – paired bones forming the anterior part of the upper jaw.
Preopercle – the cheek bone lying in front of the gill cover or operculum and behind the eye.
Prey – animals that are the food of predators.
Pterygiophore – bone or cartilaginous elements supporting the fin rays.
Pyloric caecum (pl. -a) – blind sac or pouch developed from the alimentary canal at the junction of the stomach and intestine.

Rare – the conservation status of a species with small or restricted populations which are not at present Endangered or Vulnerable, but which are at risk.
Ray – a rod-like fin support (see branched ray, unbranched ray, soft ray, spine).
Reticulate – forming a network.
Riffle – shallow, rocky river reach with turbulent flowing water.
Rostral – pertaining to the anterior part of the snout or rostrum.
Rugose – rough or wrinkled.

Safe – the conservation status of a formerly threatened species that is now considered to be relatively secure.
Scute – a shield-like bony plate.

Serrate – bearing small saw-like teeth or barbs.
Scientific name – the official name of a species consisting of two words, the first for the genus name and the second a species name. Each species has only one valid scientific name.
Snout – the front end of the head, the head section before the eyes.
Soft ray – a flexible, segmented fin ray.
Species – a particular kind of organism; the fundamental taxonomic unit. Members of a species have a common ancestor and share features unique to the group. In nature different species usually do not interbreed.
Spine – pointed bony fin support; spines may be smooth (simple) or serrated (with barbs).
Standard length (SL) – the length of a fish measured in a straight line from the tip of the snout to the end of the caudal skeleton (as indicated by the axis of flexure of the caudal fin rays).
Striae (striated) – fine grooves forming lines on a scale.
Substratum (pl. -a) – the bottom surface of a habitat.
Subterminal – below the end point; with reference to mouth position indicates snout protrudes slightly beyond mouth.
Superior – above.
Swimbladder (airbladder, gasbladder) – a thin walled, gas-filled bladder or sac in the body cavity. The bladder may be free from (termed physoclistous), or connected to (physostomous) the alimentary canal by a thin open duct.
Synonym – one of two or more different names applied to the same taxon.
Syntype – one of a series of specimens on which a species is described and named.

Tactile – pertaining to the sense of touch.
Taxon (pl. taxa) – any taxonomic unit (e.g. family, genus, species).
Taxonomy – the theory and practice of describing, naming and classifying organisms.
Terminal – at the end, or furthest point, of.
Thoracic – pertaining to the chest or thorax.
Threatened status – the status of a species or population that has deteriorated through natural or unnatural causes to the point where it may be considered as Rare, Vulnerable or Endangered.
Total length (TL) – the overall length of a fish measured in a straight line from the tip of the snout to the tip of the tail.
Triploid – having a threefold number of chromosomes.
Truncate – with a straight edge; square-cut.
Tubercle – small horny projection on the head, fins or body.
Turbid(-ity) – muddy or murky water due to the presence of suspended particles.
Type(s) – the specimen(s) on which a species is described and named (see holotype, syntype).

Unbranched ray – a simple, usually flexible, segmented fin ray.
Unculus (pl. -i) – small horny projection from a single cell in the skin.

Vent – the external opening of the intestine, anus.
Ventral – on or near the lower surface of the body (underside).
Vermiculation – short wavy line or stripe.
Vertebra (pl. -ae) – bony or cartilaginous segment of the backbone or vertebral column.
Vertebrate – an organism with a segmented spinal column or backbone.
Villiform – like fine bristles or velvet.
Viscera – all discrete internal organs such as the heart, gut, liver, etc.
Viviparous – giving birth to live young.
Vlei – a marsh or shallow body of water with emergent vegetation (Afrikaans).
Vomer – median bone in the front of the palate (roof of the mouth), often bearing teeth.
Vulnerable – the conservation status of a species likely to move into the Endangered category in the near future if the threatening factors continue operating.

Weberian apparatus – a complex structure of modified anterior vertebrae in Otophysan fishes (cyprinids, characins, catfishes) forming a chain of small bones linking the swimbladder and the inner ear.
Wetland – an ecosystem which is periodically flooded.

Zonation – the sequence of changing ecosystems along a river from its source to its mouth.
Zooplankton – minute animals drifting in the water column.

SELECTED REFERENCES AND READING LIST

General works on southern African fishes

Balon, E.K. 1974. *Fishes of Lake Kariba, Africa.* TFH, Neptune City. 144 pp.

Bell-Cross G. & J.L. Minshull. 1988. *The Fishes of Zimbabwe.* National Museums and Monuments of Zimbabwe, Harare. 294 pp.

Bowmaker, A.P., P.B.N. Jackson & R.A. Jubb. 1978. Freshwater fishes. pp. 1183–1230. In M.J.A. Werger (ed.) *Biogeography and Ecology of Southern Africa.* W. Junk, The Hague.

Bruton, M.N., P.B.N. Jackson & P.H. Skelton. 1982. *Pocket Guide to the Freshwater Fishes of Southern Africa.* Centaur Publishers, Cape Town. 88 pp.

Bruton, M.N. & H.M. Kok. 1980. The freshwater fishes of Maputaland. pp. 210–244. In M.N. Bruton & K.H. Cooper (eds) *Studies on the ecology of Maputaland.* Rhodes University, Grahamstown and the Natal Branch of the Wildlife Society, Durban.

Crass, R.S. 1964. *Freshwater fishes of Natal.* Shuter & Shooter, Pietermaritzburg. 167 pp.

Harrison, A.C., K.E. Shortt-Smith, J.H. Yates, R.A. Jubb, G. Rushby, & C.T. Flamwell. 1963. *Fresh-water Fish and Fishing in Africa.* Nelson, Johannesburg. 210 pp.

Jubb, R.A. 1961. *An Illustrated Guide to the Freshwater Fishes of the Zambezi River, Lake Kariba, Pungwe, Sabi, Lundi, and Limpopo Rivers.* Stuart Manning, Bulawayo. 170 pp.

Jackson, P.B.N. 1961. *The Fishes of Northern Rhodesia.* The Government Printer, Lusaka. 140 pp.

Jubb, R.A. 1965. Freshwater fishes of the Cape Province. *Annals of the Cape Provincial Museums* 4, 1–72.

Jubb, R.A. 1967. *Freshwater Fishes of Southern Africa.* Balkema, Cape Town. 248 pp.

Kenmuir, D. 1983. *Fishes of Kariba.* Longman Zimbabwe, Harare, 135 pp.

Le Roux, P. & L. Steyn. 1968. *Fishes of the Transvaal.* S.A. Breweries Institute, Johannesburg. 108 pp.

Pienaar, U. de V. 1978. *The Freshwater Fishes of the Kruger National Park.* National Parks Board of Trustees, Pretoria. 91 pp.

Poll, M. 1967. *Contribution à la Faune Ichthyologique de l'Angola.* Diamang Publicações Culturais (75), 381 pp.

Books or articles of special interest

Check-List of the Freshwater Fishes of Africa (CLOFFA), vols 1–4. Editors J.

Daget, J-P. Gosse, G.G. Teugels (vol. 4 only) & D.F.E. Thys van den Audenaerde. (Vol. 1, 410 pp (1984)), (Vol. 2, 520 pp (1986)), (Vol. 3, 273 pp (1986)), (Vol. 4, 740 pp (1991)).

Crass, R.S. 1986. *Trout in South Africa.* Macmillan, Johannesburg. 207 pp.

de Moor, I.J. & M.N. Bruton. 1988. *Atlas of Alien and Translocated Indigenous Aquatic Animals in Southern Africa.* South African National Scientific Programmes Report No. 144, 310 pp.

Eschmeyer, W.N. 1990. *Catalog of the Genera of Recent Fishes.* California Academy of Sciences, San Francisco. 697 pp.

Hecht, T. & P.J. Britz. 1990. *Aquaculture in South Africa. History, Status and Prospects.* The Aquaculture Association of South Africa, Pretoria. 58 pp.

Hecht, T., W. Uys, & P.J. Britz (eds). 1988. *The Culture of the Sharptooth Catfish, Clarias gariepinus in Southern Africa.* South African National Scientific Programmes Report No. 153. 133 pp.

Jackson, P.B.N. 1975. Common and scientific names of the fishes of southern Africa. Part 2. Freshwater fishes. *Special Publication of the J.L.B. Smith Institute of Ichthyology (14),* 179–198.

Lévêque, C., M.N. Bruton & G.W. Ssentongo (eds). 1988. *Biology and Ecology of African Freshwater Fishes.* ORSTOM, Travaux et Documents (216), Paris. 508 pp.

Lowe-McConnell, R. 1975. *Fish Communities in Tropical Freshwaters.* Longman, London. 337 pp.

Nelson, J.S. 1984. *Fishes of the World,* 2nd ed. Wiley-Interscience, New York. 523 pp.

Skelton, P.H. 1987. *South African Red Data Book – Fishes.* South African National Scientific Programmes Report No. 137, 199 pp.

Skelton, P.H., M.N. Bruton, G.S. Merron and B.C.W. van der Waal. 1985. The fishes of the Okavango Drainage system in Angola, South West Africa and Botswana: Taxonomy and distribution. *Ichthyological Bulletin of the J.L.B. Smith Institute of Ichthyology* (50), 21 pp.

Trewavas, E. 1983. *Tilapiine fishes of the genera Sarotherodon, Oreochromis, and Danakilia.* British Museum (Natural History), London. 583 pp.

Welcomme, R.L. 1979. *Fisheries Ecology of Floodplain Rivers.* Longman, London and New York. 317 pp.

Useful addresses

Museums with fish collections

- J.L.B. Smith Institute of Ichthyology, Private Bag 1015, Grahamstown 6140, South Africa.

- Albany Museum, Somerset Street, Grahamstown 6140, South Africa.

- The Natural History Museum of Zimbabwe, P O Box 240, Bulawayo, Zimbabwe.

- The State Museum, P O Box 1203, Windhoek, Namibia.

- The South African Museum, P O Box 61, Cape Town 8000, South Africa.

Angling Associations & Record Officers

- South African Anglers Union (SAAU): The Hon. Secretary, P.O. Box 1303, Edenvale 1610, South Africa.

- SAAU Records Officer (freshwater): Mr R.A. van der Merwe, P.O. Box 93, Pullen's Hope 1096, South Africa.

- Zimbabwe Angling Records, P.O. Box 942, Harare, Zimbabwe.

    or :

- J. Minshull, Department of Ichthyology, National Museum of Natural History, P.O. Box 240, Bulawayo, Zimbabwe.

- The Angling Society of Malawi, P.O. Box 744, Blantyre, Malawi.

- The Freshwater Angling Association of Namibia, P O Box 613, Windhoek, Namibia.

Nature Conservation/Fisheries Authorities

- Botswana
    Fisheries Officer, Department of Animal Health & Production, Ministry of Agriculture, Private Bag 003, Gaberone.

- Lesotho
  Fisheries Officer, Fisheries section, Department of Livestock Services, Private Bag A82, Maseru.

- Malawi
  Chief Fisheries Officer, Department of Fisheries, P O Box 593, Lilongwe.

- Namibia
  Directorate Nature Conservation and Recreation Resorts, Private Bag 13306, Windhoek.
  Secretary, Fisheries and Marine Resources, P O Box 13355, Windhoek.

- South Africa
  Cape: Chief Directorate Nature & Environmental Conservation, P Bag X9086, Cape Town 8000.

  Natal: Natal Parks Board, P O Box 662, Pietermaritzburg 3200, South Africa.

  Orange Free State: Department of Nature & Environmental Conservation, P O Box 517, Bloemfontein 9300.

  Transvaal: Chief Directorate Nature & Environmental Conservation, Private Bag X209, Pretoria 0001.

- Zambia
  Chief Fisheries Research Officer, Headquarters Department of Fisheries, P O Box 350100 Chilanga.

- Zimbabwe
  Department National Parks and Wildlife Management, P O Box 8365, Causeway, Zimbabwe.

Aquaculture

The Aquaculture Association of South Africa, P O Box 72467, Lynnwood Ridge, Pretoria 0040.

INDEX TO SCIENTIFIC AND COMMMON NAMES

Acanthopagrus berda 356–7
Aethiomastacembelus 339
Aethiomastacembelus frenatus 340
Aethiomastacembelus shiranus 340–1
Aethiomastacembelus vanderwaali 341–2
African lungfishes 83, 89–91
African mottled eel 107
African pike 208–9
Afrika-bontpaling 107
Afrika-greepvis 209
air-breathing catfishes 227
alestiine characins 200
Amarginops 213
Amarginops hildae 214
Amatola barb 134–5
Amatola-ghieliemientjie 134–5
Ambassidae 85, 347
Ambassis 347
Ambassis gymnocephalus 347–8
Ambassis natalensis 348
Ambassis productus 349
Amphiliidae 82, 218
Amphilius 221
Amphilius laticaudatus 221
Amphilius natalensis 222
Amphilius uranoscopus 223
Anabantidae 86, 333
Angola-happie 299
Angolan happy 299
Anguilla 104
Anguilla bengalensis labiata 107
Anguilla bicolor bicolor 106–7
Anguilla marmorata 108
Anguilla mossambica 105–6
Anguillidae 35, 36, 81, 104
annual killifishes 267–72
Aplocheilichthys 274
Aplocheilichthys hutereaui 275
Aplocheilichthys johnstoni 274–5
Aplocheilichthys katangae 276–7
Aplocheilichthys myaposae 276
Aplocheilidae 267
Astatotilapia 299
Astatotilapia calliptera 300
Atherina 350
Atherina breviceps 350
Atherinidae 85, 350
Austroglanididae 211, 215
Austroglanis 215
Austroglanis barnardi 215–16
Austroglanis gilli 216–17
Austroglanis sclateri 217
Awaous 363
Awaous aeneofuscus 363

bald glassy 347–8
balk-ghieliemientjie 120–1
balk-juweelvis 294
banded jewelfish 294
banded tilapia 320–1
bandvin balk-ghieliemientjie 121
barbs 83, 117, 128–64
Barbus 119, 128
Barbus aeneus 168–9
Barbus afrohamiltoni 162
Barbus afrovernayi 157
Barbus amatolicus 134–5
Barbus andrewi 165–6
Barbus annectens 136–7
Barbus anoplus 35, 132–3
Barbus argenteus 159
Barbus barnardi 145
Barbus barotseensis 137
Barbus bellcrossi 137–8
Barbus bifrenatus 142–3
Barbus breviceps 135
Barbus brevidorsalis 144
Barbus brevipinnis 139
Barbus calidus 153–4
Barbus capensis 171
Barbus choloensis 159–60
Barbus codringtonii 173
Barbus dorsolineatus 164
Barbus erubescens 154
Barbus eutaenia 155
Barbus fasciolatus 147
Barbus gurneyi 133
Barbus haasianus 148–9
Barbus hospes 157–8
Barbus kerstenii 162–3
Barbus kimberleyensis 167–8
Barbus lineomaculatus 138–9
Barbus macrotaenia 146–7
Barbus manicensis 163
Barbus marequensis 172
Barbus mattozi 161
Barbus miolepis 155–6
Barbus motebensis 134
Barbus multilineatus 156–7
Barbus natalensis 169–70
Barbus neefi 140
Barbus pallidus 140–1
Barbus paludinosus 160–1
Barbus poechii 151
Barbus polylepis 170–1
Barbus radiatus 148
Barbus serra 164–5
Barbus thamalakanensis 144–5
Barbus toppini 146

382 INDEX TO SCIENTIFIC AND COMMON NAMES

Barbus treurensis 135–6
Barbus trevelyani 158–9
Barbus trimaculatus 150–1
Barbus unitaeniatus 141
Barbus viviparus 143
bariliins 119
Barnard se klipbaber 215–16
Barnard se rower 205
Barnard's robber 205
Barnard's rock catfish 215–16
Barotse barb 137
Barotse-ghieliemientjie 137
barred minnow 120–1
Basses 283
beekforel 264–5
Beira barb 148
Beira-ghieliemientjie 148
Beira killifish 269
Beira-kuilvissie 269
Berg River redfin 123–4
Bergrivier-rooivlerkie 123–4
black tilapia 328–9
blackback barb 145
blackspot climbing perch 335
blokkies-dikkop 366–7
blotched catfish 231–2
blougroen kuilvissie 270
bloukurper 325–6
blouwang-sonvis 284–5
bluegill sunfish 284–5
blunttooth catfish 230–1
Bo-Zambesi-geelvis 173
Bo-Zambesi-moddervis 186
Bo-Zambesi-skreeubaber 252
boel-ghieliemientjie 149–50
boogstreep-ghieliemientjie 143
Border barb 158–9
borrelbaard skreeubaber 256
bostreep-ghieliemientjie 164
botterbaber 225–6
bowstripe barb 143
breëbalk-sitarien 198
breëband-ghieliemientjie 146–7
breëkop-slaper 361
breëkopbaber 235–6
breëstert-bergbaber 221
breëstreep-ghieliemientjie 136–7
broadband barb 146–7
broadbarred citharine 198
broadhead catfish 235–6
broadhead sleeper 361
broadstriped barb 136–7
broadtail mountain catfish 221
brook charr 264–5
brown squeaker 249–50
brown trout 261–2
brownspot largemouth 318
bruin skreeubaber 249–50
bruinforel 261–2
bruinkol-grootbek 318
Brycinus 201
Brycinus imberi 201

Brycinus lateralis 202
bubblebarb squeaker 256
bulhaai 343–4
bull shark 343–4
bulldog 34, 98
Burchell se rooivlerkie 123
Burchell's redfin 123
burrowing goby 364
butter barbel 225–6
butter catfishes 224
Buzi-baber 214

canary kurper 298
Cape galaxias 259
Cape kurper 338
Cape moony 359
Cape silverside 350
Caprivi killifish 271–2
Carassius 118, 189
Carassius auratus 189–90
Carcharhinidae 81, 343
Carcharhinus 343
Carcharhinus leucas 343–4
carp 188–9
catfishes 210
cave catfish 234–5
Centrarchidae 86, 283
Characidae 84, 199
Characin families 193
characins 84, 199
checked goby 366–7
chessa 195–6
Chetia brevis 297
Chetia flaviventris 298
Chetia welwitschi 299
Chiloglanis 240–1
Chiloglanis anoterus 242
Chiloglanis bifurcus 242–3
Chiloglanis emarginatus 243–4
Chiloglanis fasciatus 244
Chiloglanis neumanni 245
Chiloglanis paratus 245–6
Chiloglanis pretoriae 246
Chiloglanis swierstrai 247
chiselmouths 173–6
Chobe sand catlet 220
Chobe-sandbabertjie 220
chubbyhead barb 132–3
chubbyhead group 132
Churchill 99
Cichlidae 86, 291
cichlids 291–332
citharines 83, 193–8
Clanwilliam redfin 153–4
Clanwilliam rock catfish 216–17
Clanwilliam sandfish 179–80
Clanwilliam yellowfish 171
Clanwilliam-geelvis 171
Clanwilliam-klipbaber 216–17
Clanwilliam-rooivlerkie 153–4
Clanwilliam-sandvis 179–80
Clariallabes platyprosopos 235–6

Clarias 228
Clarias cavernicola 234–5
Clarias gariepinus 229–30
Clarias liocephalus 232–3
Clarias ngamensis 230–1
Clarias stappersii 231–2
Clarias theodorae 233–4
Clariidae 82, 227
claroteid catfishes 211
Claroteidae 211
cloudy squeaker 251
Clupeidae 84, 109
common mountain catfish 223
copperstripe barb 156–7
Coptostomabarbus 118, 149
Coptostomabarbus wittei 149–50
Cornish jack 94
Croilia 364
Croilia mossambica 364
Ctenopharyngodon 118, 190
Ctenopharyngodon idella 190–1
Ctenopoma 334
Ctenopoma intermedium 335
Ctenopoma multispine 336
Cubango kneria 115
Cubango-skulpoortjie 115
Cunene dwarf happy 295
Cunene happy 310
Cunene kneria 114
Cunene labeo 186–7
Cyprinidae 83, 117
Cyprinodontidae 273
Cyprinodontiformes 84, 266
Cyprinus 118, 188
Cyprinus carpio 188–9

dashtail barb 151
dikbek-happie 302–3
dikkop-ghieliemientjie 132–3
Distichodontidae 83, 193–8
Distichodus 194
Distichodus mossambicus 194–5
Distichodus schenga 195–6
donker slaper 360
Drakensberg minnow 127–8
Drakensberg-rooivlerkie 127–8
driekol-ghieliemientjie 150–1
driekolkurper 327–8
dusky sleeper 360
dwarf barb 144
dwarf citharine 196–7
dwarf sanjika 121
dwarf stonebasher 100
dwerg-ghieliemientjie 144
dwerg-klipstamper 100
dwerg-sitarien 196–7

East-coast barb 146
East-coast lungfish 91
eastern bottlenose 95–6
eastern happy 300
Eastern Cape redfin 124–5

Eastern Cape rocky 337
eels 104–8
electric catfish 238–9
elektriese baber 238–9
Eleotridae 85, 360
Eleotris 360
Eleotris fusca 360
Eleotris melanosoma 361
estuarine round-herring 109–10
European perch 289–90
Europese baars 289–90

fiery redfin 126
finetooth squeaker 256–7
flathead mullet 351–2
freshwater goby 363
freshwater mullet 352–3
freshwater pipefish 354
fyntand-skreeubaber 256–7

Galaxias 258
Galaxias zebratus 259
Galaxiidae 82, 258
Galaxiids 258
Gambusia affinis 278–9
geel ghieliemientjie 163
geelbek-paling 105–6
gestreepte kuilvissie 271–2
gevlekte baber 231–2
gevlekte sandbabertjie 219
gewone bergbaber 223
ghost stonebasher 101
Gilchristella 109
Gilchristella aestuaria 109–10
Glossogobius 364
Glossogobius callidus 365
Glossogobius giuris 365–6
gobies 363
Gobiidae 85, 363
golden sleeper 362
goldfish 189–90
goldie barb 140–41
goldie barbs 139
gorgeous barb 137–8
Gorongoza kneria 116
Gorongoza skulpoortjie 116
goud-ghieliemientjie 140–1
goudvis 189–90
goue slaper 362
graskarp 190–1
grass carp 190–1
grawende dikkop 364
green happy 306
greenhead tilapia 331–2
Greenwood se happie 308
Greenwood's happy 308
greepvis (Afrika-) 209
Grens-ghieliemientjie 158–9
groen-happie 306
groenkop-kurper 331–2
grootbek-baars 286–7
grootbek-geelvis 167–8

384 INDEX TO SCIENTIFIC AND COMMON NAMES

grootbek-skreeubaber 254
grootskub-geelvis 172
grootskub-harder 353
grootvlek-skreeubaber 253
guppie 280–1
guppy 280–1

Hamilton se ghieliemientjie 162
Hamilton's barb 162
Hemichromis 294
Hemichromis elongatus 294
Hemigrammocharax 196
Hemigrammocharax machadoi 196–7
Hemigrammocharax multifasciatus 197
Hemigrammopetersius 204
Hemigrammopetersius barnardi 205
Hepsetidae 84, 208
Hepsetus 208
Hepsetus odoe 209
herrings 84, 109
Heterobranchus 236
Heterobranchus longifilis 236–7
Hilda's grunter 214
Hippopotamyrus 96
Hippopotamyrus ansorgii 96–7
Hippopotamyrus discorhynchus 97
humpback largemouth 312
Hydrocynus 205
Hydrocynus vittatus 206–7
hyphen barb 142–3
Hypophthalmichthys 117
Hypophthalmichthys molitrix 191
Hypseleotris 362
Hypseleotris dayi 362
Hypsopanchax 277
Hypsopanchax jubbi 277

imberi 201
Incomati chiselmouth 174–5
Incomati rock catlet 242–3
Incomati suckermouth 242–3
Inkomati-beitelbek 174–5
Inkomati-suierbekkie 242–3
introduced cyprinids 187
Israeli tilapia 330–1
Israelse kurper 330–1

Johnston se lampogie 274–5
Johnston's topminnow 274–5

kaalkop-glasvis 347–8
Kaapse galaxias 259
Kaapse kurper 338
Kaapse maanskynvis 359
Kaapse spierinkie 350
Kafue killifish 270–1
Kafue-kuilvissie 270–1
kanariekurper 298
kapenta 110–11
Kariba-kurper 326–7
Kariba tilapia 326–7
karp 188–9

kleinbek-baars 287–8
kleinbek-geelvis 168–9
kleinskub-geelvis 170–1
kleinskub-rooivlerkie 125
kleintand-saagvis 345–6
klipbaber 217
Kneria 112, 13
Kneria auriculata 113
Kneria maydelli 114
Kneria polli 114
knerias 83, 112
Kneriidae 83, 112
kolstert-ghieliemientjie 157
kolstert-muskietvis 279–80
kolvin-stekelpaling 341–2
koperstreep-ghieliemientjie 156–7
kortsnoet-beitelbek 174
kortstekel-suierbekkie 246
kortstert-pypvis 355
kortvin-paling 106–7
kortvlerk-ghieliemientjie 139
kromkop-grootbek 312
Kunene dwerg–mondbroeier 295
Kunene-happie 310
Kunene-moddervis 186–7
Kunene-skulpoortjie 114

Labeo 118, 176–87
Labeo altivelis 180–1
Labeo ansorgii 186–7
Labeo capensis 178–9
Labeo congoro 183–4
Labeo coubie group 183
Labeo cylindricus 184–5
Labeo forskahlii group 184
Labeo lunatus 186
Labeo molybdinus 185
Labeo niloticus group 180
Labeo rosae 181–2
Labeo rubromaculatus 179
Labeo ruddi 182–3
Labeo seeberi 179–80
Labeo umbratus 177–8
labeos 83, 117, 176–87
labyrinth fishes 333–8
laeveld-kurper 314–15
laeveldse suierbekkie 247
Lake Tanganyika sardine 110–11
langbaard-ghieliemientjie 141
langstekel-glasvis 349
langstert-stekelpaling 340
langvin-grootbek 315
large-scale mullet 353
largemouth bass 286–7
largemouth breams 311–18
largemouth squeaker 254
largemouth yellowfish 167–8
largescale yellowfish 172
largespot squeaker 253
leaden labeo 185
leopard squeaker 255
Lepomis 284

INDEX TO SCIENTIFIC AND COMMON NAMES 385

Lepomis macrochirus 284–5
Leptoglanis 218
Leptoglanis cf *dorae* 220
Leptoglanis rotundiceps 219
ligroos-happie 307
Limnothrissa 110
Limnothrissa miodon 110–11
line-spotted barb 138–9
live-bearers 278–82
Liza 353
Liza macrolepis 353
longbeard barb 141
longfin eel 105–6
longfin largemouth 315
longspine glassy 349
longtail spiny eel 340
longvis 90–1
loodvis 185
lowveld largemouth 314–15
lowveld rock catlet 247
lowveld suckermouth 247
luiperdkol-skreeubaber 255
lungfish 90–1
lynkol-ghieliemientjie 138–9
lynvin-ghieliemientjie 160–1

Madagascar mottled eel 108
Madagaskar-bontpaling 108
makriel 225–6
Malapteruridae 34, 82, 238
Malapterurus 238
Malapterurus electricus 238–9
Maluti minnow 127–8
Maluti-rooivlerkie 127–8
manyame labeo 180–1
manyame-moddervis 180–1
manyspined climbing perch 336
Marcusenius 98
Marcusenius macrolepidotus 98
Marico barb 134
Marico-ghieliemientjie 134
Mastacembelidae 81, 339
Megalopidae 84, 102–3
Megalops 102
Megalops cyprinoides 102–3
meshscaled topminnow 275
Mesobola 119
Mesobola brevianalis 119–20
Micralestes 202
Micralestes acutidens 203
Microphis 354
Microphis brachyurus 355
Microphis fluviatilis 354
Micropterus 285
Micropterus dolomieu 287–8
Micropterus punctulatus 288
Micropterus salmoides 286–7
miljoenvis 280–1
Mochokidae 82, 240
moggel 177–8
Monodactylidae 85, 358
Monodactylus argenteus 358–9

Monodactylus falciformis 359
moonies 358–9
Mormyridae 83, 92
Mormyrops 93
Mormyrops anguilloides 94
Mormyrus 94
Mormyrus lacerda 95
Mormyrus longirostris 95–6
Mortimer se happie 309
Mortimer's happy 309
mosquitofish 278–9
mountain catfishes 218
Mozambique tilapia 325–6
mudfishes 176
Mugil 351
Mugil cephalus 351–2
Mugilidae 85, 351
mullets 351–3
multibar citharine 197
muskietvis 278–9
Myxus 352
Myxus capensis 352–3

Namakwa-ghieliemientjie 157–8
Namaqua barb 157–8
Namib happy 303
Namib-happie 303
Nannocharax 197
Nannocharax macropterus 198
Natal moony 358–9
Natal mountain catfish 222
Natal topminnow 276
Natalse bergbaber 222
Natalse geelvis 169–70
Natalse lampogie 276
Natalse maanskynvis 358–9
nembwe 317–18
neobolins 119
Neumann's rock catlet 245
Neumann's suckermouth 245
newelrige skreeubaber 251
Nile tilapia 330
nkupe 194–5
noordelike skulpoortjie 114
northern kneria 114
Nothobranchius 35, 37, 267
Nothobranchius furzeri 270
Nothobranchius kafuensis 270–1
Nothobranchius kuhntae 269
Nothobranchius orthonotus 268–9
Nothobranchius rachovii 272
Nothobranchius sp. 271–2
Nyl-kurper 330

ocellated spiny eel 341–2
Okavango rock catlet 244
Okavango suckermouth 244
Okavango tilapia 322–3
Okavango-kurper 322–3
Okovango-suierbekkie 244
olyfkurper 317–18
Oncorhynchus 262

386 INDEX TO SCIENTIFIC AND COMMON NAMES

Oncorhynchus mykiss 263–4
Oos-Kaapse rooivlerkie 124–5
Oos-Kaapse kurper 337
Ooskus-ghieliemientjie 146
Ooskus-longvis 91
oostelike bottelneus 95–6
oostelike happie 300
Opsaridium 119, 120
Opsaridium sp. 121
Opsaridium zambezense 120–1
orange-fringed largemouth 297
Orange River labeo 178–9
orangefin barb 155
oranjerand-kurper 297
Oranjerivier-moddervis 178–9
oranjevlerk-ghieliemientjie 155
Oreochromis 324
Oreochromis andersonii 327–8
Oreochromis aureus 330–1
Oreochromis macrochir 331–2
Oreochromis mortimeri 326–7
Oreochromis mossambicus 325–6
Oreochromis niloticus 330
Oreochromis placidus 328–9
Oreochromis shiranus 329
Orthochromis 295
Orthochromis machadoi 295
osoog-tarpon 102–3
Otjikoto tilapia 321–2
Otjikoto-kurper 321–2
oxeye tarpon 102–3

papermouth 161
papierbek 161
Parakneria 112, 115
Parakneria fortuita 115
Parakneria mossambica 116
Paramormyrops 100
Paramormyrops jacksoni 101
Parauchenoglanis 212
Parauchenoglanis ngamensis 212–13
pennant-tailed suckermouth 242
pennant-tailed rock catlet 242
Perca 289
Perca fluviatilis 289–90
Percidae 86, 289
perskop-grootbek 316
perslyf-moddervis 183–4
Petrocephalus 99
Petrocephalus catostoma 99
Phalloceros caudimaculatus 279–80
Pharyngochromis 300
Pharyngochromis acuticeps 301
Phongolo rock catlet 243–4
Phongolo suckermouth 243–4
Phongolo-suierbekkie 243–4
pike (African) 208–9
pink happy 307
pipefishes 354–5
platkop-harder 351–2
Poecilia reticulata 280–1
Poeciliidae 278

Pollimyrus 100
Pollimyrus castelnaui 100
prag-ghieliemientjie 137–8
Pristidae 81, 345
Pristis microdon 345–6
Protopteridae 83, 89–91
Protopterus 89
Protopterus amphibius 91
Protopterus annectens brieni 90–1
Pseudobarbus 119, 122
Pseudobarbus afer 122, 124–5
Pseudobarbus asper 122, 125
Pseudobarbus burchelli 122, 123
Pseudobarbus burgi 122, 123–4
Pseudobarbus phlegethon 122, 126
Pseudobarbus quathlambae 122, 127–8
Pseudobarbus tenuis 122, 126–7
Pseudocrenilabrus 295
Pseudocrenilabrus philander 38, 39, 296
Pungwe chiselmouth 175–6
Pungwe-beitelbek 175–6
purple labeo 183–4
purpleface largemouth 316

rainbow happy 305
rainbow killifish 272
rainbow trout 263–4
red barb 147
redbreast tilapia 323–4
redeye labeo 184–5
redfin minnows 122–8
Redigobius 366
Redigobius dewaali 366–7
rednose labeo 181–2
redspot barb 162–3
redtail barb 133
reënboog-happie 305
reënboog-kuilvissie 272
reënboogforel 263–4
requiem sharks 343
Rhabdalestes 203
Rhabdalestes maunensis 204
river goby 365
river sardine 119–20
riverbream 356–7
riverine haplochromines 293
rivier-dikkop 365
rivier-rondeharing 109–10
riviersardyn 119–20
rock catfish 217
rock catfishes 215
roof-bottelneus 94
rooi ghieliemientjie 147
rooiborskurper 323–4
rooikol-ghieliemientjie 162–3
rooineus-moddervis 181–2
rooioog-moddervis 184–5
rooiskub-moddervis 183–4
rooistert-ghieliemientjie 133
roosvlerk-ghieliemientjie 159
rosefin barb 159

INDEX TO SCIENTIFIC AND COMMON NAMES 387

saagvin 164–5
saagvin-suierbekkie 245–6
sagkopbaber 232–3
Salmo 261
Salmo trutta 261–2
Salmonidae 84, 260
Salvelinus 264
Salvelinus fontinalis 264–5
sand catlets 218
Sandelia 337
Sandelia bainsii 337
Sandelia capensis 338
Sargochromis 304
Sargochromis carlottae 305
Sargochromis codringtonii 306
Sargochromis coulteri 310
Sargochromis giardi 307
Sargochromis gracilis 310–11
Sargochromis greenwoodi 308
Sargochromis mortimeri 309
sargos 304–11
sawfin 164–5
sawfin barbs 152
sawfin rock catlet 245–6
sawfin suckermouth 245–6
sawfishes 345
scaly 169–70
Schilbe 224
Schilbe intermedius 225–6
Schilbe yangambianus 226
Schilbeidae 82, 224
seabreams 356–7
seelt 192
sekelvin-ghieliemientjie 148–9
Serranochromis 311
Serranochromis altus 312
Serranochromis angusticeps 313
Serranochromis longimanus 315
Serranochromis macrocephalus 316
Serranochromis meridianus 314–15
Serranochromis robustus 317–18
Serranochromis thumbergi 318
serranos 311–18
sharptooth catfish 229–30
Shire spiny eel 340–1
Shire tilapia 329
Shire-kurper 329
Shire-stekelpaling 340–1
short-tail pipefish 355
shortfin barb 139
shortfin eel 106–7
shorthead barb 135
shortsnout chiselmouth 174
shortspine rock catlet 246
shortspine suckermouth 246
Sibayi goby 367
Sibayi-dikkop 367
sicklefin barb 148–9
sidespot barb 140
sigsag-ghieliemientjie 155–6
Silhouettea 367
Silhouettea sibayi 367

Siluriformes 210
Siluroidei 82, 210
silver barb 159–60
silver carp 191
silver catfish 225–6
silver labeo 182–3
silver robber 203
silversides 350
silwer karp 191
silwer moddervis 182–3
silwerbaber 225–6
silwer-ghieliemientjie 159–60
silwer-rower 203
silwervis 161
skakel-ghieliemientjie 142–3
skerptandbaber 229–30
slangbaber 233–4
slanke glasvis 348
slanke happie 310–11
slanke klipstamper 96–7
slanke rooivlerkie 126–7
slanke rower 204
sleepers 360
slender glassy 348
slender happy 310–11
slender redfin 126–7
slender robber 204
slender stonebasher 96–7
slimjannie 356–7
smalkop-grootbek 313
smallmouth bass 287–8
smallmouth yellowfish 168–9
smallscale redfin 125
smallscale yellowfish 170–1
smalltooth sawfish 345–6
smoothhead catfish 232–3
snake catfish 233–4
snawelvis 98
snoutfishes 83, 92–101
soft-rayed minnows 129–50
southern deepbody 277
southern kneria 113
southern mouthbrooder 38, 39, 296
Sparidae 86, 356
spelonkbaber 234–5
spikkel-baars 288
spikkel-kuilvissie 268–9
spikkel-skreeubaber 250–1
spinefin barbs 150
spiny eels 339–42
spiny-rayed fishes 283
spook-klipstamper 101
spottail barb 157
spottail mosquitofish 279–80
spotted bass 288
spotted killifish 268–9
spotted sand catlet 219
spotted squeaker 250–1
squeakers 240, 247–57
stargazer mountain catfish 223
stekelrige kurper 336
stompkop-ghieliemientjie 135

388 INDEX TO SCIENTIFIC AND COMMON NAMES

stompkoppie 99
stomptandbaber 230–1
straightfin barb 160–1
streep-rower 202
streeplampogie 276–7
streepstert-ghieliemientjie 151
striped robber 202
striped topminnow 276–7
suckermouth catlets 240–7
suidelike dieplyf-kuilvissie 277
suidelike mondbroeier 296
suidelike skulpoortjie 113
sunfishes 283
swaarddraer 281–2
swaardstert 281–2
swartkol-kurper 335
swartkurper 328–9
swartrug-ghieliemientjie 145
swordtail 281–2
sykol-ghieliemientjie 140
Syngnathidae 84, 354
Synodontis 247
Synodontis leopardinus 255
Synodontis macrostigma 253
Synodontis macrostoma 254
Synodontis nebulosus 251
Synodontis nigromaculatus 250–1
Synodontis thamalakanensis 256
Synodontis vanderwaali 256–7
Synodontis woosnami 252
Synodontis zambezensis 249–50

Tanganjikameer-sardyn 110–11
tank goby 365–6
tarpons 102–3
tench 192
tenk-dikkop 365–6
Thamalakane barb 144–5
Thamalakane-ghieliemientjie 144–5
thicklipped happy 302–3
thinface largemouth 313
Thoracochromis 302
Thoracochromis albolabris 302–3
Thoracochromis buysi 303
threespot barb 150–1
threespot tilapia 327–8
tiervis 206–7
tigerfish 206–7
Tilapia 319
Tilapia guinasana 321–2
Tilapia rendalli 323–4
Tilapia ruweti 322–3
Tilapia sparrmanii 320–1
tilapiines 319

Tinca 118, 192
Tinca tinca 192
topminnows 273–7
topstripe barb 164
tralielampogie 275
Treur River barb 136
Treurrivier-ghieliemientjie 135–6
trouts 260–5
tsungwa 317–18
Tugela labeo 179
Tugela-moddervis 179
turquoise killifish 270
Twee River redfin 154
Tweerivier-rooivlerkie 154

upjaw barb 149–50
Upper Zambezi labeo 186
Upper Zambezi squeaker 252
Upper Zambezi yellowfish 173

Varicorhinus 118, 173
Varicorhinus nasutus 174
Varicorhinus nelspruitensis 174–5
Varicorhinus pungweensis 175–6
varswater-dikkop 363
varswater-harder 352–3
varswater-pypvis 354
veelbalk-sitarien 197
vleikurper 320–1
vundu 236–7
vurige rooivlerkie 126

westelike bottelneus 95
western bottlenose 95
whitefish 164, 165–6
wimpelstert-suierbekkie 242
witvis 165–6

Xiphophorus helleri 281–2

Yangambi botterbaber 226
Yangambi butterbarbel 226
yellow barb 163
yellowfishes 166–73

Zambesi knorbaber 212–13
Zambesi-pappagaaivis 97
Zambesi-happie 301
Zambezi grunter 212–13
Zambezi happy 301
Zambezi parrotfish 97
Zambezi-suierbekkie 245
zig-zag barb 155–6

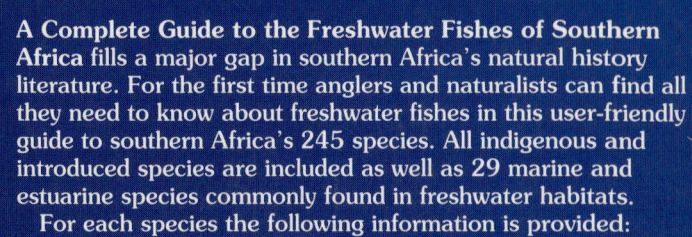

A Complete Guide to the Freshwater Fishes of Southern Africa fills a major gap in southern Africa's natural history literature. For the first time anglers and naturalists can find all they need to know about freshwater fishes in this user-friendly guide to southern Africa's 245 species. All indigenous and introduced species are included as well as 29 marine and estuarine species commonly found in freshwater habitats.

For each species the following information is provided:
- a meticulously detailed painting
- a distribution map
- symbols indicating size, conservation status and uses
- a description of the fish, its distribution, biology, ecology and uses
- for angling species the appropriate angling technique is indicated
- English, Afrikaans and scientific names for each species
- keys to families, genera and species help the angler or naturalist to identify species.

Introductory chapters introduce the reader to issues such as freshwater fish habitats, the factors that influence their distribution, their anatomy, ecology and biology, conservation and the interaction between humans and fishes.

Dr Paul Skelton, who was born in Johannesburg, is the curator of freshwater fishes at the JLB Smith Institute of Ichthyology in Grahamstown. He has done extensive work on the systematics and conservation of African freshwater fishes and he has published numerous articles and addressed international conferences on these topics.

ISBN 1 86812 350 2